RACE, GENDER, AND CLASS

Guidelines for Practice with Individuals, Families, and Groups

Larry E. Davis □ Enola K. Proctor

The George Warren Brown School of Social Work
Washington University

PRENTICE HALL, Englewood Cliffs, New Jersey 07632

Library of Congress Cataloging-in-Publication Data

Davis, Larry E.
    Race, gender, and class : guidelines for practice with
  individuals, families, and groups / Larry E. Davis, Enola K.
  Proctor.
      p.   cm.
    Bibliography: p.
    Includes index.
    ISBN 0-13-750118-8
    1. Social case work. 2. Counselor and client. 3. Family social
  work. 4. Social group work. 5. Group counseling. I. Proctor,
  Enola Knisley. II. Title.
  HV40.D247 1989
  361.3'2--dc19   89-3471
                                                            CIP

Editorial/production supervision and
 interior design: Joan L. Stone
Cover design: Lundgren Graphics, Ltd.
Manufacturing buyer: Peter Havens

©1989 by Prentice-Hall, Inc.
A Division of Simon & Schuster
Englewood Cliffs, New Jersey 07632

Printed in the United States of America

10 9 8 7 6 5 4 3 2

ISBN 0-13-750118-8

PRENTICE-HALL INTERNATIONAL (UK) Limited, *London*
PRENTICE-HALL OF AUSTRALIA PTY. LIMITED, *Sydney*
PRENTICE-HALL CANADA INC., *Toronto*
PRENTICE-HALL HISPANOAMERICANA, S.A., *Mexico*
PRENTICE-HALL OF INDIA PRIVATE LIMITED, *New Delhi*
PRENTICE-HALL OF JAPAN, INC., *Tokyo*
SIMON & SCHUSTER ASIA PTE. LTD., *Singapore*
EDITORA PRENTICE-HALL DO BRASIL, LTDA., *Rio de Janeiro*

Contents

Preface

One of the realities of practice is the fact that worker and client often are of different gender and come from different ethnic, racial, and socioeconomic backgrounds. Research is conclusive that race, gender, and class are salient issues to clients and that the helping process is affected by demographic differences between worker and client. Our practice and teaching experiences convince us that students and practitioners are often ill at ease when working with clients whose backgrounds differ from their own. Although the practice literature does address these issues and extensive research has been conducted, most teachers, students, and practitioners lack ready access to information that can provide guidelines in these practice situations.

This text addresses the salience, consequences, and implications of race, gender, and class differences between worker and client. The chapters reflect the best available empirical evidence and practice theory. In addition, the text provides practitioners with guidelines for managing practice situations when race, class, and gender are significant issues in individual, family, and group practice.

The knowledge base regarding the impact of race, class, and gender differences between worker and client is rapidly expanding. We now know much more than we did just five years ago about the way demographic differences affect the helping process. It is also increasingly possible to separate what is known from myth or supposition. For example, many people assume that clients always prefer workers similar to themselves, although the empirical literature does not lend total support to this assumption.

In most settings, workers have daily encounters with clients whose race, gender, and class differ from their own. Many practitioners know intuitively that these attributes affect their ability to help clients, yet they have neither the time nor resources to review the vast range of literature required to help them grapple with these issues. For many, their professional education occurred at a time when this knowledge was less well developed or when professional training programs were less committed and sensitive to these issues.

In recent years, the identification of knowledge and skills related to practice with oppressed racial, gender, and economic groups has become an increasingly visible priority for professional education. As a result, many educators are searching for materials that can readily present content on the impact of race, class, and gender.

Much of the knowledge pertaining to these issues is scattered among separate research reports or isolated theoretical discussions which focus only on one of the demographic factors. Moreover, these variables have been explored in many different disciplines, including social work, psychology, education, counseling, and psychiatry. As a result, it has been difficult for students, practitioners, and teachers of practice to investigate this wide range of materials and derive implications from the information. This text aims to provide a comprehensive yet succinct overview of the theory and research relevant to practice in situations of race, gender, and class differences.

The central theme of this text is what we refer to as the phenomenon of difference. Upon observing a major demographic difference, both client and worker begin to think and perhaps feel differently about each other and the helping relationship. Visible differences are likely to be translated into other underlying differences. Research findings from the social sciences indicate that perception of another person's race, gender, or socioeconomic status often triggers assumptions and expectations about the other's attitudes, beliefs, competence, and behaviors. Whether these assumptions are correct or incorrect, they have implications for the helping relationship. Thus, the demographics of race, gender, and socioeconomic status themselves convey or trigger assumptions and impact upon individuals' perceptions of each other.

Whether individuals are similar or different in terms of these demographic attributes has further consequences for the helping relationship. When individuals perceive that others are similar to themselves in important attributes such as race, gender, or class, two important consequences occur. First, similar individuals are likely to assume that they view the world similarly, and hence conclude that the other's reading of reality is valid and his or her advice can be trusted. Second, because of their similar world views, they are more likely to be attracted to each other and to want to continue their interaction.

Conversely, when individuals differ on such important attributes, they are likely to assume that they experience and view the world differently. The validity and usefulness of a dissimilar other's advice is viewed as suspect; its applicability is questioned. In turn, the attraction between dissimilar persons and their desire to interact is often reduced. We are most concerned about the consequences of observable differences between helper and client. Upon the perception of racial, gender, or class differences, the relationship between client and worker is likely to be adversely affected. Thus, the text focuses less on the importance of similarity than it does on the consequences of difference.

Clients who perceive that they differ from their helper in terms of race, gender, or socioeconomic status are likely to experience three major concerns. These concerns are:

1. Is the helper a person of goodwill? That is, does this person have my best interests at heart? Does he or she dislike me, or people like me? The client's answer to this question determines the extent to which the client will initially *trust* the helper to be a person who values the client, wants to help, and will pursue the client's best interests.

2. Does the worker have professional expertise or mastery of skills that can resolve my problems? That is, is this person adequately skilled or trained as a practitioner? The answer to this question will also affect the client's trust in the worker. The central issue, however, is the worker's *competence*, or capacity to be helpful.

3. Does the worker have sufficient understanding of my social reality or my world view? That is, is this person sufficiently familiar with people like me? Will this person understand my life experiences? The answer to this question will determine the extent to which the worker is seen as *credible*, and the extent to which advice and suggestions can be accepted as valid and meaningful.

A negative response to even one of these questions may seriously jeopardize the helping relationship in that both attraction and trust are likely to be diminished.

These questions are especially likely to be directed toward some groups of helpers, and a negative response may be more likely depending on the worker's race, gender, or class. For example, minority clients may be more likely to challenge the goodwill of white helpers than that of minority workers. On the other hand, competence, or the mastery of helping skills, may be questioned more frequently when helpers are minority or female than when they are white or male. The extent to which a helper is at risk of receiving a negative response on one of the three questions is influenced significantly by the client's history of interactions with that group and by the status which society ascribes to its members. For example, men are ascribed a higher social status than women and, as such, are often viewed as more capable even when they are not. With respect to the practitioner's understanding of the client's social reality, women are believed to have a greater understanding of men than men have of women. Similarly, minorities are generally believed to have greater knowledge of the social realities of whites than whites have of minorities.

Current research findings and practice wisdom do not suggest that situations of race, gender, or class differences between worker and client should be avoided. We suggest, instead, that practitioners become cognizant of the treatment implications of their own personal demographics, that they become informed about client groups from whom they differ, and that they understand the implications of those differences for the dynamics of interpersonal helping. Most importantly, they should enlarge their own repertoire of helping responses so they will be prepared to respond in the way most helpful to the client. This text contributes toward these ends. Chapters, 5, 10, and 15 condense the discussions of race, gender, and socioeconomic status into actual guidelines for practice.

ACKNOWLEDGMENT

We owe a special indebtedness to our Dean, Shanti Khinduka. He provided us with continual encouragement, support, and the resources to complete this book. We are grateful for his leadership and friendship. We appreciate also Assistant Dean David Cronin's diligence in providing secretarial support in the preparation of these chapters; Michael Sherraden's continued belief that this book could be completed and that it would make a contribution to the field; Michael Powell's assistance in locating innumerable lost references and citations; and the long hours of word processing accomplished by LaVon Marshall, Gail Deering, and Cynthia Jones. Many students helped us keep abreast of current references. We offer particular thanks to Beverly Brown, Treva Gressman, Angelene Hayes, Clarice Mason, Carla Merry, Allyn Schmidt, and Belinder Williams. We are grateful to Maeda Galinsky, Nancy Vosler, and Vered Slonim-Nevo, our colleagues who read and offered helpful comments on early drafts of portions of the book.

Our collaboration in co-teaching a course in human behavior, in which we wrestled with the implications of race, gender, and class in social work practice, sparked the idea for this book. The book, which we originally estimated to be a two-year project, was finally completed in its fifth year. This book was a joint effort, with each of us making equal contributions throughout. Over the years of its preparation, we often disagreed vehemently over what to say and how to say it. This process provided checks and balances to the correctness of each of our individual world views, and, we believe, enhanced the final product.

Finally, we express our gratitude to our families and friends, who encouraged us to "finish the book!" in spite of the many hours its preparation consumed.

DEDICATION

To our parents, Kires and Clara Davis, and John and Helen Knisley, who taught us to care.

Larry E. Davis
Enola K. Proctor

1

Race as an Issue in Practice

In many helping relationships, worker and client belong to different ethnic or racial groups. Indeed, most helping professionals are white, while many of their clients are nonwhite. Cross-racial helping encounters are likely to increase as the United States' racial demographics continue to change. Nonwhites (American Indians, Asians, Hispanics, and Black Americans), who now comprise 12 percent of the populace, are expected to make up 35 percent of the total U.S. populace by the year 2020 (Davis, Haub, and Willette, 1983). Moreover, the percentage of minorities graduating from U.S. colleges and universities is decreasing (*Time*, 1985), thereby further reducing the potential pool of minority practitioners. Hence, while the number of nonwhite clients seeking services will be increasing, the number of nonwhite professionals available to provide services to them will have decreased. The implications of these demographic facts for the helping professions are clear: Practitioners can expect to see increasing numbers of clients who are racially different than themselves.

The terms *race* and *ethnicity* will be used interchangeably in our discussion despite the fact that they are not synonymous and differ technically in meaning. However, they are so often used interchangeably in the literature, we have elected not to make the distinction in our own discussions. We felt such an attempt would have only confusing results at best. We also wish to make note of our use of the terms *minority* and *ethnic minority*. In recent years the term (minority) has been expanded to include a wide and diverse group of individuals (e.g., groups determined by gender, age, and sexual preference). In contrast, the term *ethnic minority* is often understood to refer only to nonwhite persons (e.g., American Indians, Hispanics, Asians, and Black Americans). Consistent with the latter usage, references made in this text to either minorities or ethnic minorities are, in fact, references to nonwhites. The factor of color rather than language or culture has been selected as the critical attribute because neither language nor culture has played such a significant role as color in affecting the life situations of so many U.S. residents (Hopps, 1982).

This discussion is further limited by its focus on the social psychological aspects of race and ethnicity rather than on political and economic aspects. We do, of course, recognize the importance of politics and economics to a broad understanding of minority-majority relations. However, to discuss these factors here exceeds the goal and focus of our efforts. We shall instead limit our discussion of race to the inspection of how the racial sentiment and consciousness of the worker and client influence the treatment process.

PERCEIVING A DIFFERENCE IN RACE

It has been stated that color and race are at once among the most important and the most enigmatic factors at work in our society (John Hope Franklin, 1969). Indeed, racial consciousness (that is, the awareness of racial distinctions) seems to develop early in life. Goodman (1952) reports that by age four or five the vast majority of children have awareness of racial characteristics as well as some awareness of the social implications of racial categories. Even by age six, children have been found to harbor racial prejudices and stereotypes; indeed, some minority children were found to hold such stereotypes toward themselves (Taylor, 1966). Hence it is not surprising that although the United States' people differ significantly in social class and culture, their relationships have been dominated foremost by observable differences in skin color.

Unlike the distinctions of language or culture, color is more readily observable: Whites and nonwhites usually have little difficulty in discerning one another. However, it has been noted that even in situations where blacks and whites cannot readily distinguish each other, race continues to be important. A somewhat extreme but comical example of this was the use of racial spotters during Harlem's heyday in the 1920s. Some nightclub establishments hired blacks, who were thought best able to make racial distinctions, to be on the lookout for light-skinned blacks who might be trying to "pass" for white and thereby gain entrance into "whites only" clubs. It is truly enigmatic that one racial group was willing to pay for the removal of individuals from another racial group whom they considered objectionable, but whom they themselves could not distinguish from individuals who belonged to their own group.

Visual differences that individuals perceive in others are likely to be translated into other underlying differences as well (Allport, 1954; Byrne and Wong, 1962). Hence, actual differences in physical color are less important than are the differences thought to underlie these colorations. In short, those who differ in color are assumed to differ in many other ways as well. One might ask how great the color difference needs to be in order for whites and nonwhites to assume or perceive other, more important underlying differences. Allport (1954, p. 103) explores this question and concludes that any perceived color difference is sufficient grounds for assuming other underlying differences. There appears to be no equation whereby so many shades of difference in skin color translate into a given degree of perceived difference with regard to other aspects of the person. To the contrary, perceived differences in skin color, at least in the United States, largely follow an all or nothing principle: Any perceived difference in color that indicates a racial difference connotes other dissimilarities, such as differences in attitudes, beliefs, and social status. Hence, perceived color differences indicative of a racial difference are not viewed to be merely color graduation differences, but rather are seen as being categorical in nature.

Indeed, even when differences in skin color cannot be observed, mere knowledge that a person is "black" or "white" is sufficient grounds for assuming other underlying differences. A great deal of social psychological theory and research, especially that on interpersonal attraction, indicates that such perception may have particular relevance and thus considerable consequence for interracial helping relationships.

While color within minority groups has been observed to exert an influence on intra-group interactions (Seymour and Kleiner, 1964; Cruse, 1967; Walker, 1982), these in-group differences in colorations are overshadowed by the greater sociopolitical significance of color between racial groups. Racial categorizations in the United States have not established in-group categories based on skin hue. For example, unlike some countries, the United States does not have Negroid groups classified as blacks and coloreds. Instead we have an either-or racial classification scheme. Individuals are black or not. For example, although children from black and white marriages may be identified during childhood as being interracial, as adults they are categorized as blacks. In short, in our society, interracial children become black adults. Subsequently, once designated nonwhite, individuals are perceived and responded to in a manner consistent with the prevailing societal attitudes held toward minorities (Ginzburg, 1962; Baker, 1964).

Hence the fundamental question for both white and nonwhite practitioners is, What does it mean for a worker or client to perceive the other's color as being different from his or her own? The answer to this question is significantly influenced by who is perceiving the difference. But we can, with some degree of confidence, state that in such instances more than observable physical differences are being viewed. Thus, a perceived difference in skin color by either worker or client may suggest other important differences which have far greater impact than a mere shade of skin color would suggest.

PERCEIVING A DIFFERENCE IN BELIEFS

Perceiving dissimilarities between one's self and others is believed to have potent and often adverse effects for those individuals involved (Rosenbaum, 1986). Generally, when individuals interact with persons of a different race, they appear to assume that racially dissimilar others also hold dissimilar beliefs and attitudes (Byrne and Wong, 1962; Stein, Hardyck, and Smith, 1965). This possibility has obvious implications for cross-racial helping relationships.

Indeed, an individual's willingness to interact, at least initially, with different-race others may be largely a function of the degree of perceived belief congruence. Support for this proposition comes from the Rokeach studies, where college students were asked to select as a friend either a person of similar race with dissimilar attitudes, or a person of dissimilar race with similar attitudes (Rokeach, Smith, and Evans, 1960; Rokeach and Mezel, 1966). In these studies, belief similarity was a stronger determinant of friendship choices than was racial similarity.

Why does a perceived difference in race, which in turn is translated into other perceived differences (e.g., attitudes), affect an individual's willingness to interact? According to "Byrne's Law of Attraction" (D. Byrne, 1971), perceived similarity has a positive effect on liking because it is reinforcing. That is, the idea that others share attitudes and beliefs similar to our own provides consensual validation, in that it confirms or affirms our conception of social reality. We like attitudinally similar others because they see things as we do, which suggests to us that we are seeing things correctly or as they "really are." Although others have offered explanations as to why perceived dissimilarity results in less attraction and perceived similarity in greater (Heider, 1958; Newcomb, 1961; McWhirter and Jecker, 1967; Rosenbaum, 1986), Byrne's interpretations and work have received the greatest attention and are clearly the most germane to our purposes here.

Consensual validation is a central issue in the pairing of any helper and client who differ on a major demographic attribute such as race or ethnicity. Clients may view the worker's racial dissimilarity as but a visual manifestation of other, more important conceptual differences. Principally, the racial difference may suggest to the client that the worker holds a different—and incorrect—view of social reality, particularly as it relates to the client and the causes of his or her problems. Thus, the therapist may be seen as incapable of understanding how things "really are," at least how they are for the client. The client may view the racially different worker as unable to understand or help with his or her difficulties. Because clients who feel that their therapist does not understand their problems experience higher dropout rates (Kline, Adrian, and Spivak, 1974; Saltzman et al., 1976), this may be the most serious problem to be faced by those therapists who work with clients who differ racially from themselves.

Consensual validation and attraction have significance for the worker as well. Theoretically, those clients whom the worker perceives as validating his or her own conception of social reality should be more attractive and reinforcing. By contrast, clients perceived as different in attitude or belief, and possessing a different conception of social reality, are likely to be viewed as unattractive. Indeed, there is evidence to suggest that the therapist-client relationship is reciprocal: Both therapists and clients receive more positive responses (Goldstein, 1971). According to Fiedler (1951), if a therapist perceives too great a difference between himself and a client, the client is likely to be viewed as being unsuitable as a client. Evidence suggests that workers respond to clients perceived as different from themselves less favorably than they do to clients perceived as similar. The worker's dislike of very needy and involuntary clients could have serious negative consequences. In the reverse situation, in which the client does not like the worker, the consequences are probably less serious (Sue, 1981). However, both situations are problematic and warrant corrective action on the part of the practitioner. As Feld and Radin (1982) suggest, practitioners who view individuals of certain racial or ethnic groups unfavorably should, whenever possible, refer these clients to other practitioners who hold more favorable racial attitudes.

The race relations literature is replete with both social psychological (Berkun and Meeland, 1958; Mann, 1958; Hraba and Grant, 1970; Kiesler, 1971) and therapeutic research (Brieland, 1969; Wolkon, Moriwaki, and Williams, 1973; Harrison, 1975; Atkinson, Maruyama, and Matsuri, 1978; Atkinson, 1983) which attests that attraction is enhanced by racial similarity. Kadushin (1972) has suggested that because of a similarity in race, individuals are likely to share similar backgrounds, values, experiences, and problems and are therefore more likely to feel comfortable with each other than are individuals who are racially dissimilar.

Does this mean that racially dissimilar workers and clients will assume that they also hold dissimilar beliefs and consequently experience very little mutual attraction? Not necessarily. Some suggest that the law of attraction paradigm is too simplistic and may be moderated by personality or situational variables (Clark and Clark, 1947; Lewin, 1948; Triandis and Davis, 1965; Novak and Lerner, 1968; Peres, 1971; Rosenbaum, 1986). Indeed, the significance of race appears to vary among individuals (Davis and Burnstein, 1981; Atkinson, 1983). In addition, the sharing of similar attitudes may be more important to some relationships than to others (Banikotes, Russell, and Linden, 1972; Sole, Marton, and Hornstein, 1975). Finally, it should be noted that the vast majority of studies conducted on belief congruence and attraction have utilized only white subjects, thus leaving incomplete our understanding of attitude congruence and racial attraction.

Despite the intuitive appeal of "Byrne's Law of Attraction" and the wealth of research that attests to the importance of attitudinal similarity in predicting interracial contacts (Byrne and Wong, 1962; Byrne and Nelson, 1965; Byrne and Rhamey, 1965; Byrne and Clore, 1967), some research has not found similarity in attitude or belief to be most important in determining the quality of interracial interaction. For example, Triandis (1960, 1961, 1965) asserts that race is more important than attitude similarity in interracial encounters. He argues that many studies that have found attitudinal similarity to be most important failed to vary the type of proposed contact adequately. Specifically, Triandis asserts that if Rokeach et al. (1960) had offered the subjects in their studies a range of social interactions which more closely resembled real world situations, race would have emerged as more important than belief. The research by Triandis and his colleagues found both race and belief to be important in affecting cross-racial interactions. However, race was found to be more salient for intimate social interactions while belief appeared to be more salient for less intimate interactions. In other words, it appears that as intimacy increases, so does the importance of the race of the individuals with whom we interact.

The controversy over which is more significant in affecting attraction—attitudes or race—has generated considerable research (Rokeach and Mezel, 1966; Sears and Abeles, 1969; Hendrick, Bixenstine, and Hawkins, 1971; Dienstbier, 1972; Hendrick, Stikes, and Murray, 1972). The present status of this controversy is perhaps summed up best as follows:

1. Belief congruence is the most important determinant of interpersonal attraction
2. When one individual knows only that another's race is different, he or she assumes belief dissimilarity
3. There is a greater tendency for prejudiced persons to assume belief dissimilarity than nonprejudiced persons
4. Race is a more frequent determinant of a person's relation to another when that relation is an intimate one (Jones, 1972)

The findings of Rokeach, Triandis, and others have significant implications for interracial therapy (Byrne and Wong, 1965; Stein, Hardyck, and Smith, 1965; Goebol and Cole, 1975). Clearly, the perception of attitudinal or belief dissimilarity that frequently accompanies racial differences can be expected to have significant effects on helping relationships.

PERCEIVING A DIFFERENCE IN STATUS

The perception of a racial difference may also result in the perception of a difference in social status. Social status refers to an individual's rank, role, and position in society (Biddle and Thomas, 1966). However, social status generally refers not only to social position but also to the value of a particular position. Social status can be either ascribed or achieved. Generally individuals have less control over those statuses that are ascribed to them (e.g., race, caste) than they do over those statuses that they achieve themselves (e.g., educator, physician). In U.S. society, color and race have had, more so than any other ascribed status, a preeminent influence on an individual's societal worth (Franklin, 1968; McKissick, 1969).

As with other determinants of social status, race or ethnicity brings with it certain expectations, privileges, responsibilities, and limitations (Berger, Fisek, Norman, and Zelditch, 1977). These influence how a person is responded to by and, in turn, perceives the larger society. Bogardus (1925a, 1925b, 1926a, 1926b), who focused his early work on the relative statuses of ethnic groups in the United States, found that the status ranking ascribed to a particular ethnic or racial group significantly influenced its social interactions with other groups (e.g., intermarriage). In addition there is strong evidence to suggest that the status ascribed to a minority group influences that group's intra-group relations (Lewin, 1948; Poussaint, 1972). That is, they may relate to each other in a manner consistent with the status ascribed to their racial group. For example, they may exhibit low levels of respect toward members of their own group.

Social status and individual worth have been ascribed in the United States on the basis of color. Hence, individuals who differ in skin color (white, nonwhite) differ also in social status. White skin color has been ascribed greater social status than skin color that is nonwhite. Thus, historically, most encounters between whites and ethnic minorities of color in the United States have been characterized by superordinate-subordinate statuses, with the person of color occupying a subordinate or lower status to that of the white (e.g., master-slave, boss-worker).

Neither clients nor workers who enter into interracial helping relationships are oblivious to these historical and, to a great extent, continuing status differences. Subsequently the question for both workers and clients who enter into interracial treatment is, "Of what consequence to the interracial encounter is the fact that, by virtue of our different race or ethnicity, we also occupy different social statuses?"

Are workers who differ from their clients on a significant social status such as race appropriate as practitioners for those clients, given the different expectations associated with their respective statuses? That is, given the dissimilarity in social expectations brought on by the dissimilarity in race, is a worker of a different race suitable as a helper? Indeed the question clients working with different race practitioners must at some point ask themselves is, "If, as it appears, my worker and I have different social statuses by virtue of our colors, is the advice that he or she offers appropriate or suitable? Will the help in the way of advice or counseling be relevant, given the social realities of our differing status?" The key concern here is whether advice coming from a different-race person is inappropriate, not because of some racist intent or motivation, but rather because the advice may be inappropriate for persons occupying different social statuses.

The above consideration bears directly on practitioner credibility. Credibility is important, as practitioners who are perceived as credible are found to be capable of exerting greater influence on their clients (Schmidt and Strong, 1970; Atkinson and Carskaddon, 1975). Practitioner credibility seems to be a function of perceived worker expertise, trustworthiness, and attractiveness to the client (Strong, 1968). Clearly, when clients and workers have different social statuses, the client may question the worker's expertise, at least with respect to the worker's ability to understand the social realities associated with the client's social status. Thus, even if the client believes that the therapist is of good will (trustworthy) and possesses adequate or even superior mastery of therapeutic techniques (expertise), the client still may question whether a worker of a different race possesses an adequate understanding of the social realities associated with the client's social status. It may be the client's attempt to address this concern that prompts the challenging and often threatening question directed toward a worker, "How can you help me? You don't know what it is to be a minority."

CONCLUSION

In this introduction to race and its implication for practice, we have reviewed the importance of perceived racial similarity and difference on helping encounters. Both clinical and social psychological research point to the potential therapeutic benefits of racial similarity between worker and client. However, we have focused foremost on the consequence of racial differences because they suggest and trigger assumptions of other dissimilarities such as differences in attitudes, beliefs, and social status. These differences, in turn, may hamper the development of a beneficial worker-client relationship.

The conceptual framework introduced here should sensitize the reader to the powerful and frequently enigmatic influences of color and ethnicity on interpersonal interactions. Moreover, it should clarify the possible consequences of racial dissimilarity for the therapeutic relationships. Finally, this discussion addressed the issues that underlie the perennial question of whether cross-racial therapy can ever be viable. The extent to which this question can be answered affirmatively will be affected significantly by the skills, training, and sensitivity of the workers who by choice or chance find themselves working with individuals, families, or groups of a different race.

2

Race and Individual Treatment

THE SALIENCE OF RACE

The Importance of Race to Clients

How important is race to clients seeking services from social agencies? Do clients approach helping encounters with expectations or preferences for the race of their helpers? Several studies have focused on these issues, and a review of their conclusions may help practitioners understand the salience of race to clients.

In many studies, subjects are shown videotapes or written case histories depicting worker-client interaction under different conditions of racial similarity, then are asked to express their preferences for worker race. Findings from such studies suggest that race may not be as important as other factors. For example, Sattler (1977) found that preference for worker was determined more by worker style (particularly directiveness) than by race. In a comprehensive study of factors influencing black clients' worker preferences, Atkinson, Furlong, and Poston (1986) found that similar ethnicity, while chosen as important 55 percent of the time, ranked fifth in importance, following (in order of priority) worker education, attitude similarity, older age, and personality similarity. Thus, while black college students preferred a black counselor over a white, other characteristics were even more important.

When these other factors are controlled for, however, subjects appear to prefer racially matched dyads. Several laboratory studies indicate that blacks, whites, and Native Americans prefer workers of their own race (Stranges and Riccio, 1970; Riccio and Barnes, 1973; Haviland, Horsivill, O'Connell, and Dynneson, 1983). While such studies have the advantage of experimental control, by definition the subjects are not therapy clients and hence the findings should be generalized only cautiously to actual clients entering treatment. Although the findings suggest that race may not be as important as other factors, such as interviewing style, it is clear that racial similarity is often preferred.

Many studies of racial preference have asked subjects to express preference for a minority or a white therapist through their response to items on interview schedules or questionnaires. Subjects in these studies include the general public, high school students, college students, and actual clients in or approaching therapy. In such studies experimenters generally have no control over, or sometimes awareness of, characteristics of the real or imagined therapist on whom subjects base their responses. However, it is generally assumed that subjects respond on the basis of prior or anticipated experiences with helping professionals and that their responses reflect actual or anticipated satisfaction with those experiences.

Several such studies reveal a preference among blacks for black workers (Barrett and Perlmutter, 1972; Jackson and Kirschner, 1973; Wolkon, Moriwaki, and Williams, 1973), especially when studies use black interviewers (Brieland, 1969). However, Parker and Davis (1983) found no evidence that blacks prefer black workers, and many black respondents who preferred black workers viewed worker competence as more important than racial similarity (Barrett and Perlmutter, 1972). Although Jackson and Kirschner (1973) also found that black college students generally preferred a black counselor, preference depended on strength of the student's racial identity. Client preference for an ethnically-similar worker was found to depend on strength of client cultural commitment. Similarly, Sanchez and Atkinson (1983) found that Mexican-American clients with a strong commitment to their own culture expressed the greatest preference for an ethnically-similar worker; clients committed to Anglo culture were least concerned about seeing an ethnically-similar worker. Most studies of client preference fail to incorporate such moderating variables as client ethnic identity.

Although considerable attention has been directed to the nature and salience of client preferences for worker race, until recently expectations and preferences have not been distinguished conceptually or operationally. Thus prior studies of preferences have sometimes assessed what race clients *want* their workers to be and at other times have assessed what race they *think* their workers will be. In a study of clients entering treatment at an outpatient mental health clinic, Proctor and Rosen (1981) separately measured client expectations and preferences for worker race. Results indicated that black and white clients alike expected their therapist to be white. Blacks did not, however, prefer white workers. Many clients stated that they had no particular preference. These responses may reflect social desirability factors or they may reflect a low relevance of therapist race for the clients studied. The study's findings confirmed the importance of distinguishing between and separately measuring clients' expectations and preferences (Rosen, 1967). Although blacks generally expected a white therapist, they clearly did not prefer a white therapist.

Studies measuring expectations or preferences of actual clients have not always controlled for the amount of contact the client has already had with the therapist. For example, Warren, Jackson, Nugaris, and Farley (1973), who queried clients about their preferences for therapist race at the time they completed therapy with a white clinician, found that black workers were preferred by 31 percent of black clients. Although the findings are generally viewed as reflecting client preferences for therapist race, they instead may reflect client satisfaction with their recently completed therapy with white therapists. Further studies are needed that focus on actual client populations, control for experimenter race, distinguish between expectations and preferences, and examine possible changes in preferences over time as a result of client contact with racially similar or dissimilar therapists.

Given the findings of this somewhat limited body of research, what should workers presume about the significance or importance of their race to the clients? The findings of available studies suggest that both minority and white clients are realistic in their expectations. That is, clients generally expect their professional helpers to be white. These expectations are consistent with data, which indicate that a very small proportion of therapists and counselors are nonwhite (Thomas and Sillen, 1976; Williams, Ralph, and Denham, 1978). Thus workers who are white can generally assume that their race will not surprise the client; conversely, minority workers meeting either white or ethnic clients should be sensitive to potential surprise clients may experience in learning that their helping professional is not white.

Workers should also realize that clients' expectations do not necessarily correspond to their preferences. Although clients generally expect a white helper, many studies indicate that minority group clients frequently prefer therapists of their own racial or ethnic groups (Vontress, 1970; Harrison, 1975). White clients seem to attach less significance to the issue of therapist race, perhaps because they presume their worker will be white (Sattler, 1977; Proctor and Rosen, 1981).

Whatever the salience of worker race to client, it is clear that the client's race is part of his or her identity and thus part of the "self" that is brought to the helping situation. Moreover, race of worker appears to be an issue of concern to clients, whether or not workers recognize and are comfortable with client's ethnicity. Thus a worker in a racially dissimilar helping dyad may need to explore the salience of his or her race directly with the individual client.

The Importance of Race to Workers

How important is the client's race to the worker? Do workers have or acknowledge preferences for working with clients of their own ethnic or cultural group? Do workers feel less comfortable or competent in working with racially dissimilar clients? These issues have not been widely investigated or even acknowledged in the practice literature; indeed these issues have been characterized as neglected, if not taboo (Draguns, 1981). However, the available evidence clearly indicates that race is an issue for workers. Race seems to become especially potent when the race of worker and client are different. It may also have importance when both worker and client are members of ethnic minority groups.

Cheek points out that conflicts in

attitudes, perceptions and values are part of the American cultural fabric in which the issues of Blacks and Whites must be addressed. These conflicts are frequently brought into the counseling or therapeutic relationship. Whites know it and Blacks feel it (1976, p. 120).

The salience of race to workers and its significance in helping interactions reflects and approximates its significance in the larger society. The extent of segregation and the depth of racism evident in contemporary society greatly limits the contact that whites typically have with ethnic cultures and with minority individuals. As a result, whites generally are not knowledgeable about minority persons, their lifestyles, and communities. Moreover, as members of the larger society and culture, white workers are likely to bring preconceived ideas and attitudes about minorities to their practice (Bloombaum, Yamamoto, James, 1968; Vontress, 1970; Siegel, 1974). In spite of the fact that interracial contacts are not unusual in the helping professions, most programs of professional education have not adequately addressed deficits in students' understandings of ethnic groups, nor do they adequately prepare them for effective work with minority group clients. As a result professionals frequently find themselves working with clients about whom they are uninformed and with whom they are ill at ease.

Characterizations of ethnic minority life and culture in professional and social science literature may compound the difficulty of white workers in understanding and working comfortably with nonwhite clients. In the early 1950s, postwar research conducted on black subjects yielded conclusions that "difficult living conditions" affected all aspects of personality in blacks, producing "a wretched internal life" (Kardiner and Ovesey, 1962). The resulting generalizations of pathology in the personality of blacks persisted for at least two decades. Whether they employed terms of "culturally deprived," "socially handicapped," "underprivileged," or "minority," social scientists widely viewed minorities as manifesting "the mark of oppression"—a term which conveyed the notion that black people "are limited or lacking in some irreversible way" (Griffith, 1977, p. 30). One reflection of widespread racism in the United States is the view among the majority, white culture that members of minority groups are not merely culturally different but are culturally disadvantaged or deprived (Hankins-McNary, 1979).

Avoiding the Racial Issue

Many whites avoid direct discussion of race, especially with minority individuals, and minimize the salience of race in interpersonal relationships. Whites prefer not to discuss racial issues due, perhaps, to their limited exposure to and knowledge of minorities. Professional helpers may even deny awareness of, or feign blindness to, their client's race, maintaining that they strive to treat minority clients like "any other" client. This widespread pattern has been identified as the "illusion of color blindness" (Cooper, 1973; Thomas and Sillen, 1976). Color blindness is often defended on the grounds that it reflects "true regard" for minority clients and ensures that all clients are treated equally. However, Griffith (1977) points out that the "any other client" in the standard of treatment tends to be any other *white* client. Disregard of the importance of client racial identity, "while at the same time ignoring the undeniable impact of the therapist's whiteness," leads Griffith to view color blindness as unrealistic and destructive (1977, p. 29). Color blindness also encourages workers to view clients in the abstract, ignoring their social realities and the impact of racism upon their development. Indeed, cultural barriers are only reinforced when workers respond to their minority clients under the illusion of color blindness.

To members of ethnic minority groups—whether in the role of client or worker—race is a significant part of history and personal identity. While white practitioners tend to minimize the importance of racial or cultural factors, minorities wonder why whites cannot acknowledge the impact of color in a racist society (Cheek, 1976). In short, race has a different salience to minorities and whites; the result in their interpersonal encounters is ambivalence and awkwardness of which, in all likelihood, both groups are aware.

Worker Confidence and Perception of Competence

The intrusion of the racial barrier in the helping relationship appears to affect the confidence with which the worker approaches the treatment situation. Higginbotham and Tanaka-Matsumi (1981) use the term "culture shock" to describe experiences in which an individual is unable to use formerly effective skills, and note that workers counseling international and minority group clients may experience an erosion of self confidence. The anxieties and insecurities experienced by workers in interracial helping situations have been widely noted (Sattler, 1977), although not systematically investigated. To Kadushin (1972) it is "obvious" that persons of similar backgrounds and experiences will feel more comfortable with each other. Chandler (1980) found that social workers from five ethnic groups acknowledged through a questionnaire that they felt more competent handling problems with clients of their own ethnic backgrounds. White workers may be particularly uncomfortable working with racially dissimilar clients. Turner and Armstrong (1981) found that white workers were more uncomfortable than black workers when working with a client of a different race. This is probably a function of minorities' greater contact with and knowledge of whites than vice versa. White workers tended to be either oversolicitous or too distant with black clients and sometimes felt incapable of providing help. Whites' lack of comfort with blacks may explain Franklin's (1985) findings that black social workers were significantly more enthusiastic about working with a black client than were white workers; black workers also gave more favorable prognoses than did white workers, should the client enter treatment.

Through selection and referral processes, workers simply may choose not to work with minority clients (Sue, McKinney, Allen, and Hall, 1974). In his classic book, *Psychotherapy, The Purchase of Friendship*, Schofield (1964) argues that workers often accept clients for treatment on the basis of characteristics that disadvantage ethnic and minority clients, such as verbal fluency and potential for insight. It is likely that the worker's sense of competence and comfort in working with racially dissimilar clients in itself has potentially significant consequences for the delivery of social services. A worker's comfort with and liking for the client are believed to bear on the development of therapeutic relationships and the eventual effectiveness of treatment (Frank, 1961; Heller and Goldstein, 1961; Goldstein, 1962; Shapiro, 1971).

This discussion of race and its salience in treatment highlights its significance for both workers and clients. Workers are less knowledgeable about and appear less comfortable with clients whose race differs from their own. Although workers probably do not express these attitudes directly to clients, they may have deleterious effects on the helping process and its outcome. Race and racial dissimilarity are clearly factors in treatment.

CONSEQUENCES OF RACIAL DIFFERENCE
IN TREATMENT

Minority clients seeking mental health or social services are likely to encounter white professionals. Recent data indicate that less than two percent of psychiatrists and doctoral level psychologists and only about eleven percent of professionally trained social workers are black (Williams, Ralph, and Denham, 1978). The numbers of minorities receiving professional training for the helping professions may be increasing ever so slightly (Williams et al., 1978), but not as rapidly as the growth of U.S. minority populations. Moreover, because few agencies intentionally match worker and client according to race, increasing the number of nonwhite professionals does not ensure that minority clients will work with minority professionals. Recent declines in minority enrollment in colleges may even reduce the future number of minority professionals (*Time*, 1985). The likelihood of racial difference between worker and client, then, is substantial and the foreseeable future offers little promise of improvement.

Once a client has approached an agency for social services and has entered a helping relationship with a racially dissimilar worker, what are the likely consequences for the process and outcome of treatment? In this section, the literature from various social psychological areas will be reviewed, including empirical studies, theoretical formulations, and the accumulated body of practice wisdom. We review the consequences of racial similarity and dissimilarity for client entry to and continuance in treatment, interpersonal communication and development of the helping relationship, accuracy of assessment, choice of interventive modality, and the attainment of treatment outcome.

Client Entry, Assignment to Treatment

The social and psychological needs of minorities are less adequately served by social agencies than the needs of whites (Sue, McKinney, Allen, and Hall, 1974; Padilla, Ruiz, and Alvarez, 1975; Griffith and Jones, 1979). Epidemiological studies indicate that minority groups utilize mental health services at a rate far below their proportion in the general population (Griffith and Jones, 1979; Root, 1985).

Moreover, mental health clinics appear to be less likely than other community institutions such as the church to serve the needs of minority persons (Hankins-McNary, 1979), and many blacks use only informal sources of help or rely on informal supports along with professional help (Marsh, 1980; Neighbors and Jackson, 1984). Puerto Ricans will usually approach family members, friends, and neighbors for help, even before consulting clergy or spiritualists. Only if none of these can help will formal treatment be sought (Ghali, 1977). Chinese Americans rely on informal social networks for information and assistance more than do whites, blacks, Chicanos, other Hispanics, and Native Americans (Endo, 1984). The reluctance to use formal services may be, in part, a function of attitudes. For example, one small-scale study revealed that Vietnamese students in the United States held less positive attitudes toward counseling than did Anglo-American students (Atkinson, Ponterotto, and Sanchez, 1984). Subjects in a study of one black community, however, had positive attitudes toward mental health agencies and professionals. They knew the locations of some mental health agencies, believed that those agencies provide helpful services, and believed that counselors can help with problems in ways that families, friends, and ministers cannot (Parker and McDavis, 1983).

Minorities' limited access to services remains as a key concern. Agency location, relationships within ethnic referral networks, and language accessibility may attract or deter prospective minority clients. Linguistic accessibility is particularly important for Hispanics. Use of bilingual/bicultural staff, including paraprofessionals, is essential in making services accessible to Hispanics and has been shown to increase utilization rates in Hispanic communities (Rogler, Malgady, Costantino, and Blumenthal, 1987).

Most empirical studies show that race is a major determinant of the type and quality of services. Race appears to affect the very earliest treatment decisions. For example, Beck and Jones (1975) found that regardless of socioeconomic status, minority clients were more than twice as likely as whites to be placed on waiting lists. This pattern may reflect, in part, the concentration of minority clients in large cities, where waiting lists are more frequent.

Minority clients are more likely than whites to be assigned to workers with lower levels of education, training, or status, for both intake and treatment. In their extensive study of the experiences of minorities at community mental health centers, Sue, McKinney, Allen, and Hall (1974) found that black clients were significantly more likely to be seen by paraprofessionals and less likely to be seen by psychiatrists, psychologists, and social workers than were whites. Native Americans saw more social workers but fewer nonprofessionals than whites, while Asian Americans were more likely to see educators and less likely to see psychologists than were whites (Sue, 1977). The authors proposed several explanations for these findings. First, through institutional discrimination, professionals may avoid seeing minority clients. Second, nonwhite clients may be matched with nonwhite therapists, who may be overrepresented among paraprofessionals with lower levels of training. Third, professional staff may prefer to work with clients who have characteristics coincidentally related to race, resulting in racially matched assignment of clients to professionals. However, after cancelling out other demographic factors, blacks were still more likely than whites to see paraprofessionals, and race remained the factor most strongly related to staff assignment.

The findings of many studies suggest that different and lower quality forms of treatment are often provided for minority clients. Studies have generally focused on three types of clients: outpatient adults seeking mental health services; children and their parents seeking services at child guidance clinics; and patients hospitalized in psychiatric clinics or hospitals. Nearly all studies of inpatient psychiatric services indicate that minority patients are provided with less intensive and less "psychologically-oriented" treatment than are whites. An exception to this pattern are findings of Winston, Pardes, and Papernik (1972) who, studying inpatients who were treated by white therapists, found no differences in length of hospitalization or use of drug therapy for black and white patients. However, other studies employing a variety of criteria indicate differential treatment by client race. Krebs (1971) found that black patients were significantly more likely than whites to be involuntarily admitted. Once confined to inpatient facilities, blacks received different forms of treatment. For example, black patients hospitalized over a four-year period were found more likely than whites to be given only drug therapy and were less likely than whites to be given intense psychotherapy (Singer, 1967). Mayo (1974) found that 80 percent of white but only 25 percent of black inpatients received individual psychotherapy. Black patients were also found to receive less electroconvulsive therapy and less group psychotherapy than whites. Even when diagnosis and level of disturbance were held constant, differential treatment for black and white inpatients was found in a study by Flaherty and Meagher (1980). Their retrospective audit of the clinic charts of 66 black and 36 white patients diagnosed as schizophrenic indicated the following: blacks were medicated twice as many days as whites; seclusion and restraint were ordered 78 percent of the days for black patients but only 46 percent of the days for whites; and black patients had significantly fewer privileges than whites. Although hospital physicians reported that recreational and occupational therapy were "routinely" ordered, less than half of black patients but more than three-fourths of white patients were found to receive such therapy. Hence therapy appeared to be "more routinely" ordered for white than for black patients. Finally, black inpatients were discharged from hospitalization more quickly than white patients (Singer, 1967; Mayo, 1974). Flaherty and Meagher (1980) found that with identical diagnosis and comparable severity, blacks spent an average of 29 days hospitalized while whites spent an average of 46.6 days. Black patients were also more likely than whites to be discharged without being referred to follow up or community support services (Mayo, 1974).

Also, in a study of children who received services at five child guidance clinics, blacks appeared to receive less intensive forms of treatment. More white than black children were provided with individual psychotherapy (Jackson, Berkowitz, and Farley, 1974). Secondary data analysis indicated that black females were at greatest risk of receiving inadequate treatment. Black females were seen more frequently for diagnostic procedures only, despite the fact that they were diagnosed as having more severe psychopathology than white boys and girls. At two of the clinics studied, no black females were seen for psychotherapy (Jackson, Farley, Zimet, and Waterman, 1978). Black children, and black females in particular, received therapy for significantly shorter periods of time than white children, although it is not clear whether termination resulted from the therapist's, the child's, or the parent's decision (Jackson et al., 1974, 1978).

The studies focusing on adult outpatients yield less consistent findings about the effects of race on the provision of treatment. In a study of outpatients Krebs (1971) found race and sex to interact, with black females significantly more likely than black males, white males, or white females to be assigned to brief crisis rather than to long-term therapy. Client assignment was independent of worker gender, experience, and professional orientation. However, in an extensive study of treatment in community mental health centers, Sue et al. (1974) found no evidence that blacks received inferior forms of treatment. In fact, blacks were significantly more likely than whites to be diagnosed at the time of intake and were more likely than whites to receive individual psychotherapy. Whites, on the other hand, were more likely to be assigned to group and family therapy. Similarly, in a study of services provided in an alcoholism clinic, Lowe and Alston (1974) found no evidence of differential treatment according to client race.

The studies reviewed above indicate that, although less clear in outpatient services, different personnel, type of therapy, and length of treatment are frequently provided to white and nonwhite clients. Minority clients often are assigned to less highly trained personnel and less intensive therapy. Moreover, their treatment is often much briefer. The evidence of racism in service delivery is clear. However, its origin and locus in policy, administration, or therapeutic interaction is less adequately understood. Evidence of overt policies directing intake workers to provide minority clients with shorter or less adequate service has not surfaced, nor would it be expected. Flaherty and Meagher (1980) suggest that racial bias is not due to hostility or contempt for black patients, but to subtle stereotyping and to staff's greater familiarity with and preference for white patients. They hypothesize that "favored" patients stay longer, and "favored" patients are generally white. White workers' discomfort in treating nonwhite clients, noted and discussed earlier, may be responsible for the unfortunate yet undeniable racial bias frequently evidenced when minority clients enter the service delivery system.

Race and Dropout

Once clients commence treatment, does race affect their continuance in treatment? Are minority clients more likely than whites to drop out of treatment? Does racial dissimilarity between worker and client affect the length of the client's duration in treatment? The findings of one study indicate that the length of time workers intend to keep clients in treatment may be a function of client race. In a study of social workers' responses to questionnaires, Franklin (1985) found that both black and white workers indicated they would keep a black client in treatment longer than a white client. These findings may reflect an expectation that the problems of black clients are more serious than those of whites, and hence, an assumption that blacks need longer treatment.

However, quite the opposite is found in actual treatment, with minorities remaining for much shorter periods of time than whites. In an early study of race and dropout, Rosenthal and Frank (1958) found that black clients were only half as likely as white clients to remain in treatment for a minimum of six sessions. Black female clients were found especially likely to miss scheduled appointments (Krebs, 1971). Although race was not found related to client continuance in a few studies (Overall and Aronson, 1963; Weiss and Dlugokinski, 1974; Gibbs, 1975), most studies support the conclusion that black clients spend significantly less time in treatment than white clients (Yamamoto, James, and Palley, 1968). Black clients are particularly likely to drop out of treatment when they are assigned to white therapists expressing prejudiced attitudes (Yamamoto, James, Bloombaum, and Hattem, 1967).

Dropout is found to be extremely high during the initial phases of treatment. Raynes and Warren (1971) found that black clients were less likely than whites to keep their first scheduled appointment in a Boston psychiatric clinic, although length of time on a waiting list appeared also to affect nonattendance. Salzman, Shader, Scott, and Binstock (1970) found that 24 percent of minority group clients failed to return for a second appointment, compared with only 3 percent of white clients. In their study of minority clients in community mental health agencies, Sue et al. (1974) found that over 50 percent of black, Native American, and Asian-American clients dropped out of treatment after their first session; the dropout rate for white clients was 29.8 percent.

According to one study, minority clients at every social economic status (SES) level had significantly fewer treatment sessions than did white clients. For example, upper- and middle-income white clients had 8 interviews while upper- and middle-income minority clients had 4.9 sessions (Beck and Jones, 1975). Similarly, in an extensive study of community mental health services, minority clients were found to complete fewer sessions than white clients. Black clients attended an average of 4.68 sessions, Native Americans attended 3.28, Asian Americans attended 2.35, Hispanics attended 5.30, and white clients attended 7.96 sessions (Sue, McKinney, Allen, and Hall, 1974; Sue, 1977).

Duration of treatment may be affected by worker race. Neimeyer and Gonzales (1983) studied 70 worker-client pairs and found that minority workers saw clients for longer periods than did whites. Minority workers averaged six sessions per client, regardless of client race. White workers averaged five sessions with white clients and only three sessions with minority clients.

Worker ethnicity also had a significant effect on "appointments kept" by Mexican-American clients, as shown in a recent community mental health study. Taussig (1987) found that Mexican-American clients kept significantly more appointments when their workers were of "other" ethnicity (Cuban, Puerto Rican, South American) than when their workers were Mexican or Anglo Americans. However, Vail (1978) found no differences in black clients' dropout rate as a function of worker race, client attitudes toward whites, patients' perceptions of worker understanding, or worker-client discrepancies in perception.

Minority clients remain at a high risk of failing to benefit from treatment, due in large part to their high dropout rate. Sue (1977) speculates that the brevity of minority clients' treatment may stem from their experiences in face-to-face interactions at community mental health centers. If, as previous studies suggest, minority clients are usually seen by white therapists, then racial differences may impede the development of trust and rapport, resulting in early termination. The overwhelming evidence, then, indicates that minority clients do not participate in treatment beyond the initial session or two, a finding that is particularly disturbing given that clients who drop out of or terminate treatment early appear to rarely seek services elsewhere (Garfield, 1971).

Interpersonal Communication

The literature reviewed above indicates that many minority clients decide on the basis of only one or two interviews not to pursue treatment. This early termination indicates that clients probably make their decisions to drop out on the basis of relatively little interaction with their workers. Initial treatment sessions are usually those in which workers attempt to create a facilitative helping climate—one in which clients may describe their concerns and develop trust and rapport with the worker, and one in which workers may assess the client's strengths, problems, and potential benefit from various therapeutic approaches. What goes wrong? How does race influence clients' decision to terminate treatment? The effects of race on interpersonal communication have probably been subject to more debate and empirical study than most other treatment issues. The accumulated body of literature indicates that race of worker and client frequently affects the amount of verbalization engaged in by the client, the nature or type of information disclosed, and the affect—or emotional tone—of the communication.

Verbalization and self disclosure. Minorities are often reported to verbalize less than whites when they are interviewed by white interviewers. Indeed, when describing their work with racially dissimilar clients, practitioners often note their inability to get clients to verbalize freely. However, few studies have empirically examined the ease or quantity of verbalization in racially similar and dissimilar dyads or compared verbalization rates of minority and white clients. In one study which did address this issue, Womack and Wagner (1967) failed to confirm their hypothesis that white interviewers were better able than black interviewers to elicit information from white interviewees. In their study subjects were white, the treatment setting was white, and the black interviewer was a psychiatrist in the Northwest. Geographical region, status, and socioeconomic factors may have affected subjects' responses.

Concealment—or reticence to verbalize—has characterized the communication of minorities and whites in the United States for many years. Pope observes "there is no reason to believe that the . . . concealment expressed so poignantly in . . . (Negro folk songs) would not serve as an obstacle to open communication, even in a professionally managed mental health interview" (1979, p. 453). Concealment has been self-protective for many minority groups of color, including Asians, Mexican Americans, Native Americans, and blacks who, with good reason feared that whites would use what they say to disparage them. Similarly, according to Smith (1981), minority clients may give only brief responses to workers' inquiries because they fear that their manner of speech will be evaluated negatively.

Workers should be cautious in making assumptions about verbally reticent minority clients; their conclusions may be inaccurate and may deter their helping relationships. In particular, workers should not conclude that such clients are uncooperative or sullen. The history of race relations in the United States should be remembered, and the justifiable concern among minority persons that what they say will be used against them should be recognized. Moreover, workers should carefully evaluate their own reactions to the style and substance of ethnic clients' verbalization, to ensure that there is no basis for the clients' fear of negative evaluation. According to Ridley (1984), the treatment experiences of blacks may be more negative than their prior experiences with whites in the larger society. Even when workers do not draw insidious conclusions about verbally reticent clients, the anxiety they feel when such clients are silent or slow in verbalization may itself negatively affect the therapeutic alliance (Tsui and Schultz, 1985).

In addition to amount of verbalization, the nature of discourse appears to be influenced by racial difference. Studies of race and its influence on interviewee behavior have focused on a number of dependent variables, including amount of self disclosure, depth of self exploration, and superficiality of response. Some studies compare the responses of black and white interviewees to the query of white interviewers; others compare the amount or depth of self disclosure in racially similar and dissimilar dyads. The latter approach enables examination of interviewees' responses to minority interviewers, but few of these studies are available.

The type of information disclosed is a significant issue for practitioners and for researchers with interest in therapy because disclosure of accurate, personally relevant information is almost uniformly viewed as essential to the helping process. Whatever a practitioner's theoretical assumptions and mode of intervention, understanding the client and the presenting problems is a crucial task in the first few sessions. Self disclosure is generally viewed by helpers in western cultures as the most direct means by which persons can make themselves known to others and, therefore, client self disclosure is assumed to be essential. Because self disclosure is viewed as possible only under conditions of trust and rapport, it has acquired significance as a signal of the quality of interpersonal encounter. Indeed, self disclosure is often viewed as a reliable indicator of client involvement in treatment, and some researchers assume that it will correlate positively with treatment outcome (Griffith, 1977).

However, persons of African descent are especially reluctant to disclose themselves to whites, due to the hardships they and their forebears experienced in the United States. A black client's unwillingness to open up to a white therapist reflects a larger unwillingness to disclose him or herself to a representative of the white world (Vontress, 1969). As Harrison (1975) notes, whites have traditionally expected blacks to tell them what they would like to hear, an expectation that contributes to a lack of openness. Moreover, virtually all minorities in the United States have prior negative experiences with whites that contribute to their tendency toward concealment of true feelings.

In situations of racial dissimilarity, interviewees may provide socially desirable responses. Sattler concludes from his review of research and technical reports that minority "respondents inhibit their replies, or give replies that conform more to the existing social or racial stereotypes in order, perhaps, to avoid generating threat and hostility" from whites (1970, p. 152). On the basis of opinion polling studies, Sattler concluded that most studies—regardless of geographical region—indicate that black respondents provided white interviewers with publicly "acceptable" responses, while more privately held and presumably true opinions were expressed to black interviewers. This strategy is perhaps best reflected in the lines of a black poet, Dunbar, in 1896 (1970):

> We wear the mask that grins and lies,
> It hides our cheeks and shades our eyes (p. 112)

In spite of its central role in counseling theories, self disclosure is not universally valued. Vontress (1969) observes that young Japanese Americans are reluctant to express their feelings in the presence of higher-status individuals and in group situations. Indeed, revealing emotions and problems with marriage, jobs, friends, family, and sex is personally unacceptable and counter to cultural norms for most Asians, although perhaps less so for Koreans (Chien and Yamamoto, 1982). LeVine and Franco (1981) found that Anglo Americans reported more self disclosure than Hispanics. Puerto Rican females and lower-class rural blacks also evidence reserve in social relationships. Molina and Franco (1986) found less self disclosure among Mexican-American men, although Mexican-American women were as likely to self disclose as were Anglo-American women. (These findings indicate the influence of gender on self disclosure, an issue to be more fully explored in a later chapter.) Studies have found self disclosure to occur less frequently among blacks than among whites (Jourard and Lasakow, 1958), regardless of social class (Wolkon et al., 1973). Thus self disclosure may be both difficult to achieve and culturally inappropriate with nonwhites.

Minority interviewees do appear to engage in more self disclosure and to explore themselves more deeply when they are interviewed by someone of their own race. In an early study involving a clinical population, Carkhuff and Pierce (1967) examined depth of client self exploration in an initial interview as a function of worker-client match.

Workers included two whites and two blacks, all of whom had completed training in the facilitative conditions of empathy, positive regard, and genuineness. Subjects included both black and white mental patients. Results indicated that clients tended to explore themselves more under conditions of racial similarity. In a similar study, Banks (1972) explored the responses of 16 black and 16 white male high school students in interviews with 4 black and 4 white workers. Again students were found to engage in greater self exploration in racially similar dyads.

Grantham (1973) found that worker race—not racial similarity with client—affected the depth of subjects' self exploration. Studying responses in a single interview, Grantham found that subjects interviewed by whites engaged in greater depth of self exploration than did subjects interviewed by blacks. Grantham hypothesized that black workers may be more concerned with issues of racial identity in the first interview than they are with immediate exploration of deeply personal issues. These findings suggest caution in accepting the salience or validity of self disclosure as criteria in first interview, initial contact situations. Particularly when race of worker and client differ or when participants are minority group members, the expectation of self disclosure and its use as an indicator of the interaction's quality may be unrealistic. Perhaps, instead, issues related to race and the necessary testing of trust are salient and should be emphasized in first sessions. Ridley (1984) cautions that black clients should not be diagnosed as pathological on the basis of their reluctance to reveal personal information. Workers who do not recognize "healthy cultural paranoia" and its role in suppressing black's self disclosure to whites risk "blaming the victim" if they inadvertently diagnose individual pathology in this situation. Indeed, such a tendency may contribute to overestimating the prevalence of paranoid schizophrenia among blacks, an issue to be more fully discussed later in this chapter.

In summary, the empirical literature generally indicates that clients engage in greater self exploration under conditions of racial similarity. On the assumption that depth of self exploration reflects the quality of interaction, this body of literature may be the clearest—indeed perhaps the only—indication of greater effectiveness of minority workers with minority clients (Siegel, 1974). However, further study is clearly needed and, in particular, study of the development of self disclosure over the entire course of therapy. Finally, the cultural inappropriateness of early self disclosure to many ethnic groups should be recognized.

Affect. Verbal reticence and reluctance to reveal personally relevant information in racially dissimilar treatment dyads may signal and be accompanied by a generalized distrust and lack of rapport. Although causal relationships have not been posited or tested, most writers imply that negatively charged affect—or at best, wariness—frequently characterizes communication under conditions of racial dissimilarity. The affect characterizing racially dissimilar treatment dyads and the white worker-minority client situation, in particular, is likely to reflect the affect of interracial encounters in larger society. Thus it should be expected that interracial treatment encounters potentially reflect a variety of negative sentiments.

Distrust and suspiciousness—i.e., minority client distrust of the white worker—is probably the most frequently mentioned barrier in interracial helping situations (Siegel, 1974). Among blacks, distrust of whites has been well documented for its survival function (Griffith, 1977) and has been viewed as a "healthy cultural paranoia" by Grier and Cobbs (1968). As a consequence of historic, pervasive, and institutionalized racism, some blacks demonstrate antipathy to all white persons. Such a pattern is likely to hamper or even preclude their ability to evaluate and react to a white worker as an individual and to enter a trusting helping relationship (Hankins-McNary, 1979). White workers who experience such a pervasive distrust from minority clients need to acknowledge its historical and cultural origin and should recognize the adaptive and survival role that distrust often serves for minorities.

Interracial encounters are often charged with negative feelings for both blacks and whites. Minority clients are likely to experience anxiety when they are evaluated by whites. Baratz (1967) found that black undergraduates, given psychological tests by both black and white graduate student experimenters, experienced higher levels of anxiety when tested by a white examiner. Similarly, Phillips (1960) found that black students manifested submissiveness, hostility, and suspiciousness in their encounters with white counselors, sentiments absent when their counselors were black. Minorities may fear the uses of or conclusions drawn from information they disclose to whites (Sattler, 1970). For some minority clients, fear may be pervasive even in the absence of grounds for it in a specific encounter (Pope, 1979). Submissiveness and overcompliance, a likely consequence of fear, were reported frequently in the practice literature from the 1950s.

Negative feelings may also occur for whites in interracial interactions. Ickes (1984) concluded from experimental study of black-white interaction that white subjects often feel responsibility and concern for making such interactions "work." Such concern not only increased the whites' behavioral involvement, but also caused them to experience interracial interaction as uncomfortable and stressful. Indeed, the discomfort of whites may be greater than that of blacks because the latter generally have more interracial contacts and, hence, are more comfortable.

The negatively charged affect often observed in racially dissimilar encounters may contribute to a generalized lack of rapport. A study by Banks (1972), although focusing only on an initial session, found that racially similar pairs of workers and high school students were rated as higher in rapport than were racially dissimilar dyads. However, worker ability to convey high levels of empathetic understanding also contributed to higher levels of rapport. A number of writers have noted the difficulty of developing rapport with minority clients (Vontress, 1970; Griffith and Jones, 1979). The challenges to rapport under conditions of racial dissimilarity are numerous and should not be ignored. Yet the underlying "healthy paranoia" should be recognized and respected.

Style of communication. Helping encounters may be viewed as one subset of more general social interaction and, therefore, may be expected to reflect all the factors that influence communication in general. To the extent that culture affects communication, then it should be expected to affect worker-client communication, particularly under conditions of racial dissimilarity. Communication encompasses both verbal and nonverbal interaction (Pope, 1979), and persons may convey messages through a variety of communication "channels." Communication channels include the verbal, the visual, the facial, the paralinguistic (voice tone, pauses, rate of speech), and the kinetic (body motion) (Mehrabian, 1972). Persons who wish to communicate explicitly and directly generally rely primarily on the verbal channel; that is, they convey the intended message through words (Pope, 1979). However, many messages that persons are not able to verbalize explicitly are expressed through other channels. Thus, a person who is uncomfortable about racial dissimilarity but chooses not to express that discomfort verbally may reveal or "leak" the true feelings through nonverbal channels.

Since communication is central to nearly all models of treatment, workers must be able to understand their clients and to be understood by them. Ability to understand the meaning of gestures, voice tone, and body posture among minority persons requires an understanding of cultural history, institutions, values, and lifestyle (Vontress, 1981). Minorities are nearly always familiar with white culture since it is conveyed as a "norm" and is widely disseminated in media, song, literature, and music. As a result, minorities are usually able to understand the communication of whites. However, minority cultures are less widely disseminated, with the consequence that whites may know little about minority persons and have difficulty understanding their communication. Since cultural groups vary both in their reliance on various channels of communication and in their styles of communicating within specific channels, clear communication is often a challenge. Ability to "read" nonverbal messages has served as a "survival mechanism" for oppressed groups (Smith, 1981; Sue, 1981). For example, blacks may spend more time than whites observing people, unobtrusively or unnoticed, to "see where they are coming from" (Sue, 1981, p. 155). As a result of such experiences, minority persons often are adept at "reading" nonverbal messages in others and at discreetly conveying intended messages through nonverbal channels.

Members of ethnic color groups may employ patterns of eye contact that differ from those of whites. Some laboratory studies indicate that black speakers and white speakers demonstrate differences in the times they gaze and look away in conversation. Whites were found to gaze while listening, and to avert their gaze while speaking; in contrast black speakers averted their gaze while listening and gazed at their partners while speaking. Whites regard visual gaze as a cue to speak, signifying that the other person is ready to listen. Blacks, however, look while speaking rather than while listening and may continue to speak when gazing at a white person (Fugita, Wexley, and Hillery, 1974; LaFrance and Mayo, 1976). Although the origin and meaning of this difference is not clear, problems in black-white communication may result. As Ickes observes,

> Blacks tend to consider it rude, confrontational, or disrespectful to maintain eye contact with a person who is speaking, whereas whites tend to consider it evasive, inattentive, or disrespectful not to do so. A common outcome of this clash of cultural expectations is that black and white participants both experience their visual interaction as somewhat awkward and uncomfortable (1984, p. 331).

According to Vontress (1981), Puerto Rican females are socialized to avoid eye contact with men. If not aware of possible cultural differences in eye gaze, white professionals may draw erroneous conclusions about minority clients. For example, if a minority client looks away while the worker is speaking, the worker may assume incorrectly that the client is not listening, is distant, or does not trust the worker. Whites also may interpret the gaze directed toward them as aggressive staring when, in fact, their minority partner's eye contact while speaking is simply a reflection of a cultural pattern. "Such crossed-up cues may prompt both to speak at the same time or be simultaneously silent" (Pope, 1979, p. 461), thus disrupting interviews and conversations.

Interpersonal space—preferred distance beween listener and speaker—also varies across cultures. According to Pope (1979), whites are most comfortable with greater space between listener and speaker (26–28 inches), while blacks prefer shorter distances (21–24 inches). Moreover, conversation appears to terminate at different distances for blacks and whites. Laboratory studies indicate that blacks tended to stop a conversation if distance between the two participants exceeded 36 inches, while whites tolerated conversation as distance increased to 44 inches. Blacks and whites who are unaware of these cultural differences tend to judge each other inappropriately. For example, minority clients may find it difficult to verbalize simply because they are too far away from the worker. These communication factors may interfere with or impede dyadic exchanges in an interview when interviewer and interviewee are of different race.

Cultural differences are evident also in verbal communication. Native Americans often communicate with an economy of language, using concrete rather than abstract words (Vontress, 1981). The language of lower socioeconomic black persons often contains pronunciation, idioms, slang, and a reliance on nonverbal communication that may be difficult for white or even middle-class black listeners to understand (Vontress, 1981). However, cultural differences do not mean deficits. The once widespread myths that black clients are nonverbal or have inferior language ability have been debunked. Smith (1977) cites a number of studies of language patterns which demonstrate that black children have the same grammatical competence as middle-class white children; moreover, their language systems are more than adequate for abstract thinking. Distinctions should be made between clients who cannot verbalize, clients who can verbalize but refuse to talk for some reason, and clients who communicate although in a manner different from that expected or desired by the listener (Smith, 1981). Workers should recognize that black clients may "jive" (trick or deceive) them through language. According to Bass, Acosta, and Evans (1982), jive talk may have several purposes. Sometimes, black dialect may represent the only mode of verbal communication available to the patient and may allow for the expression of feelings that otherwise may not be expressed in therapy. At other times, jive may serve to block the expression of some of the patient's inner feelings. Jive may also be used to maintain distance with the worker, especially when the client's past relationships with other whites were negative. Workers must assess client cues and use of jive language and, where appropriate, ask the client to interpret to ensure understanding of what is said. In short, they must check to see if they accurately understand what their different-race clients attempt to communicate.

It is logical to assume that minority professionals are better able than white professionals to understand the communication of minority clients. Indeed, Schumacher, Banikiotes, and Banikiotes (1972), who studied familiarity with black language, found that black students did better than did white students, who in turn scored better than white professionals. However, Bryson and Cody (1973) reported that black counselors were not significantly better than white counselors in understanding black clients.

Although minority group members are likely to be exposed to and, therefore, be familiar with the verbal communication of whites, white language often sounds different to them. For example, in contrast to black speech, white language is characterized by stress on standard grammar and precise enunciation. Cheek suggests that to most blacks, white speech sounds nasal, formal in style, or clipped in sound. White conversation may seem subdued and intellectual, symbolized by "square" expressions like "golly" and "gee whiz." Because emotions are controlled and tones are quiet in the communication of whites, "Blacks suspect that whites only . . . emotionally express themselves when they've been drinking, or when they escape from the presence of people who know them in their routine roles . . ." (Cheek, 1976, p. 54). If they are unaware of how U.S. society has put special meaning on certain words and social situations, whites may unknowingly offend nonwhite clients. Words or phrases like "boy," "auntie," "Uncle Tom," "you people," "sold down the river," "Chinaman's chance," "Jew him down," "Scot-free," and "in a coon's age" may convey the white speaker's insensitivity to or lack of awareness of racist connotations.

Cheek (1976) also notes racial differences in the content of conversation in dyads or small groups. Black-black conversation frequently focuses on such content as white people and their racist attitudes, forthcoming social events, mutual friends, and being black in America; moreover, conversation may be marked by slang, laughter, gestures, Black English, and assumed intimacy. Black-black communication generally serves purposes of relaxation, furthering mutual interests, or maintaining relationships. In contrast, black-white conversations generally focus on such content as the weather, school or work, mutual acquaintances, the news or current events, or activities of interest to whites, and only rarely on social events that are not work-related. Such conversations often have a restrained style, emphasis on grammar, and little use of slang. Black-white communication serves functions of obtaining or maintaining positions, of demonstrating a capacity to get along, or obtaining or keeping business connections. Cheek observes that these contrasting styles and differing points of emphasis have produced conflict and lack of communication. This has been particularly true of the conditions faced by blacks in therapeutic situations. Black clients are met by white practitioners who apply the only standards they know (typically those taught in professional training, which has ignored the black experience). Standards are usually based on white values and white expectations for judging the appropriateness of verbal and nonverbal behavior. Research has pointed out that black interviewers elicit greater linguistic elaboration than do white interviewers and that there is low linguistic compatibility between black students and white counselors. Such findings lead to the not surprising conclusion that there is greater facility in communication among persons who are similar in characteristics. Other data are found to generally support the contention that blacks do not feel psychologically comfortable or verbally free in a completely white-oriented clinical or therapeutic situation (Cheek, 1976, pp. 55–56).

Since most forms of helping are dependent on language as the basic tool of communication, it is imperative for mental health professionals to discard stereotypes about the limitations of the language of minority clients (Smith, 1977). Furthermore, effective treatment requires worker skill in understanding and clearly communicating with the client. Workers must be able to attach both connotative and denotative meaning to the client's language in order to understand and relate empathically with the client. As Vontress observes,

> So many customary counseling techniques require instantaneous comprehension. Paraphrasing, reflection, and interpretation presuppose an understanding of the client's language. In order to reflect accurately what the client is experiencing and feeling, the counselor should be able to derive meaning from the totality of an individual's communicative behavior on the spot (Vontress, 1981, pp. 96–97).

The literature reviewed above and the honest reflection of practitioners who have worked with racially dissimilar clients reveal that such understanding is not easily attained. Lower-class blacks in particular often speak with pronunciation, idioms, and slang that are difficult for white and black middle-class counselors to understand (Smith, 1981; Vontress, 1981). Workers often wish to conceal their inability to understand their clients and continue the dialogue, hoping to catch up later. Instead, they become increasingly confused. Personal fluency in the client's language is, of course, the ideal (Vontress, 1981). However, for a variety of reasons, workers fail to understand clients; in such cases, the most honest response is to ask for an explanation or repetition. Such requests not only enhance the likelihood that the worker comprehends what the client says; they also convey the worker's genuineness, sincerity, and interest in the client.

Given that conversation is the primary means of engaging in the therapeutic relationship (Wohl, 1981) and given the challenges that race poses for communication, it should be no surprise that the clinical literature is replete with references to problems in these regards. Early treatment sessions are often characterized by uneasiness, testing, and uncertainty about what the other participant is really thinking, feeling, or communicating. These events should be recognized for what they are—reflections of difference and unfamiliarity—and should not be interpreted devoid of their racial origin and meaning. Nor should such difficulties be erroneously interpreted as negative transference reactions, as signals of client resistance, or as indicators of client deficiency or inappropriateness for treatment. Although resistance may occur in interracial treatment and although some clients or workers may be unable to work under conditions of racial dissimilarity, all awkwardnesses in communication do not signal poor prognosis. Rather, communication difficulties may more appropriately be viewed as reflections of cultural segregation in U.S. society, as indicators of strangeness experienced in close contact with persons of another race, and as appropriate reactions to anticipated or conveyed stereotypical attitudes and behaviors (Griffith and Jones, 1979).

Assessment

One of the earliest tasks confronting workers in the initial stages of helping is understanding, assessing, or diagnosing the client's problem. Almost all approaches to practice view accurate and thorough assessment as central to the success of treatment. Assessment generally serves as the basis for subsequent treatment decisions, including the identification of outcomes for pursuit and the choice of interventive method for attaining those outcomes (Proctor and Rosen, 1983).

According to traditional social casework theory, assessment may be viewed as entailing three distinguishable components. First, workers must obtain a variety of information: about the client, his or her environment, the client's constraints and resources, the client's problems, and the desired objectives. This task requires communication skills of the worker such as those reviewed in the preceding section. Second, the worker must interpret the information that has been obtained. Interpretation generally involves comparison, even implicitly, of the client's current situation to some set of norms. This involves attribution of the client's problem to some source or cause, or analysis of how the client's current behavior may be functional or reinforcing. Hollis describes this aspect of assessment as weighing "up the facts to see where the trouble lies" (1964, p. 129). A third component of assessment is classifying or categorizing the problem (Hollis, 1964), or affixing a diagnostic label. Classification may enable professionals to describe the problem in readily understood terms, may facilitate comparisons between the client and other persons, or may serve administrative and statistical purposes.

Assessment may focus on the client as a person, on the client's problem behavior, on the client's milieu, or on a combination of those factors. Errors in assessment may occur (1) when a problem is labeled or identified in the absence of supportive evidence or facts, (2) when the worker fails to detect or observe a problem that does exist in fact, or (3) when the worker fails to reach a complete understanding of the client. Because assessment involves, most centrally, judgments about persons and their lives, and because racial dissimilarity typically involves situations of unfamiliarity or lack of knowledge, racial effects on the accuracy of assessment would be expected. Indeed, Vontress (1981) views the accurate diagnoses of culturally different clients as even more difficult than communicating with and relating to them. In this section, literature about the effects of racial similarity/dissimilarity on assessment and literature on assessment of minority clients will be reviewed for each aspect of the assessment process.

The obtaining of information.   Does race affect the type and amount of information clients convey to workers? Do the problems and concerns clients express to workers vary according to client race? The literature on interpersonal communication reviewed above indicates that racial dissimilarity between interviewer and interviewee in initial contacts may suppress the amount of verbalization, hence the amount of information obtained, from the interviewee. Moreover, information that is obtained is likely to be less personally relevant, less "deep," and more "socially acceptable." In a study focusing on interviewee problem description, Shosteck (1977) found that blacks were more likely to report certain types of problems to black interviewers than to white interviewers: Specifically, blacks were more likely to mention to black interviewers problems of poor housing, high housing cost, poor job opportunities or unemployment, poor schools, and racial segregation. On the other hand, black respondents were more likely to mention to white interviewers than to black interviewers such problems as inflation, high taxes, and poor street conditions. The researchers concluded that black respondents were more likely to mention problems with potential racial significance or sensitivity to black interviewers than to white interviewers.

Do the problems that clients present vary as a function of client race or ethnicity? That is, are white clients, black clients, Asian-American clients, and Native American clients likely to present different issues and concerns to the workers and agencies from whom they seek help? This question has been neither thoroughly nor systematically addressed, although some pertinent data are available. Black college students did not present significantly different problems than did white students when seeking help from a university counseling center (Baum and Lamb, 1983). However, findings from another study indicate significant differences in types of help requested by black clients and white clients (Wood and Sherrets, 1984). Although overall more alike than different, black clients were more likely than white clients to indicate they sought certain kinds of help:

1. help in dealing with legal issues or agency, such as social services or schools
2. assurance about their mental health status

3. medication
4. referral to an appropriate community agency

These differences suggest that black clients may seek more direct and immediate types of services, at least from agencies perceived to represent the majority white society.

In a similar study of these issues, client reason for seeking help was found to vary more by race or ethnicity than by client gender, income, or marital status. Evans, Acosta, Yamamoto, and Hurwicz (1986) studied Hispanics, blacks, and Caucasians who sought help from a psychiatric outpatient clinic, with respect to their reasons for seeking help. In all three ethnic groups, most clients wanted an informed collaborator in resolving their emotional concerns; however, this request was more frequent among Caucasians than Hispanics and blacks. Hispanic clients, more so than blacks or Caucasians, perceived their problems as residing outside themselves, and therefore sought more action from their workers than they expected to exert themselves. Similarly, Hispanics and blacks were more likely than Caucasians to hope that the worker would resolve their problems. It should be noted that cultural differences in client presentation of a problem might influence workers' perception of client motivation. For example, workers were found to perceive clients as more motivated and with a better prognosis when their reasons for seeking help were intrinsic rather than extrinsic (Schwartz, Friedlander, and Tedeschi, 1986).

Another study sheds light on the types of problems for which Chicano clients sought help at community mental health clinics in South Texas. Gomez, Zurcher, Farris, and Becker (1985) found that 74 percent of the clients reported an emotional problem, 46 percent reported family problems, 40 percent sought assistance with a social problem. Substance abuse was a problem for 35 percent of clients, employment and finances for 30 percent, and relationship problems were identified by 21 percent of clients. Obviously, clients identified multiple areas as problematic.

Cultural norms may influence the form in which clients express their problems. According to Lorenzo and Adler (1984), mental illness and psychological problems are viewed by the Chinese as shameful, whereas physical problems are not. Therefore, Chinese clients often express emotional crises as somatic complaints (Leong, 1986). Their expression of problems as physical even affects the referral process; Chinese individuals often take their problems first to medical professionals, who then refer them for psychosocial treatment.

Liss, Welner, Robins, and Richardson (1973) studied the symptoms of white and black psychiatric patients and concluded that several symptoms were significantly more frequent among blacks. These included dull affect, delusions, hallucinations, psychomotor retardation, decreased need for sleep, increased speech, and fighting. Depressive affect was significantly more frequent for whites. Similarly, Skilbeck, Acosta, Yamamoto, and Evans (1984) studied self-reported psychiatric symptoms of black, Hispanic, and white applicants for outpatient therapy and found that Hispanics and whites checked more numerous and more intense symptoms than the norm, while the reported symptoms of blacks were fewer and less intense.

Racial factors are also likely to affect the worker's comprehension of problems and information provided by clients. When vocabulary and paralinguistic communication differ across ethnic groups, workers may err in understanding information the client provides. The worker's subjective impressions of the client may be erroneous when worker and client are of different cultural groups. As Stewart explains,

> when counselors and counselees share the same culture, counselors intu-
> itively rely on shared assumptions to flesh out client intentions of counselees,
> and draw upon personal knowledge to fill in gaps in the client's back-
> grounds. When the cultures of the participants in counseling differ, coun-
> selors often lack implicit inferences to create coherent images of counselees
> (1981, p. 61).

Workers may, on the basis of existing assumptions, fail to seek certain information from clients or make inaccurate assumptions about information they do obtain.

Interpretation of assessment data. The interpretation of data obtained in an assessment—that is, the judgment of health or problems—may be vulnerable to the effects of racial difference because of factors related to the professional knowledge base and to worker familiarity with minority cultures. White middle-class norms pervade social science and professional knowledge; indeed, notions of mental health, normality, and even physical health are based on data from white cultures (Sue, 1977). White middle-class norms may be discriminatory when universally applied across populations and situations (Sue, 1981). The white middle-class value base from which criteria derive may not be recognized, with the result that persons who vary from the criteria will be judged as deviant. For example, "autonomy" and "competence" reflect white middle-class notions of maturity, and many ethnic minority groups place little value on "insight" (Sue, 1981). In contrast, noises, hallucinations, or temporary visions are part of religious practice in some Hispanic or South American cultures and do not indicate the disturbance or pathology they imply in dominant western culture (Vontress, 1981; Malgady, Rogler, and Costantino, 1987).

Racial stereotypes also affect workers' interpretation of information about racially dissimilar clients. Wampold, Casas, and Atkinson (1981) tested this possibility in an analogy study in which white and minority graduate students were presented with information about hypothetical persons and asked to make judgments based on the data presented to them. White students were more susceptible than the minority trainees to the influence of stereotypes when processing information about ethnic minorities. Stereotypes prevented them from distinguishing actual information about the client from their own prior, albeit incorrect, assumptions. Indeed, the stereotypes held by mental health workers may contribute to differential diagnosis of minority clients in mental health service systems.

Findings from another study revealed that black students' problems were assessed differently than whites', in spite of the fact that their presenting problems did not in fact differ (Baum and Lamb, 1983). The problems of black students were more often assessed as involving school work, while those of white students were more often seen as involving mood and interpersonal relationships.

Assessment is further affected by worker race. Jones and Gray (1985) report that black psychiatrists' and white psychiatrists' responses reflected differences in the rate, order, and frequency with which various problems were seen in black clients. For example, black psychiatrists reported depression as the most frequent presenting problem for black men, while white psychiatrists reported work-related problems as most frequent. The investigators suggested that white psychiatrists may be less likely to perceive depression as a presenting problem for black men because it is not consistent with racial stereotypes.

An important aspect of problem interpretation is the attribution of causality, or assessment of the problem's origin. According to traditional social casework theory, thorough problem assessment requires analysis of factors in the client's personality or the environment that contribute to the difficulty (Hollis, 1964). Moreover, attributing causality to various components of the client's situation is necessary for locating points for intervention. There is considerable evidence that cultural factors are associated with differences in perceptions of causal events, or attribution of causality. Blacks have been found to be more external in orientation than whites (Gurin, Gurin, Lao, and Beattie, 1969; Davis and Proctor, 1981), where locus of control refers to perception of events as influenced by factors external or internal to the person's control. For many minority groups, external or societal factors may be more potent influences on their situations than intrapsychic factors (Sue, 1981). Even when evaluating the contribution of prior childhood experiences to current presenting problems, black clients tend to focus less on experiences within the family than on systems surrounding the family (Smith, 1981). Smith concludes that "minorities are inclined to perceive mental health as situationally or environmentally determined," while whites tend to view mental health as independent of situations (1981, p. 164).

Such differences in attribution are likely to affect the accuracy of problem assessment when the races of a worker and client are different. Many models of practice are predicated upon assumptions that the problems of individual clients are caused by intrapsychic, or personal, disturbances. Professionals so trained generally attribute causality to personal factors. Thus workers and minority clients often view the world, and more importantly view causation of the client's problem, differently (Smith, 1981). As a result, the client may conclude that the worker doesn't understand the problem and, therefore, is unable to help.

Worker and client must address, at some point in treatment, the question of how much and what kind of change should be sought in the client's situation (Draguns, 1981). In this regard, again, race is often an important factor. For example, work with minorities—and in particular with blacks—often needs to go beyond psychological adjustment to incorporate change in environments or the social system (Smith, 1981). Workers must, therefore, be able to assess the strengths and weaknesses in a client's culture, the client's functioning within that culture, and the stresses within the larger social system. Moreover, both minority and white workers should be able to determine when the source of their client's problems is racial and socioeconomic, or personal and independent of race and socioeconomic factors.

Hankins-McNary (1979) cautions that when minority workers identify with clients only on a racial level, they may err in their attribution of problems in one of two ways. On the one hand, they may overestimate the role of race in the client's situation and attribute most, if not all, of the client's problems to external societal factors. The "mark of oppression" theory (Kardiner and Ovesey, 1962), or the assumption that racism has inevitable and detrimental effects on the personalities of blacks in the United States, encourages workers "to look for and find only evidence of psychopathology in blacks" (Maultsby, 1982). In short, pathology is seen as inextricably linked to race. On the other hand, minority workers may deny identification with the client, overlook race, and attribute all problems to individual factors rather than such social issues as discrimination. To avoid these errors, professionals who work with ethnic clients should assess personal, interpersonal, and social system functioning; moreover, they should be able to attribute causality to internal or external forces in a manner appropriate for the particular client, the client's problem, and the client's own perspective on problem attribution. Such a capacity requires workers to understand events as clients see them and to appreciate the client's world view, even if it differs from their own.

Classification and diagnosis. A number of questions surround the issues of race and diagnosis. An obvious issue is true variation in incidence of various disorders by race; that is, do blacks, whites, Hispanics, and

Asian Americans actually experience differences in types and rates of disorders? Another issue is diagnostic bias, which results in the over-representation of certain diagnoses in various racial groups even when rates of true incidence do not differ.

In spite of the significance of these issues, surprisingly little research has addressed the relationship between race and diagnosis (Wright, Scott, Pierre-Paul, and Gore, 1984). However, early writings about ethnic clients reflect the operation of racial bias in diagnosis. For example, prior to 1950 the psychological functioning of blacks was viewed as immature and fixated at childlike levels. Blacks, therefore, were believed to be less susceptible to mental illness than whites. "Depression, paranoia, and suicide were rarely diagnosed because Blacks allegedly lacked the mental development presumed to be requisite for their etiology" (Griffith and Jones, 1979, p. 226). Consistent with their presumed fixation at immature levels, acting out tendencies and hysteria were frequently diagnosed among black clients. However, after World War II, white therapists who had worked with black servicemen acknowledged their psychological disturbances and wrote of their susceptibility to mental illness. Causation generally was attributed to centuries of social and economic oppression resulting from racism in U.S. society. While such a view may seem to reflect progress in professional thought, it is disturbing to realize that personality "impairment" in blacks was often viewed as irreversible. In the 1960s blacks who experienced psychosocial difficulties were generally seen as culturally deprived. Because the cause of their problems—cultural deprivation—was viewed as different from the cause of problems experienced by whites, diagnosis and often treatment were also different for blacks.

Contemporary literature on race and treatment continues to suggest the operation of racial bias in diagnosis. When assessment focuses on the client's global personality rather than on specific behaviors or problems, there appears to be a risk that minority clients will receive different labels or diagnoses than white clients. Particularly in psychiatry, black patients are frequently assessed as hostile, not motivated for treatment, not "psychologically minded," impulse ridden, primitive in character structure, and possessing few ego strengths (Hankins-McNary, 1979). More widespread in professional literature are assumptions that black clients have negative self concepts and poor impulse control. These labels persist in spite of the strength of black families to buffer society's derogatory messages to black children (Smith, 1977) and in spite of blacks' ability to endure the frustrations and stresses of racism and economic deprivation (Jones, 1979). Workers also perceive rage in minority clients, ignoring the fact that oppression is a daily reality for most minorities and that the rage provoked by the environment often must be repressed, displaced, sublimated, or internalized (Jones, 1979).

The venting of rage may often appear inappropriate if considered only in relation to the immediate precipitating event. However, provocations in the life of the average Afro-American are longstanding and cumulative. Therefore, although the immediate provocation may be minor, when it is seen in light of myriad other precipitating events, the combination may result in the release of pent-up anger." (Jones, 1979, p. 114)

Minority clients, and especially blacks, are often characterized by professionals as suspicious and paranoid. Although it may be difficult for white workers to distinguish between fears of oppression that are founded and those that are actually pathological, workers should recognize that for members of historically oppressed minority groups, suspicion and paranoia may represent well-developed survival mechanisms (Jones, 1979; Ridley, 1984).

Minority clients are often diagnosed as concrete in their thought; that is, they are assumed to be preoccupied with the specific and actual in the environment rather than with the symbolic or the generalized (Jones, 1979). White workers often view concreteness as a reflection of deficient intelligence or mental health (Jones, 1979). However, a primary focus on pragmatic and basic realities of existence need not be viewed as excluding the capacity for abstract thinking. In many situations concrete thought is appropriate, demonstrating that a client is in touch with his or her social reality; abstraction, in such cases, might reflect denial and escapism. Jones (1979) contends that abstract and concrete thinking are equally valuable processes and appropriate depending on the circumstances. Thus workers should assess thought patterns in functional terms rather than always viewing concreteness as an indicator of impaired capacity.

Standardized diagnostic instruments may be particularly vulnerable to racial bias. Most existing diagnostic tests are based on and reflect norms derived from white populations and fail to provide baselines for different ethnic groups. For example, behaviors, feelings, and beliefs that are customary in many Hispanic subcultures may be keyed as reflecting pathology on standardized tests such as the Minnesota Multiphasic Personality Inventory (MMPI) (Malgady et al., 1987). Mistrust between client and tester, client misunderstanding of the testing purpose, and erroneous interpretation of results also increase the probability of cultural and ethnic bias of standardized diagnostic tests (Sattler, 1970; Smith, 1977; Hankins-McNary, 1979).

Adebimpe asserts that

unless the factor of race is taken into consideration in the construction and validation of a psychiatric rating scale, the possibility of . . . discrepancies exists whenever the scale is used for ethnically mixed patient groups (1981, p. 283).

Evidence to date suggests that the MMPI test, in particular, is susceptible to cultural influence. For example, the MMPI may lead to false positives in the diagnosis of schizophrenia among blacks (Adebimpe et al., 1979). Among American Indian patients, MMPI scores appear to be more influenced by cultural group than by pathology. According to the research of Pollack and Shore (1980), the test scores of patients diagnosed with schizophrenia, nonpsychotic depression, situational reaction, and antisocial alcoholism did not differ markedly among patients of the same cultural group; the scores of different cultural groups, however, did differ. These findings suggest that test scores vary with ethnicity, not pathology. Thus "the use of the MMPI in a cross-cultural setting amplifies the risk of a false perception of the patient's psychological state" (Pollack and Shore, 1980, p. 949).

Studies have insufficiently explored the effects of racial difference in testing. Moreover, in existing studies of racial effects in standardized personality testing, differences in subject age and measurement of independent variables complicate the comparison of results across ethnicity (Sattler, 1970). However, similar to findings of studies involving race and IQ testing, black subjects appeared anxious but were less hostile with white examiners than with black examiners (Sattler, 1970).

Empirical studies of racial effects in diagnosis tend to follow one of two methodologies. One approach is the analogue study, in which professionals are asked to make an assessment on the basis of a "stimulus" case study, in which client race is varied. In such studies, differences in worker assessment are attributed to worker racial bias. The advantage of analogue studies is their control of all factors other than race that could contribute to variability in diagnosis, such as the nature and severity of the presenting problem. The only factor that varies is designated client race, and differences in diagnosis are attributed to the worker's reaction to client race. The second approach is the archival study, in which the diagnoses given to clients of various racial and ethnic groups are compared. An advantage of this approach is the reliance on data regarding actual clients, about whom the assessor has an opportunity to gather detailed information. However, this methodology precludes distinguishing between the effects of racial bias in the assessor and true difference in prevalence and severity of disorders among clients.

Data from the best designed studies indicate that actual prevalence of mental disorder does not vary significantly by race or ethnicity. Overall, nonwhites are no more likely than whites to experience mental disorder or to be admitted to treatment facilities (Cockerham, 1981). Any variance in the incidence of mental disorder overall or of specific diagnoses by race is probably due to socioeconomic factors, which are significant (see Chapter 12 of this text).

However, clinical diagnosis often varies by race. For example, in both analogue and archival studies, blacks receive significantly more diagnoses of schizophrenia than do white patients (Lane, 1968; Sattler, 1977); this is particularly so when MMPI scores are used in diagnosing schizophrenia (Adebimpe, Gigandet, and Harris, 1979). In an extensive archival study of nearly 14,000 clients in 17 mental health centers in Seattle, Sue (1977) found that blacks were significantly more likely to receive diagnosis of personality disorder and were less likely to be diagnosed as experiencing transient situational disturbances than were white clients. However, diagnoses given to Native Americans, Asian Americans, and Chicanos were not significantly different from those assigned to white patients. In a field study, Baskin, Bluestone, and Nelson (1981) examined differences in the diagnoses assigned to black, white, and Hispanic patients in a New York psychiatric outpatient clinic in 1968. The findings indicated that ethnic minority patients received different diagnoses than white patients. Black patients were more likely to be diagnosed as alcoholic and schizophrenic, while Hispanic patients were more likely to be diagnosed as having depressive/affective disorders, transient situational disturbances, and nonpsychotic disorders. In addition, more Hispanic patients were diagnosed as mentally retarded than other groups.

White student social workers were found to assign more diagnoses of severe emotional problems to black than white clients, while black students viewed black clients as healthier than white clients (Wallace, 1977). According to Wright et al. (1984), the symptoms contributing most to misdiagnosis in blacks include suspiciousness, hallucinations, delusions, and flat or inappropriate affect. Overemphasis of hallucinations, suspiciousness, and delusions by white assessors may contribute to the overdiagnosis of schizophrenia among blacks, as might the "masking" of anxiety behind an appearance of hostility (Mayo, 1981). More recently, Skilbeck et al. (1984) found that black patients were more likely than white or Hispanic patients to be diagnosed by therapists as severely disturbed, even when their symptoms were the same or milder. Even neuropsychological tests of central nervous system functioning have been found subject to racial effects, resulting in misclassification of normal minorities as brain damaged (Adams, Boake, and Crain, 1982).

The evidence, however, is not unanimous. Other studies have failed to detect expected differences in diagnoses by client race (Dorfman and Kleiner, 1962; Krebs, 1971). Such findings, however, sometimes raise other concerns. For example, one analogue study found that black clients were rated by social workers as having less psychopathology than identically described white clients (Fischer and Miller, 1963). Similarly, Merluzzi and Merluzzi (1978) report that white graduate students in counseling rated black-labeled cases as more positive than identical cases that were unlabeled or labeled white. These findings may reflect workers' overcompensation to avoid negative racial bias; or they may reflect worker acceptance of behavior in blacks that would trigger concern if displayed by whites. From their analysis of case records of hospitalized blacks and whites, de Hoyos and de Hoyos (1965) found that fewer symptoms were recorded for black inpatients than for whites. The investigators hypothesized that white mental health professionals had less contact with and therefore less information about black patients.

Such findings raise the possibility that failure to detect an existing disturbance may in itself be a form of inaccurate diagnosis. Lewis, Balla, and Shanok (1979) concluded from epidemiological data, case records, and clinical observation that psychopathology frequently goes unrecognized, unreported, and untreated among black delinquent populations. Affective disorders, and in particular depression, may be underdiagnosed among blacks (Jones, 1980; Adebimpe, 1982). White assessors often fail to detect somatic complaints, a common symptom of depression, in blacks (Wright et al., 1984). According to the clinical observations of Lewis et al. (1979), black delinquent children referred for psychiatric evaluation often are dismissed as having character disorders in spite of clear evidence of psychotic or organic problems. They assert that professionals often ignore symptoms in black children that would be recognized as pathological in whites. Their observations indicate that treatment facilities fail to admit—or admit and then quickly discharge or transfer to correctional facilities—seriously disturbed black delinquents. Their review of epidemiological data further indicates that abuse and neglect often go unrecognized and unreported among black delinquent children.

Failure to diagnose existing problems may be due to efforts by white professionals to avoid the bias of racism and overdiagnose pathology among blacks.

> It has been our experience that, as a result of efforts to avoid possible overdiagnosis, Black delinquent children and their parents must demonstrate flamboyantly psychotic behavior before they are recognized as being in need of treatment . . . The economically deprived environment from which the Black delinquent often comes, the behaviors with which he is charged, and his adolescent stage of development influence the white diagnostician to dismiss even the most bizarre and illogical acts as manifestations of normal ghetto difficulties. That his behavior is usually considered deviant and inappropriate by his own family and even by his peers is often disregarded (Lewis et al., 1979, pp. 59–60).

In summary, literature reveals clear evidence of racial bias in assessment. Some studies show that ethnic minority patients are overrepresented in certain diagnostic categories, and other studies show that their problems go undetected. A few studies fail to find evidence of the influence of race in diagnosis. Sattler (1977) concludes that diagnostic judgment is not systematically biased against minority clients, and that, even when race appears to play a role, the exact nature of its effect and manner of operation are unknown. However, there is substantial evidence that nonwhites often receive different diagnoses than whites, even when their symptoms and problems are the same.

Practitioners should be wary of the potential consequences of inaccurate diagnosis. To the extent that assessment is inaccurate, outcomes pursued and the interventive method chosen may be inappropriate. Such treatment is unlikely to resolve clients' actual problems, resulting in the perpetuation of suffering (Lewis et al., 1979). In addition, clients diagnosed inaccurately, especially when they are diagnosed with a particular problem in the absence of supporting evidence, may experience "a career of mistreatment from which escape is difficult" (Adebimpe, 1981, p. 279). Finally, misdiagnosis of minority clients is likely to perpetuate racially stereotyped notions of psychopathology and personality.

Racial bias in assessment may vary across settings, geographical regions, professional training of workers, and diagnostic procedures. Its incidence may depend, most directly, on the diagnostician's knowledge of and familiarity with minority cultures and communication patterns. It should be recognized, however, that assessment is fundamentally an aspect of judgment, and neither the process nor product of assessment is absolute. Such judgments are especially prone to error under conditions of dissimilarity. Therefore, diagnostic accuracy and reduction of racial bias remain critically important for the helping professions.

Choice of Intervention

Once client problems have been assessed, the worker must select an interventive approach for their remediation. Choice of intervention may be based on a variety of factors, including empirical support for its effectiveness, its appropriateness for the presenting problem, worker comfort and expertise in employing the intervention, and its acceptability to client (Cormier and Cormier, 1979; Rosen, Proctor, and Livne, 1985). Given the extent to which racial dissimilarity affects assessment of clients and their problems, it is also a major influence on worker selection of interventive approaches.

The therapeutic relationship has long been recognized as a central—if not primary—means of intervention. In traditional social casework and in numerous psychological theories of helping (most notably Rogerian client-centered therapy), the relationship between worker and client has been regarded as a "core" or basic element in determining effectiveness (Rogers, 1962; Proctor, 1982). Some have viewed its role as so central that treatment gains are believed to vary directly with the quality of the relationship (Parloff, 1961). Such assumptions are challenged by those who assert that the therapeutic relationship may be difficult to achieve under conditions of racial dissimilarity. For example, Griffith observes that "given the history and current status of black-white relations, a mutually accepting relationship may be difficult to achieve between the white therapist and black client. Cultural differences and ingrained attitudes toward blacks may interfere with the white therapist's ability to convey accurate empathy, respect, and appreciation for the black client" (Griffith, 1977, p. 31). Wohl (1981) questions whether an "outsider" can deliver, express, and communicate aspects of the therapeutic relationship such as empathic understanding with a minority group client. However, there is a modest body of empirical support for the effectiveness of empathy in interracial treatment situations (Carkhuff and Pierce, 1967; Banks, 1972).

In challenging the assumption that the therapeutic relationship is universally applicable, Wohl (1981) observes that the nature and elements of a "good human relationship" are probably different in various cultural groups. Some of the interventions involved in the therapeutic relationship—such as acceptance, respect, empathy, and regard—may be consistent with a particular culture's norms while others may not be (Wohl, 1981). Certainly the abilities to assess the appropriateness of various relationship techniques and to engage in a relationship with a racially dissimilar client depend on the worker's knowledge of and skill in communicating with the specific minority group.

Worker-client racial dissimilarity may influence the development and content of transference and counter-transference phenomena. Race-related assumptions and fears of both worker and client may be mobilized and may hamper both the formation of transference and accurate perceptions of each other (Curry, 1964; Cavenar and Spaulding, 1978; Jackson, 1983).

Fry, Fry, Kropf, and Coe (1980) studied the influence of race on worker-client interaction in a laboratory study. Both black and white counselors were more expressive with black clients than they were with white clients. The authors hypothesized that counselors may have perceived black clients to have more active and assertive lifestyles, thereby concluding that a more directive and expressive style would be effective. However, given the fact that most counselor training programs place a heavy emphasis on attending skills, counselors' extensive use of expressive skills with black clients may indicate that professionals select different interventive approaches for use with minority clients.

Client race and choice of intervention.   The appropriateness of various interventive approaches for minority group clients has also been debated, with some of the arguments clearly rooted in racist and stereotypical assumptions. For example, early stereotypes that blacks were not "psychologically minded" and possessed few ego strengths often resulted in treatment decisions that they could benefit from only limited interventive approaches, such as support (Hankins-McNary, 1979). In the 1960s, workers were advised of the appropriateness of role-playing techniques for the "motoric," "noncognitive," and "anti-intellectual" styles of black clients (Smith, 1977).

Contemporary practice literature encourages workers to use action-oriented, nontraditional helping approaches with minority clients rather than techniques oriented to verbal insight. Smith (1981) indicates that minority clients may reject regressive, intrapsychic models of treatment which assume that resolution of childhood conflict will alleviate current difficulties. Because behavioral approaches emphasize functional relationships between the client's behavior and sociocultural environment, and because treatment goals generally are guided by the client's values rather than by theoretical standards of normality, behavioral and cognitive-behavioral approaches are often advocated for workers treating culturally different clients (Hayes, 1980; Higginbothan and Tanaka-Matsumi, 1981; Maultsby, 1982; Turner, 1982).

In the same vein, Gomez et al. (1985) encourage workers to explore and draw on "psychocultural" data when working with Chicano clients. Worker exploration of client past behavior and relation of that behavior to current problems was found strongly associated with Chicano client satisfaction. Also found important were (1) considering client cultural beliefs and natural helping systems, (2) developing and reinforcing of clients' positive self concept as Mexican Americans, and (3) allowing clients to use their preferred language. Insight-oriented psychoanalytic approaches have been criticized as uneconomical and irrelevant to the needs of many Hispanics (Ruiz, 1981; Rogler et al., 1987).

Because the family, not the individual, is the most important unit in many Asian cultures, family treatment—or at least treatment oriented to the family—may be more appropriate than individual treatment for Asian clients (Chien and Yamamoto, 1982). However, this may be less important for third and fourth generation Asian Americans. Leong (1986) advises use of structured approaches with Asian Americans, rather than approaches characterized by ambiguity. Therefore, workers are often encouraged to emphasize problem-solving activities and worker authority, and to minimize reliance on insight-oriented interventions, with Asian-American clients.

With Native American clients, workers are encouraged to rely on nondirective communication techniques that restate, clarify, summarize, reflect, and convey empathy (Lewis and Ho, 1975). Confrontation and introspection are likely to conflict with the client's cultural norms.

Thus, treatment methods may need to be differentially selected and modified to fit the client's ethnic culture (Rogler, Malgady, Costantino, and Blumenthal, 1987). Workers should incorporate folk remedies, spiritualism, language, values, and sex-role issues consistent with the client's culture (Kreisman, 1975; Delgado, 1977; Ghali, 1977; Szapocznik, Scopetta, and King, 1978). Especially important is incorporation of the minority client's "world view." For example, to Puerto Rican and Asian clients, there is no division between mind and body (Delgado, 1977; Tsui and Schultz, 1985); a treatment focus on only the emotional component of the person may be bewildering to the client and counterproductive. Among Native American communities, traditional curing practices are community-based, nonanalytic, and do not involve others in the client's personal social network (Dingles et al., 1981). Thus professionals should not expect family members to be involved in problem analysis or treatment. Native American clients are likely to present a passive, expectant, and hopeful attitude toward the practitioner, and may resist active involvement in introspection and self disclosure (Dingles et al., 1981). In summary, workers should ensure that interventions are appropriate and acceptable to the client; race and ethnicity are likely to bear upon both acceptability and appropriateness. In particular, ethnicity is likely to impact significantly on the client's preferred style of participating in the helping effort.

Recognizing the importance of tailoring an intervention to the client to ensure its cultural appropriateness, a few cautions are in order. First, workers should avoid stereotypical assumptions that minority persons are less capable than whites. Unfortunately, black clients are still sometimes seen as "culturally disadvantaged" (Smith, 1977). Such a view contributes to a tendency to seek a "less than best" treatment for "less than capable" clients. The capacity of minority clients to benefit in various treatments is not in question; rather the issue is appropriateness of the intervention.

Second, workers must be able to individualize clients within minority groups (Smith, 1977). In particular, they should recognize the variability within a particular ethnic group and the differences between subcultures. As Rogler notes, "treatment decisions cannot be based (solely) on a simplistic criterion such as a Spanish surname" (1987, p. 567). American Indians, for example, are extremely heterogeneous, residing in over 250 federally recognized tribes, 9 distinct geocultural regions, and different urban, rural, and reservation settings. Intertribal differences in values and attitudes may be greater than differences between Indians and non-Indians (Dingles, Trimble, Manson, and Pasquale, 1981).

Hispanics also vary widely and Asians comprise Chinese, Japanese, Filipino, Vietnamese, Korean, and many other groups. They also vary, within each of these groups, in their degree of acculturation to the dominant culture, with the result that their behaviors and attitudes also vary (Tsui and Schultz, 1985). Thus workers may need to assess within-group differences, relying on such methods as racial self-designation (asking clients how they describe their ethnicity) (Leong, 1986; Malgady, Rogler, and Costantino, 1987; Rogler et al., 1987). Racial identity scales also may be used (Atkinson, Maruyama, and Matsui, 1981). For minority clients acculturated to and assimilated into the majority culture, race may be a minor consideration in the selection of treatment.

Finally, it should be recognized that, to date, there is very little evidence that client preference for treatment methods varies by ethnicity. In a study of college students' preference for various counseling styles, Anderson (1983) found no differences in the preferences of black, Mexican-American, and white subjects. Similarly, in a study of clients at a community mental health center, Taussig (1987) found no differences in Mexican-American and Anglo-American clients' responses to early goal setting in counseling. Therefore, practitioners should be cautious in assuming that client ethnicity necessitates differential selection or modification of interventions.

In short, there is no evidence that specific treatment approaches are inherently appropriate or inappropriate for clients of particular minority groups. However, there are persuasive arguments that certain interventions are probably more or less consistent with the norms of various minority cultures. Although methods should not be chosen on the basis of race alone, they should be selected with the client's ethnicity in mind. No one set of techniques is earmarked as "ideal" for counseling minority clients (Smith, 1977), but some techniques will be more consistent with the client's cultural norms. Thus race and ethnicity should be viewed as central influences on, albeit not the final determinant of, the worker's chosen treatment approach.

Worker race and intervention. Does intervention vary by worker race? That is, do black workers, Hispanic workers, and white workers select different methods for working with clients? This issue has received very little empirical attention. According to one study, black workers were found to give more directions and interpretations, while white workers were more likely to reflect client feelings. Fry, Fry, Kropf, and Coe (1980) explored the influence of worker race on intervention in a laboratory study. Each of sixty black and white counselor trainees in clinical and counseling psychology conducted a 15-minute interview with four actor clients: one black male, one black female, one white male, and one white female. Verbatim typescripts and audio tapes of client-therapist verbalizations were judged by trained raters for frequency of attending and expression responses. Results indicated that black counselors were significantly more expressive (giving more directions and interpretations) than were white counselors, who made more attending responses (reflection of client feelings) than did black counselors.

Franklin (1985) found that black social workers were more likely than white social workers to describe their theoretical orientation as systems/ecological and behavioral, and were less likely than white workers to indicate a psychodynamic orientation. Moreover, black workers were more likely than white workers to indicate that they would use nondirective treatment for a black client. Franklin sees this as reflecting the black practitioner's effort to create a nonthreatening atmosphere, and establishment of an egalitarian relationship consistent with empowerment of helping models.

TREATMENT EFFECTIVENESS

Although racial bias offers a variety of threats to social service delivery, the bearing of ethnicity and racial dissimilarity on treatment effectiveness is probably the most critical issue. Administrators, practitioners, and consumers of the helping professions daily confront such challenging questions as: Can professional helpers work effectively with racially dissimilar clients? Are minority workers more effective than white workers with minority group clients? Can the effects of racial prejudice, mistrust, and unfamiliarity be countered so that workers can use their helping skills and clients can attain desired outcomes? These issues are of central importance to those involved in professional education, to those delivering social services, and to clients. Yet in comparison with other issues pertaining to race and treatment, the actual evaluation of effectiveness has received surprisingly little attention.

The evaluation of treatment effectiveness is usually approached from a set of judgments—by either the worker, the client, or another observer—as to whether various outcome criteria have been attained. Such criteria generally include two types: *intermediate outcomes,* conditions that, although not constituting final treatment goals, are viewed as facilitative or necessary for treatment; and *ultimate outcomes,* those conditions that address the client's reasons for seeking help and that, therefore, reflect the objectives toward which treatment is directed (Rosen and Proctor, 1978, 1981). The literature on race and treatment reflects attention to both these types of outcomes. Most studies evaluate the impact of worker-client racial similarity or dissimilarity on intermediate outcomes such as understanding, client satisfaction, and quality of the helping relationship. A smaller body of literature has focused on ultimate, or long-range outcomes, such as task accomplishment or treatment effectiveness under varying conditions or race.

Attainment of Intermediate Outcomes

Several studies support the widespread assumption that racial similarity between worker and client facilitates the treatment climate. For example, Sladen (1982) found that worker empathy, worker-client similarity, and attraction were judged to be higher when worker and client were of the same race. These findings are limited by an extremely small sample and by the measurement of subjects' perceptions of counseling process variables only in response to an audiotape.

Some studies have explored actual client perceptions of workers under varying conditions of race. Phillips (1960) found that white counselors were less successful than black counselors in establishing rapport with 17-year-old black male high school students. Focusing on evaluations of treatment at a child guidance clinic, Warren, Jackson, Nugaris, and Farley (1973) found that almost half of the black parents reported feeling alienated from and poorly understood by their white therapists. Workers were seen as supportive but not familiar with or understanding of the problems of black clients; however, 80 percent reported they would be willing to return to the worker. A weakness of this study is its failure to compare the effectiveness of black workers versus white workers. In another study, each client was interviewed by four therapists, thereby enabling evaluation of the effects of worker race and training (Banks, Berenson, and Carkhuff, 1967). The eight black clients studied reported a willingness to return to the black worker, but few were willing to see the white workers again. Interpretation of these findings is complicated by inability to distinguish the effects of race from worker training, as each worker represented different conditions of experience and counseling orientation. These studies, however, are widely cited as indicating the difficulties of creating facilitative treatment conditions, or attaining intermediate outcomes, when race of worker and client differs.

The findings of a recent study suggest that white clients may perceive white workers more favorably than they do minority workers. Lee, Sutton, France, and Uhlemann (1983) studied the perceptions of Caucasian high school students toward Caucasian, Chinese, and East-Indian Canadian counselors. The students related the counselor's expertness, trustworthiness, and attractiveness after viewing videotaped interviews of the workers. The white worker was perceived significantly more favorably than either of the two minority workers.

Worker cultural sensitivity was found to affect blacks' perceptions of white workers in a recent study. Culture-sensitive workers, those who acknowledged the role that race might play in client problems and who expressed interest in exploring that further, were rated as significantly more culturally competent by blacks than were workers who did not acknowledge the role of race (Pomales, Claiborn, and LaFromboise,

1986). The racial identity of black participants was also important; those with strong concerns for black identity rated the culture-sensitive workers the most expert.

One of the most important elements in cross-cultural helping is worker credibility—that is, the client's perception of the worker as an effective and trustworthy helper. According to Sue and Zane (1987), the underutilization of therapy by minorities may be due in large part to their failure to perceive professionals as credible. Achieving a perception of credibility in cross-cultural helping encounters is a complex and delicate task. Certainly, in the words of Dingles et al., it is "more than impression management" (1981, p. 250); workers in cross-cultural situations are perceived by many audiences—including client, family, staff, and indigenous peers—among whom skills must be confirmed and borne out through observation and personal experience.

A few studies have focused on worker credibility. Atkinson, Maruyama, and Matsui (1978) asked Asian-American college students in an analogue study to listen to an audiotape and rate the credibility of workers portrayed as Asian American or Caucasian. The students rated the Asian-American workers as more credible and someone they would be more willing to see for professional help. Similarly, Native American high school students gave more positive ratings to counselors introduced as American Indian than to counselors introduced as non-Indian (Dauphinais, Dauphinais, and Rowe, 1981). Porche and Banikiotes (1982) found client perception of worker competence to vary by worker gender and race. Male and female adolescents perceived white female workers as most expert, followed by black males and white males; black female workers were perceived as least expert. These findings, however, are not consistent with other findings of more favorable perceptions of black females. Green, Cunningham, and Yanico (1986), for example, found that both black subjects and white subjects expected black female counselors to be more helpful than white counselors. Finally, Peoples and Dell (1975) found that both black and white subjects rated a black counselor as more helpful and competent than they did a white worker; however, these findings should be interpreted cautiously since only two workers were involved.

Other studies have explored the influence of race on worker-client attraction. A study by Porche and Banikiotes (1982) is one of the few reporting greater attraction for white than for minority counselors among minority clients. Black adolescents were more attracted to white counselors, especially white females, than to black counselors. Counselor race did not have a main effect on students' perceptions of worker expertness or trustworthiness.

This same study, however, highlights the importance of attitudinal similarity between workers and clients. Overall, workers portrayed as having attitudes dissimilar to those of the students were rated significantly lower in terms of attractiveness, trustworthiness, and expertness. Several other studies indicate that attitude similarity may be more important than worker-client racial match (Peoples and Dell, 1975; Furlong, Atkinson, and Casas, 1979; LaFromboise and Dixon, 1981).

Another study suggests that regardless of worker race, minority clients were significantly less satisfied with counseling than were white clients (Neimeyer and Gonzales, 1983). However, this dissatisfaction may have been directed toward the mental health system in general, rather than toward the particular worker and treatment they experienced, since these same minority clients did not perceive their treatment as less effective than did white clients. Yet workers should not conclude that all racial or ethnic minority clients will be dissatisfied. Gomez et al. (1985) found that Chicano clients were highly satisfied with the casework services they received from community mental health centers. However, their study did not compare clients from different ethnic groups; consequently it is not possible to determine whether Chicano clients were as satisfied as white clients.

Other studies have failed to find evidence that racial dissimilarity impedes the attainment of intermediate outcomes. In several studies, black and Native American client satisfaction has been found to be independent of racial dissimilarity (Cimbolic, 1972; Ewing, 1974; Dauphinais, LaFromboise, and Rowe, 1980; Proctor and Rosen, 1981), suggesting that minorities who are paired with white workers may be as satisfied as white clients. Another study (Mulozzi, 1972) indicated that racially matched and racially mismatched dyads were not significantly different in levels of empathy, congruence, and unconditionality or regard, as perceived by clients. Black clients did, however, perceive less regard from white workers than did white clients. Neither black nor white clients rated their relationships with black workers more favorably than they did those with white workers. Similar results were reported by Bryson and Cody (1973), who explored the relationship between race and extent of client understanding of workers. They found that white clients understood their black workers as well as they did their white workers, and black clients understood white workers as well as they did black workers. Finally, Roberts and Attkisson (1983) found no differences in the mean satisfaction scores of anglo, black, or Hispanic clients at an outpatient community health center. Thus several studies indicate that clients experience understanding, satisfaction, and facilitative conditions in their relationships with racially dissimilar workers.

Some studies indicate that workers are more affected by race than are clients. In spite of the fact that black clients did not rate black workers more favorably than white workers, Mulozzi (1972) found that white workers viewed themselves as more empathic when working with white clients. Bryson and Cody (1973) also reported that workers felt more capable in situations of racial similarity. They found that both black and white workers reported higher levels of understanding with clients of their own race; black workers reported that they understood black clients better than white clients, and white workers understood white clients better than black clients. Clearly, more research is needed to clarify these relationships, but existing evidence suggests that racial dissimilarity may affect workers' assessments of effectiveness in attaining intermediate outcomes more than it affects the judgments of clients.

Attainment of Ultimate Outcomes

Surprisingly little empirical study has explored the influence of race on attainment of ultimate treatment outcomes, or actual client change. Studies from testing situations highlight the importance of this issue. In his review of such studies, Sattler (1970) concluded that white experimenters sometimes appear to impede the performance of black children. Specifically, their performance was impaired by the presence of a white experimenter when the tasks involved cognitive or decision-making skills; however, racial effects were not as definitive in experiments involving motor skills. Studies with older subjects were not as likely as those involving children to find adverse effects from racial dissimilarity. Pope (1979) reported an unpublished study focusing on the effects of racial dissimilarity on verbal conditioning. The study indicated that for subjects low on racial prejudice, race did not affect success of the conditioning procedure. However, racial effects were evident for highly prejudiced subjects; white prejudiced subjects appeared to depreciate the positive reinforcement provided by the black experimenter, negating the effects of conditioning. These findings have important implications for social service deliverers: They suggest that minority children may not perform as well with white workers as they would with racially similar workers, and that highly prejudiced white clients may not gain from treatment with minority workers.

Are social service interventions differentially effective for clients of varying ethnic or racial groups? The findings of one study suggest this possibility; at least they suggest that different interventive styles may be effective for black and for white workers working with white clients. Merluzzi, Merluzzi, and Kaul (1977) found that an "expert" style, emphasizing worker knowledge, was more effective for black workers in producing attitude and behavior change among white clients; for white workers, however, a "referent" style, emphasizing similarity to client, was most effective. Indeed, the black experts were more effective than the white experts, although white workers were perceived as more expert than were blacks. These differences suggest that white workers may benefit from emphasizing their similarity to clients, while black workers need to highlight their professional expertise.

In addressing the role of race on treatment success, many studies rely on global ratings of treatment effectiveness. Such studies indicate that racial dissimilarity does not impair treatment success as much as is generally anticipated (Krebs, 1971; Warren et al., 1973). In an analogue study, black college students rated black counselors as more effective than white counselors (Gardner, 1972). However, in a field study of clients' experiences at a mental health center, Lerner (1972) found that black clients did not significantly differ from white clients in their attainment of treatment outcomes. Cimbolic (1972) also found that race did not determine black clients' ratings of effectiveness so much as did the level of worker experience.

In a study of treatment effectiveness at a multicultural university counseling center, Neimeyer and Gonzales (1983) found that race did not affect counseling effectiveness as measured by worker and client ratings of perceived relief, understanding, and coping. In this study, it was interesting to note that although white workers provided significantly shorter treatment than did minority workers (especially to minority clients) and nonwhite clients were significantly less satisfied than white clients, racial differences between worker and client did not seem to hamper actual treatment effectiveness. However, several races were grouped together in the "nonwhite" group, and this may have obscured a clearer picture of racial effects.

Finally, in their study of clients receiving services at Family Service Association of American agencies, Beck and Jones (1975) found that black clients fared better, in terms of overall change scores, with black workers than with white workers. Conversely, white clients with black workers also showed better than average results, although the differences were not statistically significant. Overall, it appeared that "black clients do somewhat better with black counselors, while white clients achieve about equally good outcomes with or without racial matching" (Beck and Jones, 1973, p. 141).

With respect to the outcome of treatment with clients of other ethnic minorities, very little is known. For example, Leong (1986) cites a void of empirical studies on this topic with respect to Asian Americans.

Thus studies in this area are markedly limited in number and in scope. However, they do indicate that racial dissimilarity does not necessarily impair a worker's ability to help a client. In fact, workers appear to be more wary than clients with regard to racial dissimilarity. This suggests that a worker's race may have less effect than his or her belief that race will affect treatment. This belief itself, however, may have effects on the initial interview and on the long-term treatment relationship. Griffith (1977) acknowledges that racial dissimilarity may have an inhibiting effect on intermediate outcomes, impairing the treatment relationship, the depth of self disclosure, and rapport. However, "while racial homogeneity may be desirable for some therapeutic issues, it is clearly not a prerequisite for effective psychotherapy as long as the therapist is sensitive to the issues around which racial influences may develop" (Griffith, 1977, p. 38).

CONCLUSION

The extensive literature addressing the issues of race and racial similarity in individual treatment yields some discernible trends. Race is a salient issue to worker and client. Clients clearly expect, though do not necessarily prefer, that their professional helpers will be white. Many clients have been found to prefer racially similar workers. Moreover, race is a factor of which minority clients are aware—when they are paired with white workers, they are not oblivious to their differences from the worker in skin color, background, and social reality. The literature indicates that workers are less knowledgeable about and less comfortable with racially dissimilar clients than they are with clients of their own race. Minority clients are more likely than white clients to be assigned to paraprofessionals and—although the data from outpatient populations is mixed—there is evidence that minority inpatients receive less adequate treatment than whites. Minority outpatients are likely to drop out of treatment, often after the first session.

In the process of treatment itself, racial dissimilarity appears to threaten the ability of workers to help clients talk about themselves and their problems. Culturally conditioned patterns of distrust and concealment pervade the helping relationship. Moreover, white professionals find it difficult to understand the verbal and nonverbal communication of minority clients unless they are familiar with the history, values, lifestyle, and institutions of the client's culture. Cultures appear to differ in the attribution of causality and in their social realities, and these differences may affect the way racially dissimilar workers and clients view problems and desired objectives. In particular, minority clients may attribute problems to social or environmental factors while white workers attribute them to personal or intrapsychic factors. The literature indicates that minority clients are more likely than whites to be assigned certain diagnoses or labels, and to be viewed as severely pathological or limited in capacity. Although certain approaches to treatment have been cited as more or less appropriate for minority clients, the consensus of available practice wisdom is that selecting interventions primarily on the basis of client race is unfounded at best, and ill-advised and potentially racist at worst.

In spite of the strains that may affect interracial treatment, little empirical study addresses the comparative effectiveness of same- and different-race treatment dyads. However, available evidence does not support the widespread assumption that workers cannot help racially dissimilar clients. Some studies, in fact, indicate that minority clients fare no worse than white clients when they are assigned to white workers. Moreover there is some evidence to suggest that—if the initial issues of familiarity and trust are satisfactorily resolved—experienced, skilled, and sensitive professionals can work effectively with racially dissimilar clients.

3

Race and Family Treatment

Race as an issue in the treatment of families has begun to receive increasing attention in the practice literature. Such attention is sorely needed as minorities make up an increasing proportion of U.S. families. The literature suggests that, despite their increasing numbers, minority families frequently underutilize mental health services and, when they do use them, are often greeted by practitioners ill-prepared to help them (Gwyn and Kilpatrick, 1981; Boyd, 1982).

Historically, it has been the weaknesses of minority families rather than their strengths that have received attention (Moynihan, 1965). This fact, it should be noted, has been true of the practice literature for white families also (Bell and Bell, 1982). However, since the late 1960s, many notable efforts have been made to point out the strengths of minority families (Billingsley, 1968; Hill, 1971; Monteil, 1973; Redhorse et al., 1978; Vega et al., 1986). This chapter focuses on treatment issues and attempts to refute the perception that the family of color is dysfunctional or pathological in its structure and functioning. Such faulty perceptions have resulted in frequent misdiagnosis of nonwhite families, consternation by those who attempt to understand and work with these families, and the use of inappropriate practice interventions.

SALIENCE OF RACE
IN FAMILY TREATMENT

Salience of Race to Family

There are a number of reports which indicate that minority families are at best hesitant to seek family therapy. Compared to white families, minority families are less inclined to seek institutional family assistance in the form of therapeutic or professional consultation (Lewis and Ho, 1975; McAdoo, 1977; Redhorse et al., 1978; Shon and Ja, 1982; Ho, 1983). Furthermore, it seems that if they do seek services, they often fail to complete the expected course of treatment (Raynes and Warren, 1971; Sue et al., 1974; Sue and McKinney, 1975; Gwyn and Kilpatrick, 1981).

It has been suggested that helping black families to accept the family therapy process has been difficult for at least two reasons: They are often assigned to white practitioners who frequently have an insufficient understanding of the social realities faced by black families, and they may have negative feelings about seeking professional assistance (McAdoo, 1977; Grevious, 1985). Clearly, as has been suggested, family therapy with blacks is still in the "incubator stage" (Foley, 1975). Certainly this fact is especially true for treatment with the low-income family (Grevious, 1985).

In working with either Asian or Native American families, Lewis and Ho (1975) and Ho (1983) point out that the culture of these families may argue against the employment of outside professionals. For many Asian-American families, the admission of problems is seen as a defect within the family. Cultural norms regulating against outside intervention make family intervention difficult. Hence, open discussion of family problems with outsiders is not likely with Asian Americans (Ho, 1983; Hsu et al., 1985). Shon and Ja (1982) do suggest, however, that an Asian therapist is generally preferable if an Asian family agrees to outside intervention.

Lewis and Ho (1985) doubt that many social workers will have the opportunity to render family counseling services to Native Americans because of their close structure and values toward keeping problems within the family. Redhorse et al. (1978) posit that there are three distinct cultural groups of American Indian family patterns. First, there is a traditional group which adheres to American Indian culturally defined styles of living and cannot relate to professionals, also preferring to ignore mainstream treatment modalities. The second group, characterized as bicultural, appears to have adopted many aspects of mainstream lifestyle, and is perhaps most receptive to outside ideas and interventions. A third group, defined as pan traditional, is overtly struggling to redefine and confirm previously lost American Indian lifestyles.

This group is even less accepting of mainstream interventions than the first group: While the first group will politely listen to the suggestions of outside professionals, the third denounces the professionals and their methodologies. The within group cultural classifications offered by Redhorse are similar to those ascribed to other minorities (Staples and Mirande, 1980; Hall, Cross, and Freedle, 1972).

What this suggests is that the response the practitioner receives may be significantly influenced by the cultural identity of the minority family. The extent to which client cultural identity supports the acceptance of outsiders will have a significant influence on a practitioner's ability to establish a viable relationship.

Despite the general underutilization of family services by minority families, many minority families do seek and receive professional assistance (Beck and Jones, 1975). We might ask, do those who seek professional services differ in some significant way from those who do not? It is possible that those clients who do hold strong preferences for same-race practitioners may not seek assistance from mainstream helpers. Avoidance behavior is possible since many minority clients who do seek help anticipate being seen by a white practitioner (Proctor and Rosen, 1981) yet prefer a same-race helper (De Geyndt, 1973; Redhorse et al., 1978).

The literature also notes exceptions to same-race preference. Minorities do, for a variety of reasons, sometimes request nonminority practitioners. A white practitioner may be viewed as offering greater treatment anonymity, and therefore be preferred. This is probably a stronger determining factor than is generally acknowledged in the literature. There are also indications that minorities may express a preference for white practitioners because they perceive white practitioners as having greater expertise. This racial status effect has been noted among virtually all minority groups (Kitano, 1969; Sue, McKinney, Allen, and Hall, 1974; Sue, 1981). Finally, Rothman et al. (1985) have noted that some Mexican-American clients have requested a non-Mexican family therapist because they felt that he or she would serve as a role model. It appears that minority families attempting to adjust to mainstream society may view the white practitioner as the best role model to assist them in their acculturation efforts. Rothman cautions us, however, not to assign therapists who violate the client's cultural expectations, but to match practitioners with clients in a culturally and situationally sensitive manner.

In sum, minority families may be either for or against treatment by a different-race practitioner. The rationale most often suggested by the literature for a same-race practitioner is he or she is likely to have a better understanding of the minority family's social reality (McAdoo, 1977; Lewis and Ho, 1985; Redhorse et al., 1978). Clients expressing a preference for a different-race practitioner may do so because they believe this practitioner will offer greater anonymity, professional expertise, or serve better as a role model.

Salience of Race to Therapist

There is evidence that minority families are among the least preferred as clients (Sue et al., 1974; Gwyn and Kilpatrick, 1981). Such a negative therapeutic history, particularly as experienced between black families and white practitioners, has caused some to ask the question, Can white therapists work with black families? (Foley, 1983). Evidence suggests that minority families seeking help, especially if they are poor, are more likely than white families to be seen by a paraprofessional rather than a professional. Moreover, race has been observed to be the most significant factor in determining if nonwhite families see a psychiatrist, psychologist, or social worker (Sue, 1976).

Bias against minority families is not too surprising, given that attraction for people is fostered, in part, by perceived similarity and prior exposure to them. Training programs for many mental health practitioners fail to provide knowledge or content about minority clients (Bradshaw, 1978; Bernal and Padilla, 1982). This absence of diverse cultural training persists even though resulting problems continue to be noted in the practice literature. For example, McKinley et al. (1970) reported that their failure to address the issue of race with minority families severely limited the willingness of minority family members to engage in disclosure and open discussions of personal materials.

It seems that fear on the part of the practitioner, however, rather than racism, may be the principle cause for such omissions (McKinley et al., 1970). At least in the McKinley et al. project, white practitioners apparently felt that mentioning race would harm the treatment process. Only upon reflection, at the conclusion of their treatment efforts, were McKinley and his colleagues able to acknowledge that their failure to discuss race was damaging to the helping process.

Other practitioners have also reported experiencing racial discomfort when working with minority families. Wold et al. (1977) reported feeling themselves to be in the minority and somewhat isolated. This feeling is probably widespread among practitioners who find themselves working alone in treating a racially different family. These feelings may be a function of the therapist's infrequent contact with a particular minority group (Davis, 1975). Moreover, such feelings may be more pervasive among whites since whites are generally in the majority. However, there is no reason to assume that feelings of isolation or discomfort may not also occur for minority family practitioners who find themselves working alone with an unfamiliar racially different group.

Despite the frequent reportings of discomfort, etc., not all white practitioners perform poorly, nor do all avoid working repeatedly with minority families. Both Sager et al. (1970) and Pinderhughes (1982) offer sound practice wisdom as to how white practitioners should work with minority families. Pinderhughes suggests that white practitioners must understand that because of their race, they (the practitioners) benefit from a system that oppresses their clients. She also contends that white practitioners working with minority families must recognize that they are, as helpers, being called on to assist in solving problems that are important for their own social functioning, as well as that of the client. Consistent with Pinderhughes' perspective, Whittaker (Sager et al., 1970) states that as a family practitioner he expects to be modified by this contact with the minority family. Sager et al. (1970) take Whittaker's point a step further and suggest that the benefit of this exchange can be reciprocal. They suggest that the white practitioner and minority families are both capable of learning things from the experience.

In review, minority families are generally not the families of choice of family practitioners. Indeed, it seems that some family practitioners may limit their contact with minority families, and if they do treat them, they often experience racial anxiety or discomfort. On the other hand, it also seems that some white practitioners have benefited from working with minority families. These practitioners report that they and their clients have been favorably changed by the experience.

Co-Therapy

Although some have not found family co-therapy to be advantageous (Rice and Rice, 1977), the family treatment literature in many instances has championed its use (Whitaker and Napier, 1972; Foster, 1981). Co-therapy, the employment of two therapists, usually a male and a female, has become a common practice technique in some settings in the treatment of families. To those who advocate its use, co-therapy is believed to offer greater role modeling possibilities to the family and greater flexibility and control to the therapists.

Some therapists who have worked with minority families have also supported the use of co-therapy. They have suggested, however, that the team be biracial. Specifically, one of the co-therapists should be white and the other a member of the minority group with whom the team is working.

The response to biracial teams in family treatment appears quite favorable. Both Hightower (1983) and Wold et al. (1977) contend that biracial co-therapy teams appear to enhance the communication process, gaining greater disclosure on the part of minority family members relative to what would normally occur if both practitioners were white.

This enhanced disclosure may, however, occur because minority family members are more willing to make comments to the nonwhite therapist. White practitioners should not view this skewed communication as an attempt by the minority family members to exclude them, but rather as the family's effort to communicate with someone whom they feel understands them. However, it is believed that the combination of white and minority therapists results in the establishment of a more positive relationship between the minority family and the treatment agency than would be established by employing only the minority practitioner.

Let us look for a moment at another dynamic that may come into play with biracial co-therapy teams. In the scenarios offered by Hightower et al. (1983), the co-therapy team was both bigender and biracial; the male was white and the female Hispanic. They mention in one example that a Hispanic family undergoing treatment reflected a "sex-role" bias, as evidenced by the male Anglo team member being addressed as doctor while the female Hispanic team member was called by her first name. The authors suggest that this choice of titles indicated a sex-role bias. While it is possible that the family members were responding solely to gender, they might also have been responding to ethnicity or a combination of the two.

Researchers (Meeker and O'Neill, 1977) have suggested that our responses to people and their responses to us are influenced significantly by their perceptions of our social status. The scenario offered by Hightower et al. (1983) as an example of Hispanic family gender bias may indeed be a case of higher status being ascribed to the male, hence affording him the higher-status title of doctor. However, the example is confounded by race, as the male was white and the minority family members may have instead been responding to the status associated with ethnicity. Clearly the bigender, biracial team is dynamically complex. Co-family therapists should be cognizant of status dynamics and learn to accept, adjust to, or modify them accordingly. Failure to do so could result in feelings of inadequacy, anger, and discomfort for the co-therapy team member to whom is consistently ascribed a lower status, due to race or gender.

Both Hightower et al. (1983) and Wold et al. (1977) suggest that team members discuss all potentially problematic racial issues that occur during the course of working with minority families. Hightower et al. (1983) assert that it is a mistake for co-therapists to ignore ethnic differences and pretend "color blindness." It is advised that co-therapists should not attempt to present a false front of "togetherness" or "pseudomutuality" (Wynne et al., 1958) to the families they counsel. Hightower et al. assert that "open communication between the members of the co-therapy team in front of the family not only strengthens the bonds of the co-therapy team, but assists the family in openly discussing their perceptions of each other" (p. 108).

In sum, co-therapy with minority families has received some favorable evaluations. It does, however, necessitate excellent co-therapist communication and the willingness of both members to discuss, between themselves and with families, racial, ethnic, and perhaps gender issues that come up during treatment. The biracial, bigender therapy team is clearly more complex in its dynamics than are teams that are not biracial. We strongly advocate that those who use this approach with their minority family attune themselves to the racial/gender dynamics, which have the potential to manifest themselves as status effects during family treatment.

Race and Family Problems

Does race of the family influence the type of problem members are likely to experience? Prior failures of practitioners and scholars to differentiate within minority family groups resulted in stereotypic perceptions of these families and their problems. In contrast to much of the earlier writings and research, minority families are currently viewed less monolithically, and their problems and cures are viewed less stereotypically. Researchers, theorists, and practitioners now point out that minority families are heterogeneous class and cultural groups (Willie, 1974; Mirande, 1977; Redhorse et al., 1978; Bagarozzi, 1980; Kitano, 1987). Considerable effort has gone into debunking commonly held misperceptions that minority families are: *matriarchal* (Staples, 1971; Dietrich, 1975); *patriarchal* (Sotomayor, 1971; Cromwell et al., 1973; Hawkes and Taylor, 1975; Mirande, 1977) and *unstable* (Billingsley, 1968; Hill, 1971; Scanzoni, 1975; McAdoo, 1978; Bagarozzi, 1980; Delgado and Humm-Delgado, 1982).

However, correcting these misperceptions does not mean that minority families are any less vulnerable. Minority families, like other families, do experience problems that are of interpersonal or intrapsychic origin; however, the minority family is also faced with significant external threats to its existence (Sager et al., 1970; Lewis and Ho, 1975; McAdoo, 1977; Pinderhughes, 1982). McAdoo (1977) has suggested that minority families have the unusual burden of caring for their members and the additional burden of trying to do so in an environment that does not reinforce positive evaluation of their ethnic group.

Problems presented to practitioners by minority families must be seen within a larger systemic framework. As Canino and Canino assert, psychopathology is not only the consequence of a sick intrapsychic reality, but also a family's environmental structure contributes to and sustains an individual's pathology (1980). We are not, however, suggesting that minority family members do not "go crazy" or experience interpersonal conflicts; rather, we are suggesting that close attention must be paid to the influence of the larger social context.

Pinderhughes has suggested that "treatment must be directed toward strengthening family structure, enhancing flexibility, and reinforcing the ability of friends, community, and the larger social system to offer effective and appropriate support" (1982a, p. 115). Without this broadened perspective, treatment effects may be short lived, and the family will return to its prior, and perhaps unsatisfactory, methods of coping. However, both the therapist and the minority family can benefit significantly from a broadened systematic perspective. Both can be helped to see how the family's adaptive behavior to a hostile environment may result in maladaptive family patterns.

In sum, minority families, like other families, are diverse in the problems they experience. As a group, however, they should not be characterized as having pathological family structures or internal difficulties. As in other families, members may experience intrapsychic as well as interpersonal problems. However, what most distinguishes the problems of minority families is that their problems are more likely to be sustained, and exacerbated, by the larger social environment. Hence practitioners in their treatment and assessment of minority families must keep a more vigilant eye on the influence of the social environment.

RACE AND FAMILY DYNAMICS

The dynamics of minority families have their roots not just in the culture of the family, but in society's reaction and response to these families. It is clear that the racial discrimination experienced by nonwhite families affects not only the family members as individuals, but the internal dynamics of the family as well (Bagarozzi, 1980).

Practitioners who wish to work effectively with minority families must have knowledge of the unique qualities of these families, along with an understanding of the family's relationships with the larger white society. In particular, family practitioners should:

1. view minority families as a social system interacting with other social systems
2. have some historical knowledge of these families as colonized or quasi-colonized people in order to make appropriate assessments
3. understand that behaviors in these families may be influenced by social structures which differ from those impacting on white families
4. perceive minority family structures as significantly affected by the wider social environment (Billingsley, 1968; Sotomayor, 1971; Harris and Balgopal, 1980; Pinderhughes, 1982).

Increasingly, the minority family is a family in transition. It has been altered significantly in the past three decades. Always considered to be different, if not deficient, relative to other families, it is now viewed to be in an even more precarious position. For example, since 1965, black families have gone from 75 percent of their households being headed by two parents to approximately 50 percent today. This change, more than any other, has influenced the family's ability to fulfill its functions. It has also influenced perceptions of and thoughts about these families. Many are now asking, Can these families survive in a society that constantly demands more of its members? For example, even the two-parent white middle-class family is experiencing the struggle of holding on in a society threatened internally by drugs, crime, and teen pregnancy and externally by foreign economic competition.

Although we do not wish to minimize the significance of culture, much of the discussion of family dynamics has to do with the impact of economic changes on minorities. Indeed, it appears that poverty has become not just an issue of economics but a significant agent in affecting the structure of minority families (Rodgers, 1986, p. 17). This is illustrated by Sotomayor's poignant description of Mexican families, which we believe is applicable to minority families in general. She states that

> the type and quality of the interchanges between the family and the external social system determine to a considerable extent the interfamily activities and its integration. The Mexican-American head of household often has been unemployed, or underemployed in menial tasks that constantly remind him of his inferior status. He has practically no access to the decision making process that could change his situation and he has no effective means of making those vital institutions respond to his needs. This damaging, limiting process invariably affects the internal functioning and the role arrangement within his family. It has adverse effects on family leadership, and on the maintenance of expected patterns of behavior, and on the integration and solidarity of specific families and their individual members (1971, p. 124).

With this brief introduction as a backdrop, let us focus on minority family relationships.

To understand families and their structural arrangements, we believe that three factors should be considered:

1. family cultures may differ in the degree to which they choose to focus their attentions or concerns on the mothers, fathers, or other family members
2. power is never unilateral, but is possessed by both the husband and wife
3. both family focus and power are relative in that our perceptions of the "proper" family relationship depend on the point of reference from which we evaluate it

Husband and Wife:
Roles, Power, Focus, and Satisfaction

Does the distribution of power between the husband and the wife in minority families differ from that of the typical white couple? Are minority families patriarchal or matriarchal? These are questions frequently raised by professionals and laypersons alike. Largely, these questions have not been adequately addressed because of the profession's ethnocentrism and the lack of unbiased conceptual terms.

Our traditional ways of thinking about husband and wife interaction have assumed that power is a dichotomous rather than a continuous variable. That is, one person is assumed to have all the power, and the other person is assumed to have none. This conceptualization has prevented family theorists and practitioners from realizing that family power is shared and that being "powerful" is relative. While one partner may have more power than the other, neither one is devoid of some power. Moreover, the balance of power between two people may shift over time. The dichotomous perspective, however, has led to perceiving and labeling families in terms of who is powerful, the man or the woman. The terms *patriarchal* and *matriarchal* suggest that power is possessed totally by either the husband or wife. The net result of labeling minority families as either matriarchal or patriarchal has, subsequently, placed these families on the defensive and obstructed our understanding of their familial relationships.

We believe that another concept important to understanding the relationships among family members is *family focus*. This concept, while similar in some ways to that of *matrifocality* (Monagan, 1985), should be distinguished from it. Matrifocality has more to do with power and decision making; family focus involves socioemotional attention and the affection which the family bestows on a particular member. The most focal person may not necessarily be the most powerful member; conversely, the most powerful member may not be the most focal member. Focus, like power, is relative and seldom the sole possession of only one person. Rather, we can think of family members as being more or less powerful, and more or less focal, relative to the other family members. Some minority groups may focus more of their attention on the mother or father than does mainstream American culture. What may be a "mother focused" family pattern may be mislabeled as a matriarchal pattern. The terms patriarchal and matriarchal, because of their pejorative connotations, have actually retarded the understanding of minority family dynamics. Family practitioners should move beyond the concepts of matriarchy and patriarchy, and look at family dynamics less rigidly.

Another impediment to the understanding of minority family dynamics is the reliance on Anglo standards. Any deviation from the standard has been viewed not merely as different, but as deficient. Thus, because Anglo families have been employed as the standard for all families, minority families with different power or focal arrangements have been seen as deviant. The "different equals deviant" mentality has strongly contributed to minority families being classified as dysfunctional—e.g., matriarchal or patriarchal. Hence, it is not surprising that minorities have found such descriptions of their families objectionable. To the extent that only Anglo standards are accepted and utilized by practitioners, nonwhite families will continue to be viewed as pathological or flawed in their male-female relationships.

From a review of the literature, it appears that power dynamics in minority families may differ from those of mainstream whites in the United States. Minority families may differ from white families in allocation of both power and focus. In black families, the female is believed to share power more equitably with her mate, and male-female relationships may be more egalitarian. This perception of black female power is held by both blacks and whites, males and females. For example, the black female is perceived as having greater autonomy, independence, and individualism than her white female counterpart (Scanzoni, 1975, 1977; Beckett and Smith, 1981). This greater parity of family power appears to have resulted from fewer sex-linked roles and tasks among black families (Scanzoni, 1977; Dietrich, 1975; Beckett and Smith, 1981). Most notably in this respect, black husbands, relative to white husbands, are likely to share more equitably in the domestic and childcare roles. It is probable that this more egalitarian power relationship has contributed to the frequent labeling of black families as matriarchal.

We believe it is also the black female's centrality of focus within the family that has contributed to the perception and labeling of black families as matriarchal. The female is believed to be the focal person in black families irrespective of the socioeconomic standing of the family (Wilkinson, 1984). In this respect, we might view the black family as being mother-focused. That is, the most focal person in the family is the mother rather than the father. A family considered to be mother-focused would not necessarily mean that the mother is the dominant or the most powerful person in the family; rather, it suggests that greater family attention revolves around the mother. This is supported by the centrality of the mother in black literature. Other ethnic groups also place the female in a focal position where she is frequently the center of family life (e.g., Jewish mothers) (Herz and Rosen, 1982). However, such focal positions do not typically result in the family classification of matriarchal.

Within Hispanic families, males appear to exert greater power than do comparable males in white families (Minuchin, 1967; Hardy-Fanta and MacMahon-Herrera, 1981). Moreover, the male-female relationship and the accompanying sex roles are likely to be more traditional in their divisions of labor (Minuchin, 1967; Hardy-Fanta and MacMahon-Herrera, 1981; Falicov, 1982; Garcia-Preto, 1982). For example, Canino and Canino (1980) state that in Puerto Rican culture, the man has the final word. However, both acculturation and socioeconomic status significantly impact on Hispanic family interactions (Vega et al., 1986). Hence, the extent to which Hispanic families follow the more traditional sex-role pattern is influenced by the degree of acculturation of the family, which in turn is significantly affected by whether the family is first, second, or later generation American. Sex roles may also be influenced by whether or not the wife is employed, an issue that will be discussed later in greater detail. Consequently, there is considerable variation within Hispanic male-female dynamics—e.g., traditional-egalitarian (Hawkes and Taylor, 1975). Moreover, such variation within Hispanic families can be expected to continue as a function of generational influence. It would appear from the literature that although the father may be most powerful, the mother is often the focal person in the family in that she is the most frequent recipient of socioemotional attention and affection.

Typically, in Asian families the father is the leader of the family. Fathers in these families are both the most powerful family member and also the most focal (Kim, 1985). Husband-wife roles are more strictly prescribed than in western cultures, with males customarily being ascribed a higher status and value. The nature of male-female family roles are, however, influenced by the type of Asian family (that is, Japanese, Chinese, Korean, etc.), in addition to social class, geographical origins of the family, and number of generations within the United States (Kitano, 1987). Despite these cultural and class variations, male-female roles are considered to be traditional: Males are primarily responsible for task function, while females attend to the social and cultural tasks (Shon and Ja, 1982). However, despite the powerful status of males in Asian families, the mother is still the recipient of strong emotional attachment.

Husband and wife roles within American Indian families also typically differ from those of Anglo Americans. Primarily, the distinction has been in the extensive involvement of a number of "non-nuclear" family members. The family structure has been viewed as "positively enmeshed," with extensive family involvement from in-laws and extended family generations (Attneave, 1982). Sex roles of males and females are largely traditional. However, like other women, female Native Americans are breaking with more stereotypical sex divisions of power and role as influences of urbanization and acculturation increase (Hanson, 1980).

In sum, while minority families have understandably resisted the pejorative lables of being patriarchal and matriarchal, their male-female relationships do frequently differ from those of whites in the United States. These differences have traditionally been viewed as instances of deviation. Most notably, these differences manifest themselves in two ways: (1) the extent to which males and females share roles and power within the family and (2) the extent to which the mother or father is the focus of family activities and interest. We believe that to be effective in working with minority families, practitioners must accept the familial cultural differences. Therapeutic approaches that attempt to undermine or ignore these culturally dictated male-female relationships are likely to end in failure. Practitioners must put aside what they believe "ought to be" and accept these families as reflecting cultural differences, not cultural pathology.

Marital Satisfaction

Another important issue for practitioners is how minorities feel about their marital relationships. That is, how do they evaluate their marriages? How satisfied are they? Perhaps even more importantly, how stable are their marriages?

There has been little research in this area with minorities in general; however, some research has addressed these issues relative to blacks and whites. Indeed, some findings have been surprising. Despite what appears to be a more egalitarian family arrangement among blacks, some research has found them to score significantly lower on measures of marital satisfaction than do whites (Scanzoni, 1975). Instances of marital disruption appear to support these reported levels of dissatisfaction, as blacks have a higher rate (66 percent) of marital dissolution than do whites (50 percent) (U.S. Bureau of the Census, 1983).

Lower marital satisfaction and a corresponding higher rate of marital dissolution seems, intuitively at least, to be at odds with the perceived sex-role equity in black families. It has, however, been suggested that the structuring of sex roles per se may have little direct effect on marital satisfaction and stability (Scanzoni, 1975). Scanzoni has suggested that higher education levels of couples have a positive effect on marital satisfaction and stability. Moreover, sex-role structures appear to be indirectly linked to marital satisfaction via education; better educated persons do tend to be more economically satisfied and hence experience greater marital satisfaction (Scanzoni, 1975). And on the whole, satisfaction at least for black husbands appears to increase with per capita family income (Ball and Robbins, 1986).

It has also been asserted that it is the black male's inability to fulfill his role as primary economic provider that contributes substantially to marital instability (Staples, 1985). However, at least one study by Scanzoni (1975) reports that the wife's full-time employment had a negative effect on marital satisfaction among black, but not among white, couples. Moreover, despite the greater numbers of women in the labor force, it is still a pervasive black and Anglo cultural expectation that men be the principal breadwinners. This incongruity between the societal expectation of the male to be the primary breadwinner and the black male's frequent inability to perform as such may undermine the husband's self esteem, frustrate the wife, and create marital dissatisfaction for both partners (Staples, 1985, p. 1010). The stability of the marital relationship may be further undermined by the necessity of the minority female's employment and by her at times higher earning power (Hampton, 1980).

Employment

Employment of husband and wife has clear impact upon family dynamics and contributes to issues that many families bring to practitioners for help. To what extent are these issues similar for families of different racial and ethnic groups? Does employment of husband and/ or wife create similar or different issues for white and minority families?

Indeed, these dynamics do seem to differ for minority and white families. For white families, the central question seems to be what the effect of wife's employment is on the family. For minority families, the central question is what the effect of husband *unemployment* is on family dynamics.

When the male is unemployed. The husband's role of the "good provider" (Bernard, 1981; see also Chapter 8), while taken for granted by most white families, is a role frequently difficult for minority males to enact. In other words, the male's position as principal breadwinner has never been the "given" for minority families that it has been for white families. Moreover, because the majority of white women now share the breadwinner role with their husbands, the male role of the good provider is largely outmoded for whites in the United States but has never been fully achieved for large numbers of minority males.

Thus, while much of the United States is struggling with the complications created by dual career couples, many nonwhite families are struggling to have at least one full-time, primary breadwinner. For example, the unemployment rate for white males is 4.6 percent, yet for black males it is 11.3 percent, and for Hispanic males it is 7.2 percent (U.S. Department of Labor, 1988). In addition, among those minorities who are employed, many are "underemployed" in that they work only intermittently. Moreover, future scenarios also appear bleak as the high school dropout rate for minority males continues to run higher than that for white males and higher than that of minority females (Attneave, 1982; Reed, 1988).

The realities that these distressing statistics reveal have had negative effects on minorities and their families. In spite of changing societal norms, the male is still often viewed as being principally responsible for the family's financial well being. Moreover, there are indications that this perception is held even more steadfastly by minority families (Sotomayor, 1971; Scanzoni, 1975; Shon and Ja, 1982). Hence, while minority males and their families may share the more traditional view of the male as principal breadwinner, they have less opportunity to fulfill this role than do white males. This disparity between ideology and practice contributes substantially to family difficulties for minorities (Staples, 1985).

Indeed, the employment difficulties of black males are believed to be a principal contributor to the increased instability of black families. One of the most powerful observations, which continues to receive the attention of family researchers, is how the structure and stability of the black family has waxed and waned as the employment rates of the black male have varied (Moynihan, 1965; Hampton, 1980). Consistently it has been shown that as the employment picture for black males improves, so does the percentage of intact stable black families. Staples (1985) contends that black families are now experiencing greater dissolution and disruption because black males are unable to fulfill their roles as economic providers.

The negative psychological impact of unemployment for males in a society that praises achievement is often devastating. Speaking of Mexican Americans, Sotomayor (1971) suggests that the frequent low status and unemployment of the male undermines his role as father, provider, disciplinarian, and protector. The consequences are a distortion of family decision-making patterns, a disruption of the family's equilibrium, and hence, a diminished capacity to deal effectively with a hostile external environment. Therefore, when assessing family dynamics, practitioners must be careful to distinguish between the family's normal structure and what is instead an artifact of the male's inability to fulfill his role as provider. For example, there is a difference between the male who voluntarily chooses to stay home as a house husband, and the male who has no employment alternatives.

When the female works.   Should the minority female work or should she stay at home? This question has by and large been moot for females of some minority groups. For example, the number of black females in the labor force has traditionally been higher than that of white females. The harsh economic reality of their families has taken much of the choice out of the question. Indeed, the minority female has often been the only family member able to find work. Hence, a more realistic question to be asked is, what are the consequences of the female's employment for the family? Pertinent to our focus here, how does her employment affect family dynamics? It appears that her employment, although largely an economic imperative, has powerful effects on the dynamics of the family. Moreover, employment of the wife in minority families has different implications than similar employment would within white families. There are at least two major factors that distinguish employment for minority females. First, as already mentioned, she has a good probability of being the only family member employed. Second, minority females earn a higher percentage of total family income than do their white female counterparts. For example, black and Hispanic females earn 82 percent and 75 percent, respectively, the incomes of their male counterparts (National Commission on Working Women, 1986). These percentages are in striking contrast to white females, who earn only 67 percent of the white males' salary. These relative income differences suggest that minority females may possess more economic clout within their families than do white females. If, as has been suggested, earning power translates into social power within the family (Blood and Wolfe, 1960), these women are more powerful within their families than are comparable white women. The impact of increasing minority female employment relative to that of minority males continues to receive considerable attention in the family literature (Scanzoni, 1975; Bean et al., 1977; Hampton, 1980; Hanson, 1980; Ybarra, 1982).

Black females have had a long history of employment and thereby have long participated in the role of "shared principal breadwinner." They have also been well prepared for that role, as evidenced by the fact that most black females are better educated than their husbands (Spanier and Glick, 1980) and 20 percent of them earn more than their husbands (U.S. Bureau of the Census, 1983).

One of the consequences of employment patterns of black families has been a more equitable sex role distribution. That is, because the female has participated so extensively in the economic provider role, other roles such as household maintenance tasks have been more equitably shared with the black male (Scanzoni, 1975; Beckett and Smith, 1981). In addition, employment opportunities for black women have enabled them to enjoy more varied and more equitable sex roles which, in turn, have contributed to their own positive evaluations of their abilities and to the more favorable evaluation of their abilities by others (Scanzoni, 1975).

It may be, however, that dissonance is created by the increasing minority male-female parity of sex roles or even role reversal (Hanson, 1980; Ybarra, 1982). It is possible that the minority male may be threatened and feel a sense of loss of authority and status. In this sense, the employment of minority females, in contrast to that of white females, has a different psychological, if not sociological, consequence for minority families. As the minority male's position is so economically fragile, the employment of the female, albeit necessary, may be more threatening than it might be to white males. Indeed, there is some evidence to suggest that the black wife's earning potential relative to that of the husband may contribute to black family tension (Hampton, 1980; Marshall, 1983). For example, black families where the wife earned more than 40 percent of the family income were the group most at risk for divorce (Hampton, 1980). This dynamic, while disturbing, is likely to continue as women, in general, make further gains in the employment sector.

Clearly, minority family dynamics are significantly influenced by the employment of females and the unemployment of males. The consequences are frequent role reversals, with the husband being challenged, if not replaced, by the wife as principal breadwinner. Despite changing sex-role expectations, society, and especially minority cultures, continues to expect males to be the pillar of financial strength for the family. Consequently, we are witnessing some minority families struggling to reconcile cultural dictates and economic imperatives. At least one study reported husbands of working Mexican-American women to be less affectively satisfied, but more economically satisfied than those whose wives were not employed (Bean et al., 1977). We would not, of course, advocate that minority women leave the labor force as a solution to this dilemma. At best, such a strategy would be a prescription for family disaster, as it is often essential to the family's survival that the female work. The obvious solution is greater employment opportunities for all minority family members. Meanwhile, family practitioners who wish to be effective with minority families must be cognizant of the fact that the employment of minority women, in view of the underemployment of minority men, has the potential to contribute to negative family dynamics.

Parenting and Socialization

Can we make any generalizations about parenting styles of minority families? Do their parenting styles differ from those of white families? The answer to this question appears to be a qualified yes.

It has been stated that minority parents have two tasks in socializing children: They must teach them to be human as well as how to be a minority (Billingsley, 1968). Minority children, if they are to function outside their community, must become bicultural. That is, they must learn the values and customs of their native culture, as well as those of the dominant white culture. Thus, minority parents face the ominous socialization task of having to prepare their children for entry into a culture not only different from their own, but frequently hostile toward them (Barnes, 1980; Chestang, 1980). Practitioners attempting to work with minority families must come to appreciate the difficulty of this task for minority parents.

Racial or ethnic differences in socialization, however, appear to be more a reflection of degree than of differing viewpoints of the parents (Bartz and Levine, 1978). For example, research indicates that, like white parents, minority parents value and teach their children autonomy and independence, but do so at an earlier age (Miller, 1975; Alvirez and Bean, 1976; Bartz and Levine, 1978; McAdoo, 1979; Peters, 1981). It appears that minority parents are responding to an insecure and uncertain environment. Children are subsequently taught early to "do for themselves" as a hedge against continued or possible family hardship (e.g., death or economic crisis) in which they may need to care more completely for themselves and/or assist in caring for others in the family. Hence, workers can anticipate that the parental role expectations for children may appear to be "more adult and unchildlike" than the child's years would suggest. Practitioners must understand that minority families, because of their at risk status, often struggle to keep themselves together socially, psychologically, and economically, and that responsible behavior is thus required of the young members sooner.

Pinderhughes (1982a) has suggested that minority parents, because of their frequent victim status, are often powerless to protect their children from illegal, amoral, and violent acts. She has suggested that parents may respond to their situations in a variety of ways:

1. In their contact with the child they may assume a more controlling and authoritative stance than otherwise to counteract the undermining of their role and authority. (This constitutes yet another determinant of fused family relationship.)
2. They may subject the child to harsh treatment to toughen the child up as preparation for coping with the powerlessness of the victim system. (Although harsh treatment may slip into abuse if carried to an extreme, it also may be perceived by others as abuse when it is not.)
3. They may ignore the situation and leave the child to deal alone with the deficits in the parental role.
4. They may interpret and explain the complexities of the victim system and powerlessness. (p. 93)

She suggests that all these strategies, except the last, cause additional difficulties for the family.

Among various minority groups, are there differences in parenting processes? Research conducted by Bartz and Levine (1978) provides some insights on this question. Their study compared the parent-child interactions of 160 black, 152 Hispanic (Mexican American), and 143 Anglo, lower- and working-class families. It appears from their findings that black families were more controlling of their children relative to the white and Hispanic families. Controlling the child's behavior was most apparent on the part of black fathers, more so in families in which the children were male rather than female. Such efforts to control their sons may be an attempt to reduce the probability that they will be harmed by a society frequently hostile to black males (Allen, 1981). With respect to interactions with children, Hispanic families were found to be least egalitarian. This phenomenon has been noted elsewhere in studies comparing black, white, and Hispanic child interactions (Durrett et al., 1975). By and large, Hispanic children, in interactions with their parents, appear to have less of a voice in decision making than do black or white children. However, Bartz and Levine report that although black families had more egalitarian parent-child interactions, the parents did not necessarily agree among themselves about the extent of egalitarianism which would be desirable. It seems that black mothers, but not fathers, were desirous of even greater parent-child egalitarianism than currently existed within the family. Among Hispanic parents, however, there was less egalitarianism in parent-child relationships, but greater agreement between the parents about how egalitarian their relationships with their children should be. The studies by Bartz and Levine (1978) and Durrett et al. (1975) provide practitioners with significant insight into the variation that may exist in normative child-parent interactions among minority families.

Before leaving this subject, the impact of social class on socialization should be noted. The socialization of children has been shown to be significantly affected by socioeconomic class (Radin and Kamii, 1965; Duvall, 1971; Walters and Stinnett, 1971). In general, lower-income families have been observed to be more authoritarian than middle-income families. Many concerned with the research in this area have noted how the failure to make distinctions between the effects of ethnicity and class has resulted in frequent confusion of the data, erroneous conclusions, and faulty attributions to minority families (Lieberman, 1973; McAdoo, 1979; Staples and Mirande, 1980). In short, characteristics frequently associated with low-income families have been cast to describe minority families. As we suggested earlier, the frequent lack of distinction of race and class as research variables requires us to use the literature in this area with caution.

The Extended Family

Historically, the extended family has been an important source of social and economic support for minorities. Even now Hispanic, Asian, black, and American Indian families continue to be noted for their inclusion of persons other than nuclear family members (McAdoo, 1978; Redhorse et al., 1978; Hardy-Fanta and McMahon-Herrera, 1981; Shon and Ja, 1982; Ko, 1986). The extended family members typically include grandparents, aunts, uncles, cousins, and sometimes close friends (e.g., "play sisters or brothers"). Hispanic families may also include "compadres" and "commadres"—godparents (Klor de Alva, 1985). These extended family positions are held in high esteem in the Hispanic community. The roles of compadres and commadres have traditionally given the occupants of these roles considerable say in matters involving the children. However, it appears that the roles of compadre and commadre are becoming more ceremonial and less substantive as Hispanics become more acculturated into U.S. society. Hence, again it is important for the practitioner to note the extent of acculturation of the families with which he or she is working. For example, a first generation Hispanic family may be less acculturated into U.S. values and norms and, hence, the godparents may exert more of the power and authority traditionally granted them. This is in contrast to Hispanic families of later generations, who may have become less traditional in their view of the role of godparents.

Despite its historical role of protector and sustainer of the family, the extended family is currently undergoing extensive change. Even though it is believed to be of continued importance in the support and survival of minority families, the extended family is becoming less common today than in the past. Moreover, some authors have even argued that the extended family may have a potentially long-term negative effect on family member achievement (Stack, 1974). It is posited that the reciprocal nature of the help exchanged between family members may retard the advancement of individuals who have opportunities for upward mobility. In either event, despite a history of greater numbers of extended family networks, minority families, like other U.S. families, are becoming decidedly more nuclear in their structure. Despite the general move away from extended families, there is evidence to suggest that minority families do continue to have greater frequencies of short-term augmented families. There are situations where a relative lives within the household for some specific period of time, usually of brief duration. However, this brief inclusion is in notable contrast to the more permanent inclusion of grandparents and other relatives.

Virtually all who have written in this area alert practitioners working with these families to take cognizance of the importance those "extra" family members have in the dynamics of the family. Thus, it is advised that these extended family members be included in the practitioners' attempts to work with the family (Redhorse, 1980; Hardy-Fanta and MacMahon-Herrera, 1981; Shon and Ja, 1982).

The Single-Parent Family

By 1990, half of all U.S. families may be headed by only one parent, with the overwhelming majority of these families (90 percent) headed by females. It is already 1990 for some minority groups. Currently, over 50 percent of all black families are headed by females (U.S. Bureau of the Census, 1984). The rate for Hispanic families is approximately 22 percent (Rodgers, 1986); however, this figure obscures tremendous variation within Hispanic groups: 40 percent of the Puerto Rican families are single-parent households, compared to only 15 percent of Mexican-American families (Estrada, 1985; Klor de Alva, 1985).

Moreover, it is also estimated that, in 1984, 54 percent of black female-headed families and 50 percent of Hispanic female-headed families were poor. Two factors, female heads of households and the poverty associated with them, have resulted in the frequent employment of the term "feminization of poverty." The causes and resulting problems associated with female-headed households have received a wealth of attention (Moynihan, 1965; Spanier and Glick, 1980; McAdoo, 1981; Guttentag and Secord, 1983; Staples, 1985; Nichols-Casebolt, 1988).

Staples (1985) suggests that the factors contributing to the rise in single-parent black families are merely a variation of the general problems of all U.S. families, and that the family structure of other racial groups is changing for much the same reasons (Staples, 1985, p. 1010). Let us look for a moment at the major contributions to this changing family phenomenon.

Two major factors have been identified as increasing the ranks of minority single-parent female-headed households: divorce and out-of-wedlock births. Of black female-headed households, 50 percent are caused by divorce or separation and another 41 percent are the result of out-of-wedlock births (U.S. Bureau of the Census, 1983). Out-of-wedlock births, especially among teenagers, are having an epidemic effect on black families. Currently over 50 percent of all black births are out-of-wedlock and 74 percent of these are to teenagers (Bureau of the Census, 1984).

While teenage pregnancy is believed to have a number of causes (e.g., ignorance, low self esteem, poor role models, etc.), we believe that the lack of positive future outlook also contributes to this social malady. To the extent that youth fail to see viable employment or professional options, they are likely to succumb to a "why not" "mentality. That is, they cannot identify events or opportunities in their lives that would be thwarted by the birth of a child; hence, why not? If youth have few future prospects for professional or career advancement, or for finding a mate who has such prospects, they may see little virtue in delaying what they perceive to be their only opportunity to accomplish anything. In other words, perceptions of poor economic futures may result in minority youth seeking, through having children, what more privileged youth seek via careers and life opportunities.

The increasing frequency of single-parent minority households has profound implications for those practitioners who work with minority families. These practitioners can expect that the majority of single-parent families will be female-headed, disproportionately poor, and also, because of the high concentration of teenage mothers, disproportionately young. These factors are likely to have the following consequences:

1. clients may be overburdened with tasks, simply because so much must be accomplished by only one person
2. because of poverty, they may be at risk of having their basic financial needs unmet (Rodgers, 1986)
3. because these young mothers may be less skilled at parenting, their children will be more at risk for child abuse and neglect

Religion and Spirituality

Attempts to understand the social dynamics of minority families without reference to religion and/or spirituality are short-sighted (Scanzoni, 1977; Redhorse, 1980; Hardy-Fanta and MacMahon-Herrera, 1981; Pipes, 1981; Delgado and Humm-Delgado, 1982). One has only to visit minority communities and to witness their abundance of formal and informal religious institutions to understand that religion plays a major role in the lives of minority families. Aside from offering hope and the fulfillment of spiritual needs, religious institutions in most minority communities are also a major source of social and political support (Scanzoni, 1977). Indeed, religion often has been the only refuge for minorities in an otherwise hostile white world (Frazier, 1964). In this sense, minority religious institutions, more so than such institutions in the white community, serve both spiritual and social purposes. It is due largely to this augmented social role, which often includes finding employment for their followers, that the spiritual leaders in minority communities are ascribed such high levels of status and prestige.

Practitioners should have cognizance of this fact. Indeed, it may be only upon the advice of the religious or spiritual leader that the family will elect to seek "professional" help. Moreover, the "professional practitioner" may better serve the client or family by assisting or acting through the religious or spiritual leader. Thus, practitioners must become familiar with the role of spiritual leaders and be willing to call upon them for help in working with minority families (Delgado, 1987). In this instance, Harris and Balgopal (1980) offer a useful conceptual framework to assist us in working with minority families. They suggest that it is not what something means to us per se, but rather what it means to the family members who view it. Thus, the practitioner who is unfamiliar with certain religious or spiritual helpers (e.g., folk healers, medicine men) must, if he is to work with unfamiliar family cultures, come to understand and appreciate religious leaders for what they mean or represent to the family and its members.

The religious affiliations of minority groups differ; for example, the vast majority of Hispanics are Catholic, while comparable proportions of blacks are Protestant. Finally, within minority groups there exists considerable diversity with respect to religious and spiritual affiliation. It appears that families that are better off financially are more involved in church activities than are those who are less well off (Richardson, 1966; Scanzoni, 1977, p. 52).

It is beyond our purpose and scope to discuss how these factors affect the family dynamics of specific minority groups. Rather we wish to point out the centrality of religion and religious leaders in the lives of minority families. In sum, religious and spiritual leaders appear to hold greater power, status, and prestige in minority communities than their counterparts do in white communities. Subsequently, to work effectively with minority families, family practitioners must often call upon these leaders for help.

FAMILY PRACTITIONER INTERACTIONS

Assessment—Involving the Family

Developing a working alliance with families is a crucial task for family therapists. However, therapeutic communication across ethnic or racial lines is often problematic (Kochman, 1981; McNeely and Badami, 1984). To what extent do such problems inhibit the development of effective working relationships between practitioners and families when their race or ethnicity differs?

Gwyn and Kilpatrick (1981) report that family therapy that takes place between minority families and white practitioners is sometimes inhibited by mistrust which, in turn, results in poor therapeutic disclosures. This basic mistrust is a consequence of negative historical and contemporary interracial experiences. Not surprisingly, part of the mistrust in communication between minority families and those trying to help them is a consequence of the practitioner being perceived as an extension of the larger society, which often acts to oppress them (Weaver, 1982). Gwyn and Kilpatrick believe that this barrier, albeit significant, can be bridged if therapists "explore and recognize their own prejudices, clarify this influence on their practice, and overtly allow the racial issue to be part of the therapeutic process" (1981, p. 265). Wortman (1981) offers advice for working with single-parent families, which we view as useful in working with minority families also: He recommends that practitioners not ask for more information than is needed. He suggests the importance of balancing how much we ask of clients against how much we give of what they (clients) came for. This comment seems well taken when working with any family in which there is a possible reason for mistrust between practitioner and client.

Alliances between minority families and white practitioners also may be hampered by perceived differences in social status. That is, the minority family perceives itself to occupy one status and the white practitioner to occupy another. Wortman believes that when families perceive such a disparity in social status, workers may have to persuade family members that their contributions to the process are valuable. Of course, as Wortman points out, their contributions are more vital than those of the practitioner. The use of paraprofessionals in the treatment of minority families is presumably advocated on the assumption that status differentials between family and therapist might be reduced, thereby enhancing the communication process.

Therapeutic communication and, hence, the worker's ability to relate to families may be hampered when the therapist and the family speak different native languages (Aguilar, 1972; Wold et al., 1977; Hightower et al., 1983). For example, Hispanic family members may speak only Spanish, or, if they do speak English, may drift in and out of Spanish and English (Aguilar, 1972; Rothman et al., 1985). The practitioner who does not speak the family's native language may feel isolated and excluded.

Some view language differences as the chief cause of client-therapist difficulties because language differences are closely aligned with differences in the ways individuals think (Wold et al., 1977). Hence, persons speaking different languages may actually be thinking about problems and situations differently. We would caution, however, against the conclusion that difference is deficiency. Little treatment literature has been written pertaining to language differences and the consequences for thinking about presenting problems. However, it seems reasonable that persons who think in different languages may experience some difficulty understanding each other's cultural perspective.

When the therapist and the family do speak different native tongues, the use of a racially-similar co-therapist or bridge person may be advisable, as Baptiste (1984) has suggested, to assist the treatment process. However, the use of translations in therapy has reportedly not always fared well either, because of frequent distortions that result in negative experiences for both practitioner and client (Abad and Boyce, 1979).

Through what other means can the alliances between practitioners and ethnic families be enhanced? Are some practitioners' styles of interacting better suited for working with specific minority groups than others? Intuitively it would seem that certain cultural styles of interacting may facilitate or impede family treatment.

The literature in this area provides us with insights into what styles might best work with American Indian families. Lewis and Ho (1985) state that social workers who attempt to get American Indians to face them squarely, look them in the eyes, and talk directly to them during family therapy will probably be perceived as rude and intimidating. They suggest that the most effective communication techniques will include clarification, summarizing, and reflection. In contrast, direct confrontative communication efforts will act to retard the therapeutic process. It is, therefore, suggested that practitioners who work with American Indians be nondirective in their treatment style (Lewis and Ho, 1985). Similarly, Attneave (1982) views confrontative techniques to be unsuitable for family treatment of American Indians; however, she also notes that being nonconfrontative does not mean being inactive (Attneave, 1982). Rather, she suggests that the practitioner should employ open-ended questions that demonstrate interest in the family, while refraining from exhibiting judgmental behaviors.

Specifically, Attneave (1982) suggests that the practitioner observe the client's cultural framework and degree of defensiveness. American Indians, it is asserted, are likely to want to discuss peripheral matters before addressing the specific presenting problem. It is common that the initial problem is essentially a masking problem, not the most serious (Attneave, 1982). By presenting other than the most critical problem first, the American Indian family members assess the interest, sincerity, and trustworthiness of the practitioner. Attneave (1982) also suggests that the practitioner's ability to establish a viable relationship with Native American families will depend on the worker's respect for Indian cultural values. For example, the practitioner, to be culturally effective, must take into account differences in world views—e.g., being part of nature vs. attempting to control nature.

It appears that family treatment with Hispanics warrants a style similar to that advocated for use with American Indians. Many have suggested that social workers begin treatment with Hispanic families with a leisurely opening (Aguilar, 1972; Mizio, 1979; Garcia-Preto, 1982). First, it is necessary to establish a climate of warmth, which is informal and personable. Jumping immediately into the middle of a serious or controversial affair may confuse Mexican-American families and make them uncomfortable (Aguilar, 1972). It has been asserted that "unlike the Anglo client who expects a professionally distant yet efficient therapist, the Puerto Rican client expects a more intimate relationship" (Hardy-Fanta and MacMahon-Herrara, 1981, p. 144). The therapist should not be unprofessional, but should adopt a warm and humanistic style of relating. For example, during the process of establishing rapport with the family, practitioners may be expected to answer questions related to their own personal background. Similarly, an emotive and dramatic tone may be more appealing to Mexican-American families than an efficient, highly structured, and contractual approach. Falicov (1982) suggests that feelings be elicited subtly rather than asking the family members to openly describe and explain their feelings and reactions. Confrontative approaches or interpretations, she suggests, will be threatening and may retard disclosure. She further suggests the use of humorous stories and anecdotes as nondirective strategies. Finally, speaking on Puerto Rican families, Garcia-Preto offers advice that is probably sound in working with all Hispanic families. She suggests that clients are "likely to respond to a therapist who is active, personal, and respectful of the family's structure and boundaries. They may speak more easily to a woman about emotional problems since women handle those concerns in the family. They may take directives more readily from a male therapist because of the authority men have in the culture" (1982, p. 178).

Those who work with Asian families have been advised to take directive styles rather than passive ones (Shon and Ja, 1982; Kim, 1985). A laidback passive approach may be perceived as a lack of expertise on the part of the practitioner. A word of caution, however; being directive does not mean having a confrontation in which the family members are caused to "lose face." This will only result in a loss of therapist credibility (Kim, 1985). By being directive, the therapist is expected, for example, to determine the order in which family members speak, how long, and upon which topic area. Shon and Ja (1982) admonish practitioners to show strict respect for the traditional roles of family members. To facilitate the practitioner's understanding of the family's interaction it may be advisable to begin treatment with the entire family (Kim, 1985). Initial communication should be directed in the order of social and power hierarchies of the family. Specifically addressing initial questions or comments to the father is a good idea as he is head of the family and, by addressing him first, the therapist reinforces his role in the family's treatment. Similarly, questions pertaining to the children should be addressed initially to the mother as they are, by cultural definition, her primary responsibility. As in working with Hispanic families, therapists working with Asian families are expected to be sufficiently open to provide the family with personal background information so that the family has some understanding of who they are (Shon and Ja, 1982). Practitioners are also expected to "read between the lines" of communication within the family, as family problems and issues are frequently discussed subtly and indirectly. Kim (1985) suggests that reframing may be especially useful in working with Asian families, as relabeling something in a positive way saves face and encourages change. This style of working with families requires practitioner patience and sensitivity to nonverbal cues. Finally, the practitioner's style should not encourage the expression of overt affection, and discussions of sexual topics should occur only after there exists a sound and positive rapport with the family.

Practice with black families may also be facilitated by the employment of certain practitioner styles. Practitioners should keep in mind that blacks in the United States have historically received less respect from this society than perhaps any other ethnic group. Hence, a style that indicates respect for them by the therapist will be positively received. As an example of demonstrating respect, the adult members of these families should be referred to, upon introduction, by their last names. The practitioner should not supplant the family's desire to be respected with his or her desire to be informal or even to establish a positive therapeutic rapport. Specifically, in the interest of establishing rapport, informality does not automatically facilitate the establishment of a sincere relationship.

A style of relating that enhances trust is another important ingredient in helping relationships with black families. Like respect, this is true whether the practitioner is white or black (Grier and Cobbs, 1968; McAdoo, 1977; Weaver, 1982). Trust may be facilitated by the worker's asking only for that information which is essential at the time.

Finally, direct styles of communicating may be well received by black families. It appears that black families, like Asian families, desire treatment approaches that are active, direct, and concrete (Gwyn and Kilpatrick, 1981; Hines and Boyd-Franklin, 1982). These clients often expect to experience tangible benefits from the treatment process.

Thus, it appears from a review of the literature that practitioner style may need to vary with families of different ethnic groups. It may also be the case that the natural styles of some practitioners will make it easier for them to work with a particular ethnic group than with another. Hence, family practitioners would do well to assess their stylistic strengths with respect to working with various ethnic groups. The literature also suggests that practitioners must be cognizant of cultural nuances that exist both between and within ethnic and racial groups. For example, family practitioners should be especially cognizant of the ethnic nuances that exist within Hispanic, Asian, Black and Native American groups. Failure to become familiar with the unique culture of each ethnic group will prevent practitioners from effectively establishing and maintaining viable relationships with minority families.

Choice of Treatment Approach

How does race affect the worker's choice of family treatment approach? Are some approaches seen as better suited for working with families of various minority groups?

The structural model has perhaps received greatest attention in the treatment of minority families (Minuchin, 1974; Kim, 1985). The structuralist emphasis on the social context has won its support from those who believe in systemic approaches in general (Lee, 1982). However, it has been suggested that even those approaches that do emphasize systems theory usually only look within the family and not to systems lying outside it—e.g., factors in the environment or community (H. C. Johnson, 1986). Johnson asserts that it is this neglect of macro system factors that leads to inappropriate "therapizing," that is, redefining emotional distress that is environmentally generated as inadequate family or interpersonal functioning (p. 300).

As we have mentioned elsewhere in this chapter, the literature on family treatment of minorities often uses the terms *minority* and *low-income* interchangeably (Canino and Canino, 1980; Gwyn and Kilpatrick, 1981). Much of what is advocated as being advantageous for minority families is clearly directed at low-income families. This has led to both uncertainty and confusion as to which modalities are best suited for minority families and which are best suited for low-income families. Canino and Canino (1980) astutely address this issue. They suggest that when ethnicity is combined with social class variations, the therapist must be something of an anthropologist. That is, therapists must familiarize themselves with customs and family relations of the relevant ethnic group. Canino and Canino (1980) argue on behalf of an ecological family approach, an approach which assumes that a person is influenced by his or her context: social, cultural, familial, political, and economic environment. In this respect, the ecostructural approach would appear to minimize the shortcomings of some structural therapists, as mentioned earlier by Johnson (1986). Canino and Canino (1980) also note the efficacy of the ecostructural family model with Puerto Rican families. That is, low-income Puerto Rican families as a subculture share certain characteristics with other low-income groups—for example, greater concern with the present than the past and frequent use of extended families. Hence, it is their contention that this model, having proven useful in the treatment of low-income Puerto Rican families, is suitable for use with other low-income ethnic groups also.

It has been suggested that black families indicate a preference for active, direct, concrete treatment approaches (Gwyn and Kilpatrick, 1981; Hines and Boyd-Franklin, 1982). Gwyn and Kilpatrick (1981) note that crisis-oriented therapy, short-term therapy, and the use of paraprofessionals are currently being utilized with black and low-income families. All of these approaches have an ecological family focus; frequently they are designed to assist immediate family situations. Even though these approaches may often be effective with minority clients, practitioners should not assume that because families are minority, interventions designed for low-income families will necessarily be appropriate. Hence, they must attempt to distinguish class factors from cultural ones. It is also important to consider the values and norms of the ethnic group in light of the theoretical assumptions of the modality.

Within the practice literature, there are frequent recommendations that a particular treatment approach is most appropriate for families of certain racial or ethnic groups. For example, it has been suggested that both blacks and Hispanics, because they frequently experience problems exacerbated by the environment, may respond favorably to structural modalities (Canino and Canino, 1980; Gwyn and Kilpatrick, 1981). Behavioral and structural approaches have been advocated for use with Asian families as the objective, concrete nature of the approach is believed to be in agreement with the group's cultural expectations of the role of the therapist (Lee, 1982; Shon and Ja, 1982; Kim, 1985). Because behavioral family techniques have also been advocated for use with families with egalitarian male-female relations (see Chapter 13), they may prove beneficial with many black families as well. Yet, due to their high structure, behavioral methods may not be advisable for working with Mexican families (Falicov, 1982). However, until more research is conducted in this area, the answer to the question, "Which modality works best with a given ethnic group?" will probably depend significantly on the skills, style, and cultural sensitivity of given practitioners.

RACE AND FAMILY THERAPY OUTCOME

Family therapy is among the newest and least researched of treatment modalities. It has been argued that there are few studies of family treatment that are well-controlled and not subject to serious methodological difficulties (Johnson, 1986). It is our belief that research in this area will see greater activity in the following decades. Presently, we are forced to rely largely on anecdotal evidence and the best of practice wisdom. Moreover, with respect to the available literature on minorities, many family treatment texts fail to make any mention of minority families. Hence, we have, at best, only begun to ask such questions as, Do minority and nonminority practitioners differ in their effectiveness as practitioners with minority families? Do minority families differ in the extent to which they experience gains in family treatment?

In the following pages, we will review this topic area in hopes that we can provide at least some rudimentary suggestions to those who are attempting to address these and other questions in their practice with minority families.

Salience of Race of Practitioner

Do practitioners work more effectively with their same-race families? This frequently asked question is of increasing concern to all practitioners as the United States becomes more racially heterogeneous. The reader may wish to consult Chapter 2 for a thorough discussion of the literature and research on racial matching at the individual level. Conceptually, at least, many of the dynamics at the individual level are applicable for families also. The family practice literature, however, has, thus far, not included much on treatment outcome as affected by race of the practitioner. The general consensus, however, among family practitioners who have written in this area, is that race of the practitioner is an important influence on the outcome of treatment with families (McAdoo, 1977; Redhorse et al., 1978; Hardy-Fanta and MacMahon-Herrera, 1981; Shon and Ja, 1982). A consistent concern seems to be that the particular value and belief system of a different race and culture may be a barrier to understanding and working with that family (Shon and Ja, 1982; McAdoo, 1977). However, the point made that a sensitive different-race practitioner is preferable to an insensitive same-race practitioner also seems well taken (Shon and Ja, 1982).

Let us briefly inspect some of the empirical practice literature that currently exists on this topic. Beck and Jones (1975) provide us with one of the few research efforts in this area. Their nationwide family study observed that blacks assigned to white therapists were significantly more likely to terminate treatment prematurely. Moreover, clients in black families matched with black counselors demonstrated better outcomes in the way of change scores. Also noteworthy is the fact that these change scores exceeded the predicted outcome scores regardless of whether they were based on the client's or counselor's reports. It should be noted that white clients matched with black counselors also appeared to experience greater positive change. In contrast, black clients seen by white counselors fell below the predicted score. These latter, black therapist-white client, improvement scores were not statistically significant, but sufficiently consistent to warrant further inspection. The authors offer no firm interpretations for their observations, but they do offer questions, which in some respect differ from those most often put forth in explaining differences in practitioner outcomes. They ask, "Has discrimination led to a tighter screening for black counselors so that they are, in fact, superior counselors? As recent entrants into the profession, are they perhaps younger and less given to psychological interpretations and more concerned about environmental problems and constraints? Are they perhaps less critical, warmer, more accepting? Are they for any reason less threatening to the insecure client?" (1975, p. 141). Needless to say, we have no way of even beginning to answer these questions. They are, however, important questions and ones that warrant further consideration and research.

Salience of Race of Family

Do some minority families respond more positively to family treatment than others? It has been suggested that a client's outcome is influenced by his or her definition of the problem. Moreover, the definition of a client's difficulty is shaped by his or her cultural beliefs, which influence problem identification. As a consequence, we can expect some variance in outcomes across groups, if for no other reason than that minority group clients have different perceptions of problem etiology and resolution. It has been asserted that, for many therapists, success or positive outcome is measured by "emotional" growth, such as the individual patient's ability to communicate and express feelings including anger and hostility (Lee, 1982). In contrast, Lee (1982) suggests that for Chinese families, the criteria for positive outcome may be based largely on physical and behavioral changes. Hence, the notion of positive family outcome may vary somewhat. This, of course, further confounds our efforts to evaluate family treatment outcomes across racial groups. Thus, the answer to the question, "Do some minority families have more positive outcomes in family treatment than others?" is strongly influenced, it would seem, by cultural perspective. However, let us look for a moment at family outcome with specific attention to different ethnic groups.

Earlier in this chapter, it was pointed out that Asians tend to view family problems as indicators of deficits within the family and thus as a stigma upon the family. Consequently they were less likely to submit themselves to family treatment. Indeed, it has been asserted that the process of entering into family treatment is not an easy one for Asian families. Shon and Ja (1982) offer two additional reasons for the reluctance of Asian Americans to enter into family treatment: (1) a lack of familiarity with western mental health concepts, and (2) a problem-solving approach that is internally oriented (e.g., a general belief that family problems are best resolved within the family). Both of these reasons are likely to affect a family's perspective of treatment and thereby probabilities of positive outcomes. Furthermore, it has been suggested that because Asian families come to treatment as a last resort, the problems they bring to therapy may be more severe (e.g., psychosis) (Shon and Ja, 1982). In addition to the above consideration, high proportions of Asian clients drop out of treatment after the first session and the average number of therapy sessions is sometimes quite low.

In contrast to some minority families, it has been suggested that Hispanic families are a "natural for family treatment" (Hardy-Fanta and

MacMahon-Herrera, 1981). It is posited that because of the Hispanic family's investment in family life, continued interdependence between the family and its members throughout adulthood, and the extended nature of the Hispanic family, which allows for the possible acceptance of the therapist into the family (*adoptado*), family treatment may be the treatment of choice for Hispanics. Hence, despite the absence of substantial outcome data on the treatment of Hispanic families, it does appear from the literature that family therapy as a mode of treatment is an effective modality in working with them.

Race and family treatment is an area of study that is in great need of empirical outcome research. At present our knowledge is based largely on anecdotal evidence. It does seem, however, that researchers are beginning to take note of this area. Until we do have further research efforts like that of Beck and Jones (1975) we must continue to rely heavily on anecdotal practice experiences.

CONCLUSION

Historically, it has been the weaknesses of minority families rather than their strengths that have received greater attention in the family literature. This chapter focused on treatment issues as they pertain to working with minority families and attempted to refute the perception that these families are dysfunctional or pathological.

Minority families have tended to underutilize family treatment services. This reluctance has been a consequence of cultural values at odds with seeking outside assistance and fear on the part of families that the person offering assistance will have insufficient understanding of the problems they experience. There are indications that minority families have preferences for and against same-race practitioners depending on their personal attitudes with respect to working with persons who are culturally different.

There is evidence to suggest that minority families are among the least preferred as clients. This apparent bias may be due, at least in part, to the lack of the white practitioner's familiarity and contact with minority families. The use of a minority and a nonminority as cotherapists may enhance therapeutic communication with the family and improve the relationship between the minority family and the agency. Problems experienced by minority families are similar to those of other families, except minority families are more at risk from the environment.

Family practitioners should understand that minority families may focus on family members differently and power may be distributed differently relative to white families—both family focus and power are culturally relative. Moreover, use of the terms matriarchal and patriarchal in describing minority families have placed these families on the defensive and obstructed our understanding of them. Marital satisfaction and stability are significantly influenced by the unemployment of minority males. However, minority families appear to experience greater egalitarianism with respect to family sex roles. Indeed, because of minority females' higher percentage contribution to the family's income, minority females are believed to exert more influence within their families than do white females in theirs.

The socialization of minority and nonminority children appears to differ. In general, minority children are taught and expected to "do for themselves" sooner as a hedge against continued or possible family hardship. There are also variations in parent-child interactions across minority groups, which are influenced by factors unique to particular minority group cultures.

The extended family is becoming less common today among minority families. Indeed, for both white and nonwhite families the percentage of single-parent families is increasing. Two factors contribute most significantly to this increase—divorce and teen pregnancy.

Given the unique importance of religious institutions to minority communities, practitioners attempting to work with minority families may enhance the process by the inclusion of religious and spiritual leaders in assessment and/or intervention efforts.

Certain practitioner styles may be more effective in working with some minority group families than others. Among those who work with minorities, structural models of family therapy have received the greatest attention. No model of family therapy has accrued evidence sufficient to conclude that it is better than others.

The outcome literature on race and family treatment is currently very rudimentary. How important the race of the practitioner is to the treatment process is still unknown. However, at least one study has found that black workers obtained better outcomes than did white workers when working with black families. Given the absence of empirical data that attest to the salience of particular strategies of interventions for work with minority families, the helping professions must rely heavily on the practice experiences of those in the field.

4

Race and Group Treatment

The issue of race and ethnicity, though often overlooked, is important in group work practice. Most group practitioners would agree with the statement by Bertcher and Maple (1974) that the effectiveness of any group is determined partially by the particular attributes or characteristics that each individual brings to the group. Indeed, race is one of the most salient attributes that individuals bring to the group setting. Moreover, because the variable of race has received some modest attention from group dynamics researchers, it is surprising to find the practice literature so devoid of attention given to race as it influences working with groups. This body of literature is, however, growing as group work texts, which in the past have omitted discussions of race and ethnicity, now are beginning to include them. In the pages to follow we will pull together the race-related group work practice, theory, and research literature that appears most pertinent to those who lead groups.

RACIAL COMPOSITION

Salience to Clients

As shown in Chapter 2, a number of studies have attempted to assess individual client racial preferences for practitioners. By contrast, little effort has been undertaken to determine client racial preferences for their fellow group members or group leaders. The question for clients with respect to the racial composition of a particular group is whether they wish to be a member of a racially homogeneous group (a group composed of all racially similar individuals) or a racially hetero-geneous group (a group composed of one or more racially different others). Although this area of research has received scant attention, the available information suggests that the actual or potential racial com-position of a group may be of significant importance to clients.

Anecdotal evidence suggests that clients do have prior conceptions of what the racial composition of a group ought to be. In an interesting discussion on the inclusion of blacks in otherwise all-white groups, Brayboy (1971) points out that "whites are reluctant to enter a group in which they are becoming a minority." A similar observation has been noted by Martinez (1977). She mentions that Mexican-American groups which she conducted did not attract non-English speakers, who if they did choose to come, did so only briefly.

It should be mentioned, however, that it is not always the non-minority person who may express reservations about joining a predom-inantly or all-minority member group. There is some indication that minority members themselves may question their inclusion in such groups (Davis, Sharfstein, and Owens, 1974). Davis and his colleagues reviewed possible difficulties in beginning an all-black group in a predominantly white hospital. While most clients were agreeable to the idea of estab-lishing an all-black treatment group, some patients were opposed to the idea. Some members questioned a black's ability to lead a group com-posed only of blacks, arguing that it would be "unnatural and illegiti-mate." It appeared that these reservations were principally a function of members' belief that they (blacks) would talk only about their blackness and not their problems.

A small group experiment by Davis (1979) suggests that blacks and whites may prefer different group compositions. White and black male college students were asked to compose groups of individuals from a hypothetical list of potential members. Results from the study indicate that blacks and whites do differ significantly in their preferences for the composition of these groups. Blacks selected approximately equal numbers of blacks and whites, while whites selected group compositions more consistent with black-white representation in society at large (e.g.,

20 percent black, 80 percent white). Hence, group leaders may experience some difficulty composing a racially heterogeneous group that is to the satisfaction of both blacks and whites. Furthermore, the results of this study suggest that factors which increase intimacy, such as a reduction in formality of the group or decrease in group size, may further increase black preferences for greater numbers of same-race group members.

Although clients are not generally afforded the luxury of selecting their fellow group members, it sometimes occurs. Boulette (1975), in her selection of Mexican-American clients for group treatment, afforded them the choice of attending an English- or Spanish-speaking group. She states that in other respects both groups are heterogeneous with regard to sex, age, and type of problem. The English-speaking group includes Mexican Americans, blacks, and whites, while the Spanish-speaking groups are essentially homogeneous, made up primarily of Mexican Americans.

Let us turn for a moment to look more closely at groups composed of similar others. It appears that even if members request a racially homogeneous group there is no guarantee that the group will not experience some difficulties. This concern has been most noted perhaps among Hispanic practitioners. For example, Cubans, Puerto Ricans, Mexicans, Columbians, and other Spanish-speaking groups are all sometimes referred to as Hispanics because they speak Spanish. However, it is false to assume that because they all speak Spanish, differences among them will be slight. In contrast to Acosta and Yamamoto (1984), who view heterogeneous compositions of Hispanic group members as presenting no problem, some have noted difficulties in constructing groups composed of more than one Spanish-speaking group (Werbin and Hynes, 1975). Based on their experiences, Werbin and Hynes caution against assuming too great a similarity between clients because each speaks the same language. They provide an excellent discussion of the difficulties practitioners might experience in composing "Hispanic" groups. They state, "we underestimated the members' feelings of identification with their respective countries until certain incidents made us aware of these feelings" (p. 398). The authors noted that, although the group members shared a common language, many slang expressions were different, with an acceptable word in one country sometimes being offensive in another. Other practitioners have also noted differences that exist among various Spanish-speaking groups (Tylim, 1982). For example, Tylim contends that Puerto Ricans may react more strongly to group termination than either Cubans or Columbians. The author also suggests that while Spanish language may be a unifying factor in the group composition, it may also limit the therapist in the individualization of clients. In that regard, the apparent harmony brought on by a common language between the therapist and the members strengthens the possibility of denial of other interpersonal and subcultural differences.

Such differences within minority groups are not limited to Hispanics. Ho (1984) suggests that even heterogeneous subgroupings of Asians (e.g., Taiwanese, Mainland Chinese, etc.) may be problematic because of various cultural differences. Hence, anyone composing groups in which there are cultural differences is left with the difficult task of constructing groups that are to the liking of all those included. Therefore, attempts to construct groups of racially similar individuals should be undertaken with cognizance that even those who look, and perhaps sound, alike may differ significantly in their various cultural backgrounds. In short, it appears that although cultural differences in racially homogeneous groups are less immediately observable than those in groups of racially dissimilar others, they continue to require the workers' sensitivity and attention.

Heffernon and Bruehl (1971) attempted to determine individual preferences for race of group leader. They conducted a study employing eighth grade junior high school black youths as subjects. Four black and four white college men without prior counseling experience were given eight hours of training in Rogerian counseling and assigned to two groups each as leaders. Each group was composed of three youths. The group sessions were conducted for a period of eight weeks. At the fifth session the youths were given a choice between continuing in counseling or going instead to the library. All the counselees of black counselors chose to attend counseling rather than go to the library, while only 11 of 23 of the counselees who had white counselors chose to return to group counseling. However, it is noteworthy that all of the black counselees of one white counselor chose to return to the group. The authors mention that this white counselor had had prior experience with black youth while the other white counselors had not. Hence, it would appear that although group members may have preferences for the race of their group leader, these preferences are subject to the influence of the group leader.

Salience to Leader

The literature indicates that it is a common situation to find a white leading a group of minority group members (Stebbing, 1972; McDonald, 1975). This scenario is not surprising in that it is consistent with the reality that there are more minorities seeking services than there are minorities providing services. Therefore, group compositions noted in the literature may reflect neither leader nor client preferences since both groups may have had little actual choice. Indeed, there are indications that black clients seeking services frequently anticipate being assigned to a white practitioner (Proctor and Rosen, 1981). Similarly, group practitioners may find themselves, because of the racial makeup of the agency's clientele, leading a group whose racial composition he or she would not have selected if given a choice.

The issue of leader preference for group composition has received little attention. Rosenbaum and Hartley (1966), using questionnaire responses, attempted to assess the attitudes of 83 group leaders in their willingness to include a black in an otherwise all-white group. The questionnaire presented a hypothetical scenario in which a practitioner was conducting both individual and group therapy in the deep South. After two years of treating a black businessman individually, the practitioner thinks that the client would benefit more from group treatment. Respondents were asked to decide if they would include the black client in their otherwise all-white therapy group. Of therapists polled, 29 (35 percent of the sample) indicated that they would place the black in the group, 38 (46 percent) indicated they would discuss the problem with the group and/or patient before deciding, and 16 (19 percent) indicated that they would not place the black in the group. These findings provide useful insights into how practitioners may respond to the issue of group integration. However, this study does not address group practitioners' reasons for including or not including minorities in their groups. What are the specific motives for member inclusion or exclusion? For example, do leaders exclude minorities from their groups because they, or the group members, personally do not wish to work with them or because they believe that the group, due to its racial composition, would be detrimental to the minority client or other group members?

It has been suggested that a referral to group treatment may be a clinician's attempt to avoid working closely with clients who, for whatever reason, arouse anxiety (Saretsky, 1977). Consistent with this notion is Sattler's hypothesis that patients of one race may create anxieties and countertransference reaction in therapists of another race. Building on this conceptualization, Green (1980) and his colleagues attempted to assess whether practitioner referrals of patients from individual to group treatment were associated with the client's race or sex. They hypothesized that certain ethnicity/gender constellations of clients and practitioners would result in disproportionately greater or fewer numbers of referrals to group treatment. This hypothesis was supported. Our attentions for the moment will focus primarily on the findings with respect to race.

Green et al. (1980) analyzed the case records of 1,920 adults who had received individual, group, or both types of therapy from a California mental health agency during 1977. Their findings indicate that white practitioners were more likely to refer clients to groups than were minority practitioners. Furthermore, leaders were significantly more likely to refer a client to group treatment if the client was of the same sex but different ethnicity. The authors assert that the findings indicate that factors other than objective technical criteria and sound clinical judgment enter the group referral equation. Hence, their findings support Saretsky's (1977) hypothesis that group referral may serve as a vehicle to distance one's self from unfamiliar and/or threatening clients. These findings are disturbing. Foremost, it is unfortunate that practitioners make referrals on the basis of personal discomfort or motives rather than on the basis of client needs.

As indicated by this discussion, the area of group practitioners' preference for racial composition of groups is not well-developed. However, the work which has been done is useful in that it may serve to caution us of our biases and suggest areas of practitioner training that may be in need of greater attention.

Salience to Group Purpose

Group purpose is often an important factor in determining group composition. For groups that have as their purpose the reduction of racial tensions and prejudices and enhancement of individuals' ethnic identities, racial composition must be carefully considered. Groups have been used to reduce prejudice and enhance racial harmony for some time (Bogardus, 1925a). In fact, it is probably in this context that race as an issue in group composition received its earliest and most consistent attention in the literature (Cobbs, 1972a; Samuels, 1972; Lieberman, Yalom, and Miles, 1973; Wilkinson, 1973). Such groups are often referred to as "interracial encounter groups" (Winter, 1971; Cobbs, 1972b; Samuels, 1972; Lieberman et al., 1973; Wilkinson, 1973). The issue of composition has been central to these groups in that they are by intent racially heterogeneous. Most discussions of interracial groups have not specified criteria for composing the racial balance of these groups. A notable exception is Samuels' (1972) excellent review of the literature on the "interracial group." Contending that group balance is an important factor for success in these groups, he advocates an equal number of majority and minority members. In his view, free interchange tends to diminish if more than 70 percent of the membership is of one race. However, he asserts that being in the minority for one or two meetings can be a valuable experience for whites, because of their normal majority status. Still, he cautions that if their situation is prolonged, members tend to speak for their race as a whole rather than as individuals, thus reducing the personal impact that is vital to group effectiveness.

Cobbs (1972a) has also added considerably to our knowledge of the significance of racial compositions. Citing the successes of such groups as Alcoholics Anonymous, he believes that problems caused in part by society may best be treated in a group context rather than individually.

Hence, he advocates treating the pathology of prejudice in evenly mixed racial settings, known as *ethnotherapy groups*. Like Cobbs, those who advocate the treatment of prejudice in integrated or heterogeneous racial groups are adhering to the *contact hypothesis*. This hypothesis views prejudice largely as a function of the absence of contact or prior negative contact. The contact hypothesis considers induced positive interracial contact to be efficacious in reducing racial prejudices. There is evidence both for and against the contact hypothesis (Cook and Sellitz, 1955; Amir, 1969); increased interracial contact has been shown both to reduce and to heighten racial tension and prejudice. It is notable that those contacts that result in the most positive outcomes occur between persons who, although belonging to different racial groups, share other similarities such as socioeconomic status.

By contrast, groups composed to enhance ethnic identity are usually homogeneous in racial makeup. The literature suggests growing use of racially homogeneous groups to enhance ethnic identity (Toldson and Pasteur, 1976; Edwards et al., 1978; Markward, 1979). Foremost among the advantages of racially homogeneous groups is the opportunity for members to candidly and openly discuss their negative feelings about themselves as ethnics. Such discussions are believed to occur less frequently in the presence of racially dissimilar others. Other advantages of homogeneous groups are potential for greater cohesion and enhanced group interaction (Goldstein, Heller, and Sechrest, 1966). However, groups intended to enhance members' sense of ethnic identity are not always racially homogeneous. For example, Sommers (1953) reports beneficial gains in the ethnic identity of Chinese, Black American, and Jewish individuals who were members of a heterogeneous group.

Although the racially heterogeneous group is frequently referred to with favor in the group work literature, not all groups need be racially mixed. Circumstances may indicate that the most effective group would be a group composed of racially homogeneous individuals. Therefore, while perhaps not the rule, the racially homogeneous group should not be viewed as a taboo composition. Hence, the racially homogeneous group should not be unduly avoided or resisted when deemed desirable or necessary by the group members or leader.

On the other hand, groups may have a heterogeneous racial composition for a number of reasons:

1. Lack of sufficient numbers of members of a particular racial group may make a homogeneous group impossible
2. Racially homogeneous compositions in specific settings may appear to have strong racist connotations, e.g., segregation or separation
3. Other client attributes may be viewed as being more critical than race, and thus result in the importance of race being subordinated

4. Group members and/or leaders may prefer racially heterogeneous group compositions

A group's purpose may significantly influence its racial composition. However, for any given situation other factors, such as member or leader preferences or the political connotations of a particular composition, may weigh heavily into the decision to make a group racially similar or heterogeneous.

RACE AND GROUP LEADERSHIP

Race is an important factor to group leaders (Wilkinson, 1973; Garza et al., 1982). For example, the race of individuals who lead groups is believed to be a critical influence on group processes and outcomes. The racial balance of a group may influence the group's demands of its leader. Indeed, racially heterogeneous groups are believed to be more difficult to lead because they heighten leader tensions and anxieties (Fiedler, 1962; Samuels, 1972; Triandis, 1976; Brown and Arevalo, 1979).

To date, most of the practice literature on mixed racial groups has focused on groups that have had whites as leaders (Sommers, 1953; Murray, Brown, and Knox, 1964; Alsdort and Grunebaum, 1969; Winter, 1971; O'Shea, 1972; Samuels, 1972; Stebbing, 1972; Walker and Hamilton, 1973; McDonald, 1975). Thus the issue of a group's racial composition has been primarily the concern of white group practitioners. Now, because of the growth in the 1960s and 1970s in the number of minority practitioners, the concerns of race and group leadership have become an important issue for both white and nonwhite group leaders.

Race and Leadership Style

The literature on race and group leadership suggests that style of leadership may be a pertinent factor in affecting the group process. A question some have asked is: Do leaders respond differently when confronted with a racially or culturally mixed group? At least with respect to work groups, the answer to this question appears to be no. Several researchers have failed to find consistent or systematic differences in the behavior styles of leaders of racially heterogeneous and homogeneous groups (Hill and Fox, 1973; Hill and Ruhe, 1974). However, it does appear that group members may respond differently. Many group practitioners have noted that they have experienced member resistance, tension, hostility, and often a general lack of trust in their work experiences with interracial groups (Samuels, 1972; Stebbing, 1972; Walker and Hamilton, 1973; Davis et al., 1974).

Informality as a style of leadership has sometimes been cited as an important quality when working with individuals from minority groups (Werbin and Hynes, 1975; Brown and Arevalo, 1979). It has been suggested that a relaxed informal style of group leadership may enhance leader-member rapport, reduce emotional distance, and increase overall group rapport. Werbin and Hynes (1975) argue that informality as a style may have special salience for group work practice with Latinos since they, more so than many other groups, traditionally rely on informal support systems. Hence, when working with certain minorities, group leaders may find it advantageous to adopt a style of leadership that is both informal and personable. However, a word of caution should be added with respect to employing an informal style of leadership: Leaders of groups that contain minorities must be very careful not to confuse informality with a lack of courtesy or respect (Brown and Arevalo, 1979). Group leaders of minorities should clearly demonstrate respect for the group members. Indeed, if one is to err as a group leader, it is best to do so in an attempt to demonstrate respect and courtesy.

Informality as a leadership style should not, however, be confused with passivity. Despite indications that a less formal style of leadership may be efficacious, there are no indications that minority group members prefer passive styles of leadership (Levinson and Jenson, 1967; Rubin, 1967; Winter, 1971; Cobbs, 1972a; Hardy-Fanta and Montana, 1982). For example, Hardy-Fanta and Montana (1982), in their treatment of Hispanic female adolescents, advocate the employment of cultural neutrality: They do not reinforce either Anglo or Hispanic cultural expectations. However, they are careful to point out that taking a culturally neutral position does not mean that the leader should take a passive leadership role during the group sessions. These suggestions are in agreement with those of other practitioners who have also found minorities to prefer active, nonpassive, styles of intervention. Consistent with this notion, Levinson and Jenson (1967) found that assertiveness of leadership influenced the participation of minority group members. Among hospitalized black schizophrenic patients, those in assertively led groups directed more speech to the group leader than those in the passively led groups. Additionally, those patients in the assertively led groups reported greater satisfaction with the group than did those in passively led groups.

In sum, leadership style appears to be an important attribute in affecting a minority member's group participation and satisfaction. Minorities may respond most favorably to a leadership style that is informal yet active. Finally, evidence of respect should be a prominent component of a leader's style if he or she hopes to be effective in leading groups that contain minorities.

Personality

As is the case with leadership style, some practitioners believe that the personality of the group leader is a salient factor in treatment (Yalom, 1975). However, those who have reviewed this area of research generally conclude that there is little known about the effects of leader personality characteristics on group processes and outcomes (Bednar and Kaul, 1978). Moreover, even less is known about the dual effects of race and personality on group processes and outcomes. Despite this paucity of knowledge, two cogent studies, both experimental, provide useful information and insight into this area. One study compares the personality styles of both black and white group leaders (Holmes et al., 1980) and the other inspects the personality dimensions of biculturalism and locus of control (Garza et al., 1982).

Holmes et al., (1980) provide one of the few studies that compares both black and white leaders on any type of personality dimension. This study attempted to determine if personality types were similar for both black and white therapists. The findings from their small group experiments indicate that "leaders" tend to be extroverted; "followers" tend to be less extroverted and more reflective, conservative, and pragmatic; and "isolates" tend to be introverted, have a flexible orientation, and prefer philosophical and independent thought. Findings from this study suggest that this personality pattern appears to be the same for both blacks and whites. Hence, at least along the personality dimensions of introversion/extroversion, the type of personality needed for leadership appears not to vary as a function of race of the leader.

Garza et al. (1982) conducted a study on ethnicity and group leadership. Foremost, they attempted to assess the effects of the group leaders' cultural identity (monocultural or bicultural) on his group behavior. Group leaders were assessed under two conditions—supportive (relaxed and friendly) and nonsupportive (tense and unfriendly). The group leaders in this study were Chicano males, and the three group members, experimental confederates, consisted of one Anglo, one black, and one Hispanic male.

Garza et al., as well as others (McFee, 1968; Valentine, 1971), posit that bicultural individuals possess better interpersonal skills for dealing effectively with individuals from different cultural groups than do monocultural individuals. Garza et al. (1982) hypothesized that high-bicultural individuals would take on a more active leadership role and would be less likely to withdraw from leadership in nonsupportive situations.

Indeed, their study found high-bicultural individuals (relative to those low in biculturalism) to be more assertive in the face of nonsupportive groups. That is, bicultural group leaders asked more questions and made more clarifying statements. They also found that the ethnicity of the group members interacted with the ethnicity of the group leader. The Chicano leader exhibited more concern by way of asking for clarification when either of the minority group members disagreed with him—e.g., was nonsupportive—than when an Anglo group member did so. The authors suggest a conceptualization offered by Triandis (1976) as a possible explanation for this occurrence: Individuals are believed to be more disturbed by disagreement from similar others because those similar to them are presumed to share similar perceptions of the world. Hence, disagreement by other minority group members results in greater efforts to obtain further clarification and understanding. However, it is possible that other group members, who are racially dissimilar to the leader, may perceive such attention as an indication of greater leader interest in or concern for those racially similar group members.

Performance

The vast majority of what is known pertaining to race and performance behaviors of group leaders has been derived from small group experimentation. Despite the nontherapeutic nature of these studies, they do provide indications of how race of the group leader may affect actual treatment situations. It seems reasonable to expect that in an interactive process the group leader not only acts upon, but also reacts to the group. Hence, it is also reasonable to expect that the racial composition of the group may influence the performance of the leader. Despite the plausibility of these expectations, however, there is little evidence to support them. Indeed, researchers who have studied the effects of racial composition on group leader performance have not found leaders to vary their leadership behaviors systematically as a function of the group's racial makeup (Hill and Fox, 1973; Hill and Ruhe, 1974; Scontrino, Larsen, and Fiedler, 1977). The failure of these studies to uncover such findings may, however, be due to the type of nontherapeutic groups typically being studied or the experimental restraints of the study itself.

Researchers have observed, however, that group members vary in their perceptions of group leader performance as a function of his or her race (Richards and Jaffee, 1972; Parker, 1976; Scontrino et al., 1977; Adams, 1978). One of the notable findings obtained from research in this area is that group members have reported perceiving racially dissimilar group leaders as being more threatening, less positive, and potentially more punitive than a same-race group leader (Richards and Jaffee, 1972; Scontrino et al., 1977).

Similarly, some research in the area of management leadership has reported considerable negative racial bias against the minority leader (Katz and Cohen, 1962; Richards and Jaffee, 1972). For example, a study by Richards and Jaffee (1972) may have significant implications for group workers. In this experimental study, 45 small groups composed completely of white members were led by a white leader, and 45 small groups composed completely of white members were led by a black leader. Three major findings were revealed:

1. The performance ratings of black leaders were significantly poorer than those of whites (despite experimental efforts to control for leader performances)
2. Subordinates with conservative racial attitudes gave poorer ratings to black group leaders than subordinates with liberal racial attitudes
3. Group members supervised by blacks behaved less cooperatively (e.g., were less accepting of suggestions, etc.) than group members supervised by whites, and some of their behaviors appeared to hinder the effectiveness of black leaders

These findings are noteworthy in that they may foretell difficulties for minority group leaders who lead groups of nonsupportive whites. Unfortunately, the study did not also include minorities as group members so that an assessment of their evaluations could also have been made. As it stands, we only have knowledge of this phenomenon as it affects cross-racial leadership for the black group leader. It is possible that similar effects may occur for the white group leader of black groups; that is, they, too, might receive negative evaluation from different-race followers. In either event, the perception of leader performance appears to be influenced, if not interfered with, by the attitudes of group members. Unfortunately, we have no clue as to whether leader response to such negative group member feedback was corrective—that is, if leader response to such negative feedback enhanced the group process or if, instead, a negative group climate was exacerbated. Not all research in this area has painted such negative scenarios. In striking contrast, some of the research on managerial leadership has indicated that minorities may be perceived by subordinates to be more considerate and supportive (Parker, 1976; Adams, 1978). However, most studies indicate that both minority and nonminority leaders working with racially diverse populations should anticipate and be prepared to cope with leader-member group tensions. Needless to say, the implications from these findings are far-reaching with respect to the establishment of trust and cohesion in racially heterogeneous treatment groups. Such negative perceptions of the group leader on the part of group members can only act to retard the development of a positive and viable treatment group atmosphere.

Finally, the racial homogeneity or heterogeneity of the group may interact with the race of the group leader to influence group member perceptions of the leader's performance. For example, Parker (1976) employed whites, blacks, and Chicanos as leaders and subordinates in a study which found that white subordinates of white leaders evaluated the performance of those white leaders more favorably when white group members were in the minority. That is, when in the numerical minority, the white group members perceived the behaviors of their same-race group leader to be more favorable than when they were in groups in which they were not the minority.

Co-Leadership

In general, co-leadership of groups has received mixed reviews. Some view co-leadership as advantageous in that it brings to the group the skills of two practitioners, who can support and counterbalance each other (Shilkoff, 1983; Corey and Corey, 1987). Others caution against its use and point to potential problems, such as competition that may ensue between the co-therapists (Middleman, 1980; Yalom, 1975). Surprisingly, the issue of race and co-leadership has received almost no attention (Yalom, 1975; Papell and Rothman, 1980; Corey and Corey, 1987). The absence of attention to race and co-leadership is even apparent in works that have been exclusively devoted to reviewing the literature on race and group work practice (Davis, 1984).

We shall limit our concerns in the brief discussion here to co-leadership teams that consist of a white and minority group leader. There are, to our knowledge, few reports of actual co-leader experiences in which one leader was white and the other minority. Two such instances of biracial co-leadership actually occurred in the treatment of families rather than groups (Wold et al., 1977; Hightower et al., 1983). However, even these reports enhance our understanding of biracial co-leadership of groups. Both reports indicate that co-leadership improved the communication within the treatment context. However, the improvement in communication was primarily a consequence of the minority client's greater willingness to disclose to the minority worker.

Moreover, the co-therapy team consisting of a white and a minority may be at risk of violating what some view as one of the principal tenets of co-leadership: that the co-leaders share equal status (Yalom, 1974). Race, as noted in Chapter 1, is a primary determinant of an individual's status in our society, and whites are ascribed higher social status than are nonwhites. Consequently, biracial co-leadership may be status imbalanced and thus at risk of experiencing status difficulties. There is evidence which suggests that differences in status, based on race, will probably result in the higher-status white co-leader being perceived and responded to as the more powerful, and perhaps more competent, of the two leaders (Berger et al., 1974). Needless to say, such group scenarios may be problematic for both the white and nonwhite co-leaders.

Unquestionably, the issue of biracial co-leadership is complex and yet potentially advantageous and problematic. Co-leaders must be sensitive to and aware of the fact that racial status effects might occur. It would seem beneficial for the white and nonwhite co-leaders to have a frank and honest discussion of this topic before sitting down with their groups. If biracial co-leader teams are to avoid adverse group and collegial dynamics, they must demonstrate to the group that both are equal in their roles as leaders and neither is the other's "helper." Indeed, they may wish to discuss this topic with the group members in the early stages of the group's development.

GROUP DYNAMICS AND GROUP PROCESSES

Intimacy, Numbers, and Balance

Group dynamics appear to be significantly influenced by the level of group intimacy, group size, and the racial balance of the group. Triandis (1961) hypothesized that race becomes more important as the possibility of intimate social contact increases. If this is true, individuals should increase their preferences for same-race individuals as the intimacy of the situation increases. In an attempt to test Triandis' hypothesis with respect to implications for group composition, Davis (1979) conducted a small group experiment in which white and black students were asked to compose groups from hypothetical lists of potential group members. The requested group compositions varied in both anticipated formality (formal-informal) and in group size (5 to 10 members). Davis found partial support for the Triandis hypothesis: For groups that were more intimate (i.e., informal rather than formal) and smaller, black subjects selected more same-race members. However, no such effects were found for white subjects. These findings suggest that, at least for blacks, race of group members may be of greatest concern in small intimate groups.

There is both anecdotal and empirical evidence of racial effects on group dynamics (Bogardus, 1925a, b, 1926a, b, 1932–1933; Moreno, 1934; Criswell, 1937; Hartley and Mintz, 1946; Allport, 1954; Berkun and Meeland, 1958; Pettigrew, 1967; Winter, 1971; Davis, 1981). Bogardus (1925a, b) and Moreno (1934) were among the first to address the phenomenon of racial ratios in small groups. Moreno (1934) contended that a group allows only a certain number of outsiders to exist within its boundaries. He refers to this "certain number" as a racial saturation point. At the racial saturation point, the group will express anxiety and aggression toward members of the out group. The end result is often racial subgroupings within the group. Allport (1954) has made similar observations; he contends that a single Japanese or Mexican child in a schoolroom is likely to be a pet, while a score will probably be regarded as a threat. Criswell researched the notion of racial cleavages or subgroupings in situations where the "majority group" was in the minority. She states: "The conspicuousness of two or three whites in an otherwise colored group seems to produce unusual racial consciousness even in young white children, and results in choices of whites simply because they are white" (1937, p. 87). Criswell goes on to suggest that there is not necessarily a linear relationship between emotional arousal and other behavior manifestations within an interracial group. For example, in her groups, she contends that whites require a certain numerical strength before competing with blacks for group leadership positions.

Researchers in other areas have also noted the significance of racial ratios and their effects on group dynamics. Pettigrew's (1967) reanalysis of Coleman, Campbell, Hobson, McParland, Mood, Weinfeld, and York (1966) indicated that the academic achievement of a student body may be affected by the racial composition of the school itself. Consistently, the literature on racial composition of neighbors and schools suggests that the racial ratio often affects whether individuals choose to leave or remain (Myerson and Banfield, 1955; Giles, Cataldo, and Gatlin, 1975; Farley et al., 1978). Davis (1981) has suggested that the dynamic underlying all of these observations (cleavages, tipping points, white flight, etc.) is a function of the majority group members feeling psychologically outnumbered. He cautions group leaders that the dynamics of their small groups may be affected by their racial compositions. It is his contention that, because white persons are so consistently in the majority, placing them in groups where they are not may produce in them a psychological state he refers to as the *psychological minority*. That is, even though they (whites) may possess numerical dominance in the group, the presence of minorities in numbers greater than 10 to 20 percent may be so physically novel (i.e., deviating too far from their prior interracial experiences) as to create concern for control and dominance of the group. Whites in this mental state are said to be psychologically outnumbered. Conversely, minorities in racial ratios greater than 10 to 20 percent, because they are so characteristically outnumbered, may feel themselves to possess greater influence and power than their numbers would suggest. Minorities in this mental state are said to be in the *psychological majority*.

There are indicators that others have witnessed the phenomenon of the psychological majority/minorityness (Winter, 1971; Ruhe and Eatman, 1977; Smith, 1981). Ruhe and Eatman created small biracial work groups of equal numbers of blacks and whites who were also equal in status (power). The authors suggest that balanced racial heterogeneity, with the accompanying equal statuses, may have caused the blacks to feel less threatened and more satisfied and whites to feel more threatened and less satisfied. These findings suggest that a group which is "racially balanced"—that is, contains equal members of minorities and nonminorities—may result in the group members being psychologically off balance.

Cooperation, Competition, and Behavior

Social psychologists have invested considerable effort in attempting to investigate the dynamics of interracial group contact. A great deal of research in this area was conducted in the 1950s and early 1960s and in this respect may be dated. This research did, however, examine individual behavior in cooperative-competitive small interracial groups. The findings from these studies indicated that blacks tended to behave differently in integrated settings than in racially homogeneous ones. As has been noted, these differences in black behavior are similar to differences in behavior of high-low status persons (Shaw, 1976). That is, blacks in these small integrated groups were found to be less assertive and more anxious. Furthermore, much of their effort was directed toward avoiding failure rather than achieving success. This has been especially noted in achievement (competitive) situations (Katz and Benjamin, 1960). Such behaviors, however, were found to be due in part to the type of competitive activity, specifically those activities viewed as requiring intellectual ability. Lefcourt and Ladwig (1965) found that black behavior in integrated groups varied as a function of the group activity. Their research indicated that this avoidance behavior on behalf of blacks was less noted in competitive situations where blacks believed that they had greater chances for success, such as musical skills, for example.

Again, it would seem wise to keep in mind that this research was conducted some years ago. Since that time, social and political advances made by blacks are believed to have significantly altered black-white relations, and blacks' reactions in integrated settings. Hence, their behavior in small groups may have also been affected.

More recently, cooperative-competitive groups have been used as a means to assess the reduction of interracial prejudice. In general, cooperative interracial group encounters have been determined successful in reducing intergroup tensions (Katz, 1955; Harding, Proshansky, Kutner, and Chein, 1969; Ashmore, 1970). Both Aronson (1975) and Weigel and Cook (1975) have found cooperative group learning experiences to have a positive effect on ethnic relations and attitudes. It is, however, consistently noted in the literature that it is not just the intergroup contact itself that contributes to the positiveness of these relations, as mere contact itself has resulted in both positive and negative effects (Cook and Sellitz, 1955; Cook, 1957, 1969; Eisenman, 1965; Pettigrew, 1967; Amir, 1969).

In looking at competition and cooperation, a sizable number of researchers have also been interested in the consequences of group success or failure on members of racially heterogeneous groups (Burnstein and McRae, 1962; Blanchard, Weigel, and Cook, 1975; Blanchard and Cook, 1976; Weigel and Cook, 1975). What are the consequences for members when interracial groups succeed or fail, or when individual members within such groups prove to be competent or incompetent? Blanchard and his colleagues (1975, 1976) have conducted small group research in an effort to answer these questions. Employing 60 white military men in small group tasks, Blanchard et al. (1975) found that subjects exhibited less attraction for a black groupmate when he performed less competently than when he performed competently. No such effects were found for white groupmates who performed incompetently. That is, incompetence on the part of whites had no negative effect on subjects' attraction for them. This study also reported that subjects liked and respected both black and white groupmates more following group success than following group failure. Black subjects who were incompetent and in unsuccessful groups were liked least of all by group members. The authors conjecture that blacks who perform incompetently fulfill already existing prejudicial stereotypes and this results in reduced attraction. By contrast, the positive influence of the cooperative group experience appears to have masked the negative effect of the white group member's incompetence, resulting in no loss of attraction for him by the other members.

In a similar study, Blanchard and Cook (1976) looked not only at the effects of perceived competence and group success, but also at the effects of helping the "less competent" group members. Again, white male servicemen were employed as subjects. Those servicemen who were induced to help a less competently performing black group member developed greater respect and liking for him than did those servicemen who merely observed the less competent black being helped by another group member. The authors suggest that this finding has important implications for the establishment of interracial groups in which whites may be functioning at a level higher than blacks. The establishment of such groups would appear to have no negative effects for the helper and instead appears to increase the degree of liking and respect for the helped person. This effect was observed whether the helpee was black or white. Thus, there is reason to believe that both blacks and whites may be positively affected by helping others in small groups. There appear to be definite benefits for interracial attraction in having group members engage in helping behaviors.

Communication, Interaction, and Culture

Much of the research on interracial communication has focused on blacks and whites and most early studies focused on group dynamics rather than small group treatment (Battle and Rotter, 1963; Katz, Roberts, and Robinson, 1965; Lefcourt and Ladwig, 1965). However, with marked consistency, the findings revealed that blacks communicate with whites in a manner congruent with their racial status of social subordinates. That is, they spoke less than whites and, when speaking, spoke more often to the white (higher-status person) than to other blacks. It must be remembered that these studies were conducted prior to the black protest movements of the late 1960s and early 1970s. More recent studies suggest that blacks, females in particular, may now take less passive roles in their communications with whites (Fenelon and Megargee, 1971; Adams, 1980). Adams (1980) conducted a study in which black females were witnessed to be assertive in their interactions with white females and more challenging of statements by white males than either white females or black males.

Although most pre-1970s studies of black and white group inter-action indicate that less communication emanates from blacks than whites, at least one study found that blacks talked more in racially mixed groups. Murray, Brown, and Knox (1964) studied interracial groups of psychiatric patients. Black patients in their study were found to direct more speech toward the therapist when in racially heterogeneous groups than in all-black groups. It is noteworthy that these interracial groups were composed of equal numbers of blacks and whites. This finding appears to be in agreement with that of Ruhe and Eatman (1977), who found that blacks in a racially mixed group expressed greater self esteem and satisfaction than those in a racially homogeneous group. Ruhe and Eatman (1977) conjectured that this effect was due to the fact that blacks may have perceived themselves to be members of a group that, because of its white group members, had greater prestige and/or status than did an all-black group.

The race of the individual to whom a statement is made continues to exert significant influence upon what is said, especially as it pertains to racial topics. General indications are that blacks and whites will respond to questions from different-race individuals with answers that are more positively stereotypic of the proper racial attitude (Triandis and Triandis, 1965; Gould and Klein, 1971; Davis, 1979). This fact has significant implications for the level of honesty of communication in small treatment groups. The presence of different-race group members may retard honest expression of true racial feelings. It is also possible that members of more racially balanced groups may speak more candidly in those groups than they would if they were the only different-race member present in the group.

Due to the recent social and political strides on the part of minorities, communication between minorities in small treatment groups can be expected to be characterized by less minority subordination and greater verbal participation than in the past. Consistent with this possibility, Winter (1971) found that in small interracial discussion groups, blacks more frequently led the group discussion than did whites. Such changes in the communication of minorities may appear to be arrogant or aggressive to those individuals whose expectations for minorities are based on the social protocol of bygone eras. Therefore, group leaders might facilitate the group's process and reduce the probability of misperceptions of the minority member's behavior by introducing the topics of race, social expectations, and social change.

As has been pointed out, the verbal reserve exhibited by ethnic groups is often a function of their distrust of members who represent the larger society (Brown and Arevalo, 1979). However, cultural prescription also contributes to reluctance to open up and discuss problems in groups and to talk directly to the group leader. Mexican Americans, especially males, have been described as being close mouthed to outsiders (Paz, 1961). Martinez (1977) found no evidence of the Hispanic male's reluctance to talk. However, he did conclude that the interpersonal formality that exists within the Mexican-American culture inhibited the expression of negative feelings toward the leader. Since Mexican-American culture is more formal than Anglo culture, participants had difficulty expressing their personal misgivings with the treatment staff. Maldonado-Sierra and Trent (1960) suggest that communication between the group leader and members of Puerto Rican and certain other Latin groups may be affected by the fact that the siblings often direct their communications to the older male sibling and not the father. The authors suggest that greater sibling-sibling intimacy and less father-sibling intimacy in some Latin cultures may foster less leader-member communication and greater member-member communication.

Asian Americans' styles of group communication may vary greatly from that of Anglos. Kaneshige (1973) provides an insightful review of how cultural factors affect the communication of Asian group members. In his view, the communication styles of Japanese Americans and Anglo Americans differ chiefly due to value conflicts regarding self disclosing and issues central to the counseling process: Asians are less inclined to engage in self disclosure of personal problems. Several factors contribute to this. First, problems are assumed to reflect a personal lack of will power. Second, extensive disclosure connotes egocentrism, while Asian culture values humility. Finally, Japanese culture emphasizes politeness and verbal reticence, which reduces the likelihood of verbal confrontation between group members.

By contrast, group members in other cultures may express emotion more readily. For example, in the absence of other racial groups, blacks may readily express feelings and disagreements (Davis, Sharfstein, and Owens, 1974), and verbally respond to each other in styles outsiders might regard as hostile. Kochman notes some differences in the ways in which blacks and whites handle conflict. He contends that whites may try harder than blacks to avoid confrontation because they equate confrontation with conflict. Blacks, on the other hand, see confrontation not as antagonism, but rather as individuals "cooperatively engaged in a process that hopes to test through challenge, the validity of opposing ideas" (1981, p. 19).

Cultural factors may not only alter to whom or how things are communicated, but also what is communicated (McNeely and Badami, 1984). Hispanic group members, for example, may express their psychological or social difficulties in terms of physical symptoms and somatic complaints (Boulette, 1975; Franklin and Kaufman, 1982; Tylim, 1982). Yet the discussion of the physical ills often gives way later in the course of greater group involvement to client expressions of interpersonal, psychological, and social difficulties.

Language itself may also have consequences for the pattern or style of communication within the group. Needless to say, if some members are bilingual while the leader or other members are monolingual, group process will be affected. Often the monolingual person feels isolated or left out and, as a result, withdraws from such groups (Martinez, 1977). At the same time, this shift back and forth from English to a native language seems to enhance group cohesion among the bilingual group members. Overall, it appears that the communication within any particular group may be significantly affected by the culture of its members. Hence, it would seem necessary for group practitioners to acquaint themselves with those cultural aspects of their group members that are believed to impinge on the group's style and manner of communication.

In addition to members responding differentially to each other, there are indications that patterns of group communication may vary as a function of race of the leader and race of the group member making the comment. As was noted above in our earlier discussion on leadership, Garza, Romero, Cox, and Ramirez (1982) found that a Chicano group leader was more inclined to make clarifying statements in response to a white group member who agreed with him than to Chicano or black group members who did so. Conversely, those Chicano or black group members who disagreed with the Chicano leader received more attention in the way of clarifying statements than did the white group members who disagreed with the Chicano leader. Again, this propensity may result in the leader giving a greater proportion of group time to one particular subset of group members than to others. This increased dialogue may appear to the other group members to connote greater leader concern for and greater rapport with those racially similar group members.

RACE AND GROUP OUTCOME

As Teresa Boulette (1975) has noted, there have been numerous disfavorable reviews pertaining to the use of groups with minorities. For example, it has been stated that "group therapy is a white, middle class approach. It insults the distinctive culture of the people. These clients do not have the necessary psychological sophistication or the needed verbal skills to use it properly" (p. 403). However, in spite of such negative reviews, large numbers of minorities are being counselled in groups: *American Indians* (Kahn, Lewis, and Galvez, 1974; McDonald, 1975; Edwards et al., 1978); *blacks* (Brayboy, 1971; Felton and Biggs, 1973; Toldson and Pasteur, 1975, 1976; Markward, 1979; Brown, 1981; McRoy and Oglesby, 1984); *Hispanics* (Boulette, 1975; Cooper and Cento, 1977; Brown and Arevalo, 1979; Delgado and Siff, 1980; Brown, 1981; Hardy-Fanta and Montana, 1982; Tylim, 1982; Comas-Diaz, 1984); *Asians* (Sommers, 1953; Chang, 1972; Mummah, 1975).

Moreover, there are numerous accounts of positive outcomes. For example, Gatz, Tyler, and Paragament (1978), in an empirical study, report significant increases in personal and educational goals for black students seen in group counseling. Also working with adolescents, Hardy-Fanta and Montana (1982) found that the group process had positive consequences for Hispanic females: Following treatment, group members could better tolerate anxiety. Others have also had some success with group treatment: black chronic schizophrenics have been found to remain longer in hospital programs (Smith and Gundlach, 1974); elderly Hispanic patients have improved in self concept and in their relationships with others (Franklin and Kaufman, 1982); blind, aged Japanese were helped to interact better with staff and peers to increase their physical abilities and enhance their levels of independence (Mummah, 1975); and other groups containing American Indians, and those containing Asians, blacks, and whites, have reported noted improvements in member self acceptance (Sommers, 1953; Edwards et al., 1978). Hence, it seems that groups are not only being used widely with minority populations, but they appear to be experiencing success.

Salience of the Group Member

Do some minorities respond more favorably than others? Indeed, are some minority groups, because of cultural values or patterns, more successfully treated as members of groups than other minorities? These are important questions and ones that remain, by and large, unanswered.

Some contend that group treatment is an excellent medium through which to deliver services to minority groups (Acosta and Yamamoto, 1984; Edwards and Edwards, 1984). For example, it has been suggested that the group format is a good medium through which to treat many Hispanics because it is consistent with aspects of Hispanic culture, such as the extended family, close sibling relationships, and strong familial ties (Maldonado-Sierra and Trent, 1960; Comas-Diaz, 1981). Others, however, have noted potential problems with treating Hispanics in groups, including their reserve in dealing openly with feelings toward the group leader and with non-Spanish-speaking leaders (Martinez, 1977).

Similar pros and cons to group treatment have been noted for other minority groups as well. For example, group treatment has been viewed as potentially less beneficial for Asians, because of their cultural reticence to be confrontative and competitive and their reluctance to interrupt others who are speaking, a common group experience (Ching and Prosen, 1980; Chu and Sue, 1984; Ho, 1984). However, these authors also indicate that there are potentially positive consequences for Asian group members as a result of their cultural values: Because Asian clients value interdependence and cooperation they may benefit from the support of other group members.

In spite of the cited advantages and pitfalls of group treatment for members of various ethnic groups, there is no empirical evidence that group treatment is more or less suitable for members of certain ethnic groups. Rather, group leaders appear to emphasize group processes that are consistent with cultural aspects of specific minority members.

Another question often asked is, Which is better with respect to successful attainment of desired outcomes, racially heterogeneous or homogeneous group compositions? A number of studies have reported findings from observations of racially homogeneous or heterogeneous groups.

For example, Fenelon and Megargee (1971) found that racially mixed groups performed less efficiently than did racially homogeneous groups. Apparently, the tension created in this racially heterogeneous group reduced the group's effectiveness, e.g., increased the time needed to complete the group task. Their study (which employed white and black college females as subjects in a series of two-person group experiments) also attempted to look at the effects of race and personality on dominant behavior. Most frequently, the high "dominant person" assumed group leadership. However, when the high-dominant white was paired with a low-dominant black, the black most frequently assumed leadership. The authors suggest that this effect was the consequence of the white not wanting to assert herself over a black. However, it should also be remembered that the study was conducted with female subjects and, despite their reported personality scores (e.g., high or low dominance), black females frequently view themselves and are viewed by others as being more competent and/or dominant than white females (Scanzoni, 1975; Adams, 1980; Wallace, 1980; Brower et al., 1987).

Other studies have also noted individual differences, but few have noted differences in group productivity. Ruhe and Eatman (1977), in a study of racially heterogeneous three-person groups, found that black supervisors, regardless of the race of the subordinates, were asked fewer questions and offered fewer suggestions than white supervisors. When the group's two subordinate members were mixed, one white and one black, the black subordinate member spoke less. However, the black member in these groups expressed greater satisfaction with the assigned tasks.

Ruhe and Eatman (1977) also found that the racial composition of the group influenced the behavior and expressed satisfaction of black group members. The authors used 96 white and black male undergraduate students. The subjects were asked to participate as subordinates and supervisors in racially heterogeneous problem-solving groups. The results from the study indicate the whites were not significantly affected by the racial composition of the group. Blacks, in contrast, were positively influenced by the racially mixed group composition. Those blacks in the racially heterogeneous groups performed their tasks more effectively and expressed a greater satisfaction with self and others than did blacks in segregated work groups. Findings from this study suggest that the integrated group had positive effects for blacks while it simultaneously had no deleterious effects for whites.

No groups appear to have been composed expressly to compare the treatment effects of racially homogeneous and heterogeneous compositions. Indeed, most commonly, racially homogeneous groups are a result of the racial demographics of a particular agency or treatment facility. However, some practitioners have reported intentionally composing treatment groups consisting of all same-race clients. For example, Davis et al. (1974) hypothesized that the formation of an adjunct all-black group in a predominantly white hospital would increase the time spent in and quality of treatment for black clients, and would facilitate discussions of race-related, clinically relevant issues. The authors point out that their formation of an all-black group was met initially with some resistance from both white staff and black clients. However, their group proved successful in enhancing both race-related treatment discussions and the length of time that blacks were found to remain in "traditional integrated" therapy.

Davis (1974) and colleagues are not alone in their view that racially homogeneous groups may enhance positive outcomes. Others also attribute the positive outcomes of group members at least partially to the racial or cultural homogeneity of their groups (Franklin and Kaufman,

1982; Comas-Diaz, 1984). Although they provide no empirical evidence, Franklin and Kaufman (1982) state that the cultural and age homogeneity of their elderly Hispanic group contributed significantly to the group's success. Group success was reflected in members' improved relationships with persons at home and enhanced positive feelings about themselves.

There is also evidence to suggest that some minority group members may respond favorably to or benefit more from experiences in mixed racial groups. Notably, blacks in interracial groups have been observed to express themselves more, experience a greater sense of self esteem, report greater levels of satisfaction with the group, and demonstrate enhanced productivity (Murray, Brown, and Knox, 1964; Ruhe and Eatman, 1977). Therefore, despite the contentions of some practitioners that the racial or cultural homogeneity or heterogeneity of the group contributes positively to client outcomes, there is little empirical evidence to support their suppositions. Clearly, more group research is needed to assess the effects of racial homogeneity or heterogeneity on client outcomes.

Salience of the Group Leader

What are the consequences of racial similarity or dissimilarity between group leader and members for client outcomes? The literature offers equivocal conclusions with respect to this question (Sattler, 1977; Parloff, Waskow, and Wolfe, 1978). This equivocation can be attributed mainly to the scarcity of studies that have looked simultaneously at groups led by minorities and nonminorities and to the failure of studies to employ sufficient experimental rigor with respect to control groups and reliable outcome measures. Also, too few studies have been racially heterogeneous, and few have studied minority group members other than blacks. The notable exception to the black-white focus of research is the study by Walker and Hamilton (1973), which employed Chicanos, blacks, and whites as group members.

In general, studies that have controlled for race of the group leader (that is, employed both minority and nonminority group leadership) have provided little indication that race of the group leader affects the outcomes of group members (Owen, 1970; Heffernon and Bruehl, 1971; Lieberman, Yalom, and Miles, 1973). For example, Lieberman et al. composed groups consisting of white and black college students for the purpose of reducing prejudice and enhancing positive racial attitudes. Both black and white group leaders were employed. It was determined that neither black nor white leaders were superior in their leadership efforts—both were successful in obtaining the desired outcomes among group members. Perhaps the most important finding of the study pertained not to leader race but to group composition: Client outcomes (positive racial attitudinal change) occurred only in the racially heterogeneous group compositions; in the racially homogeneous groups, no significant attitudinal change occurred.

Heffernon and Bruehl (1971) and Owen (1970) also failed to find differences in the effectiveness of white and black group leaders. The Heffernon and Bruehl groups were composed of eighth grade black boys who were referred to the school counselor. No difference was found in member attitude change as a function of group leader's race. However, blacks appeared to prefer black group leaders, with the exception of those youths who had a white counselor who had had prior experience in interacting with blacks. One study (Phillips, 1960) that did report a difference in the effectiveness of white and black group leaders concluded that white leaders were less effective with black students. Although no actual data were collected on client outcomes, it was suggested that this difference in leader effectiveness was a function of lack of prior experience of the white leaders with black clients. It is noteworthy that in both the Heffernon and Bruehl (1971) and the Phillips (1960) studies, prior experience in working with a particular ethnic or racial group appears to play an important role in the potential for positive outcomes.

Most studies to date have failed to employ both whites and nonwhites as group leaders. Consequently, we generally inspect only the effects of the white group leader on minority group clients. Furthermore, the minority group subjects consist principally of blacks, while other minorities remain grossly underrepresented. Hence, we know comparatively little regarding the salience of the minority group leader's race on client outcomes and much of what we do know is limited only to blacks. However, the indications are that the race of the group leader does have the potential to affect group treatment outcomes via its effect on group processes and perhaps greater member readiness to remain in the group. It appears that race may be an important attribute if for no other reason than that it has served to limit therapist familiarity and experience in working with certain client populations.

Salience of the Modality

Is there a group modality best suited for use with minority clients? Are there modalities that are better suited for treating ethnically homogeneous or heterogeneous client compositions? The present state of the group treatment literature makes an assessment of answers to these questions difficult. Yet it does appear that various theoretical approaches are being employed with particular minority groups. For example, the following orientations have been identified as being useful in group practice with minorities: *gestalt* with American Indians (McDonald, 1975) and blacks (Felton and Biggs, 1973; Smith and Grundlach, 1974); *behavioral and/or cognitive approaches* with Asians (Ho, 1984) and Hispanics (Boulette, 1975; Comas-Diaz, 1981); *psychoanalytic* with culturally heterogeneous Latino groups (Werbin and Hynes, 1975) and Puerto Ricans (Maldonado-Sierra and Trent, 1960); *social goals model* with Chicanos (Brown and Arevalo, 1979); *short-term/crisis intervention* with Hispanics (Normand et al., 1974); *Rogerian* with racially heterogeneous groups of Chicanos, blacks, and whites (Walker and Hamilton, 1973); *client-centered* with groups composed of both blacks and whites (Redfering, 1975).

Unfortunately, the rationale for the use of a particular theoretical orientation often goes unstated. For example, literature in this area frequently fails to indicate why practitioners selected a particular model or theoretical orientation. Hence, it is sometimes unclear if a particular theoretical approach was selected because it was consistent with certain ethnic or cultural aspects of a specific population, if it was selected at random, or if the selected orientation was one most familiar to the practitioner.

However, a few practitioners have advocated the use of a particular theoretical orientation and have offered rationales for their choice. McDonald (1975), in his treatment of American Indian women, stated that he employed a Gestalt approach because he thought that it was most relevant to the here and now problems confronted by the relocated American Indian woman. Comas-Diaz (1981) puts forth a strong argument for the employment of behavioral group techniques with Puerto Rican women. She, like Hayes (1976), contends that behavioral approaches may be more relevant for minority clients not because such clients lack the cognitive abilities to benefit from abstract/intellectual approaches but because behavioral approaches enable them to better learn the relationship between behavior and rewards in society. Hence, minorities may better learn how to manipulate the environment and control the principal contributor to many of their difficulties. Brown and Arevalo (1979) advocate the social goals model of group work in practice with Chicanos, asserting that Chicanos and many other minorities often need structural environmental change. They suggest the social goals model of group work more than other models because this model focuses on structural aspects of society (e.g., institution and societal responsibilities). Brown and Arevalo go on to suggest that the social goals model is uniquely applicable to minorities, as many of their difficulties are due to dysfunctional social institutions and the inability of government to carry out its responsibilities.

Despite advocacy by practitioners for certain group models, the literature indicating the comparative efficacy of these different theoretical orientations with specific racial, ethnic, or cultural groups is sparse. Comas-Diaz (1981) conducted one of the very few studies that attempted to vary the theoretical focus and assess its effects on a given ethnic population. She compared the effectiveness of a control group (no treatment), a cognitive group, and a behavioral group approach to the reduction of depression among low-income Puerto Rican women. Twenty-six clients, diagnosed as depressed on the Beck (1967) depression scale, were randomly assigned to one of the three groups. The therapist was a Puerto Rican female so the group was homogeneous in terms of culture and gender. Results indicated no difference between the cognitive and behavioral approaches, both of which resulted in significantly better client outcomes than the control group. However, a five-week follow up indicated that the amelioration of depression had been maintained most by those clients treated under the behavioral approach.

At present there exists insufficient empirical validation to indicate which, if any, group modalities work best with which ethnic, racial, or cultural groups. In general, however, it does appear that a significant number of those models advocated for use with minorities are those that focus on cultural sensitivity, concreteness, active leadership, immediate attention to problem resolution, and a clear recognition of the importance of the environment as a contributing factor to the client's problems.

CONCLUSION

In this chapter we have reviewed many aspects of race that have the potential to affect group practice. There is some evidence that whites and minorities may prefer different racial compositions; neither whites nor minorities appear to like being greatly outnumbered. The language spoken in the group may also be important. For example, if some members speak Spanish while others do not, the nonbilingual speakers may become isolated. Furthermore, cultural differences that exist within various racial groups (e.g., Hispanics or Asians) may influence group member interactions significantly.

Practitioners have also exhibited preferences for various race clients. In what appears to be an attempt to distance themselves from certain clients, white practitioners have been observed to refer clients to groups more so than minority practitioners. In general, clients are most likely to be referred to group treatment by a same-sex different-race practitioner.

Group purpose has also influenced group composition. Groups composed of all same-race members have most often had the enhancement of ethnic identity as their goal. In contrast, racially heterogeneous compositions are often constructed to reduce racial antagonisms.

Leading racially heterogeneous groups may be more difficult than leading racially homogeneous groups. In working with minorities, informal leadership style that is active and respectful of the group members may be advantageous. The personal qualities needed for group leadership do not appear to vary across racial groups. Being bicultural, that is, having knowledge of both cultures, appears advantageous to leading heterogeneous cultural groups, especially if the groups are initially nonsupportive of the leader. Leaders appear not to vary their leadership behaviors as a function of the racial composition of their groups. However, it does appear that group members may respond differentially to the leader depending on race. Group leaders who differ in race from group members may be perceived, evaluated, and responded to less positively than same-race leaders. Leaders who differ in race from their group members may receive less cooperation. Biracial co-leadership may enhance communication in racially heterogeneous groups. However, biracial co-leaders must remain alert to the possibility of one leader being perceived as the leader and the other as merely his or her helper.

Group dynamics are significantly influenced by the racial composition, size, and task of the group. Group members may experience psychological discomfort in groups whose racial compositions vary greatly from those with which they are familiar. Minorities have been observed to behave less assertively in racially mixed groups. It also appears that blacks who perform incompetently in groups will receive less positive response than similarly performing white group members. It may be beneficial to the group process to have members of racially heterogeneous groups engage in cross-racial helping experiences as such experience appears to enhance member-member attraction. Cultural factors may influence the content and direction of communication in biracial groups. There is also evidence that both minorities and whites tend to provide same-race group members with more honest feedback.

The practice literature in this area is rarely empirical, however; there are many anecdotal reports of successful group experiences with minorities. There is no evidence which suggests that group treatment is more or less suitable for any particular ethnic group. Furthermore, there is little evidence that either racially homogeneous or racially heterogeneous groups are superior in their outcomes. It does seem, however, that racially heterogeneous groups are better at enhancing positive interracial attitudes than are groups that consist of all same-race members.

Very few studies have attempted to assess the effects of the group leader's race on group member outcomes. Furthermore, reports from studies involving race of leader and group outcomes are mixed. However, these studies are consistent in that they have found that prior group leader experience in working with minorities appears to have beneficial effects for the group.

Although a variety of group modalities have been recommended for work with minority clients, there is currently insufficient evidence to suggest that one group modality is more effective than another. However those modalities that are most consistently recommended for use with minorities tend to focus on cultural sensitivity, concreteness, active leadership, the environment, and immediate attention to problem resolution.

5

GUIDELINES
FOR PRACTICE
When Race Is Salient

The previous four chapters examined in detail the impact of race on individual, family, and group treatment. Regarding some issues, the research findings are seemingly contradictory or inconclusive. However, some clear trends are evident, as reflected in the conclusions of each chapter. Most importantly for the practitioner, we can derive some implications—some guidelines—for practice where race is salient.

PREPARING FOR PRACTICE

First, practitioners must be prepared for practice situations in which race is salient. Although it is possible for race to be salient even when the helper and client are of the same race, this discussion focuses on situations in which race of helper and client differ. The occurrence of client-helper racial dissimilarity may vary for practitioners and settings. However, as noted in earlier chapters, the changing demographics of U.S. society ensure that for most workers and most fields of practice, client-helper racial dissimilarity is likely to increase.

As was evident in Chapter 1, race affects not only the assumptions drawn about others but also the comfort levels experienced in interpersonal relationships. Individuals are most comfortable with persons who are racially similar and are most likely to experience anxiety with those individuals who are racially dissimilar. Deliberate effort is required to reduce such a pervasive interpersonal dynamic. Therefore practitioners—who are themselves subject to the same fears and anxieties as other members of our society—cannot be expected to automatically "rise to the occasion" and comfortably and competently respond to the needs of racially dissimilar clients. Rather they should prepare for practice in situations of racial dissimilarity long before the client presents himself or herself.

What is required for adequate preparation? First, knowledge of minority populations is essential. Workers cannot help those whom they do not adequately understand. Race and ethnicity are major influences on our beliefs and ideas. Therefore, practitioners must be knowledgeable about the social consequences of race, culture, and ethnicity in general. More specifically, they must know the history, norms, and cultural values of the particular minority group with which they plan to work. A variety of resources can enhance the practitioner's knowledge of minority groups. They include books that describe the history and culture of minority groups, community cultural centers, and ethnic festivals. Other helpful resources include workshops, special university courses, and sessions at professional symposia and conferences. In addition, we recommend that white practitioners obtain supervision or consultation from minority practitioners. Finally, personal experiences that put the practitioner in contact with ethnic minority culture are also valuable. For example, minority newspapers and radio stations can be important sources of information.

A second aspect of preparation involves self examination—and, where needed, modification—of racial attitudes and values. Racial prejudice is extensive, and not even well-intentioned helping professionals escape its impact on thoughts, attitudes, and values. In many respects, and especially with regard to racial prejudice, professional development requires modification of personal perspectives and values. Even professional values may conflict with the values of ethnic and minority groups. For example, many practice theories and assumptions reflect western, middle-class values (e.g., individualism and self determination) that conflict with the familialism and group responsibility valued by many minority groups. Professionals should strive to be aware of their own racial stereotypes and cultural values which are at odds with those of their minority clients.

Personal experiences of being in the numerical minority can facilitate the awareness of racial attitudes and dynamics. Such experiences may raise anxiety about being racially outnumbered. Such anxiety or discomfort, however, should not be equated with racism. If workers interpret their feelings of anxiety as indications of their dislike for the client and subsequently begin to behave in a manner consistent with that interpretation, the treatment process will be impaired. Most practitioners will probably never feel as comfortable working with racially dissimilar others as with racially similar others. It is important for helpers to understand that their feelings of anxiety or discomfort with racially dissimilar clients may be largely a function of the novelty of interacting with them. Indeed, there are indications that if practitioners continue to work with different-race persons, the comfort level they experience with those persons is likely to increase.

A third aspect of preparation is developing a wide repertoire of helping responses. As shown in Chapter 2, communication and assessment skills, particularly patterns of eye contact, expression of feeling, physical distance, and directiveness, are likely to vary for particular racial and ethnic groups. Just as clients differ, the interventive behavior of workers must be varied. The practitioner's task is to be able to respond in ways that are comfortable and helpful to the client. A practitioner's own customary, comfortable way of communicating may not be the most culturally sensitive or effective with all minority group clients. Instead, a different style or approach of communicating may be most suitable with certain minority groups.

MANAGING EARLY TREATMENT INTERACTION

The initial encounter appears to have a great influence on whether interaction will continue (Newcomb, 1947; Mizio, 1972; Weissman et al., 1973). Therefore, if rapport is to occur at all, it must be enhanced at the earliest encounters. Thus, one goal of practitioners in interracial treatment should be increasing the client's attraction to treatment and to the helper for a period of time sufficient for a "natural" development of rapport. Fortunately, repeated contact itself appears to foster increased positive feeling (Zajonc, 1968).

What should occur in the earliest encounters? First, racial difference and its potential salience should be acknowledged. Acknowledgment, by the worker, of a worker-client racial dissimilarity will convey to the client the worker's sensitivity and awareness of the potential significance of race to the helping relationship. It will also convey to the client that the worker probably has the ability to handle the client's feelings regarding race. It is probably best to introduce this topic by asking if the client has racial concerns and issues, rather than problems. Obviously the most likely answer to the question, "Do you have problems with my race?" is no! Thus we suggest a question such as, "How do you think my being white and your being nonwhite might affect our working together?" Or the practitioner might ask, "If during the course of our meetings you have concerns or issues pertaining to race, please feel free to discuss them." If the client hastens to assure the worker that race is not an issue, the worker can reply, "I don't think it will be a barrier either. But if at any time you feel that I don't understand something you say or mean because our backgrounds are different, I hope you will feel free to tell me. I want to help and I will work hard at understanding you and your situation." If, on the other hand, the client prefers not to work with a racially dissimilar worker, an opportunity has been provided to make such feelings clear. The most important message conveyed by the worker's initiative in acknowledging the racial issue is his or her desire to understand and help the client, and his or her ability to discuss what is often a sensitive issue.

Second, while indicating a willingness to work hard to understand and help the client, the worker should acknowledge that his or her own social reality is probably different from the racially dissimilar client's. The worker should not be too modest to indicate to the client prior personal or practice experiences that enable the worker to better understand racial factors that are important to the client.

Third, the worker should establish a basis for client trust. As elaborated in earlier chapters, minorities have experienced a history of mistreatment and have subsequently developed what is sometimes referred to as "healthy paranoia" in their interactions with outsiders. Hence the worker may be required to exert considerable effort to establish client trust. Toward this end, we suggest that only information absolutely necessary for assessment be asked for initially. Workers can also demonstrate trustworthiness by maintaining confidentiality and by prompt availability for appointments.

Practitioners should be certain to convey respect. For members of minority groups, whose history is marked by degradation by the majority society, professional courtesies are very important. Practitioners should greet minority clients with handshakes, proper introductions, and references by titles (Mr., Mrs.) and last name.

Genuineness should also be conveyed. White workers should refrain from using "hip language" or ethnic slang or phrases. Phoney or superficial attempts to relate to clients will not be appreciated.

Culturally appropriate attending skills and nonverbal behaviors should be used. (The reader should see the preceding four chapters for specific behaviors.) Workers should listen attentively, summarize and reflect back to ensure accuracy of understanding, and offer options in room arrangement so that minority clients can select interpersonal distances that are most comfortable.

Practitioners should convey a basis for credibility. The client should be shown that the worker is capable of offering help. The credibility issue may be different for various racial combinations. For white workers and minority clients, the primary credibility issue is likely to be the adequacy of the worker's knowledge of minority social reality. Minority clients may accept as sufficient the white worker's therapeutic skill but question the sufficiency of his or her knowledge of the client's social reality. It may not be possible to allay this concern immediately. However, as noted above, the first step is for the practitioner to acknowledge the potential significance of race to the client. Careful listening and accurate reflection will also enhance and demonstrate the worker's understanding of the client's situation. Minority workers may emphasize their credibility by displaying academic and professional credentials. In addition, since the possibility of informal contacts in close-knit or small ethnic communities is sometimes great, it is important that minority workers assure minority clients of professional confidentiality. In the final analysis, the worker's conveyance of credibility is as valid as is his or her depth of preparation, expertise, and knowledge of the minority client's world view.

Finally, it is important in early helping sessions to define and structure the helping process. Ethnic groups may vary in their expectations for the roles and activities of helping. Ambiguity regarding these important issues may increase discomfort, and open clarifying discussion can be reassuring and enabling.

ENSURING CULTURAL APPROPRIATENESS OF THE TREATMENT PROCESS

The cultural appropriateness of the helping process should be ensured. A critically important aspect of this involves assessment. Culturally appropriate means of obtaining information should be employed. For example, early self disclosure should not be expected from most minority clients. The validity of any questionnaires, tests, and measurement procedures should be explored in detail. Most importantly, the validity of the client's problem view and problem priorities should be respected.

Goals of treatment should be acceptable to and appropriate for the client. Along with personal change issues, social and environmental factors should be assessed and change in these areas should be considered. All goals should be consistent with maximizing the client's competence and maintenance of natural support systems.

The cultural appropriateness of interventions should also be evaluated. As shown in each of the four preceding chapters, ethnic clients are likely to have different preferences and comfort levels with such aspects of intervention as directiveness, ambiguity, self disclosure, and emphasis on empathic understanding.

Clearly, all practitioners are not suited to work with all clients. In particular, practitioners must decide when race is a barrier to their effective practice with certain clients. We do not advocate that workers avoid cross-racial helping situations. Indeed, we believe that most practitioners can work successfully with those clients whom they are sufficiently motivated to help. However, practitioners should know when to refer a client for whom racial issues preclude effective treatment. Practitioners should also know to whom such referrals are appropriate. This requires familiarity with community resources, and especially with minority agencies and professionals.

ANTICIPATING SUCCESS

In spite of all the threats to cross-racial helping, we conclude by encouraging practitioners to recognize and anticipate the potential for the effectiveness of cross-cultural treatment. Although race clearly affects the process of helping, there is no conclusive evidence that racial dissimilarity necessarily impairs the outcome of helping. In fact, there is ample evidence that experienced, sensitive, and skilled workers can be effective with racially dissimilar clients. The practice literature suggests that the guidelines offered in this and the four preceding chapters should contribute largely toward such success.

6

Gender as an Issue in Practice

The world has long been divided for the sexes. The influence of gender on childhood activities, communication styles, and division of household and marketplace labor has been recognized for years. Its impact on daily life is reflected in such expressions as "boys will be boys," "woman's intuition," and "men at work." Increasingly, we recognize that gender has pervasive and fundamental consequences for every aspect of life. Around the globe, gender is assumed to reflect not only anatomy, but personal competence as well. Gender dictates the paycheck, occupational opportunity, and status. And of course, gender and gender differences affect the way in which worker and client interact with and perceive each other.

This section of the text explores the influence of gender on workers' and clients' perceptions of each other, assumptions of the other's capabilities, and style of relating to one another. The distribution of the sexes among both workers and clients makes gender a salient issue for social work. Due in large part to societal restrictions on their personal and occupational development, women constitute the majority of help-seekers in many fields of practice. For example, women outnumber men among those seeking mental health services, nursing home residents, recipients of public welfare services, and health care consumers.

Moreover, the majority of social workers and an especially high proportion of direct practitioners are women. In many practice situations, therefore, women are likely to be helping women. Given the salience of gender in the larger society, their interactions and perceptions of each other are likely to be affected by gender-based assumptions and stereotypes. Yet in spite of the high proportion of women among both helpers and clients, worker-client gender difference is to be expected in many situations. Few agencies systematically match clients on the basis of gender; male workers are likely to work with women, and women workers often have male clients.

How do men and women perceive, assess, and evaluate each other in our society? How much do they really differ, and what are the sources of our presumptions about their differences? How, in turn, is gender likely to affect workers' and clients' perceptions of each other? Research findings from the social sciences indicate that perception of another person's gender often triggers certain assumptions, expectations, and interpersonal responses. Because gender is such a fundamental aspect of personal identity, appreciation of "maleness" and "femaleness" is an important component of understanding another person, and in particular is important in the worker's comprehensive assessment of the client. However, problems arise when reactions to another person are based on gender alone or when gender-based assumptions and stereotypes are inconsistent with and overshadow the other's individual abilities and characteristics. In such cases, sexism intrudes on perceptions.

Feminists and those concerned with discrimination against women initiated social work's awareness of the often negative experiences of women in helping encounters. As such, the focus on gender in this text grows from and is indebted to these concerns. Yet our focus is the consequence of gender—both male and female—on the provision of individual, group, and family treatment. Thus we explore gender not only as a woman's issue, but also in terms of its consequences for male workers and clients. Sexism affects not only perceptions of women, but also the perceptions and expectations of men. Women are discriminated against in terms of pay, housing, violence, and perceived personal autonomy (Proctor, 1985); however, men too are an "exceptionally vulnerable group" (Epstein, 1980), experiencing cancer, accidents, homicide, suicide, and liver disease more often than women and, of course, having dramatically shorter life spans.

Although the organization of this book provides for separate discussions of sex, race, and class, readers should recognize that gender is not only a middle-class concern. Indeed, combinations of race and gender, or gender and socioeconomic status, place many individuals in triple jeopardy.

Because the already voluminous literature on gender continues to grow, any gender-related discussion must be focused and specific. The gender issue has important historical, political, economic, psychological, and sociological aspects. A comprehensive consideration of these issues is beyond the boundaries of this book, although practitioners and administrators of social services should be familiar with the full range of these issues. The purpose of this chapter is more limited. It aims to identify the assumptions that are triggered by the perception of gender, and to explore the implications of gender for interpersonal interaction and helping.

PERCEIVING A DIFFERENCE: THE "OPPOSITE" SEX

Perception of gender and of gender differences between persons is inevitable. Developmental psychologists believe that gender is incorporated into children's definitions of self and awareness of others by the age of three (Sears, Rau, and Alpert, 1965; Green, 1974). Among adults, the perception of gender appears to be a critical factor in processing other information about a person. According to Spence and Sawin, "when they encounter another, men and women . . . assign the person to a gender category and attempt to determine whether that person exhibits, in quantitative sense, an adequate number of gender-appropriate characteristics" (1985, p. 60).

What are the "gender categories" and "gender-appropriate characteristics"? How are such assignments made? The categories of male and female, of course, are quite distinct, and the characteristics by which they differ are extensive. Indeed, Bem observes that there appears to be no other dichotomy in human experience with as many entities attached to it as the distinction between male and female. Tavris and Wade observe, "in every society in every century . . . males and females are (assumed) different not only in basic anatomy, but in elusive qualities of spirit, soul, and ability. They are not supposed to do the same things, think the same way, or share the same dreams and desires" (1984, p. 2). So different, we assume, are male and female that we speak of the "opposite" sex. Moreover we see them as different, not just in degree, but in kind (Bem, 1981).

To sensitize our understanding of how gender may influence the perceptions of workers and clients, some of the major areas in which males and females are presumed to differ in the United States will be briefly reviewed. Some of these assumed differences seem to be largely myth, while others are borne out by data. Following the overview of differences, the discussion will focus on the source and consequences of the differences.

Roles

Bem has observed that "the distinction between male and female serves as a basic organizing principle for every human culture. Although societies differ in the specific tasks they assign to the two sexes, all societies allocate adult roles on the basis of sex and anticipate this allocation in the socialization of their children" (1981, p. 354).

Although women's sex-role attitudes have changed over time, with women at all socioeconomic levels moving toward more egalitarian roles (Mason, Czajka, and Arber, 1976), roles for men and women continue to differ in some important aspects. The husband role continues to carry different expectations, obligations, and rewards than the wife role. Even more clearly, mother and father roles differ dramatically in responsibility, weekly time demands, and the intrusion on personal and occupational roles.

Occupational roles also continue to be sex-segregated. Although women increasingly move into traditionally "male" occupations, most women work in a limited number of women's jobs (secretarial/clerical, sales, domestic work, waitressing, and hairdressing) (Tavris and Wade, 1984).

Thus the expected roles of women and men continue to differ dramatically. Our expectations that the sexes "do different things" are likely to influence workers' and clients' perceptions of each other. With respect to helping, clients may view social work as a more appropriate role for women, and as less appropriate for men. Indeed, the majority of social workers, and an especially high proportion of direct practitioners, are women. In community mental health centers, women comprise 11.9 percent of psychiatrists, 28.3 percent of psychologists, 56.2 percent of social workers, and 94.1 percent of nurses (Russo and VandenBos, 1981). Clients may therefore expect their helpers to be female in the "lower-status" professions and male in the higher-status professions.

Interpersonal Behavior and Personality Traits

Male and female interpersonal behavior also is expected to differ in many ways. Males are often expected to be powerful, aggressive, and rational, while females are assumed to be submissive, warm, and expressive (Rosenkrantz et al., 1968; Broverman et al., 1972). Men continue to be seen as more influential than women, and women as more susceptible to influence than men (Eagly and Wood, 1982, 1985). Women are seen as better communicators, especially at sending and receiving nonverbal messages (Hall, 1978). Women generally see men as sexually aggressive, although women are widely assumed to behave seductively with men. Indeed, male-female interaction is so charged with overtones of sexual attraction that straightforward expressions of warmth are inhibited, and, when conveyed, may produce discomfort for women (see Chapter 7, p. 149).

Such expectations stem from the assumption that personality is sex-specific. "Masculine" behavior is expected from men; "feminine" behavior from women. Given the notion that men and women are "supposed" to be different in temperament, behavior, and personality, gender differences in standards of mental health are not surprising. The now classic study by Broverman et al. (1970) demonstrated that *healthy* adult men and women were expected to display different patterns of behavior and different personal traits. Moreover, the standards of mental health for men and women differed not only in kind, but also in value: The expectations for healthy men were the same as those for healthy adults, while healthy women were expected to be different from healthy adults.

Ways of Thinking

Men and women are widely assumed to think differently. Women are seen as impulsive, while men are assumed to be logical and deliberate. Indeed, clear thinking has been seen as part of the male domain. Such assumptions have not been substantiated, as research has failed to identify clear and consistent differences in men's and women's mathematical, spatial, and verbal activity (Deaux, 1985). However, differences in attribution, or the way men and women see cause and effect, have been substantiated. Girls and women tend to attribute failure to their own lack of ability, while boys and men tend to attribute failure to the difficulty of the task or to the teacher or evaluator of the task performance (Dweck, Davidson, Nelson, and Enna, 1978). Differences in attribution are also suggested by findings that men and women show different patterns of symptoms when depressed. Women display greater indecisiveness and self dislike, while men display decreased social interest and a sense of failure (Hammen and Padesky, 1977). Recently hypothesized, but not yet thoroughly tested, are differences in men's and women's paths to moral development. Gilligan (1982) hypothesizes that women's moral judgments emphasize attachment, caring, and a balancing of conflicting responsibilities, while men's reflect separation, individuation, and justice.

Ability, Achievement, Motivation, and Evaluation

Women's abilities and the motives for their behavior also are assumed to differ from men's. For example, women may be perceived to work because they want to buy luxuries, rather than because they want to work, or for economic reasons (Tavris and Wade, 1984). Neither are women seen as ambitious or driven toward success, as are men. In fact, women have been assumed to avoid or even fear success (Horner, 1969). The findings of research, however, cast serious doubt on assumptions of gender differences in motivation or ambition. Rather than fearing success, women seem to perceive accurately that success is not available to them or that it will not be equitably rewarded (Condry and Dyer, 1976). Desire for achievement and ambition follows perception of realistic opportunities for achievement (Epstein, 1981).

Although motivation and ability does not vary by gender, performance evaluation does. Even when the performance of men and women is perceived as equal, their behavior is evaluated differently. Research indicates that in group and organizational contexts women are perceived, evaluated, and rewarded less favorably than males when performing leadership tasks (Rice, Bender, and Vitters, 1980; Wiley and Eskilson, 1982). Particularly in the evaluation of qualifications for occupational selection and promotion, males are perceived more favorably than females (Nieva and Gutek, 1980).

The pro-male bias in evaluation is probably due to differences in attribution. Women who are perceived as performing well tend not to be given credit for their performance; instead, their success is attributed to factors other than ability, such as luck, extra effort, or the ease of the task performed (Nieva and Gutek, 1980; Hanson and O'Leary, 1985).

It is in the area of ability and achievement that the dissimilarities between men and women most clearly move from the realm of mere "difference" to that of "deficiency." Indeed, regarding achievement, even women sometimes accept the view that "even the best women are lesser men" (Tavris and Wade, 1984, p. 3).

SOURCES OF GENDER DIFFERENCES, REAL AND ASSUMED

Where gender differences are real, what is their basis? Where they are mere fiction, why does their acceptance persist? Three major bases of assumed gender differences—physical differences, status inequity, and stereotypes—will be identified and briefly explored.

Physical, Biologically-Based Differences

Very few biologically-based male-female differences have been substantiated. Maccoby and Jacklin (1974) do persist in their view that males evidence more aggression by age six, as a function of biology. Yet although males and females differ anatomically, genetically, and hormonally, none of these factors have been found to influence specific behaviors in a direct and simple way (Tavris and Wade, 1984). Indeed, laboratory research in which conditions other than biological differences are controlled generally fails to substantiate the sex differences that people perceive in their everyday lives (Eagly and Wood, 1982). In short, the behavior of men and women is not really very different, and the biological basis for any perceived differences is not very sound.

Socialization and Sex-Role Stereotypes

Gender differences in behavior, opportunity, and achievement are, in part, a function of sex-role stereotypes and the socialization through which they are perpetuated. Girls are socialized from early infancy to pursue different activities and interests than boys. Even gifted girls and women continue to experience different models and rewards (Kerr, 1985). For example, it is the anxiety women acquire, and not genetic differences in quantitative ability, that appears to explain women's avoidance of math. "Math anxiety" has been identified as a crucial "filter" keeping women out of the sciences (Sells, 1978, 1980; Tobias, 1982).

Deaux and Lewis (1984) demonstrated that gender stereotypes involve several separate components, including personality traits, role behaviors, occupation, and physical appearance. In short, we have a broad and diverse "network of associations linked together under the umbrella of gender stereotypes" (Deaux, 1985, p. 68). A study by Deaux and Lewis of how we *think about gender* revealed complex interrelationships between the components of stereotypes. They found that information about one component (occupation, for example) implicated or led to conclusions about other components (personality traits, for example). Thus, a complex network of assumptions is triggered and processed. "Self-fulfilling prophecies . . . thus may begin to operate before potentially disconfirming information is available, ensuring the perpetuation of gender stereotypes" (1984, p. 1003). Thus gender stereotypes are comprehensive, and are triggered on the basis of specific and limited perceptions.

Status Inequity

Another more sociological source of potential difference in male-female behavior is social status. Increasingly, pervasive gender differences in power and status are recognized as contributing to differences in the expectations of, perceptions of, and actual behavior of men and women (Kahn and Gaeddert, 1985).

Status differences between males and females are evident in interpersonal relationships, wages for work performed, and acts of crime and violence by men against women. Economic status differences are apparent in the workplace, where women earn less than men, married women earn less than single women and married men, and black wives are paid less than black husbands. (Tavris and Wade, 1984, p. 272). Status differences likely also underlie the tendencies of women, but not men, to interrupt educational and professional pursuits for the demands of family life, and to geographically relocate for spouse. The view that rape expresses and perpetuates male status, power, and dominance over women was articulated by Brownmiller over a decade ago (Brownmiller, 1975).

Gender affects our perceptions of others because gender is so often associated with status. As we observe the world, we see individuals distributed into social roles that vary in status. Generally, men are in high-status roles and women are in low-status roles. As Kiesler observes,

> Clearly, current American reality, and that in other countries, is that women are a success less often than men in all activities to which the word, success, is commonly applied. In business, in the professions, in the arts, in athletics, and in the university, one observes that the most successful persons, on the average, are men. Whatever the causes, be they socialization practices, hormonal differences, de facto or purposeful discrimination, role prescriptions, or beliefs, men are the most influential, best paid, and most respected members of the occupations (1971, p. 203).

So consistent is the pattern between gender and status in our reading of the world that we begin to depend on gender as a cue for status. While, in fact, gender and status are often associated, gender comes to trigger expectations about status. Eagly and Wood explain, "the inferences that people make on the basis of gender in any one context are a product of the meaning that gender actually has in the larger society" (1985, p. 247). In short, we observe, over time and situations, men in positions of higher status than women; by association, we come to perceive the status of a particular woman as lower than that of a particular man.

We thereby come to hold different expectations of men and women. Gender, along with age and race, functions as a "diffuse status characteristic" (Eagly and Wood, 1985), an attribute that signals or conveys other, more pervasive information and therefore serves as a basis for more general expectations. Because we so often observe (accurately) that men outnumber women as successful achievers in many occupations, we begin to assume (inaccurately) that a woman's performance is generally less worthy than a man's. Kiesler has labeled this cognitive bias, based on past information about a group and leading to expectations of present inferior performance, as *actuarial prejudice*. We observe the performance of a group, and formulate expectations about the behavior of individuals.

Hence, gender, because of its status implications, serves in our perceptions as a signal of a person's ability and competence.

Similarly, people of higher status are perceived not only as more competent, but also as having the right to exercise influence, or make demands of others. Once again, perceptions of the world around us affect our expectations and perceptions of the individuals with whom we interact directly: "Because men are typically observed holding higher status positions than women, they will be thought to possess more legitimate authority, which results in power over others and the ability to resist other's demands" (Eagly and Wood, 1982, p. 916). Meeker and Wietzel-O'Neill (1977) observe that high-status people are expected to, and thus generally do, take the lead in group participation. Observed differences between men and women tend to become assumed and expected indices of capability (Deaux, 1985). Men have been leaders, thus men are expected to lead, and they are perceived as more competent leaders. Of course, their behavior is also evaluated and rewarded more highly. Success may be neither expected nor perceived in women, even when their behavior is similar to that of the successful man.

CONSEQUENCES OF PERCEIVING
GENDER DIFFERENCES

When one individual perceives another and, inevitably, notices the other's gender, what are the consequences? What expectations and perceptions of an individual occur as a function of gender? Is one's perception of the other automatically and inevitably limited by gender? Are behaviors, traits, and potential gender-specific? Is fate sealed by the perception of gender? Maybe. Maybe not.

The findings of Bem's (1981) research indicate that individuals differ in their tendency to rely on gender in their perceptions and evaluations. Individuals who are highly sex-typed in self concept (that is, who strongly identify themselves as masculine or feminine) are more likely to perceive and draw conclusions about others on the basis of gender. Moreover, such factors as perceptiveness, values and personal taste, liking of the other person, age, life circumstances, and situational factors also influence the salience of gender in individuals' perceptions of others (Spence and Sawin, 1985).

Practitioners can recognize and perhaps then limit their tendencies to make assumptions about clients on the basis of gender. If we recognize that stereotyping is more extreme when we have limited information about a person, we can ensure that our assessments are complete and that we check out the validity of our (often gender-based) assumptions. If we recognize that gender becomes especially salient when perceiving a person whose behavior falls below our levels of acceptability (Spence and Sawin, 1985), we can exercise caution with clients who are particularly needy or who differ markedly from ourselves. We should also recognize that we are less likely to expect and perceive behaviors in one sex that have been assumed more typical of members of the opposite sex (such as competence, strength, and leadership in women).

But what about clients? What conclusions are they likely to draw on the basis of perceiving *our* gender, or from the fact that we are of the same or different sex? To clients who are astute readers of social status, worker gender may trigger assumptions about professional competence. Male helpers may be seen as generally higher in status; female helpers may be seen as less skilled and less competent. However, the helping professions may be somewhat unique in that women may be assumed more competent in terms of empathic understanding than are men.

Clients who have incorporated society's pervasive sex-role stereotypes may assume that males and females are fundamentally different. For them, worker-client gender differences may raise serious issues, including questions about their ability to benefit from working with a helper of the opposite sex. Among those questions may be, "If gender has such pervasive consequences for life experiences and if the two sexes are not only different, but opposite, is a member of the opposite sex capable of understanding me? Will my situation and life experiences be understood? Will his (her) advice, interpretations, or suggestions be relevant to me?" In short, "Will I be able to work with this person?"

Such concerns are not unfounded. As this chapter's brief review indicates, the sexes do differ, not only anatomically, but more profoundly in their presumed competence. Even where men and women are very much alike, society continues to expect and assume differences and to perceive and reward their behavior inequitably. In that important respect alone, the social reality of men and women differs significantly. Thus, again as with the issue of race, an observable physical difference often implies more fundamental, underlying, and pervasive differences.

BUT AREN'T THINGS CHANGING?

Women's roles and status in society and men's roles in personal relationships have undergone substantial change in recent years. Haven't such changes reduced the impact of perceived gender differences on the ability of opposite-sex persons to work together? Indeed, some important changes have occurred, and others have begun. As subsequent chapters will show, standards of mental health and of healthy family life are not now as sex-typed as they once were. Yet some differences persist, and the residual effects of some previous differences are evident. Assumptions, expectations, and perceptions often lag behind and retard behavioral changes.

While change is viewed with great acclaim by those longing for a less sexist and less sex-typed society, it also may produce uncertainty, a less welcomed consequence. During periods of change, many men and women question their own sex roles, the bearing of gender on their own experiences, and their future options. Thus, increasingly, issues related to sex-role change may be brought to professional helpers. Periods of change are also marked by unpredictability, wariness, and uncertainty in interpersonal—and especially in male-female—relationships. In short, men and women may not know what to expect not only from themselves but from each other, personally and professionally.

It remains clear that gender stereotypes, fundamentally, are a relatively accurate reflection of a person's experiences with men and women, of social reality. So long as their social reality differs, men's and women's perceptions and expectations of each other will also differ. Thus, change in social reality—that is, change in society's reliance on gender for the assignment and rewarding of social roles—is necessary before any change in sex-role stereotypes and in the significance of gender for interpersonal relationships can occur (Eagly and Wood, 1982; Proctor, 1985).

7

Gender
and Individual
Treatment

THE IMPORTANCE OF GENDER TO CLIENTS

Is worker gender a concern to clients as they approach social service agencies? Do clients have expectations or preferences regarding helper gender? A number of studies have explored these issues and may prove helpful.

Early findings reflected a clear preference for male helpers. Chessler's (1971) study of adult outpatients participating in therapy in New York City indicated an "overwhelming" preference for male rather than female therapists, especially among female clients. The preference for male therapists persisted regardless of client age, marital status, or religious affiliation. Male clients based their requests for male therapists on their greater respect for "a man's mind," their general discomfort with and mistrust of women, and their anticipated embarrassment about discussing sensitive issues—particularly sexual issues—with women. Female clients had more confidence in and anticipated that they could relate better to male therapists. In short, gender reflected competence, and male therapists were viewed as more competent by both men and women.

Several studies suggest that preference for worker gender may vary according to the presenting problem. Both male and female college students have been found to prefer male counselors—older male counselors in particular—when their problems involved vocational problems; only clients experiencing personal problems preferred female counselors (Fuller, 1964; Boulware and Holmes, 1970; Lee, Halberg, Jones, and Hasse, 1980). Similar results were reported in a study of Native Americans' preferences for worker gender (Haviland, Horswill, O'Connell, and Dynneson, 1983). Older male workers were expected to be more understanding of vocational problems, more experienced, more knowledgeable, and able to give better advice.

The findings of more recent studies, however, suggest increasing receptivity to female workers. Johnson (1978) found that when worker gender mattered to the college students, they tended to prefer a counselor of their own gender. However, males expressed preference for female counselors more frequently than had been evidenced in prior studies. Simons and Helms (1976) studied preference for worker gender among two groups of women—female undergraduate college students and beauty salon customers. Women in both groups preferred female workers, anticipating that women counselors would be more interested in and better able to understand their problems than would male counselors. Moreover, they expected more initial interview comfort, more comfort following the interview, and lower levels of anxiety in interviews with female rather than male counselors. They also expected to be able to disclose more freely and felt they could more easily ask questions of female counselors. College students preferred single female counselors, while beauty salon customers preferred married female workers.

The importance of worker gender to clients may be related to sex-role expectations. Among the college students studied by Johnson (1978), worker gender was salient to students who also had more stereotyped and more traditional sex-role expectations for workers. Students who did not express a preference about the gender of their worker tended to have flexible, androgynous sex-role expectations of their worker (similar expectations for male and female workers).

Male and female clients' expectations for the behavior and style of their workers have been the subject of several studies. Although the findings are not consistent, there is evidence to suggest that males and females prefer different qualities and behaviors in their workers. In one study, women clients' expectations for their workers reflected characteristics stereotypic of the male sex role (i.e., autonomous, dominant, aggressive, persistent, controlled, confident, and orderly). Conversely, men's descriptions of the ideal therapist reflected stereotypic female sex roles (i.e., nurturant, emotional, outgoing) (Greenberg and Zeldrow, 1980). In another study, women clients preferred expressive behaviors, such as sympathy, support, warmth, and understanding—characteristics consistent with feminine sex roles. Instrumental or "masculine" traits vere rated lowest (Highlen and Russell, 1980).

Other studies report differences between men's and women's expectations for worker behavior that are not as readily linked to sex-role expectations. Women clients, more than men, report expecting their workers to be attractive, trustworthy, confrontative, genuine, tolerant, and nurturant (Hardin and Yanico, 1983; Subich, 1983). Men, more than women, expected workers to be directive and self-disclosing. Men and women did not differ in their expectations for worker empathy, expertness, and concreteness (Hardin and Yanico, 1983). Yet unlike these findings, Sipps and Janeczek (1986) found no differences between males' and females' expectations.

In terms of their own participation in the helping process, women expected to be more motivated and assume more responsibility than men. Women also expected to have a more positive outcome than did men (Subich, 1983). Subich viewed these findings in terms of women's greater comfort in sharing emotional concerns and stronger inclination to engage in interpersonal interactions, thereby leading them to anticipate more positive outcomes than do men.

In summary, early studies of client expectations and preferences for worker gender reflect a consistent preference for male workers among both men and women based on the assumption that male workers are more competent, particularly for certain types of presenting problems. However, such preferences may be changing. More recent studies reflect a more complex pattern of client preference and suggest that client preferences may reflect assumptions that the behavior of male and female workers may be different. Underlying client preference for worker gender may be assumptions or stereotypes about sex roles, and their impact on worker behavior. Thus, worker exploration of client preferences for worker gender may need to incorporate discussion of client's preferences for the worker's interactive style, which may be more salient than worker's gender itself.

Preferences regarding worker gender may also vary among various client populations. Marecek and Johnson (1980) note that more highly-educated individuals, younger clients, and women are more likely than other client groups to prefer female therapists. Although further study is needed, recent studies suggest that the preference for female workers, especially among women clients, may be increasing.

SALIENCE OF GENDER TO WORKERS

How important is the issue of gender to workers? Do workers prefer to work with clients of their own gender? Do they assume that gender affects their competence or skill as professional helpers? Like the issue of race, gender has not been widely acknowledged as a salient issue for workers. Yet there is considerable evidence that gender—their own and their clients'—is incorporated in workers' attitudes and assumptions about their helping abilities.

Preferences for Client Gender

In an early survey of practicing psychotherapists, Schofield (1964) found that a majority of psychiatrists, psychologists, and social workers preferred to work with women clients. Indeed, females were seen as the "ideal patient." Among psychiatrists with single-gender caseloads, 75 percent saw only female clients. Psychologists and social workers were equally likely to see only females or only males. Further, a recent study indicates that social workers have more female clients than do other mental health professionals (Knesper, Pagnucco, and Wheeler, 1985).

However, Maracek and Johnson do not believe that caseloads accurately reflect worker preference for client gender. In the first place, male-worker female-client dyads are likely, given the prevalence of women clients and male psychiatrists and psychologists. In addition, in many agencies workers have little control over the composition of their caseloads. Further study of worker preference for client gender is needed, incorporating such factors as client age, marital status, presenting complaint, and behavior.

Preferences for Gender Match

Many workers seem to desire worker-client gender match. Clopton and Haydel (1982) asked 236 psychologists to indicate the worker characteristics desirable for a certain client situation, along with the actual worker to whom they would refer the described client in their own community. Workers preferred worker and client to be of the same sex, especially when the client sex was the same as the subject's own. Children, however, were referred significantly more frequently to female therapists than would be expected, given the availability of female therapists. Thus, women and children were referred to female workers and men were referred to male workers.

Impact of Worker Gender

What assumptions underlie the preference of workers for clients of one gender or the other? It is interesting to note that although male workers were willing to refer female clients to either male or female workers, adult male clients were referred almost exclusively to male workers. Apparently male-worker female-client dyads were more acceptable than were female-worker male-client dyads to the men studied. The women, on the other hand, referred most female clients to female workers. The referral patterns of the men studied may reflect less an emphasis on gender match in helping relationships (given their willingness to refer women to male workers) than a reluctance to place women in a "dominant" or leadership position over men.

Male workers may prefer to work with female clients because they can communicate more easily with women. Lerman (1978) suggests that self disclosure and expression of emotion are difficult for many male workers, especially when they work with male clients. However, the results of two studies suggest that male workers do not see themselves as any less effective with women clients. While acknowledging that worker gender has some effect on helping, most male workers doubted that women clients can relate more easily to a female therapist; only 33 percent of females agreed with this view (Sherman, Koufacous, and Kenworthy, 1978). Similarly, in his study of male social workers in direct service positions, Kadushin (1976) found that only 3 percent reported difficulty in understanding female clients. Nearly half did acknowledge that female clients sometimes found it difficult to talk to them about sex, childrearing, or "women's problems" due to the clients' belief that a man could not understand them. Even more frequently, they reported, female clients attempted to convert professional relationships into personal relationships by being manipulative, seductive, or overly dependent. Such situations caused discomfort and anxiety for some of the workers. The male social workers were not troubled by their need to express acceptance, gentleness, and nurturance to either male or female clients. Most had responded to emotional male clients in gentle, compassionate, and comforting ways, with only 6 percent reporting discomfort or anxiety in such encounters.

The fact that most workers are male and most clients are female highlights the issues of sexual attraction and sexual intimacy in helping encounters. According to a task force of the American Psychological Association (1975), many workers are unprepared to handle these issues. Although the extent of this problem is believed to be small, it is serious and significant for those involved, and therapists were seen as unprepared to handle it. In the view of the Task Force, "the male therapist has considerably more power in the therapy situation than the female patient, a classic situation for the operation of sexual politics" (p. 1170). In addition, sexual intimacy prevents the worker from remaining objective and conducting therapy in a manner beneficial to the client's interests.

The worker's sex-role stereotypes are likely to influence the importance of gender in helping. Workers, as members of the larger society, have been exposed to sex-role stereotyping in their own socialization. Thus their attitudes toward women are likely to be similar to those found in the general public. Many theories of personality, human development, and psychotherapy reflect sexist notions (Harris and Lucas, 1976; Howell and Bayes, 1981), thereby adding to the probability that workers may hold very traditional attitudes. Thus workers should examine their attitudes and confront any ambivalence about changing sex roles (Sherman, 1976).

A number of studies indicate that male and female workers hold significantly different attitudes regarding women and sex roles, with those of females being significantly more liberal (Brown and Hellinger, 1975; Davenport and Reims, 1978; Sherman, Koufacous, and Kenworthy, 1978). Female workers not only held less stereotyped views than male workers, they were also significantly better informed. Male therapists evidenced gaps in their knowledge of the psychology of female sexuality, menstruation, pregnancy, childbirth, and menopause (Sherman et al., 1978). Thus gender appears to affect workers' sex-role attitudes and their knowledge of women's issues.

Sex-role attitudes do not seem to vary by profession. Although Brown and Hellinger (1975) found significantly more "contemporary" sex-role attitudes among psychiatric nurses, no differences have been reported between psychiatrists, psychologists, and social workers (Brown and Hellinger, 1975; Sherman, Koufacous, and Kenworthy, 1978). Moreover, Davenport and Reims (1978) found type of curriculum (sociological versus psycho-dynamic) did not influence the attitudes of social work toward women.

Worker ability to respond appropriately to clients may be influenced by gender and sex roles. For women workers, the authority of the professional role may be especially problematic, given cultural pressures on women to be deferential, warm, and empathic. Because women have not been seen as authority figures in this society, the competence of women workers may be challenged by clients, female as well as male.

For male workers, the situation is different. The authority of the helping role is consistent with traditional masculine socialization. The challenge for the male worker is to temper authority with empathy. Because "males bring to their role as therapists a cultural heritage which has not encouraged the open expression of feelings, intimate sharing between peers, or a sensitivity to the emotional states of others" (Kaplan, 1979b, p. 118), their capacity for clinical empathy may be inhibited. Men may experience particular difficulty in accurately assessing the emotional states of women.

Carter (1971) goes one step further, asserting that women are better therapists than men. She sees helping as more natural for women because understanding, nurturance, and responsiveness have been fostered in their development. The "basic biological makeup and sex-role learning" for men is cognitive, while for women feelings dominate.

Although male workers are quick to grasp concrete difficulties and formulate coping alternatives, women's emotional responsivity enables them to impact on clients in a feeling way (Carter, 1971). In particular, Carter sees women as more competent than men when working with severely disturbed individuals (to enable developmental progress); female delinquents and post-adolescent women (to establish sexual identity); and female hysterical patients (to resolve disturbed mother-daughter relationships). This issue will be explored more fully later in this chapter, as empirical evidence about the effectiveness of men and women workers is systematically examined.

GENDER AND ITS CONSEQUENCES
FOR TREATMENT

The gender of worker and client has major consequences for both the process and outcome of treatment. This section of the chapter will explore the impact of gender and gender similarity on client entry and assignment to treatment, assessment, worker-client communication, and choice of treatment goals and method.

Client Entry and Assignment to Treatment

The majority of social work clients are women (Rauch, 1978), and social workers are more likely than other professionals to have a high proportion of female clients (Knesper et al., 1985). Some agencies, such as rape crisis centers, shelters for victims of domestic violence, and clinics for family planning, pregnancy counseling, and abortion, provide services specifically for women. Women outnumber men among recipients of public welfare assistance, child welfare services, and services for the aged. Women utilize mental health services more often than men, whether those services are delivered in private practice, outpatient clinics, private psychiatric hospitals, general psychiatric hospitals, or community mental health centers (Schofield, 1964; Chesler, 1971b; Rauch, 1978; Benedek, 1981; Russo and Sobel, 1981; Taube, Burns, and Kessler, 1984). Only in state and county mental hospitals and in public general hospitals do men outnumber women as the recipients of mental health services (Russo & Sobel, 1981).

The high proportion of women among clients reflects the fact that women request help more often than men. Women apply for outpatient counseling and mental health services nearly twice as often as men (Brown and Kosterlitz, 1964). Gender does not appear to affect the acceptance of applicants for treatment; two studies indicate that equal proportions of males and females seeking help were accepted as clients

(Brown and Kosterlitz, 1964; Rice, 1969). Marital status influenced women's (but not men's) chances of being accepted for mental health treatment: 91 percent of married women, but only 67 percent of single, divorced, or widowed women, were accepted as clients. Socioeconomic status influenced men's (but not women's) acceptance. Middle- and upper-income males were significantly more likely than lower-income males to be accepted for service. Women accepted for treatment were found to be more seriously troubled than were males who were accepted for treatment (Brown and Kosterlitz, 1964). As a consequence, women may be more likely than men to remain disturbed but untreated.

Gender differences in helpseeking. Holding constant the number and seriousness of problems, women appear more likely than men to ask for help. Asking for help, displaying emotion, and expressing distress are more consistent with women's traditional roles than with men's. Moreover, in the view of Chesler (1971), psychotherapy has been a "socially approved" institution, a safe "haven," for middle-class women with problems.

Men, on the other hand, are often expected to be strong. Asking for help has been equated with weakness, and therefore may be avoided by men. Men often prefer to "tough out" their problems, rather than seeking professional help. Men may not make extensive use of counseling as long as helpseeking is seen as a reflection of weakness (Collison, 1981).

The findings of several studies confirm these tendencies. Women have been found to be more willing than men to talk to someone about personal and vocational problems (Boulware and Holmes, 1970), as well as more likely to seek medical and psychiatric care (holding constant the number of physical and psychiatric illnesses experienced) (Phillips and Segal, 1969). Sanchez and Atkinson (1983) found that among Mexican Americans, women had more favorable attitudes toward using counseling services than did men. Also, women were found to seek help at earlier stages of distress than men (Kirshner, 1978b). According to Padesky and Hammen (1981), men require a more severe level of depression than women in order to seek help from either a friend or a professional.

There is some evidence that men experience negative consequences for expressing problems and seeking help. Phillips (1964) found that females were less likely to want to associate with males portrayed as displaying paranoid, depressed, neurotic, schizophrenic, and phobic-compulsive behaviors than with females suffering similar complaints. Phillips observed, "If a man in our society is expected to be better able to cope with his illness, and is rejected for not doing so, he may be more hesitant to make his illness public by seeking professional help" (p. 687).

Cleary, Mechanic, and Greenly (1982) also suggest that sex roles and helpseeking norms permit women to complain more readily, and afford them greater convenience and flexibility for scheduling and using helping services. In short, the sick role may be more compatible with women's obligations.

Tracey et al. (1984) found that gender and type of help offered influenced college students' interests in obtaining help. Men were more likely to express interest in getting help when the help focused on external factors (ability to manipulate the external environment), while females expressed more interest when the help focused on internal factors (self-change).

The helpseeking behavior of men and women for mental health problems was the focus of an extensive investigation by Veroff (1981), who interviewed a national sample of 2,264 adults. Women were found to seek help more often than men. Of the sample, 66 percent were women and 34 percent were men. The findings revealed helpseeking to be a complex phenomenon, one whose frequency varied not only by gender, but by age and education as well. Helpseekers were likely to be women, to be young or middle-aged people with at least a high school education, and to have at least median income level.

Women had and used informal supports more often than men. Both men and women without informal supports were less likely to seek help than were those with such supports. Veroff speculates, "If talking with friends is a well-practiced and relieving way to deal with problems, perhaps it is an easy extension to talk with a professional to obtain similar relief" (1981, p. 194).

According to Veroff, women have been socialized to view their problems as personal failures; thus they believe that change in themselves will relieve their problems. Middle-aged women, in particular, "who feel inadequate, who do not feel good about themselves in a variety of ways, who feel unable to cope, are the most likely to deal with their problems by seeking professional help" (1981, p. 196). In summary, women utilize helping services more frequently than men due, in part, to differences in socialization regarding helpseeking. Women learn to ask for help, while men learn that acknowledging problems and seeking help lead to rejection.

Client gender and propensity to problems.   Women may also seek help more often than men because of gender differences in the number of problems actually experienced. This issue will be explored in greater depth in a later discussion of gender and differential diagnosis. For now, however, it should be noted that studies of health care suggest that gender differences in utilization reflect differences in objectively experienced problems (Cleary, Mechanic, and Greenly, 1982) rather than socialized patterns of helpseeking.

Among children, boys, who tend to have more health problems than girls, are more likely to visit the doctor; "among adults, women have more minor, acute illness than men, and women visit the doctor more often" (Ross and Duff, 1982, p. 128). Sex differences in the use of health services are greatest for young adults and lessen with advancing age. After age 45, women continue to have more physician visits, excluding sex-specific conditions, but men exceed them in frequency of hospital stays (Verbrugge, 1985).

Cleary, Mechanic, and Greenly (1982) hypothesized that sex differences in health care utilization would result from various processes in disease occurrence, illness perception, and illness behavior. Thus, they developed a model that distinguished among and measured separately:

1. the occurrence of symptoms as a medical problem
2. the decision to seek care
3. the actual seeking of care
4. follow up care and compliance with medical advice

Actual sex-related factors such as pregnancy and childbirth were controlled for. Sex differences in utilization were found to stem from actual chronic health conditions (that is, real differences in health), not merely differences in detection, reporting, or helpseeking behavior. Whether or not this model and these conclusions also apply to the utilization of mental health services awaits further study.

Women as an underserved population. Despite the fact that women represent the largest proportion of clients in most mental health facilities and in many types of social service agencies, Russo and Sobel (1981) argue that women frequently remain an underserved group. Close scrutiny reveals that women are overrepresented only in facilities that treat disorders congruent with sex-role stereotypes, such as depression (Russo and Sobel, 1981). In facilities that treat disorders incongruent with societal sex roles—such as alcoholism and drug abuse—women show much lower rates of utilization than males and, indeed, may be underserved and untreated. Although women's use of illicit drugs does not differ from that of men's (Burt, Glynn, and Sowder, 1979), men and women have different rates of entry to treatment programs, reflecting the problems of access experienced by women whose disorders are incongruent with sex role stereotypes (Sobel and Russo, 1981). Adequate utilization data are not yet available regarding services for women's special needs, such as rape and domestic violence. Also lacking are adequate diagnostic categories and hence utilization data for "problems of living" women often experience as a result of poverty, economic dependence, and sex discrimination. Finally, it should be recognized that accurate data on men's and women's use of private practice mental health care is obscured by the typical use of global summaries, preventing analysis by age, gender, and race (Russo and Sobel, 1981).

Client gender and type of service provided. Once clients apply and are accepted for service, a series of decisions are made about treatment, one of the earliest being the type of treatment most appropriate for the client. Such decisions may form the basis of referral, for assignment to a particular service within an agency, for assignment to a worker, or for choice of a particular type of treatment. These decisions appear to be based only partly on the nature of the client's problem or on diagnosis. Client attributes, including gender, also may play a significant role.

Whether or not disposition of an application for services varies by client gender has been the focus of several studies. In his study of treatment provided to over 2000 clients at 17 community mental health centers, Sue (1976) did not find any significant variation in client assignment to inpatient or outpatient services by gender. However, other evidence suggests that gender influences the type of agency through which treatment is provided. Ozarin and Taube (1974) examined data on inpatients in public and private mental hospitals, public and general hospitals' psychiatric units, VA hospitals, and federally funded community mental health centers. They found that men were more likely to be admitted to public mental hospitals, while women were more likely to be admitted to private hospitals. In particular, men exceeded women by almost 50 percent in psychiatric units of public general hospitals.

Dispositions of psychiatric patients in hospital emergency rooms also appear to vary significantly by client race and gender. White females are more likely to be referred to outpatient mental health clinics, while nonwhite females are more likely to be admitted as inpatients, treated simply in the emergency room, or referred for brief treatment (Gross et al., 1969; Gale, Beck, and Springer, 1978). While nonwhite females are slightly more likely to be hospitalized than white females, nonwhite males are most likely to be hospitalized. The investigators interpret such patterns as indicating that white females are most likely to receive "optimistic" dispositions, perhaps because white male residents are making the decisions (Gross et al., 1969).

In their study of referrals of clients to individual or group therapy at a university affiliated outpatient mental health clinic, Brodey and Detre (1972) found that women were more often referred to individual treatment, while men were seen as best suited for group treatment. However, in a more extensive study involving 17 community mental health centers, Sue (1976) found that assignment of clients to individual or group therapy was not influenced significantly by client gender.

Rice (1969) found that although similar percentages of males and females were referred to individual psychotherapy, different patterns or symptoms were associated with the decisions for men and women. Males assigned to individual therapy rather than group treatment were more likely to have significantly greater symptoms of anxiety, personal unhappiness, and low self esteem; to have had prior psychotherapy; and to have a prognosis of longer and more frequent therapy. For females, none of these variables discriminated between those accepted for individual therapy and those referred to group, suggesting that treatment decisions for females may be based on more subjective criteria.

Client gender, sex roles, and assignment to worker. Are male and female clients assigned to workers differently? Findings by Sue (1976) indicate that client assignment to type of worker (i.e., professional or paraprofessional) did not vary significantly by client gender.

However, client gender clearly appears to influence assignment with respect to worker gender. Shullman and Betz (1979) found that when intake workers assigned clients to other agency workers, both males and females matched worker and client on the basis of gender 70 to 80 percent of the time, regardless of presenting problem. However, when the intake worker continued to work with the client, less gender pairing was found. Female clients, in particular, were kept by male and female intake workers. This may reflect preference of both male and female workers for women clients. Barocas and Vance (1974) found that while male counselors had an equal number of male and female clients, female counselors had mostly female and relatively few male clients. Assignment of male clients was more likely to reflect gender match; male clients were likely to be assigned a male worker, while female clients were referred to either male or female workers. The authors viewed these findings as reflecting a bias against placing women in positions of dominance over men.

Client Continuance in Treatment

Once clients begin treatment, what, if any, bearing does gender have on their continuation? Are males or females differentially likely to drop out of treatment? Is client dropout related to worker gender? Does worker-client gender pairing affect dropout or length of clients' stay in treatment?

Client gender and dropout. The data on client gender and dropout are not conclusive. In one of the earliest studies of this issue, Cartwright

(1955) found that male clients were more likely to terminate treatment early, while females tended to continue. However, other studies have failed to find a relationship between client gender and dropout from outpatient services (Frank et al., 1957; Affleck and Garfield, 1961; Rice, 1969).

There is evidence that female dropouts differed from male dropouts in terms of personality (Heilbrun, 1961). Females who dropped out tended to have lower achievement needs, to have less autonomy, to be less dominant, and to display more deference than females who continued. Male dropouts tended to have higher achievement needs, to be less deferent, more autonomous, and more dominant. Heilbrun concluded that the client who conforms most closely to the expected cultural stereotype of femininity or masculinity tends to terminate early. His later work focused on tolerance of ambiguity among female clients and suggested that among females, higher tolerance for ambiguity was associated with earlier departure from counseling, lower ratings of counseling readiness, and less actual improvement.

Among clients who do not drop out of treatment prematurely, is gender related to the duration of a client's stay in treatment? The evidence is, once again, inconsistent. Two studies indicate that male outpatients stayed in treatment longer than did females (Cartwright, 1955; Brown and Kosterlitz, 1964). Another study, however, found that female clients stayed in treatment nearly twice as long as male clients (Fabrikant, 1974). This finding has been interpreted as reflecting victimization, in that females are kept "dependent for as long as possible" (Fabrikant, 1974, p. 96) by male workers (Abramowitz et al., 1976a, b). Although Abramowitz et al. (1976b) reported that male workers saw female clients for significantly longer periods than male clients, a later study that controlled for degree of client's impairment revealed no differences in treatment duration for male and female clients (Davidson and Abramowitz, 1980). Chesler (1971), in her study of middle-income outpatients in New York City, found that clients who requested either female or male workers were in treatment twice as long as clients who stated no preference for worker gender. In particular, male clients who requested a male worker remained in treatment longer than any other group, including women clients with a male worker. Overall, there is little evidence of a relationship between client gender and treatment duration (Chesler, 1971; Del Gaudio, Carpenter, and Morrow, 1978).

Worker gender and dropout. Other studies have focused on worker gender and its bearing on client dropout. Two studies suggest that clients of male workers are less likely to drop out than clients of female workers. Clients of male workers at a university counseling center were found significantly less likely to drop out after the first and second sessions than were clients of female workers, regardless of counselor experience level, client gender, type of problem, or problem severity (Epperson, 1981; Epperson, Bushway, and Warman, 1983).

There is some evidence that clients are less likely to drop out after an intake interview with a female worker. Betz and Schullman (1979) found that both male and female clients were more likely to return for counseling after intake with a female counselor. After seeing a female counselor, 83 percent of male clients and 85 percent of female clients returned for individual counseling; following intake with a male counselor, 68 percent of males and 69 percent of females returned for counseling. Although rate of client return was not a function of assigned counselor gender alone, when a client had a male worker for intake and was assigned to a male worker for counseling, both male and female clients had significantly lower return rates than under all other conditions of gender. Level of counselor experience did not affect return rates in either of these studies.

Some studies have focused on worker gender and its bearing on the duration of treatment for clients who do not drop out. Carpenter and Range (1982) found that worker variables taken together accounted for only 3 percent of the variance in treatment duration, and that worker gender itself did not impact on client's duration in therapy. Helms (1978), however, found that female workers saw their clients for a significantly longer period of time than did male workers.

Worker-client gender match and dropout. Jones and Zoppel (1982) found that gender match had a clear impact on length of treatment: Clients paired with a same-gender worker remained in treatment significantly longer than clients with a worker of the opposite sex. However, gender match did not significantly affect who initiated termination, worker or client.

Interpersonal Communication

Because verbal communication is the basic medium of most helping approaches, it is important to examine the effects of gender of both worker and client on communication. Only a few studies have focused on the overall bearing of gender on quantity of client verbalization. Scher (1975) reports that female clients and workers are more verbal than their male counterparts. In another study, males' and females' responses to questions about "neutral" topics were similar in length, but males were more productive than females in responding to questions about intimate topics (Siegman, 1977).

Verbalization appears to be affected by interviewer affect and gender. Males have been found to verbalize most when interviewed by a male interviewer whom they expected and found to be warm; they were less productive when they expected and found his behavior to be cold. Females, however, reacted differently to male interviewers, responding more productively when the male interviewer was cold than when he was warm (Pope, 1979). The findings suggest that warmth and friendliness on the part of a male interviewer, especially when exaggerated, may have threatening and seductive tones for female interviewees and hence inhibit their productivity (Maracek and Johnson, 1980). Pope observed that a male interviewer is perceived differently by male and female interviewees, even when he conducts their interviews similarly. These experimental findings alone should not be viewed as indicating that male therapists should behave coldly to female clients. They do suggest, however, that gender and interviewer style may affect the interviewee's comfort and verbal productivity.

Self disclosure.   Helping processes generally focus on problems and issues that have personal relevance to the client. It is widely assumed, therefore, that client self disclosure is necessary in order for the worker to learn about and understand the client. Numerous studies provide evidence that gender is an important factor affecting the ease and level of self disclosure.

Although the evidence is not uniform (Doster and Strikland, 1969), several studies report that women seem to engage in more self disclosure than men (Jourard and Lasakow, 1958; Dimond and Munz, 1967; Hill, 1975). Socioeconomic status also appears to influence the self disclosure of men and women. In one study, working-class women evidenced the most self disclosure, and working-class men evidenced the least (Hacker, 1981). Married women also were high disclosers. Cozby (1973) observes that no study has reported greater male disclosure.

Why do males engage in so little self disclosure? Societal norms and sex-role expectations of men and women probably contribute to sex differences in self disclosure. Men are seen as better adjusted psychologically when they do not self disclose about personal problems, while females are seen as better adjusted when they do self disclose (Derlega and Chaikin, 1976). Competition and traditional U.S. male stereotypes of toughness, confidence, and self reliance may serve as barriers to emotional intimacy among men. Too, men lack role models of self disclosure. Lewis (1978) observes that, although men have more same-sex friendships than women do, the friendships of men typically are not intimate, nor are they arenas for self disclosure. Homophobia is often assumed to prevent emotional intimacy among heterosexual men, but there is no conclusive evidence regarding this assumption (Lewis, 1978).

Even within friendships, then, men appear to experience difficulty in revealing weaknesses while women experience difficulty in revealing strengths, patterns that reflect conformity with sex-role expectations. Hacker found that in their friendships with women, men revealed their strengths; in their friendships with men, women revealed their weaknesses. In both same- and mixed-gender friendships, no women were found to reveal strengths but not weaknesses, and no men were found to reveal weaknesses but not strengths. The role of sex-role socialization is further supported by the findings of Stokes, Childs, and Fuehrer (1981), that sex roles were better predictors than gender of both males' and females' self disclosure to intimates. In their view, ability to disclose to intimates requires both stereotypically masculine traits (such as assertiveness) and feminine traits (such as expressiveness and comfort with intimacy). They suggest that males who are reluctant to self disclose may lack the necessary "feminine" abilities, while females who don't disclose may lack the "masculine" traits.

The reluctance of males to self disclose and the consequences of such reluctance for treatment have been widely discussed by practitioners. Male clients have been described as uncommunicative of their needs and feelings, unable to be intimate with another person (Carlson, 1981), even as "hidden," and having difficulty benefiting from treatment (Scher, 1981). Because effective counseling generally requires an atmosphere of intimacy, this situation is often disheartening to workers.

Must workers conclude that male clients are simply unable to self disclose? Probably not. Several studies have focused on situational factors that influence level of self disclosure. The findings of these studies offer some clues as to factors that may increase the level of client disclosure. Stokes, Fuehrer, and Childs (1980) found that when communicating with a stranger, males were even more willing to self disclose than were females. As level of intimacy increased, however, women were more willing to self disclose than were men. These findings suggest that men and women may not differ very much in their willingness to reveal personal information to the worker in the early stages of helping, a time when the worker is more like a stranger or acquaintance than like an intimate.

Gender of worker may also influence a client's willingness to self disclose. Some evidence indicates that clients may self disclose more when their worker is female. Regardless of the level of facilitative condition in the worker's communication, clients of women at a university counseling center explored themselves more deeply than did clients of men (Grantham, 1973). However, women workers may be more likely than men to perceive their clients as low disclosers, perhaps because they are more comfortable with and expect more self disclosure (Strassberg and Anchor, 1977).

Other studies suggest a different, and not totally consistent, picture of the role of worker gender. College students were found to disclose more to a person of the opposite sex (Brooks, 1974), although dyads containing a female, whether client or worker, had more disclosure than did all-male dyads. Hacker (1981), however, found that self disclosure for both men and women was greater in same- rather than in cross-sex dyads. Men were not more confiding to women than to men, and women did not engage in unreciprocated self disclosure with men.

Sex-role behavior of worker also may influence level of client self disclosure, even more than worker gender, according to one study. Feldstein (1979) reports that both male and female clients disclosed more to workers who displayed a feminine-type style in interaction (responsive, warm, supportive, and emotional) than they did to workers who had a masculine-type style (action-oriented, cognitive, assertive). Males disclosed most to female workers with feminine style, and least to female workers with masculine style. The influence of worker inter-active style is further indicated by findings that reciprocity—one person's self disclosure in response to the disclosure of the partner—increases level of self disclosure (DeForest and Stone, 1980; O'Kelley and Schuldt, 1981). Subjects in a role-play paradigm were found to increase their disclosure in response to increasing intimacy of disclosure by worker, although women clients consistently responded with higher levels of intimacy than males.

Clients also appear to increase their level of self disclosure with more attractive (Kunin and Rodin, 1982) and higher-status workers. However, research suggests that the direction of influence of status may differ for male and female clients. Brooks (1974) reports that males disclosed more to interviewers described as having high professional status, while females disclosed more to low-status interviewers. Moreover, although interviewer status did not affect subjects' responses to female interviewers (Brooks, 1974), high status increased the amount of self disclosure directed toward male interviewers (Brooks, 1974; Kunin and Rodin, 1982).

The studies reviewed above suggest that self disclosure often varies according to several factors. These studies suggest female clients may be more willing than male clients to self disclose to workers. The data also suggest that male workers may have more difficulty than female workers in eliciting disclosure from clients, especially male clients. However a warm, responsive interpersonal style and the worker's own provision of self disclosure to the client seem to have promise as means of increasing clients' self disclosure.

Expression of affect. In a study of clients presenting educational and vocational problems at a university counseling center, Fuller (1963) found that during both intake and counseling, female clients expressed significantly more feelings than did male clients. More feeling was expressed in pairs that included a female, regardless of whether the female was a client or a counselor. Clients who had expressed preference for male workers expressed less feeling than did those with no preference. Among clients working with male counselors, expression of feeling was higher when the counselor had a higher level of experience. Matching male clients to male therapists did not increase the expression of feeling.

Interviewer sex-role behavior was found to also influence client expression of feeling. Feldstein (1982) found that clients expressed more feeling with feminine than with masculine workers.

Howard, Orlinsky, and Hill (1969) studied the affect of male and female therapists in response to their work with women clients. Male workers, more often than female workers, were found to experience unpleasant feelings in dealing with female clients. Female workers, on the other hand, experienced more positive and gratifying feelings when working with female clients. Female workers with female clients did experience dependency demands from patients, often when the female worker noticed a lack in nurturing feelings. The experience of erotic transference feelings in male workers corresponded to feelings of embarrassment and transference resistance in female clients.

Assessment

The assessment of client problems, a task essential to the success of treatment, may also be influenced by gender. According to social casework theory, assessment involves attending to information about the client and problem, interpreting the obtained information, then classifying, categorizing, or assigning a diagnosis to the problem. The potential effects of gender on each of these components will be explored, and empirical evidence regarding the role of gender will be reviewed.

Problems presented and information obtained. The findings of several studies indicate that women experience and present to workers a greater number of problems than do men. In studies of outpatient clients and in surveys of randomly selected community residents, women have been found to cite more symptoms than men (Brown and Kosterlitz, 1964; U.S. Department of Health, Education, and Welfare, 1970; Helms, 1978; Cochrane and Stapes-Roe, 1981). In addition, women's symptoms indicated that they were more seriously disturbed than men (Brown and Kosterlitz, 1964).

Men and women also appear to differ in the frequency with which certain types of problems are presented to helpers. Although a few studies, in which unmarried college students were studied, fail to find gender differences in depression (Hammen and Padesky, 1977; Padesky and Hammen, 1981), most studies show that women experience more depression than men (Moskol, 1976; Cochrane and Stopes-Roe, 1981). In fact, Benedek (1981) reports that two-thirds of all clients experiencing depression—the most common psychiatric problem encountered—are women.

Women are also more likely than men to experience feelings of inadequacy and self criticism (Chesler, 1971b; Cochrane and Stopes-Roe, 1981), problems with personal identity (Bond, 1982), and anxiety or an anticipated nervous breakdown (U.S. Department of Health, Education, and Welfare, 1970; Chesler, 1971b; Moskol, 1976; Cochrane and Stopes-Roe, 1981). Women experience more transient situational disorders than men (Gove and Tudor, 1973), often related to transitional crises—changes in relationships, education, jobs, or living arrangements (Moskol, 1976). Finally, more women contemplate or attempt suicide, although more men actually commit suicide (Chesler, 1971b; Gove and Tudor, 1973; McIntosh and Jewell, 1986).

Men seem to experience fewer and different problems. Men are more likely than women to present problems related to alcohol consumption, homosexuality, changes in vocation, and aggression (Chesler, 1971b; Collison, 1981). Loneliness causes men to seek help, presenting issues of identity and intimacy (Carlson, 1981; Collison, 1981). Crises also bring men to therapy, including being left by a spouse, loss of a mate or a child through death, loss of job, or serious physical illnesses or disability. Intimacy is a frequent issue for men in crisis (Carlson, 1981).

Padesky and Hammen (1981) report that although the degree of depression among college students did not differ, the sexes reported very different symptoms. Depressed men were more likely to express symptoms of social withdrawal, problems with memory and concentration, sleep disturbance, and tension (cognitive and somatic symptoms). Women's symptoms were more likely to include lack of confidence, apathy, and sensitivity to criticism (Padesky and Hammen, 1981), consistent with other findings that women blame themselves for their depression (Calhoun, Cheney, and Dawes, 1974).

Why do women and men present such different patterns in problems and symptoms? Phillips and Segal (1969) believe that the sexes' actual experience of symptoms does not differ, although their attentiveness to them and willingness to express them does. They administered a standard checklist of physical and psychiatric symptoms to men and women on two occasions one year apart. They concluded that although there were no significant differences in experience of illness, women were more likely to perceive and express signs of emotional difficulty that men were reluctant to acknowledge.

Others, however, believe there are real differences in actual experience of disturbance, with women experiencing more stress and mental illness. Verbrugge (1985) reports that women suffer more frequent, but less serious, illness and disability than men, and that they experience more daily and long-term stress, less happiness about life, and more dissatisfaction with their roles than men.

A number of contributing factors are cited by those who see women as experiencing more actual stress than men. Gove and Tudor (1973) believe the role of women in modern industrial society contributes to mental illness. First, women traditionally have been limited to one role (homemaker), while men have had two roles (household head and worker). Roles are sources of gratification, and those with multiple roles can shift their focus if one role is unsatisfactory. Second, the primary role of women, that of raising children and keeping house, is frustrating, has low prestige, and is discrepant with educational and intellectual attainment. Moreover, housework is unstructured and invisible. Lack of role specificity may lead women to perceive that their activity is dependent upon men's. Such factors leave women at risk of not developing a personal identity and increase the likelihood that they will experience problems of low self esteem (Bond, 1982).

However, women who choose to add a role, via employment, also add to their lives the demands of their jobs, the experience of wage discrimination, and the strain of even longer days due to the household chores for which they remain responsible. Verbrugge (1985) suggests that women have either too little social involvement (homemakers) or too much (employed women with excessive demands).

High-risk women.   Certain groups of women experience even greater risk. Young, poor women evidence the greatest increase in rates of depression (Carmen et al., 1981). Divorced and separated women experience more feelings of "impending breakdown" than men or any other group of women (Chesler, 1971b). Women who have never married and women employed outside the home have been found to report fewer symptoms than other women (Chesler, 1971b; Cochrane and Stopes-Roe, 1981). Powell and Reznikoff (1976) found that female college graduates with contemporary sex roles had higher levels of psychiatric distress than did women with traditional sex-role orientations, suggesting that conflicts between personal needs and traditional cultural expectations may contribute to their problems.

Gender and worker attention to client problems.   Carmen, Russo, and Miller (1981) charge that workers are sometimes inattentive or disbelieving of some problems female clients present. For example, reports of incest or rape have been interpreted as fantasy or wish. One study focused on the attentiveness of workers in response to problems expressed by male and female clients. Workers were asked to listen to audiotaped presentations of either a male or female client in which the client expressed presenting complaints, facts and concerns about social behavior, facts and concerns about vocation, and other general information. Both male and female workers recalled fewer facts and concerns expressed by the female client. Male workers asked significantly more questions related to social concerns for a female client than they did for a male client who had identical concerns, perhaps reflecting an assumption that social concerns are more relevant to the treatment of female clients. Male and female workers were equally attentive to the vocational concerns of male and female clients, and indeed, on a recall test, workers recognized more vocational facts presented by the female client.

Other studies have focused on worker gender. Carmen, Russo, and Miller (1981) report that female workers were better able to retain client information on both recall and recognition tasks than were male counselors; female workers may have been more attentive to needs and concerns expressed by their clients. Women workers are also reported to exhibit greater sensitivity to disturbances in family relations and sexuality (Jones and Zoppel, 1982).

Interpretation. Clinical assessment requires more of workers than just receiving, accurately hearing, and retaining concerns presented by clients. Workers also must interpret and evaluate the information they receive, often by comparing the client's current situation with some more desirable state. Thus norms, or standards of healthy optimum functioning, are involved in clinical assessment. In our society, definitions or standards of optimum, healthy behavior have been based, in part, on notions of appropriate male and female sex roles. To the extent that these definitions differ for men and women, and to the extent that helping professionals incorporate society's definitions of appropriate behavior in standards of mental health, the norm or standard against which assessment is conducted will be different for men and women.

Responses to an American Psychological Association task force survey reflected the use of traditional sex roles as a basis for assessing mental health. Psychotherapists frequently have considered female clients' attitudes toward childbearing and childrearing as an index or reflection of their emotional maturity, and dependency and passivity have been seen as norms for women (APA Task Force, 1975). Berlin asserts that whether or not the majority of therapists ever accepted the Freudian belief that women had weaker capacities, "they have incorporated into their behavior the myth of a natural feminine role in which all normal women could find satisfaction" (1976, p. 492).

Gender and mental health. Over the past fifteen years, several studies have addressed the question of whether clinicians' standards of mental health are different for men and women. The most "classic" study of this issue was conducted by Broverman, Broverman, Clarkson, Rosenkrantz, and Vogel (1970). Clinical psychologists, psychiatrists, and social workers were given a questionnaire and the following instructions: One group was asked to indicate items descriptive of a mature, healthy, socially competent man; a second group was asked to describe a mature, healthy, socially competent woman; and a third group was asked to describe a mature, healthy, socially competent adult person. Male and female clinicians were found to agree that notions of mental health for adult males corresponded closely to those for healthy, competent adults. However, notions of mental health for women were different. Specifically, healthy adult females were seen as more submissive, less independent, less adventurous, less objective, more easily influenced, less aggressive, less competitive, more excitable in minor cases, more emotional, more conceited about appearance, and having their feelings hurt more easily. The findings indicated that the general standard of health (adult, sex-unspecified) was applied only to men, while healthy woman were seen differently.

In addition to the controversy sparked, this study stimulated extensive attempts at replication in different settings, at different times, using different measures, and with different populations. Some of these studies replicated the findings of Broverman et al., finding further evidence of different standards of mental health for men and women (Nowacki and Poe, 1973; Neulinger, Stein, Schillinger, and Welkowitz, 1979).

However, some latter studies reflected change in the attitudes of women practitioners. Thus, while male practitioners continued to reflect traditional views of women, women practitioners saw the healthy person, the healthy male, and the healthy female as similar (Maslin and Davis, 1975). For example, women social work students were found to describe the healthy women as more independent, less emotional, more objective, less excitable, more logical, more sophisticated, and less easily hurt than did male practitioners, who expected healthy females to be more stereotypically feminine.

Studies of mental health professionals provide further evidence that females' definitions of mental health may be less stereotyped than those of males. Aslin (1977) found that women therapists held the same standards of mental health for adults, females, wives, and mothers, while male therapists had significantly different standards of mental health for adults and for females, wives, and mothers. Similarly, Leichner and Kalin (1981) found that the sex-role ideology of male psychiatrists was more traditional than that of feminist women.

According to findings of studies conducted in the 1970s, clinicians began to accept a wider range of behavior in women. Specifically, it was viewed as appropriate for women to add stereotypic "male" characteristics to their repertoire of behavior, although there was no corresponding tendency to add "feminine" characteristics to the views of healthy males (Kravetz and Jones, 1981; Marwit, 1981). Increasingly, then, definitions of mental health—at least for women—appeared to become more androgynous, reflecting Bem's view that fully effective human functioning involves integration of both masculinity and femininity.

It should be noted that most studies reviewed above relied on questionnaires to elicit workers' descriptions of rather abstract stimuli, such as "the optimally healthy" female or male. This methodology emphasizes gender as the only salient cue and therefore may evoke more sex-role stereotyping than would typically occur when specific individuals are rated (Stricker, 1977; Smith, 1980).

Indeed, Stricker believes that "widely cited conclusions concerning a double standard of mental health and negative evaluations of women are premature in light of the data. They may ultimately prove to be correct, but we do not have sufficient evidence at the present time to reach sweeping positions" (1977, p. 21). Smith (1980) cautions that in order to prove that sex bias has harmful effects in counseling, it must not only be demonstrated that clinicians hold sex stereotypic concepts about women, but also that

1. assessments reflect sex-role stereotypes rather than the true characteristics of the client
2. the stereotypes lead the clinician to behave in specific ways, which express bias
3. the stereotyped recommendations of the therapist must be perceived and accepted by the client

Perceiving a need for intervention.   In order to explore the impact of gender and sex-role stereotypes on workers' perceived need for intervention, a different methodology has been employed. Such studies usually involve providing workers (or other subjects) with a specific client's history and description of client behavior, varying the gender of clients across subjects while holding other factors constant, and analyzing differences in workers' perceived need for intervention.

In a few studies client gender did not influence workers' assessment or perception of the need for intervention (Zeldow, 1975; Gomes and Abramowitz, 1976). In other studies, however, the impact of gender was clear. In some cases, female clients were seen to have greater need for intervention, even when presenting problems identical to those of male clients. The problems for which women were seen to need intervention more than men included schizophrenia (LaTorre, 1975), "nonconforming career goals" (e.g., engineering) (Thomas and Stewart, 1971), and sexual assertiveness (Mintzer and Halpern, 1980).

Other types of behavior, however, were seen as reflecting less need for intervention for female than for male clients. Miller (1974) found that social workers, psychologists, and psychiatrists saw passivity and depression as healthy when the client was assumed to be female. The view that passivity is more appropriate for women suggests that less may be expected from them. In another study, depression, alcoholism, and schizophrenia were seen as more serious for males than females, but only by more experienced workers (Lowery and Higgins, 1979).

Thus, findings from several studies suggest that although women as a group are seen as less mentally healthy than men, in clients actually presenting themselves for treatment, the problems of men will be seen as more serious.

Age seems to affect workers' perceptions of the seriousness of problems for women. Personal and social problems were seen as more serious for women than educational and vocational problems, except among women under 25 years of age (Hill, Tanney, Leonard, and Reiss, 1977; Helms, 1978), and anxiety was seen as more serious for younger women than for older women (Hill et al., 1977).

Gender and perception of clients. Other studies have explored the role of client gender on workers' overall perceptions and clinical judgments of clients. Concerns have been repeatedly expressed that workers may judge female clients more harshly. For example, Carmen, Russo, and Miller charge that clinicians use "inaccurate and demeaning labels" (1981, p. 1325) for female clients, citing the example that a male may be labeled "assertive" but a female with similar behavior might be labeled "castrating."

Not all studies support such concerns, however. Malchon and Penner (1981) found that male clients and clients with masculine sex-role identities were seen as less attractive, less competent, and less likable, and as being less mentally healthy than were female clients and clients with feminine characteristics. However, the perceptions of women were influenced by their sex-role behaviors, while the perceptions of men were not so influenced. Sex-role congruent females (those with feminine characteristics) were seen as more attractive, better adjusted, and as having a better chance for improvement than sex-role incongruent females. Perceptions of men were not affected by sex-role congruence.

Settin and Bramel (1981) report that clinical judgment is influenced by client gender and social class. Psychologists' evaluations were most favorable to the middle-class male, then the working-class female, then the middle-class female, and finally the working-class male. These findings may indicate that less is expected of the working-class female than the middle-class female.

Attribution of problems. Gender also appears to influence the attribution, or explanation of causality, of client problems. Women often view personal problems or problems in their families as due to their own weaknesses (Calhoun, Cheney, and Dawes, 1974). Women are often socialized to believe that "if they were better women," they would not experience personal difficulties. "Such socialization has been a strong message that a change in self might relieve problems" (Veroff, 1981). Women are less likely to attribute their problems to external circumstances than are other groups, such as the poor, the less educated, and the aged.

Moreover, because women traditionally have been seen as responsible for the family, they often seek treatment "for problems that they perceive as their own but that actually involve the whole family and cannot be solved by the women alone" (Klein, 1976, p. 93). Workers should be alert, therefore, to the extent to which presenting problems involve other family members or the family unit itself. In such cases, others' responsibility for the problems should be explored with the woman, in an effort to help her recognize the limits to her share of responsibility.

Workers have been criticized for their attribution of women's problems to individual weakness and their failure to consider social, environmental issues sufficiently in their assessments (Stephenson and Walker, 1981; Kravetz, 1982; Sheridan, 1982). Such a focus leads to the often inappropriate application of psychiatric or individual-change orientations to problems that have social, legal, or economic roots (Stephenson and Walker, 1981).

A different kind of error often characterizes workers' perceptions of black women. Too often, psychiatrists assume internal strengths among black women and attribute their problems to external factors (American Psychological Association, 1975). Thus personal problems may go undetected, contributing to the tendency of psychiatrists to see a better prognosis for black women than for white women (Schwartz and Abramowitz, 1975).

It is increasingly evident that men, as well as women, feel the consequences of gender-role strain. Heretofore, neither workers nor male clients themselves have sufficiently considered social factors, particularly sex-role issues, in their assessments of the problems of men. Obviously, men's difficulties should also be assessed in light of individual (within-the-person) and environmental (social, interpersonal) factors.

Worker gender, too, may influence the attribution of client problems. According to one study, female workers were more likely than male workers to accept clients' own attributions and explanations of their problems (Compas and Adelmen, 1981). In particular, women workers were more likely than male workers to rate female clients' external attributions of their problems as accurate.

Gender and diagnosis. Once clients have presented their problems and concerns to workers, diagnoses or classifications of problems often are made. Do the diagnoses of male and female clients differ? If so, what factors contribute to such differences? Do gender differences in diagnosis reflect true differences in problem incidence, or do they reflect bias in the methods or diagnosis?

The data are clear that, just as men and women seem to present different symptoms and concerns, their diagnoses also are different. Women are more likely than men to receive diagnoses of neurosis (Gross et al., 1969; Dohrenwend and Dohrenwend, 1976), anxiety (Levine, Kamin, and Levine, 1974), manic depressive psychosis (Dohrenwend and Dohrenwend, 1976), depression (Weissman and Klerman, 1977), transient situational personality disorders (Levine et al., 1974), and hysteria (Lerner, 1981; Jones and Zoppel, 1982). Men are more likely than women to be diagnosed with personality disorders (Dohrenwend and Dohrenwend, 1976), obsessional disorders (Jones and Zoppell, 1982), alcoholism and drug abuse (Gross et al., 1969; Baskin, Bluestone, and Nelson, 1981), and as sociopathic (Gross et al., 1969). Although there are no consistent sex differences in rates of diagnoses for schizophrenia (Dohrenwend and Dohrenwend, 1976), the most recent findings suggest sex differences in age of onset, symptomatology, and age of hospitalization. Moreover, in a study of diagnoses assigned to male and female psychiatric patients, Abramowitz and Herrera (1981) found that even after controlling for actual level of pathology, female patients were perceived by both male and female psychiatrists as more psychosomatic, more interpersonally sensitive, more depressed, more hysterical, and as evidencing more pathology in general than were male patients.

Certain groups of women experience even greater risk. Rates of depression have increased most among young, poor women (Carmen et al., 1981). Stress is especially high among middle-age women, as evidenced by the high suicide rates for those aged 35 to 55 (Verhoff, 1981). Divorced and separated women are found to experience more feelings of "impending breakdown" than men or any other group of women (Chesler, 1971b). Those with fewest symptoms include women who have never married and women employed outside the home (Chesler, 1971b; Cochrane and Stopes-Roe, 1981). Powell and Reznikoff (1976) found higher levels of psychiatric distress among female college graduates with contemporary sex roles, suggesting that conflicts between personal needs and traditional cultural expectations may contribute to their problems.

Finally, minority women are at "double jeopardy" for certain problems. They are more likely than white women to experience wage discrimination, unemployment, competition for educational and job opportunities, and pressure to "prove" their competence (Olmedo and Parron, 1981). Minority women are three times as likely as white women to die from hypertension (National Center for Health Statistics, 1976). Their higher risk of victimization and domestic violence, which is sometimes accepted as the norm or seen as inevitable given the unresponsiveness of social service and law enforcement agencies, may lead to serious problems of self esteem and helplessness (Olmedo and Parron, 1981).

Whether these patterns reflect differences in workers' applications of diagnostic labels, or whether they reflect true differences in incidence of disorder, has been widely debated.

The symptoms and diagnoses of women are often seen as indicative that women experience more, and more serious, disturbances than do men (Brown and Kosterlitz, 1964; Levine et al., 1974). Data from clinical evaluations, institutional records, impressions of professional helpers, client responses to structured interviews, and community surveys lead many to conclude that women experience more mental illness than men (Gove and Tudor, 1973; Levine et al., 1974). Dohrenwend and Dohrenwend (1976) view general comparisons of psychiatric disorder among men and women as meaningless. Instead, they argue, analysis should focus on consistent relationships between gender and different types of disorder. The important, yet unanswered, question is, "what is there in the endowments and experiences of men and women that pushes them in these different deviant directions?" (p. 1453).

Factors contributing to gender differences. If, indeed, women experience more problems than men, why? What factors contribute to gender differences in incidence and diagnosis of mental health problems? Several explanations have been proposed. First, the role of biology has been suggested. Although the precise operation of chromosomal, genetic, and endocrine factors is not fully understood, such biological factors are seen as contributing to depression in women (Weissman and Klerman, 1981). Premenstrual tension and use of oral contraceptives also may be linked to depression, although the effects are probably minor. Sex differences in biochemistry may also contribute to gender difference in age at first hospital admission for schizophrenia (Lewine, 1980, 1981). Men are younger when symptoms of schizophrenia first occur and are at greatest risk for first hospitalization during their twenties. Women are at greater risk during their thirties. These differences seem not to vary by culture. Hormonal factors may trigger schizophrenia earlier in predisposed men than in women; alternatively, certain hormones might act as suppressors in women.

Others point to social explanations for women's vulnerability to problems. Women's socialization, especially cultural prescriptions to be devoted to others in a society that values self sufficiency and independence, is seen as creating stress (Lewis, 1981). Moreover, society's views of women as dependent, subjective, passive, noncompetitive, and illogical may contribute to negative self concept and depression (Van Hook, 1979). Indeed, Chodoff (1982) views traditional female sex roles as near caricatures, and cautions that social roles may foster unhealthy behavior in women. And, as previously discussed, many view the limited roles traditionally available to women as contributing to depression and dependence.

Such factors leave women at risk of not developing a personal identity and increase the likelihood of low self esteem (Bond, 1982). Such views are supported by evidence that unmarried women have lower rates of mental illness than unmarried men, while married women have higher rates than married men (Weissman and Klerman, 1981).

Employed women, while adding a role and potential source of gratification to their lives, also add the demands of their jobs and the experience of wage discrimination. Their days become longer, because they remain responsible for household chores. Female homemakers have too little social involvement, while employed women face excessive demands (Verbrugge, 1985).

If social roles do contribute to mental illness, then gender differences in incidence would be expected as men's and women's roles change. Kessler and McRae (1981), who assessed trends in emotional distress of men and women since World War II, found a decrease in women's symptoms over the past two decades. However, the symptoms of homemakers were constant across the decades, suggesting that outside employment may protect women from some stress.

Finally, gender differences in diagnosis are viewed by some as reflecting neither sexism in worker interpretations nor true differences in men's and women's problems. Instead, gender differences in diagnosis are seen to reflect problems in current diagnostic practice.

For example, the definitions of various disorders may derive from behaviors unique to one gender's sex roles and thereby nearly exclude the behavior of the other gender. The phenomenon of "hysteria" is nearly a caricature of the stereotypic feminine personality and role; not unexpectedly, therefore, its diagnosis has been applied nearly exclusively to women who, according to critics, have learned the feminine role very well (Howell, 1981; Lerner, 1981; Chodoff, 1982).

Another problem involves use of incidence as a measurement. Since women live longer than men, incidence data artificially inflate the apparent incidence of mental illness in women. Use of rates (i.e., so many cases per 100,000) would enable truer comparison of problems between men and women.

Instruments used in diagnosis also may contribute to gender bias. For example, stress scales usually focus on individual factors in the experience of stress, and exclude aspects of stress related to interpersonal relationships and situational factors. As a result, the stresses most often experienced by women, such as those related to family roles and size, sex discrimination, poverty, violence, and sexual assault, may not be reflected in stress inventories (Makosky, 1980). Stress scales, then, may underestimate stress in women. Vocational inventories used in career counseling also may be biased. The forms used for men often contain three times as many scorable occupations as do forms used for women (Brodsky, 1980).

Worker gender and diagnosis. A final concern regarding the relationship of gender to diagnosis is that of worker gender. From earlier discussions, it was apparent that male and female workers appear to differ in their attention to and interpretation of client presenting problems. The results of several studies suggest that their diagnoses may differ as well.

In several studies, men were found to respond in more negative and less accepting ways than women did. For example, Farina et al. (Farina and Hagelauer, 1975; Farina, Murray, and Groh, 1978) found that men were less accepting than women of former mental patients. Jones and Zoppel (1982) found that women workers used more socially desirable terms than did male workers to describe female clients. Male workers used such adjectives as "affected," "awkward," and "conceited," without also using adjectives connotating interest or appealing qualities. Female workers were more likely to use adjectives such as "capable," and "intelligent," reflecting more personal competencies and strengths of both male and female clients. Similarly, Haan and Livson (1973) found that male psychologists were more negative in their evaluations of clients (both male and female) than were female psychologists. However, Werner and Block (1975) re-analyzed this data and found no basis for the conclusion that males and females differed systematically in assessment.

One of the most methodologically advanced studies of gender and diagnosis used actual clinic data and controlled for severity of client problem. In this study, Abramowitz and Herrera (1981) found that worker gender had a significant effect on ratings of client pathology. Male workers rated both male and female clients as more psychosomatic, more hostile, more paranoid, more psychotic, and more excited than did female workers. Moreover, worker gender appeared to influence even patients' own characterizations of themselves. Both male and female patients who were interviewed by male therapists characterized themselves as more obsessive, more compulsive, more psychotic, more hostile, and as manifesting more severe symptoms than did those patients interviewed by female therapists. It might be concluded that the more negative perceptions of male workers affected patients' perceptions of themselves.

Because gender accounted for a small portion of the variance in diagnosis overall, the investigators viewed these data as repudiating "charges of virulent sexism in the clinical marketplace" (p. 601). Yet, because the gender effects were consistent and clear, their impact on diagnosis was confirmed. Moreover, the findings suggest that reported differences are based on true sex bias rather than sampling artifacts.

Although their assessments are less negative, female workers have been found to perceive more problems and greater need of intervention than males (LaTorre, 1975; Zeldow, 1976; Helms, 1978). According to Helms (1978), this may reflect the greater ability of women workers to facilitate client revelation of problems. However, women workers are also reported as less empathic about clients' problems than men (Hill et al., 1977) and as having less positive personal reaction to clients than do male workers (Dailey, 1980). Dailey suggests that because female workers themselves place high value on emotional expressiveness and self reliance, they may have negative reactions to clients whom they see as lacking these qualities.

The findings of one study reflect the injection of sex and romanticism into men's diagnosis of female clients. Masling and Harris (1969) report that male assessors not only differed from female assessors in their administration of the Thematic Apperception Test, their behavior was also different with female clients. Male workers spent more time administering the test to female clients and gave them more test cards with sexual and romantic themes.

The conduct of assessment and diagnosis appears also to be influenced by social distance between worker and client. Male and female workers appear to make significantly more positive clinical judgments of, and to perceive less deviance in, clients of their own sex than those of the opposite sex (Fischer et al., 1976; Hayes and Wolleat, 1978). The more severe diagnoses and less optimistic prognoses assigned to young, poor, minority women (Carmen et al., 1981) may be another reflection of social distance. According to Gross (1969), white male psychiatrists can least appreciate, from their own past social experience, the behavior of such clients. As sociocultural distance between worker and client increases, diagnoses become less accurate.

Gender and prognosis. To the extent that gender influences both the standards used for assessment and worker behavior in assessment, it might be expected also to influence the choice of treatment outcomes and expectations for client improvement. Do workers perceive different prognoses for male and female clients? Are the prognoses for male clients more or less favorable than those for female clients? The findings of some studies suggest that the prognoses for male and female clients do not differ (Miller, 1974; Zeldow, 1975). However, Abramowitz et al. (1976a) reported that workers made more favorable prognoses for female than for male patients. Other studies suggest that it depends. For example, LaTorre (1975) reports that female schizophrenics were expected to have better outcome than male schizophrenics, but for clients described as obsessive-compulsive, the prognoses of males and females were similar. Schwartz and Abramowitz (1975) found that experienced, but not inexperienced, psychiatrists made different prognoses for men and women clients, with experienced practitioners making less favorable prognoses for women.

Whether male and female workers focus on different goals and outcomes for clients has been the focus of some studies. Billingsley (1977) reported that, regardless of client gender and pathology, female workers chose more "masculine" treatment goals for their clients, while male workers chose more "feminine" goals. Similarly, female workers (in a study involving a young client's struggle with a decision about whether to relocate in order to pursue education or whether to remain near a fiancee) were found more likely than males to emphasize educational goals (Burlin and Pearson, 1978). However, both male and female workers indicated that if they were actually working with this client, they would encourage the client to make her own decision. Finally, Fischer (1976) reported that male social workers were more likely than female social workers to emphasize home- and family-oriented goals.

Whether, in fact, the goals of male and female clients differ has received little attention. However, workers have been advised to consider client gender and the effects of sex-role socialization when formulating goals and objectives. Stricker (1977) views exploring and expanding the alternatives available to clients as a very important agenda in any helping. Women clients may need help in exploring the role of stereotypes in perceived conflicts between femininity and achievement (Horner, 1972; Oliver, 1975), reduced independence (Van Hook, 1979), and pursuit of the pleasure of others before self (Berlin, 1976). Berlin observes that many women "have lost track of who they are or what they want to be. This loss of self is pervasive and the overriding goal must be to reestablish a clear identity based on broadened indicators of respect. For women in counseling, virtually all their efforts must be directed toward discovering more about themselves and acting on this new information and awareness" (1976, p. 493).

With male clients, too, the impact of gender on treatment goals should be explored (Collison, 1981; Lewis, 1981). Through a "sex-role analysis" (that is, exploration of societal factors' influence on personal experiences) (Kravetz, 1982), a comprehensive range of potential goals can be identified. The need for changes in environment, situations, or relationships (Van Hook, 1979) should be considered in addition to traditional intrapsychic or socioemotional goals. Harris and Lucas caution that workers should be "concerned about the degree to which they may reinforce rather than resolve social and intrapsychic conflicts in their clients by steering them toward an adjustment model of mental health that is based on traditional sex-role stereotypes" (1976, p. 394). Yet Gomes-Schwartz cautions that the advocacy and pursuit of androgenous functioning is just "as much a value judgment as the prescriptions of submissiveness or dependency" (1981, p. 865).

Intervention

Once client problems have been assessed and desired treatment outcomes formulated, the worker must select an interventive approach. The roles that gender may play in this selection are numerous and complex. Client gender, itself, may influence the worker's choice of intervention. Indeed, certain treatment approaches are seen by some as inappropriate (e.g., traditional psychotherapy) or inherently appropriate (e.g., feminist therapy) for clients. Worker gender also may influence interventive behavior in the way male and female workers respond to clients and their presenting problems. Research focusing on these issues will be reviewed.

Client gender and the choice of intervention. Choice of intervention on the basis of client gender has been viewed by some as *the* defining characteristic of sexist therapy (Zeldow, 1978). Helms (1979), for instance, believes that for counseling to be "minimally sex fair," men and women should receive the same interventions. From a different perspective, however, Stricker (1977) believes that treating men and women similarly can be sexist as, for instance, when the treatment procedures are appropriate only for men. There is some evidence that male and female clients prefer different interventive behaviors. Men were more likely than women to find "honest feedback" from their worker to be helpful. Women, on the other hand, were more likely to find worker activities to be helpful when they focused on encouragement to take risks, insight, empathy, and support (Persons, Persons, and Newmark, 1974).

Do workers choose treatment approaches on the basis of client gender? Are different approaches used with male and female clients? The evidence from several studies suggests that workers often do choose treatment approaches on the basis of client gender. For example, workers appear more likely to choose the following interventions for female, than for similarly described male, clients: "supportive relationship treatment" (Miller, 1974), "nondirective, permissive" treatment, and "encouragement" (Fischer, 1976). For male clients, on the other hand, workers were more likely to choose insight-oriented treatment and interpretation (Miller, 1974). In their analysis of worker intervention as judged from audiotapes of therapy sessions, Cooke and Kipnis (1986) found that both male and female workers told female clients what to do significantly more often than they did male clients. On the other hand, workers provided explanations of thoughts, feelings, and behaviors to male clients significantly more often than they did with female clients. Moreover, workers used stronger influence tactics, those requiring a response from the client, significantly more often with female than with male clients.

Workers' reliance on drugs seems to vary according to client gender (Del Gaudio et al., 1978; Lowery and Higgins, 1979). More than two-thirds of all psychotropic drugs, including tranquilizers and anti-depressants, are prescribed for women (Carmen, Russo, and Miller, 1981; Fidell, 1981). More drugs are prescribed by male than female psychiatrists, particularly for female clients (Carmen et al., 1981). Lowery and Higgins (1979) found no evidence that client gender influenced social workers', psychiatrists', and psychologists' choices of electroconvulsive therapy, outpatient psychotherapy, and hospitalization, although vocational counseling was recommended more often for clients of the workers' own gender. According to Schwartz and Abramowitz (1975), it depends on worker orientation. "Traditional" psychiatrists saw dynamic therapy as less worthwhile for men than for women, while "less traditional" psychiatrists considered it more worthwhile for men.

While these patterns might be viewed as sexist by some, others believe that client gender can impact on the inherent appropriateness or inappropriateness of particular interventions. For example, it is frequently argued that female clients should be treated only with feminist interventions. Feminist therapies view the problems of women as related to social roles (Alyn and Becker, 1984). They assume that the ego development of women does not depend on relationships with men; that women have assets such as sensitivity, capacity to nurture, and strength to be assertive and aggressive (Radov et al., 1977; Thomas, 1977), and that the goals of treatment should maximize client choice and autonomy (Moskol, 1976; Thomas, 1977). Intrapsychic conflicts are understood and treated in terms of their relationship to social forces, in particular to social restrictions and economic discrimination (Radov et al., 1977). The treatment relationship between worker and client reflects equality and the client is seen as responsible for decision making and problem solving (Washington D.C. Feminist Counseling Collective, 1975; Thomas, 1977; Brodsky, 1980). Contracts often are utilized to limit worker influence to specific negotiated areas, and the client is free to accept or reject the therapist's influence. Therapists are seen as catalysts, but not leaders or directors for change (Thomas, 1977). Workers may self disclose and present themselves as models of autonomy and competence. Confidence in the client's ability to take charge and succeed is conveyed. Alyn and Becker (1984) observe that feminist therapy resulted in significant improvement in self esteem and sexual knowledge among chronically and profoundly disturbed women.

Other interventive approaches are advocated as uniquely appropriate for male clients. Workers are advised to proceed slowly and carefully, and to confront previously hidden emotions with concern and support (Scher, 1981). Rational, analytical approaches, including an explanation of how procedures work, are also advised for male clients (Bruch, 1978; Carlson, 1981). Bruch (1978) urges workers to consider the preferences and personal styles of male clients as individuals and, where possible, to select compatible treatment approaches. For example, he suggests that behavioral approaches, with instructions, guided practice, contrasts, and self-management components, may be best for "conventional, realistic, and investigative" men; that use of reading or audiovisual programmed learning materials may be best for men who desire a high degree of structure; and that exploration of feelings and symbolic processes may be valuable interventions for "expressive, intuitive, emotional, and liberal" male clients.

Worker gender and the choice of intervention. Several studies have explored possible differences in the ways male and female workers respond to clients. The therapeutic relationship and, in particular, workers' expression of empathic understanding have long been recognized as a key element of intervention. Therefore, the comparative abilities of male and female workers to perceive feelings and to express empathy have been extensively studied. The findings of several studies suggest that women can "decode," or perceive and interpret, emotions more accurately than men (Hall, 1978). Moreover, women workers are reported to be more empathic with clients than male workers (Abramowitz, Abramowitz, and Weitz, 1976), even with angry male clients with whom they felt less comfortable (Johnson, 1978). Yet, women also were more likely than men to feel anger toward such clients, suggesting that they were more expressive of strong feelings in general than men. Hill (1975) reports that women workers become even more empathic with experience. The magnitude of detected gender differences in worker empathy has increased in recent years, probably due to the increasing precision of measuring instruments and power of methods for data analysis (Maccoby and Jacklyn, 1974; Hoffman, 1977).

A number of explanations have been offered for women's heightened sensitivity to and expression of feelings. Women in U.S. society are socialized toward interpersonal sensitivity and may, as a result, be better able to communicate empathically (Johnson, 1978). Moreover, oppression is hypothesized to increase females' sensitivity to nonverbal messages, although Hall (1978) notes that young girls also can decode better than young boys, and questions whether young girls are influenced by oppression. Alternatively, Hall suggests that, through evolution, females may be "wired" from birth to be especially sensitive to nonverbal cues or to be quick learners.

Beyond the helping relationship, does the interventive behavior of women differ from that of men? Rivero and Bordin (1980) found no evidence of such differences. However, Robyak (1981) reports that gender influences worker choice of method of influence. Workers at a university counseling center were provided with a client description and asked to identify strategies for facilitation of change. Strategies were analyzed in terms of method of social influence: expert, referent, and legitimate bases of power. Women chose "legitimate" methods of influence significantly more often than men. Such strategies focus on client voluntary status and commitment to change. Men chose "expert" methods of influence more often than women, with both male and female clients. Women appeared more comfortable with expert methods of influence with female clients but not with male clients, perhaps because they did not expect males to defer to their expertise.

Focusing on worker attempts to influence clients, Cooke and Kipnes (1986) studied audiotapes of actual psychotherapy sessions. Male workers were found to be more active, in that they used significantly more influence tactics and interrupted their clients more frequently than did female workers. Male workers were particularly more likely to use the influence tactic of "focusing," which involved attempting to make the client reflect on his or her own behavior. Women workers spent more session time listening to their clients rather than actively seeking to influence them. These findings may reflect cultural patterns calling for men to be more active and women to be more passive, according to the researchers. However, other studies have failed to detect gender differences related to worker style of influence (Rivero and Bordin, 1980; Paradise, Conway, and Zweig, 1986; Robyak, Goodyear, Prange, and Donham, 1986).

Worker-client match and the choice of intervention. The interventive behavior of workers with same- and opposite-sex clients has also been explored. Some studies report that both male and female workers were more empathic and elicited more feelings with same-sex, rather than opposite-sex clients (Olesker and Balter, 1972; Hill, 1975). In two similar studies, however, gender match did not appear to affect level of empathy (Breisinger, 1976; Petro and Hansen, 1977).

Concern often has been expressed that male-worker female-client relationships are "just one more power relationship in which (women clients) submit to a dominant authority figure" (Chesler, 1971a, p. 269), making it difficult for women clients to experience independence. Even when the male worker tries to help the female client gain insight and learn new patterns of behavior, there is concern that female clients may repeat their habitual styles of relating to men (Van Hook, 1979). Too, they may respond to their workers emotionally, attempting to maintain and control the relationship. However, Heatherington and Allen (1984), who studied the communication patterns between client and worker for evidences of power, failed to find support for their hypothesis that communication between female clients and male workers would reflect the client in a one-down position. The messages exchanged between workers and their female clients were found to be neutral, suggesting that the issue of control was not salient. In fact, messages between workers and male clients reflected unequal control, with one party more dominant than the other. Compared to communication involving female clients, the questions and answers exchanged between worker and male client were more likely to assert or relinquish control in the relationship. Parker (1967) reports that male workers were less directive with female than with male clients; however, Hill (1975) reports that greater experience enabled workers to become more active and directive with opposite-sex clients.

Concerns also have been expressed about female-worker male-client relationships. Carlson (1981) cautions that deference by female workers to male clients might reinforce traditional sex-role stereotypes. Women workers should reserve assurances of worth for later phases of helping, when it is clear that they are responses to genuine issues that have been explored in treatment, and not traditional female behavior with men. Female workers are advised to be accepting, firm, direct, and clear in identifying and interpreting the behavior of male clients.

Classic psychoanalytic writings suggest that when analysis is stalemated, switching to a different-gender worker may change the content of transference and enable the patient to be much more accessible to analysis (Mogul, 1982). When gender of worker and client differs, transference may focus on important heterosexual emotional relationships or on client identification with or wish for love from the parent of the opposite sex.

In summary, gender is clearly salient to the selection of an interventive approach. There is evidence that client gender influences preference for intervention and workers' choice of helping approach. Many argue that interventions are differentially appropriate for female or male clients. The gender match between worker and client itself is seen by some as a potential interventive influence. There is evidence that male and female workers intervene differently. It should be noted, however, that the current state of knowledge reflects clinical observation and opinion more than it does empirical evidence. Indeed, Sheridan sees "the central problem in the therapy-gender debate [as] the discrepancy between what we can prove and what we suspect" (1982, p. 82). Until more evidence is available, gender itself should not be a sufficient factor to either choose or exclude an interventive approach. Rather, interventive methods should be chosen on the basis of their potential for alleviating client problems and for attaining desired outcomes. The bearing of client gender on these issues should, however, be explored. Finally, it should be recognized that sexism, like racism, may be as much a function of what is not done as what is done (Sheridan, 1982). For example, providing male and female clients with equal levels of empathy could be considered sexist if the female client needs more action and less empathy.

Treatment Effectiveness

The bearing of gender on treatment effectiveness remains the most critical issue. Those who design, administer, and deliver social services face such issues as whether client satisfaction with services, evaluation of helper ability, and actual benefit from treatment are influenced by gender. The role of gender in treatment effectiveness will be explored in two respects. First, the impact of gender on the establishment of a facilitative treatment relationship with the client (or attaining intermediate outcomes) will be examined. Issues related to client satisfaction with treatment, comfort with the worker, and perception of the worker as a competent skilled professional will be discussed. Second, the impact of gender on resolution of the client's presenting problem (or attainment of ultimate treatment outcomes) will be explored.

Client gender and intermediate outcomes. Do male and female clients evaluate the helping relationship differently? This issue has been the focus of several empirical investigations. The findings of several studies suggest that women clients have more favorable reactions than men clients. For example, female clients were reported to give more positive evaluations of workers (Carter, 1978) and to experience higher levels of unconditional positive regard (Feldstein, 1982). Moreover, the positive relationships experienced by female clients may be reciprocated by workers. Kirshner, Genack, and Hauser (1978) found that less experienced workers reported greater satisfaction with female clients than with males. Client gender did not affect the satisfaction reported by more experienced workers.

However, women clients also appear to face some risks. Jones and Zoppell (1982) report that regardless of worker gender and professional discipline, women clients were more likely than male clients to feel disparaged by their workers. Female clients working with male workers were particularly vulnerable. These problems will be discussed in the section on gender match.

Worker gender and intermediate outcomes. How does worker gender impact on the quality of the helping relationships? Several studies focusing on client evaluations of workers indicate that clients evaluate female workers more favorably than they do males. Women workers were seen by clients as more expert, more trustworthy, more relaxed, warmer, and friendlier than male workers (Carter, 1978; Banikiotes and Merluzzi, 1981). Diagnostic feedback from a female was perceived as significantly more accurate than that from a male (Zeren and Bradley, 1982). Moreover, clients with female workers tended to be more satisfied in general than were those with male workers (Howard, Orlinsky, and Hill, 1970; Kirshner et al., 1978; Jones and Zoppel, 1982). The positive evaluations of female workers may contribute to client self disclosure and self exploration, as reported earlier. As Carter observes, "although the present research does not provide specific evidence for this connection, it seems reasonable that if clients perceive female counselors as warmer, friendlier, and more trustworthy, they may be more willing to disclose to them" (1978, pp. 33–34).

The evidence in favor of female workers is not unanimous, however. Two studies report that male workers are perceived more positively than females, albeit on different dimensions. Feldstein (1982) found that male counselors were rated higher than female counselors on expertness, trustworthiness, and attractiveness, and Kunin and Rodin (1982) report that male counselors were seen as more intelligent than female counselors. Although the nature of problems may influence client preference for male or female worker, the findings of one study revealed no significant differences in clients' perception of male and female counselors' credibility (Lee, Hallberg, Jones, and Haase, 1980).

Several studies indicate that client evaluation of helpers is complex and may be influenced by factors that interact with gender. In particular, client evaluations of female workers seem to be influenced by such factors as worker sex-role orientation, ascribed level of expertise, amount of self disclosure, race, and office decor. These factors do not affect client evaluations of male workers. A description of the worker as "highly experienced" enhanced college students' perceptions of female workers, but not their views of male workers, a finding that may reflect stereotypic assumptions that women are generally less competent than men, unless they are described as particularly capable (Merluzzi, Banikiotes, and Missbach, 1978). Merluzzi (1981) found that although sex role of male workers did not influence client evaluations, egalitarian female workers were seen by clients as more expert than were traditional female workers (Merluzzi, 1981). The findings of two other studies also suggest that acting in ways counter to traditional sex roles enhances clients' perceptions of female workers. Specifically, engaging in high levels of self disclosure (Merluzzi, Banikiotes, and Missbach, 1978) and occupying an office with "humanistic" decor (Bloom, Weigel, and Trautt, 1977) had the effect of reducing clients' perceptions of their competence. Clients' views of male workers were not affected by worker self disclosure, leading Merluzzi et al. to hypothesize that the "trappings" of professional role may be more important for women workers than for men. However, Bloom et al. (1977) found that office decor affected client perceptions of male workers as well, although in different ways than for women. Men in "humanistic" offices were seen as more credible than males in traditional offices.

Race and gender were found to interact to affect clients' perceptions in a study by Porche and Banikiotes (1982). Male or female workers were described to black adolescents, who were asked to rate the workers' expertness, attractiveness, and trustworthiness. White female counselors were viewed as most expert and black female counselors were viewed as least expert by both boys and girls. White and black male counselors were seen as equally expert, and as less expert than the white female counselor but more expert than the black female.

Gender match and intermediate outcomes. The effect of worker-client gender match on workers' reactions to clients has not received much attention. Kirshner, Genack, and Hauser (1978) addressed this question, with findings that are interesting but may have rather limited implications. Less experienced, but not more experienced, male counselors at a university counseling center reported greater satisfaction working with female undergraduate clients. The satisfaction level of more experienced workers was not affected by the gender of undergraduate clients.

Considerable attention has focused on clients' responses to worker-client gender similarity, and the findings suggest some inherent risks. For example, Carlson (1981) believes that male clients may not be prepared to accept confrontation from a female worker and may react with anger, defensiveness, and attack. Male clients may presume bias in female workers and therefore may reject their interpretations. Other risks cited by Carlson include the possibility of sexual overtures by male clients to female workers, and refusal to focus on feelings. However, these observations are not consistent with findings by Feldstein (1979), who reports that male clients talk more about themselves and experience greater satisfaction with female workers than with male workers. It should be noted that male clients were more satisfied with "feminine" counselors (i.e., warm and supportive) than with "masculine" (i.e., directive) counselors, regardless of counselor gender.

Considerably more attention has focused on reactions of female clients to worker gender. Although Scher (1975) found no bearing of gender match on client's reactions and Jones and Zoppel (1982) assess our knowledge of this issue as "equivocal," the findings of several studies indicate that gender match has a positive effect for female clients. Howard, Orlinsky, and Hill (1970) found that women clients experienced greater satisfaction when working with female, rather than male, workers. Female clients who worked with male workers felt more anger, inhibition, and depression and saw their workers as demanding and detached (Orlinsky and Howard, 1976). They saw themselves as being less open and self-critical, and getting less encouragement, than did women with female workers, and found therapy to be significantly less supportive, though not necessarily less beneficial. Further analysis indicated that two groups of female clients reacted particularly strongly to worker gender. Young single women with male workers wished for more active input from the therapist, experienced fear and anger, felt more inhibited, and viewed the therapist as more detached and demanding. However, they did not experience therapy as less productive or of less benefit than those who had female workers. A second group for whom worker gender was clearly significant was depressed women. Those working with female workers experienced more encouragement, gained more insight, felt less inhibited, expressed themselves more openly, and were more satisfied than were those with male therapists.

Schwartz and Abramowitz (1978) also believe physically unattractive female clients to be at risk for poor therapeutic relationships with male workers. They found physical attractiveness in female clients to increase male workers' perception that client dropout was likely. Moreover, male workers reduced the number of worker "rapport building responses" (head nods, smiles, and supportive statements) with physically "unattractive" female clients.

Client gender and ultimate outcomes. Given the many ways in which men's and women's experiences in helping encounters differ, the question remains: Do they have different chances of experiencing change in the problems for which they originally sought help? Are men or women any more likely to experience positive outcomes from treatment? In spite of the evidence reviewed above, that women clients are more likely to be satisfied with their helping encounters, the evidence from outcome studies indicates that, overall, male and female clients have the same chances of actually benefiting from treatment (Cartwright, 1955; Luborsky et al., 1971). However, the gains experienced by women may be more long lasting, according to data on gender and recidivism rates among adult mental health clients. Turkat (1980) reported that among both whites and blacks, men were more likely than women to be readmitted as mental health clients.

Do male and female clients respond differently to various treatment approaches? Do treatment type and gender of worker and client influence outcome? The findings of some studies suggest they do. Sloane, Staples, Cristol, Yorkston, and Whipple (1976) found a strong, though not significant, tendency for females to improve more than males from analytically-oriented psychotherapy. Males and females did not differ in the extent of gain they experienced from behavior therapy.

Marecek, Kravetz, and Finn (1979) studied women's evaluations of treatment and found that although a very high percentage (72 percent) reported that therapy had been very helpful, ratings varied by treatment orientation and client political orientation. Clients in feminist therapy reported significantly more positive evaluations of therapy than did those in traditional therapy. Women in feminist therapy were more likely to rate their experiences as very helpful (67 percent) than were women in traditional therapy (38 percent). Similarly, women in traditional therapy were more likely to rate their experiences as mixed or not helpful (17 percent) than women in feminist therapy (1 percent), and liberal women found traditional therapy less helpful than did moderates, conservatives, or radicals.

Worker gender and ultimate outcomes.   Several studies have addressed the influence of worker gender on client outcome, in an effort to determine whether the clients of male or female workers fare better. Some clear gender differences were detected. For example, in a comprehensive study of worker gender and client outcome, clients of female workers were found to attain more positive outcomes than clients of male workers. Jones and Zoppel report, on the basis of both worker and client ratings, that male and female clients who were seen by women workers had better treatment relationships, reported more energy, and experienced more improvement. Moreover, in retrospective reports of the treatment processes, both male and female clients perceived women workers as more effective than men in terms of actual interventive behavior. It should be noted that gender was not a decisive influence on outcome: "although women clients in same-gender pairings did tend to show greater change, male workers did not prevent women clients from demonstrating significant improvement" (1982, p. 271).

Jones and Zoppel conclude that women workers are seen by clients "as more accepting, attentive, and comprehensible, and in general (as) forming more effective therapeutic alliances, which in turn, tended to promote more successful outcomes" (p. 271). Consistent with findings discussed earlier, male workers gave blaming or judgmental descriptions of clients and female workers in general did not. Such attitudes are likely to reduce the effectiveness of the helping relationship and, hence, the favorableness of outcomes. Jones and Zoppel see the study as indicating that the term "sex bias" does not do justice to the complexity of the impact of gender in psychotherapy; instead, they suggest that differences in male and female workers' attitudes, behavioral skills, and emotional capacities actually are at issue.

In spite of such findings attesting to their effectiveness, women practitioners may not recognize their own competence. The results of two studies indicate that, regardless of client gender, male workers are more likely than female workers to perceive improvement in their clients (Strassberg and Anchor, 1977; Kaschak, 1978). Furthermore, one of those studies revealed interesting differences in male and female workers' attribution of improvement. Male workers attributed client change to their own interventive techniques, while female workers viewed client characteristics as responsible for change. These findings are consistent with female workers' greater tendency to perceive positive characteristics in clients, as discussed earlier. However, their perception that clients— and not their own skills—contribute to positive treatment outcome may indicate that women workers have less confidence in their own professional competence.

Worker-client match and ultimate outcomes. Whether gender match of worker and client enhances treatment outcome has been the subject of considerable discussion and debate. Many feminists have expressed the view that women clients should always have women workers. The women workers studied by Fabrikant (1974) believed that women are more effective than men in working with female clients, regardless of treatment orientation or type of client.

Others argue that the merits of gender match depend on the particular client, situation, and problem. For instance, although she is not opposed to all counseling of women by males, Van Hook (1979) argues that depressed women are vulnerable to perpetuating patterns of dependence on men when their workers are males. With women workers, on the other hand, depressed women have an opportunity to identify with a woman who does not share a "helpless" perception of the world. The female worker can more convincingly challenge the client's perceptions, help her recognize available choices, and explore more effective means of coping with her situation (Van Hook, 1979).

Female clients experiencing abortion, rape, or physical abuse may also benefit from female workers, with whom they can develop greater and more immediate rapport (Mogul, 1982). Mogul notes, however, some potential advantages to using male workers in such crisis work; for example, a male worker might help such a client avoid generalizing her anger from a particular man in her experience to men in general.

The findings of several studies confirm the benefits of gender match. Persons, Persons, and Newmark (1974) asked clients to list helpful and unhelpful characteristics of their therapists and to describe changes they experienced as a result of therapy. Although all clients reported improvement, and women indicated more gains than men, women with female therapists and men with male therapists reported the most improvement. Beck and Jones (1975) also report that male clients improved more with a male worker, rather than a female worker. Kaschak (1978), however, found (in a study of 75 clients of male and female workers) worker-client gender match enhanced outcome only for female clients. Male clients perceived greater improvement with female, rather than male, workers.

Kirscher et al. (1978) also studied improvement as a function of therapist and client gender among clients in brief therapy and found that worker-client gender match enhanced improvement in only one problem area—personal relationships—and only for female clients who worked with experienced female therapists. The investigators concluded that although women clients appeared more responsive in general and women workers appeared more effective, the results fail to provide substantial support for gender matching in brief therapy.

Studies in which particular treatment interventions are specified, such as systematic desensitization, indicate that therapist-client gender match generally does not enhance outcome (Cotler, 1970; Pucel and Nawas, 1970), although the need for more extensive study of this issue using larger samples of male clients has been noted (Cotler, 1970). Pucel and Nawas believe that sex pairing is not relevant to the efficacy of desensitization due to "the clarity and specificity of the operations of the desensitization technique, along with the amply demonstrated fact that these very operations are solely responsible for the effectiveness of the procedure . . ." They continue that, because "the transactions in the typical desensitization experiment or treatment are highly engaging and absorbing; the individual often becomes oblivious to anything beyond the scenes which the therapist asks him to imagine" (1970, pp. 106–7). However, these results may also reflect the stringent limitations to worker-client contact in experimental situations; in many studies, clients are exposed only to tape recordings of worker voices. The results of one study in which client contact was not so limited did evidence some gender effects. Geer and Hurst (1976) found that female workers were more effective than male workers with male clients, while male workers were more effective than females with female clients.

Finally, from a study of gender, verbal activity, and treatment outcome of 36 university students and their 23 counselors at a university counseling service, Scher (1975) concluded that gender of client and gender of counselor did not significantly influence outcome. Therapeutic success was experienced generally by male clients seeing experienced therapists and by female clients working with inexperienced counselors, leading the investigator to suggest that outcome depends more on what is done than on gender of participants.

What conclusions can be drawn from the research on gender and outcome? Does gender of either worker or client bear significantly on the effectiveness of helping? Or are gender effects limited to the process? Obviously, the studies reviewed show an inconsistent picture. In some studies, in some types of treatment, addressing certain types of client problems, gender—especially worker gender—appears to affect outcome. In particular, Mogul (1982) believes that because gender affects the helping relationship and transference, in particular, gender "can be powerful enough to substantially affect outcome" with some clients, in shorter forms of treatment, and with less experienced or less skilled workers.

While acknowledging that male and female workers may plan and conduct their treatment quite differently, Zeldow (1978) concludes that "there is no current evidence of sex-related difference in therapeutic outcome." And Mogul concurs that particularly if treatment is long-term, insight-directed, and thorough, "the outcome of treatment . . . is less affected by therapist sex than by the therapist's training, experience, personality, and self-awareness" (1982, p. 9).

In the final analysis, it is evident that sufficient high-quality research on this issue is lacking. Articles descriptive of clinical situations deal with only a few clients and focus on only a very few factors. Even empirical studies are limited by methodological factors, generally major ones involving the control of significant variables. Gomes-Schwartz notes that "controlled psychotherapy studies in which the gender of the patient and/or therapist is related to outcome or process are almost nonexistent" (1981, p. 865). In particular, quality studies focusing on client outcome are lacking, although "this is the primary type of data that is mustered in support of the benefits of feminist therapy and consciousness-raising groups" (p. 865). As Parloff et al. conclude, we have "not much directly relevant research, not much consistent quality, and not much by way of results" (1978, p. 23) and gender, by itself, seems not to be a powerful or consistent predictor of outcome. On the other hand, our current knowledge may be limited by conceptual and methodological weakness in research to date, weakness future studies may overcome, enabling eventual understanding of the strength and pattern of gender influences.

CONCLUSION

Some clear trends are evident in this voluminous literature about gender effects in individual treatment. First, it is evident that worker gender often matters to clients. Traditionally, male workers have been perceived as more competent, particularly for problems with vocational relevance. Preference for women workers has increased of late, particularly among female clients with personal problems.

Women seek help at earlier stages of problem development than men. Women present more problems for professional help and outnumber men as clients except for a few problem types and in a few service settings. Referral patterns and caseloads indicate that women and children, but rarely male clients, are assigned to female workers. Women have been the "preferred" clients, perhaps because they are seen as easier to communicate with. Gender does not have clear effects on dropout or treatment duration.

Women present more problems involving affect, self esteem, and anxiety, while men present more problems involving substance abuse and violence. Social roles and sex-role socialization, in all likelihood, contribute to gender differences in problems and in helpseeking.

Regarding communication and the helping relationship, male and female workers face different challenges. Women workers appear to be more skilled at assessing client emotional states, expressing feeling, and establishing rapport; male workers, however, may be seen as more competent and may have more skills in directive and authoritative interventions. The assessments of male workers appear to be more negative. Women, as both clients and workers, are more likely than males to self disclose.

Women clients are seen as less healthy than men, but men are seen as having more serious problems and greater need of intervention. The problems of women are diagnosed and treated differently than are those of men. Women are more often treated with drugs or supportive therapy; more directive and insight intervention is offered to men.

With respect to outcome, there is evidence that women clients evaluate helping more favorably than do men. Moreover, in general, female workers are evaluated more favorably by clients than are males; however, there is some evidence that male workers are seen as more expert and credible.

8

Gender
and Family
Treatment

Family treatment, perhaps even more than other kinds of helping, is affected by gender differences between participants and changes in societal sex roles. Gender and sex-role stereotypes are likely to influence practitioners' theories about family life, assumptions about healthy families, and assessment of family problems. And, of course, sex roles and gender affect the problems and relationship patterns that families present to practitioners. Hare-Mustin notes, from a feminist perspective, "nowhere do the inequities in society affect more women in their daily lives than in the family" (1979a, p. 32).

This chapter will explore the impact of gender issues on family treatment. For example, the significance of worker gender to family members and the effects of using a single worker or a co-therapy team will be considered. In addition, the chapter will explore the influence of gender on family problems, the assessment of those problems, and the worker's interaction with family members. Finally, the bearing of gender on the choice and effectiveness of various treatment methods will be considered.

Although gender and sex roles have a major impact on family life and the treatment of families, many important issues have not been thoroughly investigated. Hence, today's family practitioners must function without the benefit of an adequate empirical knowledge base. However, it is possible to systematically examine the way in which gender and sex roles impact on the treatment of couples and families, and to identify the best available knowledge as a guide for responding to those issues.

GENDER IN FAMILY TREATMENT

Salience of Gender to Families

When couples or families seek professional help, is the worker's gender an important issue to them? The family treatment literature has not addressed this question thoroughly or systematically. Indeed, studies of family members' preferences for male or female workers are virtually nonexistent. In one study that incorporated this issue, men considered the therapist's sex and race to be less important than the fee charged and the therapist's recommendations (Guillebeaux, Storm, and Demaris, 1986). Haley (1976), too, assumes that clients are much more concerned about the competence of workers than their gender. He acknowledges, however, the possibility that gender might influence the coalitions which may develop between worker and family members. Worker gender may also be important to couples in signaling worker attitudes. For example, couples might assume that women workers' marital attitudes and values would be less traditional.

There is some evidence that clients perceive the skills of male and female family therapists differently. Epstein and Jayne (1981) report that while "verbally active" female workers were seen as both supportive and competent, "verbally active" males were seen as competent but not necessarily supportive. The researchers concluded that male workers must work harder than female workers to be seen by clients as supportive.

However, verbally active males were rated as more "in charge" than were verbally active females, suggesting that "even though subjects attributed high competence and support to females, they were less willing to accord them the position of being 'in charge' of the situation, a role traditionally held by males" (Epstein and Jayne, 1981, p. 507). Thus, clients may be less likely to perceive women practitioners as being "in charge" and male practitioners as being supportive.

Family therapists (and especially verbally dominant male workers) were perceived less favorably by men than by women. This may support prevailing clinical impressions that male clients are more resistant in family treatment than are females. Moreover, Epstein and Jayne (1981) found that clients with traditional sex-role attitudes gave more favorable ratings to female than to male workers. The ratings of male and female workers by androgynous individuals were not significantly different. Such findings suggest that the question of client preference for worker gender may not be a simple issue, but may, instead, vary according to worker style, client gender, and client sex-role attitudes.

Salience of Gender to Workers

How significant are gender-related issues to family therapists? Do therapists prefer to work with male or female members of families? Do they encounter particular kinds of issues in working with men and women? Finally, do male and female practitioners face different issues in their work with families?

There is little evidence that family therapists prefer to work with one gender or the other. Rather, therapists seem to encounter different challenges in working with male and female family members. It is interesting to note that the family treatment literature directs considerably more attention to issues confronting female workers than it does to those facing male workers. This is so in spite of the fact that the most common model for marital treatment is believed to be that of a husband and wife working with a male practitioner (Rice and Rice, 1975). This may reflect the assumption that gender poses fewer problems for men than for women, due perhaps to their predominance in the field or to their presumed competence.

What issues are likely to arise when a male therapist works with a couple? This question is addressed only briefly in the family literature, but two frequent problems are noted. The first is collusion: That is, when male practitioners work with couples, the female member of the couple may perceive collusion between the worker and her partner (Reese-Dukes and Reese-Dukes, 1983). Another problem is anger of the female client toward the male worker; Hare-Mustin (1978) observes that female clients who struggle with traditional female roles may direct their anger toward the male family therapist.

Female family therapists may face a more extensive set of problems. First, as in practice with individuals and groups, clients may lack respect for and doubt the professional competence of female family therapists (Hare-Mustin, 1978). This issue is discussed more fully in Chapters 7 and 9. Second, similar to the risks faced by male workers, female family therapists may experience problems over alliances (perceived or real) with one of the partners in the families with whom they work. If the female family therapist seems to have an alliance with the husband, the wife may see her as seductive; on the other hand, if she has an alliance with the wife, the husband may perceive the women as "ganging up against him" (Ficher and Linsenberg, 1976). Even when the female worker needs to form a temporary alliance to encourage expressiveness in a submissive female client, the male partner may perceive collusion and resist (Ficher and Linsenberg, 1976). Such problems become accentuated by the personal styles of clients. For example, female workers in authority roles may amplify the inferiority of passive males, and aggressive male clients may compete with female workers for dominance of the relationship (Ficher and Linsenberg, 1976).

Other problems for female workers may result from inconsistencies between traditional female roles and the requirements for interventive behavior. For example, the assertion of authority and power required in the structural-strategic family treatment models may be problematic for some women workers (Caust, Libow, and Raskin, 1981). These therapies require expertise and assertiveness, behaviors that differ both from traditional, stereotyped female behavior and from the professional styles comfortable to many women workers, such as reliance on indirect influence, attractiveness, and empathy. Although difficult for some women, structural and strategic approaches do enable female workers alternatives to stereotyped, nurturant, expressive interventive roles. This issue is discussed later in this chapter.

However, female family therapists may have some advantages. Their socialization may have heightened their abilities to be empathic, open, and intimate, and they often have more personal experience than do male workers relevant to problems in child development and parenting. Moreover (albeit on the basis of limited research), their attitudes toward family issues appear to be more liberal. According to the research of Hare-Mustin and Lamb (1984), female family therapists were found to have more liberal attitudes than did male family therapists. In general, workers involved in family therapy with adolescents and their families had more liberal attitudes toward such issues as breast feeding, child-rearing abilities of working mothers, and male-female relationships.

Co-Therapy

Given the fact that family treatment frequently involves both male and female clients, it is not surprising that male-female co-therapy teams are often advocated. Proponents of co-therapy cite numerous merits, among which the modeling function is prominent. Co-therapists are seen as able to model flexibility in sex-role relationships (Foster, 1981), cooperation in leadership, and healthy male and female behavior, which may be particularly important for some couples (Mitchell, 1969). Also, with male-female co-therapy teams, both husband and wife are more likely to perceive that their own feelings are heard and understood by someone who has had similar feelings and conflicts (that is, the worker of their own gender) (Reese-Dukes and Reese-Dukes, 1983).

The use of male-female co-therapy teams also reflects the assumption that worker gender has an important influence on the clients' ability to learn from the family practitioner. Indeed, the assumption that male workers are better models for husbands and fathers, while female workers are better for wives and mothers, prevails in much of the family treatment literature. The presence of both male and female practitioners as models for couples appears to be particularly important in certain situations. For example, Igelhart (1982) sees male workers as important role models for husbands who are working toward role shifts; when the husband feels alone in his struggle, the male worker's sharing of his own experiences and personal adjustments may be especially welcome. Similarly, Hare-Mustin (1978) views female workers as potentially good models of competence, positive self image, high aspirations, and assertive behavior for wives and mothers.

Beyond the potential benefits for clients, co-therapy may have some advantages for workers as well. For example, co-therapists can provide feedback to each other about the impact of interventions on the family; can alternate between listening and intervening; and can provide freedom for each one to engage with the family in a variety of ways (Foster, 1981).

However, there are also disadvantages to co-therapy. First, obvious dissimilarities between worker and client may interfere with modeling and, hence, with client learning, regardless of gender match. For example, male clients may feel uncomfortable with male workers who freely and easily express emotions, just as female clients may see highly competent women practitioners as too far removed from their own experiences to serve as good models (Margolin, Talovic, Fernandez, and Onorato, 1983). In such cases, clients may have difficulty identifying with the same-sex family practitioner and even feel that their own interpersonal difficulties are accentuated by comparison to the same-sex worker (Mitchell, 1969). Co-therapy may be problematic also when families push workers into parental roles, so that the male worker becomes "father" to the family and the female worker becomes "mother" (Bell, 1975). These roles may be problematic because they interfere with the practitioner's therapeutic tasks. Finally, co-therapy teams may be problematic if they model and reinforce patterns of behavior that are discrepant with those of the family. If co-therapy teams model nontraditional sex roles to families who adhere to traditional roles, family members may feel unable to relate to and benefit from the therapists. The reverse of this situation is also possible, with the same problematic consequences. That is, when the co-therapists model traditional roles to nontraditional families, the treatment gains may be shortchanged.

The most widespread criticism of co-therapy teams is their tendency to model stereotypical sex roles in relationships and reinforce patterns of behavior that are oppressive to women (Hare-Mustin, 1978). Rice and Rice (1977) charge that most co-therapy teams model traditional male-instrumental, female-expressive patterns. That is, the female member of the co-therapy team frequently is given or assumes responsibility for client feelings, while the male member of the team takes responsibility for providing the interpretations. Indeed, the "co-therapy team in which the female rather than the male therapist is the senior member is virtually unheard of" (Rice and Rice, 1977, p. 192). As in the larger society, males are ascribed leadership positions because of higher social status. Co-therapy teams who desire a different allocation of responsibility must counter society's gender expectations. (The influence of status expectations on co-therapy treatment teams has been discussed also in Chapters 3, 4, and 9.) A major challenge to co-therapy teams is to maximize the family's ability to relate to the team's style of interaction and, hence, enhance the potential gain from treatment, yet to refrain from reinforcing patterns of behavior that are oppressive to women.

The extent of these problems is not clear, given the paucity of data. Although co-therapy has been widely espoused among family therapists and marriage counselors, its merits or effects have rarely been directly tested in studies of treatment outcome (Gurman, 1975; Gurman and Kniskern, 1978). Recent studies in the area of sex therapy show that treatment by a single worker is just as effective as that by dual-sex co-therapy teams, casting doubt on the widespread assumption that co-therapy is important in sex therapy (LoPiccolo, Heiman, Hogan, and Roberts, 1985). According to another study, not all couples are equally responsive to the modeling of the therapy team. Epstein, Jayne-Lazaras, and DeGiovanni (1979) report that clients' evaluations of their workers were more positive when the modeled pattern of dominance between workers was similar to the couple's own pattern. However, overall, "male-dominated" couples were less likely to change in response to what the therapists modeled.

Until more data are available, practitioners involved in co-therapy might well heed suggestions from the literature in order to optimize the potential advantages and minimize the disadvantages. It is recommended that members of co-therapy teams have similar training and status, regard each other as equal peers, and avoid assigning each other gender-related tasks (Rice and Rice, 1977; Hare-Mustin and Lamb, 1984). Moreover, the office used for their joint work should be a neutral one (belonging to neither one), and the co-leaders should begin working with the family at the same time to guard against the formation of individual sets of relationships (Rice and Rice, 1977). Finally, they should be able to recognize and confront and support each other, and reach agreement about the goals of treatment (Mitchell, 1969).

Gender and Family Problems

How does gender influence the problems that family members bring to treatment? Do men and women experience, identify, and define family problems differently? While there is no clear evidence that the sexes identify and define problems differently, it appears that women take initiative for seeking family treatment and for presenting the problems for consideration. Most often, families come for treatment because the mother is distressed (Hare-Mustin and Lamb, 1984). A study of men participating in marriage and family treatment revealed that in nearly half the cases, the wife initiated treatment; one-fourth of the men agreed to participate in therapy only because of the spouse's threat of separation or divorce. One-third of the men studied initiated therapy themselves, and in only a few cases were the spouses equally involved in initiating treatment (Guillebeaux, Storm, and Demaris, 1986). Fathers may be less likely than mothers to present problems or complaints because responsibility for family life has been ascribed to her. Frequent problem presentation by the wife, however, should not be taken "as evidence of the wife's demanding personality or of the husband's inability to satisfy her" (Margolin et al., 1983, p. 136). Gender also may influence the types of issues and concerns family members present. Emotional and affective issues may be of greater concern to women than to men (Margolin et al., 1983).

Many women do not know what their partner wants or expects to be worked on in family treatment. According to Margolin et al., "although neither sex is particularly accurate in predicting what the other desires before therapy begins, women are even less accurate than men" (1983, p. 137). Women seem to err on the side of overestimating what they perceive their husbands want. Margolin suggests that this may stem from their lack of information about what their spouse wants. However, it is also probable that the woman's lower self confidence may contribute to her perception that her spouse is pervasively dissatisfied with her or their relationship.

As problems become translated into goals for treatment, Margolin et al. (1983) caution that workers should take care to examine particular problems within the context of overall family patterns. For example, if only very specific problems are addressed, more pervasive or longstanding patterns of family dynamics may not be recognized and addressed.

FAMILY DYNAMICS

Practitioner perspectives on family problems, and, hence, family treatment, are likely to be affected by the current flux in society's views of the "healthy" family. The traditional view of family has been one of an employed father who is a "good provider" (Bernard, 1981), a full-time homemaker mother, and children. This view is now generally recognized as atypical. However, the values associated with it may continue to influence family practitioners and their treatment. Schwartz noted, after her review of the literature, that "there is . . . a remarkable amount of dismay expressed by family therapists that the father is no longer the head of the house . . ., and intervention strategies are often based on helping the father to reassert his power" (1973, p. 68). This situation may be perpetuated if the training of family therapists and marriage counselors continues to be based on literature and theory that reflect traditional assumptions about family roles (Alonso and Rutan, 1981). For example, only recently has the family literature explored alternative roles for husbands and fathers (Lewis and Pleck, 1979), and very rarely is it recognized that the demands of family life may conflict with the personal development of men and women. In short, the definitions of healthy family life prevailing in the treatment literature may not have kept pace with changing societal norms.

The balance between individual pursuits and family responsibility is a crucial issue in the understanding of healthy family life. Traditionally, it has been assumed that married individuals, but in particular married women, should obtain their identity and satisfaction from within the family unit. However, the balance between individual and family roles has been increasingly recognized as important. Feminist concerns about the personal development of women sparked interest in the way in which family life may optimize or hinder the personal development of its members. Similar concerns have been extended to men's individual and family roles (Safilios-Rothschild, 1969; Lewis and Pleck, 1979; Iglehart, 1982).

The costs of various roles should be considered for both individuals and the family unit. Traditional roles for men and women may be associated with both family stress and mental health problems for individuals. For example, traditional roles for men emphasize task achievement but the suppression of emotion and self disclosure (Cohen, 1979). Obviously, such a role may impair intimacy and be dysfunctional for family relationships. Similarly, women may pay a psychological price for traditional roles: The data are clear that married women are more likely to experience depression than are single women or married men (Gove, 1972). Family practitioners should be sensitive to the contribution of men's and women's social roles to personal and family problems.

In the discussion that follows, we shall examine some traditional assumptions about families in the light of current research findings. The influence of gender and sex-role issues on several areas of family dynamics will be considered. The topics include power, employment, household division of labor, parenting, and sexuality. These issues are involved in many of the problems for which families seek professional help. They are reviewed with the aim of helping readers to become better informed, and to explore their own assumptions in the light of new information.

Power

Power is a central issue in family dynamics. Prevailing norms clearly imply traditional sex roles for men and women, with the power of the husband virtually "guaranteed" by society's expectation that men will be older, bigger, better educated, and come from a higher social class than their wives (Hare-Mustin, 1978). In short, all of his statuses are expected to be higher than his wife's, ensuring him the "strength, credentials, experience, special knowledge, and training on which power, in part, is based. Marriages in which this is not the case are regarded as deviant" (Hare-Mustin, 1978, p. 182). The power of men is reflected also in traditional expectations that women will give up activities or place of residence in order to adjust to the preferences and needs of men. Of course, after giving up these interests, women have been left to depend on the marriage to meet their needs for economic support and status.

Although it has been less obvious, traditional roles also leave men dependent on women. Specifically, men have been dependent on women for the fulfillment of their own emotional needs as well as those of other family members. Men have also depended on their wives to fulfill parenting responsibilities (Szinovacz, 1984).

However, this mutual dependence should not be construed as equality or even parity. Women have been dependent on men in areas that are critical for family and individual survival (economics, status), while men have depended on women for matters often seen as less important (emotional expressiveness, housekeeping, parenting). Indeed, the fact that fathers do not participate more actively in making decisions about children may reflect the unimportance of those issues to them (Hare-Mustin, 1978).

What are the implications of these social norms and expectations for family treatment? First, it appears that many family therapists continue to assume that traditional sex roles are critical for healthy family functioning (Hare-Mustin, 1978) and, therefore, support such roles in the families with whom they work (Maracek and Johnson, 1980).

This is reflected in family practitioners' concern with tracking power in families. Often the a priori goal in family treatment is strengthening the husband's power in the family, while weakening that of the wife (APA Task Force, 1975). Burke and Boudendistel (Burke, 1982) analyzed family theory and practice and concluded that power relationships in families are more likely to be seen as pathological when the woman is more powerful; very rarely were women legitimized as heads of household or seen as independent and powerful decision makers in their families. According to Schwartz, who reviewed social work content in the areas of human growth and development and family casework, "Aggressive, controlling, domineering qualities in women are punished by the ultimate label—castrating—while there is no such negatively charged equivalent for the male who overpowers and thus, devitalizes a woman. It is acceptable, even admirable, if the mother is able to set limits in her family, but God help her in the casework if she is the dominant member of the family" (1973, p. 69).

So long as a couple's balance of power approximates that which is sanctioned and expected by society, their dynamics are neither questioned nor seen as problematic. Indeed, Hare-Mustin (1978) charges that the power balance of sex roles is usually disregarded except when the woman has considerable power, in which case the family therapist may "rush in" to restore power to the male partner. Solidifying the power of men in family decision making has been seen traditionally as central to enhancing overall family health. The fact that men typically have more power and status outside the home than women do is overlooked, with the result that treatment often perpetuates a power imbalance. As previously noted, such an imbalance may contribute to the lower self esteem of women (Hare-Mustin, 1978, 1979b). Thus, theories such as Minuchin's have been criticized for "demanding that the father resume control of the family and exert leadership as Minuchin leads and controls the sessions" (Hare-Mustin, 1978, p. 184).

The influence of traditional sex roles on family problems may be apparent in some less obvious ways. For example, they may influence family generational boundaries and the development of alliances, as when mothers use daughters or sons as confidants beccause of their own isolation from an absent or distant father or other adults (Hare-Mustin, 1979a).

Thus the conflicts that couples bring to treatment often have their roots not just in the interaction between two individuals in a marriage, but in the social roles of those two individuals. The inequity in the larger society is often reflected in women's stressful, inferior positions in families. Family therapists, then, need to be sensitive to the possibility that their assessments, conduct of sessions, and homework assignments may "intentionally or unwittingly" reinforce stereotypic roles for the man, the powerful doer, and for the woman, the dependent nurturer (Hare-Mustin, 1978, p. 184). Indeed, "traditional family therapists who seek to restore family functioning by reinforcing conventional roles may be perpetuating the causes of unhappiness and conflict in the family by their actions" (Hare-Mustin, 1979a, p. 32).

Employment

How does the wife's employment affect family dynamics, and to what extent does it cause problems for husbands? These often-asked questions reflect the traditional view that employment is the primary responsibility of the husband. Indeed, the converse question—Does the husband's employment produce problems for wives and influence family dynamics?—is rarely posed, reflecting the assumption that the "good provider" role belongs to the husband (Bernard, 1981).

Of course the "good provider" view is outmoded: In most couples without children and in most families with school-age children, both male and female are employed (U.S. Bureau of Census, 1982). High unemployment among males, divorce rates, economic insecurity, and desire for personal achievement through employment have led scores of women, married or not, to enter the workplace. In spite of changed norms, however, husbands continue to be seen as responsible for their families economically, and sharing the provider role with wives is suspected to increase family conflict. That is, husband and wife are assumed to compete over the role of economic provider. The focus of researchers, therefore, has been the extent to which wife employment produces stress, dissatisfaction, or other negative outcomes for couples, and, in particular, for husbands who might feel threatened in their ability to fill the "good provider" role.

What do those studies reveal? Overall, wife employment appears to have negligible effects on the health or marital adjustment of either men or women (Booth, 1979; Smith, 1985). Regardless of the specific criterion (physical adjustment, companionship, communication, or tension), comparisons yielded no differences in adjustment as a function of wife employment. One study did find that husbands of employed wives experienced higher levels of depression and lower levels of self esteem than did men whose wives were not in the labor force (Kessler and McRae, 1982). However, this distress was not found to be due to any increased childcare or household responsibilities nor to competition with the wife over the provider role. Indeed, wife's earnings and husband's self esteem were positively correlated. Negative effects of wife employment appear to be due to failure to share domestic roles. Men most likely to feel distressed were those who engaged in the least amount of household labor and who performed the fewest family chores. These findings counter traditional assumptions that husbands of employed wives react unhappily to either wife employment or to their own increased burdens of home and childcare.

Indeed, employment seems to contribute to the self esteem, elevated mood, and overall mental health of wives and mothers (Kessler and McRae, 1981; Gore and Mangione, 1983). Positive effects of employment for women, including social and psychological rewards, are widely reported (Bernard, 1972; Gove, 1972, 1973; Pleck, 1985). The critical factor in explaining well being for both husbands and wives appears not to be wife employment per se; rather, it appears to be the extent to which family members accommodate her employment by participating in household tasks and feel that they have coped well (Houseknecht and Macke, 1981).

Moreover, recent data dissuade us from assuming that either men or women are immune to work-family conflict; indeed, work and family appear to produce potential conflicts for *both* men and women. Pleck et al. (1978) found, in a national sample of married workers, that men and women experienced a similar degree of conflict: 35 percent of all married workers with children reported experiencing moderate to severe conflict between work and family roles. Moreover, similar conditions were associated with conflict for both men and women: Those conditions included long work hours, high psychological involvement with work, frequent overtime, work shifts other than traditional day shifts, inflexible work schedules, and psychologically demanding work. Under these conditions, family adjustment was lessened, happiness with the marriage was reduced, and individuals experienced a decreased sense of overall well being. However, the critical predictor, once again, was not the actual level of conflict experienced between work and family roles but rather the individual's feeling of having coped well with such conflicts. Consistent with this, Barling's (1984) findings indicate that when the husband's work-related experiences are negative, the wife's marital satisfaction decreases. Positive or constructive work experiences for husbands, however, can enhance marital satisfaction in wives.

The above findings suggest a focus on family cooperation and maintenance, rather than on intra-family competition and conflict. As Oppenheimer suggests, families must be viewed as units in the larger social system, "not just as small groups faced with the internal problems of maintaining good relations among members" (1977, p. 404). When we place the family in the context of the larger social system and recognize the preeminence of economic survival and enhancement, husband-wife compatibility becomes more important and economic competition between them becomes less important.

Household Division of Labor

A central question, given the above discussion of employment issues, is the extent to which household labor is shared by husband and wife. Studies reveal that wives continue to do most of the housework and childcare, even when they are employed. Krausz (1986) concludes that traditional sex roles exist in most households. Married women employed full-time spend an average of 39 hours per week on their jobs, plus 25 hours a week on housekeeping. In comparison, married men spend approximately 48.5 hours per week on the job and 12.6 hours on household responsibilities (Pleck, 1983). These data reveal that professional women are more likely than professional men to alter their work hours and job performance in order to manage household and childcare responsibilities. Thus, not only do women spend more time on household duties, but they also are more likely than men to reduce their time on the job for such duties.

Husbands do seem to increase their involvement when their wives are employed. Recent data indicate that husbands of both employed and unemployed wives have increased their domestic involvement. Pleck reports that husbands do 32 percent of the couple's total family work when the wife is employed, in contrast to 21 percent when she is not. However, men's increased involvement is primarily time spent in the house with children, but not time directly spent on housework or actual childcare. Overall, husbands of employed wives increase their time on family responsibilities about one half hour per day (Pleck, 1985). It is interesting to note that husbands do more family work when there are no children, and do least when children are of preschool age (Pleck, 1983). These findings are consistent with other reports that role overload among employed mothers is most likely when children are of preschool age (Staines, Pleck, Shepard, and O'Connor, 1978) and that marital satisfaction for women is lowest at this stage. Families with preschool children have more household and childcare responsibilities than do families at any other stage in the life cycle. These dynamics point to the likelihood of family stress and dissatisfaction over household division of labor among couples with young children.

Have there been changes in the extent to which couples share household responsibilities? Pleck (1985) believes that recently there have been both behavioral and attitudinal changes, with husbands increasing their family involvement. Yet only a minority of the population believe that men should take part in more housework and childcare than at present. Overall, men do not want to participate in housework. Moreover, only about one-third of women report that they want greater husband participation in housework and childcare. Perhaps women who have an investment in maintaining their relative monopoly of family roles resist their husbands' increased involvement (Pleck, 1985). It is interesting to note that although about one-third of women report that they want greater husband participation in housework and childcare, slightly more than one-half of men believe that their wives want them to do more. Hence, in a sizable minority of cases, husbands think their wives want more help when, in fact, their wives do not. Findings such as this indicate the role confusion and discrepant expectations currently experienced among American families. This situation is a dilemma not only for the couple, but also for the practitioner who attempts to help them understand and resolve problems regarding division of household responsibility.

Does the sharing of household labor vary by race or socioeconomic status? These issues are discussed in other chapters, but it is important to note here that these issues frequently are different for whites and minorities or middle- and working-class families. For example, there is some evidence that norms regarding husband participation in housework vary by socioeconomic status, even more than does actual behavior (Scanzoni, 1979a). In middle-class families, where egalitarian division of labor is valued, women may brag or even exaggerate about how much housework their husbands do. Ferree (1984) suggests that such exaggeration serves to protect the wives' own image as liberated. Among working-class families, however, it is more acceptable for wives to complain about how little their husbands do, even when their husbands help considerably; such complaining may be self-serving for both husband and wife in that it reflects their conformity with the norm that housework is the wife's domain. These findings, while perhaps appearing incongruous, highlight the possible lack of agreement between what couples do and what they think is "in vogue." Therefore, practitioners may have to sort out what families actually want for themselves versus what they think they should want.

Parenting

How does gender affect the participation of family members in childcare responsibilities? Do men and women differ in the way they parent, in how much time they spend with children, and in their feelings about each other's participation in childcare? How do these differences affect the issues that families present to practitioners for help?

Some research indicates that mothers bring to parenting greater empathy, affiliation, and sensitivity to nonverbal cues and social skills; fathers, on the other hand, place greater emphasis on skill mastery, autonomy, and cognitive achievement. Fathers tend to be less comfortable with intimacy, and mothers uncomfortable with impersonal situations (Rossi, 1984). Research further suggests that fathers impact positively on children's, and particularly daughters', cognitive development (Radin, 1982). If mothers and fathers have different emphases and strengths in parenting, the proportion of time a child spends with each parent may have consequences for the child's development. These findings have clear implications for single-parent families, which will be discussed in a later section. Rossi speculates that because "men bring their maleness to parenting, as women bring their femaleness" the effect of increased father involvement may be to enhance gender differences in children (1984, p. 10). This does not imply, of course, that fathers should reduce their involvement in childcare, but, rather, that the nature of their involvement should become less custodial and more nurturing.

Childcare, of course, has been traditionally "assigned" to women. Women's dissatisfaction with such automatic assignment, along with men's reluctance to share those responsibilities, often contributes to the family problems and dissatisfaction presented to family practitioners. Of course, father involvement may be limited by traditional roles and by preoccupation with work (Raubolt and Rachman, 1980). However, the amount of time the sexes spend parenting seems to be changing. Pleck (1985) reports that husbands, particularly of employed wives, are increasing their involvement with children. However, mothers are still responsible for most of the parenting, even when they are employed full-time and their children are very young. In fact, the co-parenting of children in intact families generally involves children over 18 months, and rarely involves younger children and infants (Rossi, 1984), in spite of the fact that infants and toddlers require the heaviest care.

Women whose husbands increase their involvement in parenting may experience, in addition to some welcome relief, some conflicts. Some women experience a decrease in close, personal involvement with their children (Radin, 1982). Many women are aware of pressure, both internal and social, to fulfill the traditional parenting roles for which they were socialized (Radin, 1982). As such, they may perceive shared parenting as a violation of, or departure from, their traditional expectations.

How do husband and wife feel about this distribution of responsibility? Recent data indicate that many wives—and particularly employed wives—are unhappy, not just because they do too much but also because their husbands do too little. Rather than a simple "exhaustion" effect, there is evidence for an "inequity effect" in terms of the wife's perception of her husband's time (Pleck, 1985). As Pleck summarizes,

> It may be that employed wives performing high levels of childcare, who wish their husbands would do more, feel they have relatively little control over the demands made on their time by children. . . . Low family participation by the husband leads the wife to be dissatisfied with the division of labor. This dissatisfaction has direct negative consequences for the wife's adjustment and well-being. Further, when wives experience this dissatisfaction, their own childcare time contributes further to poor adjustment. This probably occurs not because childcare is exhausting, but because the level of childcare feels inequitable. Thus, the potential issue in the dual-earner family seems to be that the husband's level of family work is too low, not that the wife's is too high (1985, pp. 114–15).

What is the experience of husbands? Many reservations about a father's participation in parenting have been expressed. It has been assumed that husbands who increase their involvement in parenting would experience role overload from trying to satisfy both traditional male roles and more modern emerging father roles (Moreland and Schwebel, 1981). In addition, concerns have been expressed that greater participation in parenting might impede men's career advancement (Radin, 1982) and increase men's dissatisfaction (Blumstein and Schwartz, 1983).

Recent data, however, suggest a quite different picture. Husbands of employed women seem to experience more problems with depression and self esteem when they *do not* increase their responsibility for childcare. It is husbands who are involved in both paid work and childcare who experience greater satisfaction and happiness with their family life (Pleck, 1985). Thus, men may be learning, as have women, the interpersonal rewards that result from participation in childcare. Moreover, actively responding to the pressures of dual-earner families provides husbands with a sense of control, a feeling that there is something they can do to respond to pressures (Pleck, 1985). Happily, it seems, "the factor that improves adjustment in the employed wife, higher husband family participation, also facilitates well-being in the husband" (Pleck, 1985, p. 117).

Also contrary to common assumptions, men appear to be quite psychologically involved with their families. According to recent research, most men are more psychologically involved in their families than their jobs, except highly educated or high-status men, who generally are more involved with work than family (Pleck, 1985). Overall, men's time in family is increasing, while women's is decreasing.

Those who remain at risk, then, may be the men and women without a variety of roles. Like the men who neglect parenting, mothers who are not employed face a unique set of problems. Mothers who spend time at home raising young children often experience social isolation and insufficient contact with other adults (Tavris and Wade, 1984). Practitioners working with families where the mother remains home with primary responsibility for child and family care should carefully examine their perceptions of family problems and the attitudes they communicate. For example, it is important to accurately perceive the wife's social isolation and to appreciate the difficulties imposed by the ill-defined, diffuse role of housewife. Workers should guard against the too frequent perception that the problems of such women are due to immaturity or inability to handle family responsibilities (Maracek and Ballou, 1981). Finally, workers should refrain from conveying disrespectful attitudes toward childrearing and domestic responsibilities, attitudes that would be particularly damaging to women who have chosen, or are considering, full-time family rearing and home care.

These issues may pose challenges for women practitioners, who by definition are professionally employed. Women practitioners may have to discount their personal resolution of the work-family dilemma, recognizing that decisions about how to combine work and family are personal ones for the client as well. The professional's responsibility is to facilitate arrangements that work satisfactorily for clients, even when those arrangements differ from the worker's personal choice. Finally, practitioners should be aware of the positive consequences in store for men who increase their family involvement: The potential benefits extend to the wife, the children, and also to the husband.

With respect to division of household labor and childcare, how much have families been affected by recent changes in sex roles? How much do families want to change the traditional allocations of responsibility? Can practitioners expect to see increasing numbers of families struggling with new and different expectations for individual and family behavior? Although sex-role attitudes may have changed, there is little evidence of change in the assignment of family responsibilities (Szinovacz, 1984). Moreover, because children are still exposed to sex-role segregated behavior in families, some experts foresee little change in the near future.

The preferences of individuals and families vary. In general, however, it appears that men prefer traditional marriages, while women prefer egalitarian relationships (Pursell, Banikiotes, and Sebastian, 1981). Moreover, the patterns of young couples may reflect the preferences of the individuals involved: Individuals with androgynous personal sex roles are found to prefer egalitarian marital relationships over traditional ones (Pursell et al., 1981). This suggests potential conflict for couples in which only one partner prefers an egalitarian arrangement.

Preferred family sex roles also may vary by socioeconomic status. For example, in the middle class, egalitarian styles may be preferred; indeed, family responsibilities may be experienced as burdensome and as interfering with personal opportunity. In lower-income families, however, family responsibilities are not as likely to be seen as personal restrictions. Instead of viewing the family as interfering with personal desires, the family is seen as a means of pooling limited resources for the protection of weaker members. According to Ferree, lower-class families may be "more aware of both the supportive and suppressive aspects of family life because the oppressive nature of the economy is more salient" (1984, p. 63). Thus, for lower-income families, struggles over changing sex roles may be less salient and, hence, may be less likely to be the focus of treatment.

For those who do struggle with these issues, the willingness and ability of spouses to negotiate, decide upon, and implement mutually satisfactory arrangements is crucial. The issue should not be cast as one in which husbands must change only for the benefit of their wives. Rather, "for the movement toward sex-role transcendence to succeed, it must profit and enhance the life quality of both men and women" (Szinovacz, 1984, pp. 189–90). Unless men can see advantages from their involvement in egalitarian relationships, they will probably resist sex-role changes.

For both husband and wife, changes related to sex roles are likely to be quite stressful (Rice and Rice, 1977). It may be especially difficult for families to move toward more egalitarian styles, with flexible, open roles based on personal preference and individual capability (Rice and Rice, 1977). Success at such change will doubtless be enhanced if practitioners can help both partners see the potential benefits for the two individuals involved and for the family unit.

Practitioners' ability to help couples with issues of changing sex roles or to treat couples already in egalitarian relationships may be limited. One source of limitation may be professional training, which, according to Alonso and Rutan (1981), continues to be based on literature and theory replete with traditional assumptions about sex roles and family behavior. The risk, then, remains that workers' perceptions of family dynamics, their focus on certain problem areas, and their chosen methods of intervention may reflect traditional assumptions about family sex roles.

Other practitioners, drawing on more recent feminist theory, might presume egalitarian family relationships to be ideal. Moreover, they might use such an ideal as a criterion for assessing the functioning of the families they treat. For example, Rice and Rice assume that "a sharing of overt and socially recognized power leads to enhanced self-esteem and promotes personal growth for both individuals" (1977, p. 5). Therefore, they urge therapists to work with couples toward equal division of labor, contracts, and schedules that focus on housework, childcare, and sex-role expectations.

How confidently can workers assume what is desirable in terms of family division of labor and role allocation? Workers should, of course, actively assess a family's sex-role behavior and division of labor, including husband and wife participation in decisions, spending, and housework and, in particular, their perception of their relationship as equitable. Further, therapists should be capable of assessing these issues in the context of their knowledge of research, social conditions, and prevailing sex-role attitudes. But their most important function, according to Berger and Wright (1978), may be facilitating family members' own clarification of values regarding the roles of husband, wife, mother, and father, and supporting the family in working toward their own desired roles. Schwartz cautions workers not to assume the desirability of male leadership within the family without exploring the facts for individual families. Practitioners should recognize the possibility that in some families husband and wife might have different areas of primary decision-making responsibility. "It depends on the people involved . . . their needs, weaknesses, strengths; the total interaction of the family" (Schwartz, 1973, p. 68).

Yet we would caution practitioners against injecting the literature's version of "ideal" family styles onto the families with whom they work. Particularly when an issue is not seen as problematic by the family or its members, workers should be cautious in attempting to help the family develop a different pattern of interaction. Even with respect to sex roles, the helping professions should not replace indiscriminant exhortation toward traditional sex roles with indiscriminant exhortation away from them (Hadley and Hadley, 1976, p. 613).

Single-Parent Families

The number of single-parent families continues to rise, due to increases in both divorce and out-of-wedlock childbearing (Norton and Glick, 1986). In all U.S. population groups (blacks, whites, the poor, and the not poor) the number of female-headed households increased by 40 percent between 1960 and 1972 and doubled between 1978 and 1984 (Freeman, 1980; U.S. Bureau of Census, 1985b). In 1984, 25.7 percent of all family groups were headed by one parent (U.S. Bureau of Census, 1985a). Nearly half of all the children in the United States are expected to live in a one-parent family at some point (Freeman, 1980).

Three times as many black families, compared to whites, are headed by a woman alone. According to recent census data, 59 percent of all black families with children, and 20 percent of all white families with children, are headed by a single parent (U.S. Bureau of Census, 1985b). This issue is also discussed in Chapter 3.

In 1984, 88 percent of single-parent families consisted of mother and children, a figure consistent over the past 15 years (Norton and Glick, 1986). The largest group of single-parent families are those headed by a divorced mother (36.8 percent). The next largest groups are never-married mothers (24.4 percent) and separated mothers (18.5 percent). Smaller proportions include families headed by widows (6.8 percent), separated fathers (2.4 percent), spouse-absent mothers (2.4 percent), never-married fathers (1.5 percent), and widowers (0.9 percent) (Parents Without Partners, 1983).

Traditionally, both larger society and helping professionals have been pessimistic about the fate of single-parent families. Problems have been assumed for both the adult heading the household and for the children. Single-parent families headed by a female and containing male children have been seen as particularly troubled. This is expressed by

Segalman and Basu, who view two adults, one of whom is employed in the marketplace, as necessary for raising a competent child. The issues confronting both women and men as single parents need to be understood by family practitioners.

Women as single parents. The extent to which families headed by a woman alone are, indeed, troubled has become an important research question. Findings of several studies point to some significant problems. The most serious problem facing single mothers is financial. The median family income for female-headed single-parent families is less than half that of male-headed single-parent families ($9,153 versus $19,950) (Norton and Glick, 1986). (See Table 1.) Practitioners working with female-headed families, therefore, need to appreciate their socioeconomic problems (see also Chapter 13).

In addition, single mothers experience strains between job and family roles and are at high risk for lowered physical and emotional well being. They simply must work longer hours and have less family time than do women in two-parent families (Weinraub and Wolf, 1983; Sanik and Mauldin, 1986). Moreover, single mothers have fewer resources of all sorts. They are more socially isolated than are married parents (Hipgrave, 1981), have less stable social networks, and receive less emotional support (Weinraub and Wolf, 1983). According to the findings of a recent study, single mothers report more anxiety over disciplining their children than do single fathers (Rossi, 1984). Moreover, single mothers with traditional sex-role expectations experience other problems if they have not developed good decision-making skills (Maracek and Ballou, 1981).

Considerable concern has been expressed regarding patterns of interaction between a single mother and her children. Some single mothers, especially those with low self esteem, may depend on symbiotic,

TABLE 1   Median Family Income in Two-parent and Single-parent Families

FAMILY INCOME (THOUSANDS)	TWO-PARENT FAMILIES	SINGLE-PARENT FAMILIES		
		TOTAL	MOTHER CHILD	FATHER CHILD
Median Income (dollars)	23,165	9,986	9,153	19,950
Mean Income	31,808	13,047	11,732	22,757

Source: U.S. Bureau of Census (1985a).

enmeshed relationships with their young children for personal gratification. According to Glenwick and Mowrey (1986), this problem is most frequent among female single parents who begin to confide in their oldest child when that child is between 9 and 13 years of age. Clinical intervention can help the mother return to her parental role and better resolve her own personal conflicts without violating the parent-child boundaries.

Of course, never-married teenage mothers are a subset of single parents of special concern to social work. They are at particular risk economically and educationally. Recent research documents the value of providing free educational daycare to their children, thereby increasing the likelihood of teen mothers completing school, obtaining post-secondary training, and becoming self-supporting (Campbell, Breitmayer, and Ramer, 1986).

Men as single parents. Increasing attention has been directed of late to male-headed single-parent families. Although increasing numbers of men have sought custody of their children following divorce and have adopted as single parents, these families remain a minority. In 1984, the father was the lone parent in approximately 3 percent of the family groups with children under 18 (U.S. Bureau of Census, 1985b). As attitudes change, men may be granted fairer consideration in determinations of child custody.

The findings of research suggest that single fathers experience many of the same problems facing single mothers. Indeed, as with single mothers, the major problem of single fathers appears to be financial (Katz, 1979). More than one-half of the single fathers studied in England experienced a drop in income due to their increased parental responsibilities and to such factors as reduction in overtime work, absenteeism necessary to care for sick children, and reduction in business-related social ties (George and Wilding, 1972). Single-parent fathers, however, are more likely to be employed than are single-parent mothers (88 versus 69 percent) (Norton and Glick, 1986), and their incomes are significantly higher (see Table 1).

Like single mothers, single fathers experience social isolation, often due to their withdrawal from former social networks (Gasser and Taylor, 1976; Hipgrave, 1981). Although single fathers receive more help from others than do single mothers, they are less likely than single mothers to make new social contacts. Divorced fathers, compared to divorced mothers, are reported to make fewer demands of their children, communicate less well, express less affection, be more inconsistent in discipline, and have less control over their children when they are with them (Hetherington, Cox, and Cox, 1976). Single fathers frequently experience anxiety over their difficulty in providing emotional support to their daughters (Rossi, 1984), and, like single mothers, experience conflicts in attempting to fulfill both parental and personal adult roles (Orthner, Brown, and Ferguson, 1976; Katz, 1979). These problems may be a reflection of the limits of their prior involvement in parenting and their lack of social support.

In spite of these problems, most single fathers are generally satisfied with their lives and are pleased by their ability to handle various roles (Orthner et al., 1976). Fathers in single-parent families, while less educated as a group than those in two-parent families, have higher levels of education than do single mothers who head families (Norton and Glick, 1986). The situation of single fathers appears to be more transitory than that of single mothers, since they tend to remarry within a two-year period (Katz, 1979). Thus, professional support for single fathers is usually needed for a short duration.

Children in single-parent families. In terms of child outcomes, male-headed single-parent families often have been assumed particularly detrimental. For example, while family literature refers to "father absence" in female-headed households, the parallel effect in male-headed single-parent families has been labeled "maternal deprivation." "Deprivation" is a clearly more ominous term than "absence." The evidence suggests, however, that when men take full responsibility for childcare, their relationship with their children can be intimate and affectionate (Risman, 1986).

An obvious problem for children in single-parent families is the increased risk of poverty. Fifty-seven percent of children in one-parent families lived below the poverty level in 1983. However, this risk varies significantly with parent gender, in that the poverty rate is twice as high for children in mother-child families as it is for those in father-child families (60 versus 26 percent) (Norton and Glick, 1986). This difference reflects not only women's lower earning ability, but also the fact that only a small minority of divorced fathers make court-ordered child support payments. Single-parent families—especially those headed by women—are characterized not only by their poverty, but also by high representation of racial minorities, high mobility, and low education (Norton and Glick, 1986). Issues in the treatment of minority single-parent families were discussed more fully in Chapter 3.

The health of children in single-parent families also appears to vary by parent gender. Hanson (1986) reports that children living with female parents were healthier than children with male parents. However, the health of the single-parent female suffered more than did that of the single-parent male. Thus, family practitioners might be alert for health risks in children when fathers are the single parents and in the mother when she is a single parent.

What can we conclude about the problems and prospects of single-parent families? Are the traditionally pessimistic views of professionals toward their fate supported by current research? Hill (1986) concludes that a major structural difference between two-parent and single-parent families is the latter's lack of personnel to fill all the expected family roles. In short, single parents, whether male or female, are likely to experience task overload. Single-parent families face more and longer periods of family instability. For example, divorce, remarriage, and re-entering the labor force constitute critical transitions for the single parent. Yet, according to recent evidence, single parents—when not experiencing poverty—can be successful (Cashion, 1982). Most problems experienced in single-parent families are transitional, not psychological (Cashion, 1982), and are often resolved satisfactorily after about two years (Segal and Yahraes, 1978).

What single parents, and female-headed households in particular, need is contact with people who are not pessimistic about the probabilities of their success (Cashion, 1982). Family practitioners, therefore, would be urged to remain openminded, even optimistic, about the success that single-parent families can experience.

Of course, professionals also need to be aware of the stresses faced by single-parent families, and the factors that can enhance the family's functioning. For example, given the evidence that social support has a positive effect on the well being of low-income single-parent families (Gladow and Ray, 1986), practitioners should help single parents better develop their support systems. In particular, Gladow and Ray (1986) suggest that workers help single parents lessen the pressure on themselves to achieve romantic relationships, while increasing the number and quality of friendships that appear to have the broadest impact on well being.

Practitioners also play an important role in facilitating the adjustment of the divorced single parent. Despite the lack of evidence that divorce has long-range adverse consequences for children (Bleckman, 1982), the time following separation and divorce is often marked by problems for parents and children. For example, because women have been dependent on marriage for both financial and emotional well being, the time period following divorce is likely to be stressful. During this period, family practitioners can provide emotional assistance, practical assistance with parenting tasks (Johnson, 1986), and assistance in locating alternative sources of social support.

Gender of worker and of single parent may affect family treatment. Shulman and Klein (1984) observe that male practitioners working with female single parents may encounter more intense transference issues than would male practitioners working with male single parents. In the latter case, children seem less intent on "inducting" the male worker into the family, and the transference issues are similar to those in therapy with two-parent families.

Domestic Violence

Another extremely important, albeit often overlooked, aspect of family dynamics is domestic violence. Family practitioners should be aware of the extent of violence between men and women and sensitive to its possible occurrence among families who come to them for help. According to research, half of all women will be battered at some time in their lives by men with whom they have significant relationships. More than one in four persons in the United States approve of slapping one's partner (Dibble and Straus, 1980). According to national surveys, within any given year, 28 percent of U.S. couples engage in physical assault (Straus, Gelles, and Steinmetz, 1980). Rather than serving as a "haven," the family is the setting most at risk for violence: Physical violence occurs between family members more often than in any other kind of relationship. Domestic violence occurs in families of all ages, races, SES levels, educational levels, and ethnic groups, perhaps reflecting the extent to which violence is valued throughout our culture. However, the incidence of domestic violence appears to be higher in low-income families, in families with limited social supports, and in "patriarchally" organized families (Finkelhor, 1983). Violence is a problem not only because of its consequences for the adults who assault each other, but also because children learn violence as a response to problems.

While a review of theories for understanding the dynamics of domestic violence is beyond the scope and purpose of this discussion, brief reference to the factors involved may be helpful. The occurrence of violence is a reflection of societal values and may be viewed as a learned, albeit ineffective, means of problem resolution. Walker (1981), who views violence multidimensionally, sees it also as a reflection of the inequality of power between men and women in society at large. Although many practitioners assume that partners share mutual responsibility for violence in a relationship, it should be recognized that such a view attributes equal power to men and women (Walker, 1981). The realities of social and economic inequalities counter such an assumption. Violence is nearly always directed to the least powerful member; hence, women, children, and the elderly are frequent targets of violence and abuse. Of course, psychological theories also are useful to aid in understanding the thoughts, feelings, and behaviors of individual family members who engage in or are victims of violence. However, Nichols (1986) points out that most family violence is carried by essentially "normal" people, and should be attributed to social rather than individual psychological factors. Often, violence in a relationship is viewed as the mutual product of two emotionally disturbed individuals. From a systems perspective, violence may be seen as a reflection of problems inherent in the relationship between two people. Such theories are useful to practitioners in their tasks of recognizing and treating family violence.

Most family practitioners have not been specifically trained to recognize family violence. As a result, they may not be aggressive enough in exploring the possible occurrence of violence in the families they treat. Assessment should be directed toward identifying the specific forms, nature, extent, and functions of violence within the family (Nichols, 1986). Recognizing the inhibitions family members may feel, the practitioner should ask about the family's use of such behaviors as slapping, kicking, biting, and hitting. Such an approach will be more productive than asking, more generally, if there is any abuse; many family members may not understand what is meant by abuse or violence and are likely to provide a negative response (Nichols, 1986). Because men and women report battering differently (Edleson and Brygger, 1986), information on violence and threatened violence should be collected from both batterer and victim.

When family violence is detected, family practitioners should be prepared to address it. In addition to their usual treatment approaches, specific knowledge and resources are required to treat this problem effectively. For example, in some cases where there is no evidence of immediate danger, training in conflict resolution and problem solving may be helpful. In cases where danger is apparent, practitioners should be able to work effectively with community resources such as safety shelters and law enforcement agencies. Practitioners need to be sensitive to the relationship between domestic violence and women's inferior status, a relationship supported by evidence of a strong link between dependency among wives and the occurrence of domestic violence (Dibble and Straus, 1980). Thus, many individuals remain in violent situations not because they are attractive or satisfying to them, but rather because those individuals have or perceive themselves to have no alternatives.

Interventions directed primarily toward raising the victim's consciousness are important, but not sufficient. Indeed, efforts aimed only at encouraging battered women to leave violent family situations may be short-sighted and insensitive to social reality. Physically and emotionally abused women who remain in violent home situations often do so because they perceive no alternatives. With a lack of employment skills, inequitable wages for women, and failure of courts and law enforcement agencies to ensure physical protection and payment of child support, battered women are indeed accurate when they perceive their options to be limited.

It is important to intervene as early as possible after violence has occurred or been detected (Geller and Wallerstrom, 1984; Nichols, 1986).

Work with the couple's families of origin, and separate work with the couple's children also may be indicated (Nichols, 1986). Whatever the form of family treatment, attention to the spouses' psychological needs is important. Yet some cautions are in order. According to some clinical research, assertiveness training with physically abused wives may be ill-advised, in fact, hazardous for such women (O'Leary, Curley, Rosenbaum, and Clarke, 1985).

This problem requires that family therapists have a comprehensive repertoire of interventions. Attention to personal consciousness raising, increased autonomy, and independence are important for the victim. Issues of conflict, anger, and power are important for the perpetrator of violence. Yet these individual and interpersonal issues are not sufficient. Also important are social, economic, and political remedies, and family practitioners need to be aware of community resources that can provide partners in a violent relationship with those remedies.

Sexual Issues

In what ways does gender affect family sexual behavior? In what ways might practitioners find their treatment of sexual issues affected by gender? How do sexual satisfaction, sexual problems, and response to treatment of sexual problems differ for men and women? Gender differences are clear, as the sexes seem to differ in levels of sexual satisfaction, types of sexual problems, and willingness to seek help for sexual issues. Although recent literature suggests a trend toward greater permissiveness and toward greater male/female similarity in sexual standards, some evidence of the double standard remains. Szinovacz (1984), in particular, notes a persistence of male dominance in the areas of sexual decision making and control. Moreover, recent data indicate that among well functioning couples, the husband usually initiates sexual activity, although these same couples report that the ideal is for initiation to be equal (Schover and LoPiccolo, 1982). Schover and LoPiccolo (1982) speculate that the power of the husband in controlling the frequency of sexual activity may also account for wives' greater dissatisfaction at the time of treatment intake.

Consistent with other findings from the population at large, husbands of couples seeking sex therapy rated significantly higher than did wives on overall sexual satisfaction (Schover and LoPiccolo, 1982). However, men and women may differ in their willingness to report sexual problems and to initiate treatment for sexual issues. Lorne Hartman (1983) suggests that husbands may appear to be more satisfied on measures of sexual functioning because they may attribute problems to their partner. Moreover, women may be more likely than men to initiate treatment when they are sexually dissatisfied, causing estimates of women's dissatisfaction derived from clinic data to be inflated.

Men and women seem to experience different areas of sexual functioning as problematic. The most common presenting sexual complaints for women are arousal and orgasm problems (LoPiccolo and Stock, 1986). For men, areas of sexual dysfunction include low sexual desire, erectile failure, premature ejaculation, and inhibited ejaculation (LoPiccolo and Stock, 1986). However, in a clinical study, similar percentages of males and females reported low levels of sexual desire (7 and 9 percent, respectively) (Schover and LoPiccolo, 1982).

Because specific treatments have been developed for specific types of sexual dysfunction, men and women—whose sexual problems typically differ—are often provided with different types of treatment. In the limited empirical research, clients have not been viewed heterogeneously (LoPiccolo and Stock, 1986), and, thus, gender differences in individuals' responses to the treatment of sexual problems have not been sufficiently investigated. Hartman (1983), who did study this question, reports treatment effectiveness did not vary by gender.

Marital Satisfaction

Marital dissatisfaction often prompts couples to seek help from family practitioners. Some couples are dissatisfied over particular issues while others are dissatisfied in general. Knowledge of factors that seem to affect marital satisfaction may be helpful for family practitioners.

U.S. men, as a group, seem to be significantly more satisfied with marriage than are women (Rhyne, 1981). Men evaluate overall marital quality more highly than women. In contrast, women are less satisfied than men with all aspects of marriage except the extent to which sexual needs are met. Only in this particular area were men less satisfied than women (Rhyne, 1981).

Are women harder to please? Are they just more prone to dissatisfaction? It doesn't seem this simple. Rather, it appears that certain factors may be differentially important to the marital satisfaction of men and women. In addition, life cycle issues affect men's and women's marital satisfaction differently. Finally, on those factors that are important to both men and women, women experience less satisfactory outcomes.

Although both sexes use the same factors in assessing marital quality, certain factors are weighted differently for men and women. For example, companionship appears to be somewhat more important to women than to men (Rhyne, 1981). On the other hand, friendship with spouse, interest expressed, and time spent with children were more important for men. For men without children, sexual gratification was the most important influence on marital satisfaction. For men with young children, the interest shown them by wives was most important, perhaps reflecting some degree of competition with their children for the wife's attention. Among couples whose children had left home, friendship was most important to men, while interest expressed by spouse and sexual gratification were most important to women. According to another study, egalitarian role relationships and perceived equity in marriage significantly increased the marital satisfaction of wives, but did not affect that of husbands (Rachlin and Hansen, 1985). Thus, there appear to be gender differences in the factors that contribute to marital satisfaction.

Second, the impact of life cycle changes on marital satisfaction seems to differ for women and men. Men's levels of satisfaction appear to remain constant over the life cycle, while those of women are variable. In particular, significant decreases in marital satisfaction were reported by women following the arrival of children (Rhyne, 1981). The bearing of life cycle stage on marital satisfaction should not go unheeded. Indeed, life cycle stage is a more critical influence than gender on overall marital satisfaction (Rhyne, 1981).

Finally, when those factors contributing to marital satisfaction are the same for men and women, wives appear to experience less satisfactory outcomes. In other words, their levels of satisfaction may be different because their life experiences are different. For example, one factor that is related to dissatisfaction for both husbands and wives is time spent on housework and childcare. Housework has long been perceived, by those who do it and those who shun it, as boring, ill-defined, unrewarded, unrewarding, and ceaseless. It should not be surprising that those who do more of it—generally women—tend to be more dissatisfied with their lives and their marriages. The data indicate that housewives, for whom housework is a central role, are more likely to use and misuse drugs, experience anxiety, and feel worthless (Tavris and Wade, 1984). Some data also indicate that increased involvement in housework leads to dissatisfaction for men (Blumstein and Schwartz, 1983). If involvement in housework is, in fact, negatively related to marital satisfaction among both men and women, and if (as research suggests) women spend 26 hours per week on housework while men spend 36 minutes, it may not be surprising that women are generally more dissatisfied than men.

Another factor that influences marital satisfaction is the number of significant roles open to husbands and wives. As noted earlier in this chapter, research confirms the advantages for both men and women in terms of health, satisfaction, and morale, of having two roles—e.g., work and family—instead of just one. Working men and women experience better health, well being, and satisfaction than do housewives (Gove and Tudor, 1973). Moreover, the absence of either the employment or marital role is associated with depression for both men and women (Gore and Mangione, 1983). The detriments of having only one role are reflected in the dissatisfaction of men who have only experienced the "good provider" role (employment) and women who have only experienced domestic roles. In fact, "where role occupancy is identical, sex differences in distress are not seen" (Gore and Mangione, 1983, p. 310). Multiple roles may be necessary for marital satisfaction among both men and women. Thus men, who are more likely to have multiple roles open to them, remain more satisfied than women.

The satisfaction of husbands, as well as the relative dissatisfaction of wives, is reflected in health and social indicators. Married men are healthier than single men, never-married men, and widowers, in terms of employment, pay, crime, physical health, suicide, accident, and life expectancy (Bernard, 1972). Conversely, married women fare worse than married men, in terms of physical and emotional health (Gove and Tudor, 1973). As Tavris and Wade observe:

> The irony is that marriage, which many men consider a trap, does them a world of good, while the relentless pressure on them to be breadwinners causes undue strain and conflict. Exactly the reverse is true for women. Marriage, which they yearn for from childhood, may prove hazardous to their health, while the opportunities for work help keep them sane and satisfied (1984, p. 274).

It seems, then, that balance between family and employment roles is important for marital satisfaction for both men and women. Rice and Rice (1977), therefore, believe that egalitarian marriages, in which individual preference or ability rather than gender dictate division of labor, may provide greater marital satisfaction and harmony. Thus, they expect couples in traditional marriages to experience more problems, and hence, to seek family treatment more often. The findings of one study are consistent with this hypothesis (Baucom and Aiken, 1984).

FAMILY-PRACTITIONER INTERACTION

Assessment

In what ways might the assessment of family problems be influenced by gender and sex roles? Do male and female family members present different issues to practitioners? Do practitioners perceive their issues differently? The literature on family dynamics reviewed above would lead us to expect some differences. Other important issues to be explored include the extent to which the procedures for assessment might be subject to sex bias and the extent to which responsibility for family problems is differentially attributed to men and women.

Worker sex roles and family assessment. As was discussed in Chapter 7, it is important to recognize the ways in which the worker's own sex-role attitudes and personal family experiences may affect his or her perception of family dynamics and assessment. Unfortunately, very little research has addressed this issue. Yet, it is suggested that practitioners' own traditional sex-role attitudes may contribute to their "dismay" when the father is not the "head of the house" (Schwartz, 1973, p. 68). If workers are typical of the rest of the U.S. population, male workers, in particular, may hold traditional values about marriage and the family. Indeed, according to Rice and Rice, "there is usually little impetus for a male to change his interpersonal relationship patterns unless personal experience has motivated him to do so" (1977, p. 3). If they are correct, then the attitudes of workers toward family sex roles may depend more on their personal family experiences than on their professional training.

Fabrikant (1974), who studied the sex-role views of family therapists, reports that both male and female therapists viewed women as able to have a full life without marriage and saw marriage as optimally a co-equal partnership. Family practitioners wanted their female clients to be less dependent on their husbands financially and socially, but to remain dependent on husbands sexually. Although Fabrikant viewed this as a reflection of a "double standard," such a view may instead reflect the value family therapists place on marital fidelity (Bergin and Silverman, 1986). Thus, we would assume the same patterns of dependence should prevail for husbands as well.

Whatever their own sex-role attitudes, practitioners should understand and respect the meaning and consequences of sex-role arrangements for families with whom they work. In such cases, social reality, or "meaning," is the key. There may be considerable room for disagreement about whether a particular pattern of role allocation is sexist or whether it is acceptable to the family. Even when the worker, the husband, and the wife all agree about what the family's division of labor is, they may not agree about what it means in terms of sex roles, or fairness. Clearly, the family's understanding of their dynamics is paramount to that of the practitioner.

Procedures for assessment. Most of the concern with gender and the assessment of family problems focuses on the influence of sex-role attitudes. According to some critics, traditional sex roles affect the concepts used for assessment of family problems. For example, according to Hare-Mustin (1978), the prevalence of such terms as "weak" or "passive" to describe men and "frigid" or "cold" to describe women reflect traditional sex-role concepts. On the other hand, the contrast between "father absence" and "maternal deprivation" may be seen to reflect bias against men, in that it places greater salience on the absence of the mother. Such concepts may result in the attribution of problems to individual factors, and a failure to recognize the role of socialization or culture.

Worker communication within the assessment interview also may be influenced by gender and sex roles (see also Chapter 7). In particular, worker sex-role attitudes may affect attention to the husband's and wife's expression of problems. For example, many workers attend more to the wife when she discusses childbearing issues and attend more to the husband when he discusses financial or employment issues (Margolin, Talovic, Fernandez, and Onorato, 1983). Hare-Mustin (1978) encourages practitioners to be sensitive to—indeed, to reinforce—emotional expression in men.

Finally, standardized instruments used in assessment should be carefully scrutinized for sexist content or assumptions. For example, Margolin and Talovic observe that some items on frequently used assessment instruments imply gender-specific responsibility for family tasks.

Attribution of problems to family members.   When workers attempt to understand the problems experienced by families, gender and sex roles may wield considerable influence. Generally, problems can be attributed to individual members, to relationships and patterns of interaction within the family, and to societal factors. In the traditional family literature, responsibility for the family's emotional well being has been assigned almost exclusively to and accepted by women (Berlin, 1976). Even those who do not go so far as to assume that the woman actually *causes* difficulties often hold her responsible for *resolving* problems. Thus, the woman often becomes the central figure in nearly every presenting problem whether it is marital, family, or parent-child (Berlin, 1976).

This tendency may reflect the concern of family therapy pioneers with the mother-child relationship. For example, many classic theorists focused on mother-child communication in their understanding of pathology. Similarly, many therapists focused on the role of mother-child symbiosis in their early understandings of schizophrenia (Libow, Raskin, and Caust, 1982), only later enlarging their focus to the entire family system.

Whatever the origin, the centrality of the mother-child relationship persists, according to findings of recent research. Kellerman (1975), who studied the attribution of responsibility for family problems by college undergraduates, found that the mother's role was seen as central in the causation of many problems. For example, such problems as mental retardation, enuresis, stuttering, tics, excess emotionality, dependent behavior, obesity, and asthma were more likely to be attributed to the mother than to the father. Only problems considered by the investigators as "masculine," such as aggression, passivity, rebellion, and athletic incompetence, were attributed more to fathers than to mothers.

Abramowitz (1977), who studied workers' attribution of child problems, suggests that attribution of responsibility depends on the child's gender. Thus, mothers were held more responsible for problems of daughters than for those of sons. Overall, however, practitioners, like the public at large, attributed more responsibility for both children to mothers than to fathers.

Involving the Family

Forming a therapeutic alliance with family members is a complex yet crucial task for family practitioners. Because more individuals are involved in the family treatment process, forming the therapeutic relationship is generally more complicated than in individual treatment. However, because several persons are involved in the problems and intervention, the literature stresses the importance of their participation in family treatment (Kaslow, 1981). Indeed, working on marital problems with only one spouse may have outcomes that are negative for the family unit, such as increased distance between spouses due to the growth experienced by the one participating in therapy. The nonparticipating spouse is also likely to perceive collusion between the therapist and the spouse in treatment. Thus, in concurrence with Rice, we urge workers to present a "firm but reasonable insistence on having both partners present" for marital treatment (1978, p. 64).

It is clear, however, that gender is a major issue in securing the involvement of family members. Specifically, practitioners often find that husbands resist participation in family treatment, and that merely getting them to come to therapy is a major issue (Weiss, 1978). Yet the father's attitude toward treatment is a central factor affecting the entire family's continued participation in the helping process (Shapiro and Budman, 1973). Thus, Whittaker (1973) viewed the "seduction" of the father in the first interview as essential.

In a study of men's participation in marital and family therapy, most men were found willing to participate even though their wives had initiated therapy (Guillebeaux et al., 1986). The study found that men most receptive to therapy were those with (1) fewer children, (2) prior experience in therapy, (3) nontraditional early childhood sex-role socialization, (4) marital problems perceived as serious, and (5) threat of divorce by wife.

Why are some men reluctant to participate in family treatment? First, consistent with the earlier discussion of patterns in problem attribution, men may assume that family problems, especially those involving children, are the responsibility of women (Doherty, 1981). In particular, when relationships between mother and child are enmeshed or overinvolved, or those between father and child are underdeveloped, fathers are likely to resist participation in family treatment (Shapiro and Budman, 1973).

Second, men may perceive as woman's domain not only the substance of therapy but also its processes of self disclosure and verbal exploration of feelings. As Rice explains, "the male spouse may feel as if he is entering . . . therapy in a 'one-down' position; not only is he likely to be 'brought' rather than to have 'sought' therapy but the arena and weapons are more comfortable for his partner" (1978, p. 64).

Third, and very much related, is the possibility that the husband perceives his wife's affinity with the worker to be stronger than his own. Indeed, if the wife relates more comfortably in therapy, by talking more freely about problems and feelings, therapists' counter-transference relationships with wives may be stronger and more positive than those with husbands (Rice, 1978). Of course, this situation itself may perpetuate the husbands' reluctance to participate.

In response to both the significance and challenge of involving men in family treatment, the practice literature provides a number of suggestions for workers. First, the participation of males should be assumed and presented as a matter of policy. Indeed, Doherty suggests that practitioners clearly and nondefensively refuse to work with families unless the husband or father also participates. In the absence of such clarity, "any fudging about wanting to have the whole family, or explaining that everyone in the family is part of the problem, tends to lower compliance" (1981, p. 24).

Once the male comes to a treatment session, workers are encouraged to ease his involvement in the helping process. Guillebeaux et al. (1986) suggest that therapists volunteer information about their credentials and qualifications and provide information about options for paying for treatment. Kaslow (1981) suggests that if child problems are central to treatment, the worker might reach out to the father in a way that establishes his sense of importance, builds his self esteem, and supports his commitment to the child. In general, the man's involvement should be kept as nonthreatening as possible and his views should be actively received (Kaslow, 1981).

Other suggestions include speaking to the male first (Haley, 1976), perhaps with a direct question such as "Mr. _____ , can you tell me what brings you and your family here today?" (Kaslow, 1981). Haley believes that any family member who seems withdrawn (more often the male) can be approached as if he or she *is* involved. Thus, he suggests that workers make use of the stereotype that the father is the household head, addressing him first and treating him as if he were in charge. This is assumed to facilitate his involvement and assumption of responsibility.

However, efforts must be taken not to perpetuate stereotypes and sexist patterns. Hare-Mustin (1979b) charges that therapists often communicate with family members in sexist patterns. In particular, women are frequently treated as inferiors and interrupted more than men (Hare-Mustin, 1979b). She urges workers to refrain from showing impatience when women talk, and encourages them to ask both husband and wife what they do.

Similarly, in the treatment of children's problems, Gurman and Klein (1980) suggest that using mothers as treatment agents rather than treating the child directly or treating both parents as treatment agents may inadvertently reinforce stereotypic assumptions that mothers are responsible for the child's problems and their resolution and, more pervasively, are responsible for overall family harmony.

Clearly, practitioners face a dilemma when they attempt to increase the involvement of family members but avoid sexist patterns while doing so. The best strategy is probably an egalitarian practice modality, in which attention is directed to both mother and father and the participation of both is expected, valued, and respected.

How does worker gender influence the involvement of family members in treatment? Are male or female practitioners better able to form therapeutic alliances? Some attention has been directed toward the comparative success of male and female workers at facilitating husband and wife involvement in treatment. Bell (1975), who observes that male workers often threaten the father and his role, believes that female workers can better enable fathers to engage quickly in treatment. However, in an extensive study of family treatment, male workers were found to be more successful than female workers in getting husbands, wives, and both husband and wife to participate in treatment (Beck and Jones, 1975). Women workers more often saw only one partner, usually the wife, and rarely saw husbands unless the wife was also seen. Husbands— who appeared to prefer a joint approach to family problems, one that also involved their wives—seemed more comfortable discussing marital and family problems with a male worker. The researchers speculated that men were less fearful that male workers would side with their wives in conflict issues. These patterns may reflect the operation of similarity and attraction principles in increasing the comfort of interpersonal relationships.

Choice of Treatment Approach

In what ways, if any, do gender or sex-role issues affect the choice of interventions in family treatment? The literature suggests that worker gender and sex roles along with family sex-role patterns have major implications for choice of intervention.

Worker gender and sex roles.   With respect to worker gender, various methods of family therapy require different patterns of worker behavior, which in turn reflect different sex roles. For example, traditional psychosocial therapies rely heavily on the helping relationship and call for worker expression of warmth and interest in the family. With such approaches, some female workers may quite comfortably call upon feminine behavior; moreover, they may use these behaviors to appeal especially to the interest of the husband or father in the family (Forrest, 1969). Such approaches, then, are very compatible with traditional female sex roles and may be very comfortable for some women practitioners. Of course, reliance on such sex roles may be uncomfortable—indeed, seem sexist—to some women practitioners.

In contrast, structural and strategic methods of family therapy require workers to have a highly flexible role, including the ability to challenge and confront family members' adherence to problematic rules and structures. This may be difficult for many women practitioners, especially those whose personal and professional behavior and roles are traditional (Libow et al., 1982). This difficulty may be accentuated when the family expects traditional sex-typed behavior from a woman practitioner, who, despite her professional status, is seen by them as first a woman.

Treatment approaches and family sex roles.   Methods of family therapy also may reflect and imply different patterns of sex roles in families. Accordingly, it may be important to consider a family's sex-role patterns and preferences when selecting an intervention. For example, Hare-Mustin sees Minuchin's interventions as modeling male executive functions for the family. "The worker forms alliances, typically with the father . . . and through competition, rule-setting, and direction, (demands) that the father resume control of the family and exert leadership as Minuchin leads and controls the session" (1978, p. 184). An unintended consequence of such an approach may be the accentuation or strengthening of traditional male-dominant sex roles in families.

Other methods may imply a strengthening of the woman's role in the family. For example, training in communication and problem solving may require and enable the wife or mother to increase her power in the family by acquiring skills usually exercised by the husband or father (Margolin et al., 1983).

The issue of sex roles also seems a complicated one for behavior therapy. According to Margolin et al. (1983), behavior therapy generally assumes or expects egalitarian family relationships. However, behavior therapists appear to take a nonpreferential stance toward couples' sex roles, to such an extent, in fact, that couples' conflicts and struggles with these issues may not be actively explored and addressed. Behavior therapists may presume that couples can, or should, automatically function in an equitable and egalitarian style, all the while failing to acknowledge or work on the conflicts created from this assumption (Margolin et al., 1983). These concerns lead some to suggest that behavioral approaches are more suited to families with already egalitarian styles than to those with traditional relationships (Weiss, 1978; Margolin et al., 1983).

At the same time, Libow et al. (1982) see the systems perspective and its associated interventions as applicable to all families, regardless of sex-role patterns. Scanzoni (1979b), however, does not advocate one treatment modality for all family situations, but advocates the choice of interventive approaches that maximize the well being, or "joint profit," of both marital partners in terms of sex-role problems and issues. That is, it is assumed that in order to benefit the family, interventions must be seen by both husband and wife as mutually beneficial.

In our perspective, treatment methods should be chosen on the basis of their relevance to issues that are significant to the family and its members. If a particular approach seems ill-suited for treating a family's problems or seems incompatible with their sex-role patterns, then an alternative approach should be explored.

GENDER AND TREATMENT OUTCOME

The bearing of gender on the outcome of family treatment remains one of the most important issues for workers. Among the questions practitioners might raise are: Do men and women differ in the extent to which they experience gain in family treatment? Are different outcomes valued and desired by men and women clients? Do male and female family therapists differ significantly in their effectiveness? Do sex roles of family members and practitioners affect family treatment outcome? Although these questions have not been adequately tested in studies of family treatment, some relevant findings are available.

Gender, Sex Roles, and Outcome Criteria

There are persuasive arguments that sex-role issues are involved in the very choice of outcome criteria. For example, therapists and couples often see agreement between spouses, or convergence of opinion on important issues, as an appropriate reflection of improvement or change. Yet, as Gurman and Klein point out, the use of such criteria "may perpetuate the assumption that convergence and conformity between spouses are a sine qua non of a happy marriage. This assumption is dangerous, because wives, heretofore, have been expected to do more converging and conforming" (1980, p. 175). Moreover, agreement or convergence per se offers little information; it may be the nature of the agreement, the consent of the spouses to agreement, and the direction of change reflected in the agreement that is significant. Of course, gender and sex roles may have implications for each of these issues.

Similarly, the stability of the relationship is sometimes used as an outcome criterion in family treatment. That is, treatment may be seen as successful when the family stays together or reunites. Again, such a simplistic approach is ill-advised and potentially complicated by sex-role issues. In particular, a focus on relationship stability or harmony may ignore the personal costs experienced by individuals who remain in the family (Klein, 1976). Of course, most often, it is the woman who experiences a balance of negative outcomes in marriage. Thus, marital status per se should not be used as an outcome criterion, and all criteria should be capable of reflecting the consequences of marital status for the individuals involved.

A quite different criterion for judging family outcomes is that of equity. Rachlin and Hansen suggest that equity can serve as a standard against which couples can assess whether to continue or dissolve a relationship. If either or both spouses believe that they are not treated fairly in their relationship, then whether their relationship can be viewed as healthy must be questioned (1985, p. 162). Yet equity appears to be a more salient influence on feelings of marital satisfaction for wives than for husbands (Rachlin and Hansen, 1985), suggesting that wives are more bothered by perceived inequity than are husbands.

General outcome indicators, such as "family functioning," are also problematic. They might fail not only to capture the specifics of a particular family's issues, but also to identify areas in which sex roles are important. More specific criteria incorporating such divergent areas as nurturance, companionship, socialization, and internal harmony, would be more valuable (Klein, 1976). In other words, it is more valuable to assess families in these terms than it is to know about their general functioning. Moreover, specific criteria provide information about the ways in which role responsibilities are allocated and performed.

As in individual and group treatment, normative behaviors in society at large may be informative when posing desired outcomes, but should not in themselves be used as outcome criteria. Again, sex-role issues are apparent. Consider, for example, the extent to which societal norms reinforce stereotypical styles of behavior such as feminine passivity and nonassertion, and masculine suppression of emotions. Families whose members behave, after treatment, in ways that approximate societal norms, need not necessarily be considered improved. Similarly, family therapists should not, in general, evaluate men in terms of their per-formance of occupation roles and women in terms of performance of housewife and parenting functions (Klein, 1976). Conversely, therapists should not automatically assume for all couples the desirability of egalitarian marital roles. Many traditional outcome indicators reflect male emphases. In particular, sexual behavior is often evaluated in terms of performance, such as frequency of intercourse and occurrence of orgasm. Less attention may be directed to intimacy and interpersonal communication, issues that may be more salient to women's sexual concerns (Klein, 1976).

In summary, traditional outcome criteria in family treatment are often problematic in terms of gender and sex-role issues. Practitioners should be sensitive to the extent to which the concerns of both male and female family members are reflected in the outcomes desired and in the criteria by which they are measured. Finally, we again would caution practitioners to formulate desired outcomes in terms corresponding to family preference.

Gender and Client Perceptions of Improvement

Do husbands and wives in family treatment perceive improvement similarly? Do they, in fact, experience improvement similarly? Given the earlier noted tendency for wives to articulate more problems at the outset of family treatment, gender differences in perception of improvement might not be surprising.

Gurman and Klein (1980) believe that women often are satisfied with, or at least settle for, only intermediate levels of change in marital therapy. That is, they often settle for changes in specific behaviors without pursuing more pervasive changes in marital behavioral patterns and sex-role attitudes.

One study focused on the relationship between gender and improvement in family treatment. Beck and Jones (1975) found that wives experienced improvement significantly more often than did husbands. Outcome scores were significantly higher for female than for male clients, regardless of worker gender. In the view of the researchers, wives often have more at stake than do husbands in the solution of marital and family problems. That is, the socioeconomic losses of marital dissolution are greater for women than for men. As a result, wives may be more highly motivated to make good use of treatment.

Worker Gender and Outcome

The bearing of worker gender on improvement in family treatment, though a significant question, has not been widely studied. In one extensive study of family treatment, male workers were found to have an advantage over female workers. Beck and Jones (1975) report that male workers were not only better able than female workers to facilitate couples' involvement in marital therapy, but also to produce better outcomes in terms of husband change. Thus, worker gender was very influential when husbands were significantly involved in treatment. However, worker gender seemed not to be a significant influence on outcome when the primary client in the family was a female.

Another study suggests that worker sex roles may also influence outcome. Epstein and Jayne (1981) report that couples whose workers were traditionally oriented males experienced fewer gains than did couples whose workers were traditional females, nontraditional females, and nontraditional males.

Factors Affecting Outcome
in Family Treatment

In what other ways may gender-related factors affect outcome in marital or family treatment? Four other factors have been identified in the literature. First, and of no surprise, whether both partners or only one participate in treatment seems to be important. Outcome studies indicate improvement is greater when both partners are seen in treatment than when only one partner is seen (Beck and Jones, 1973; Gurman and Kniskern, 1978).

A second factor found to influence outcome was wife commitment to marriage. Beach and Broderick (1983) report that wife commitment to marriage accounted for a significant amount of variance in marital satisfaction before therapy, marital satisfaction after therapy, and gains experienced in therapy. Interestingly, husband commitment was not a significant factor in satisfaction or improvement.

Third, the sex-role orientations and behaviors of couples seem to influence their eventual marital satisfaction and treatment outcome. Femininity—a construct that includes socialization and emotional sensitivity—was reported by Burger and Jacobson (1979) to predict couples' satisfaction with their relationship and their problem-solving abilities. Similarly, Baucom and Aiken (1984) report that wife level of femininity prior to treatment was significantly associated with increases in marital satisfaction for both husband and wife at the end of treatment. This may indicate that the quality of emotional expression and the wife's sense of "togetherness" in marriage strongly influenced the couple's response to treatment. It is interesting that, once again, the wife's sentiments but not the husband's are influential. Masculinity in both husband and wife, which generally reflects instrumental, problem-solving skills, was found significantly related to stability of the relationship six months after treatment (Baucom and Aiken, 1984).

Finally, the relationships among treatment modality, gender, and outcome in family treatment are of interest. Whether husbands and wives, fathers and mothers, respond differently to various treatment modalities is an issue of major importance to family practitioners. Baucom and Aiken (1984) report that after 10 weeks of behavioral marital therapy, significant but small changes in both husbands' and wives' masculinity scores (problem-solving abilities) were evident. Thus, the responses of both sexes to this modality are similar. This important question warrants further attention in family treatment research.

CONCLUSION

This chapter demonstrates the importance of gender in family treatment. Gender continues to influence, if not determine, family roles. Men are expected—by society and many family practitioners—to be more powerful than women and to be the primary breadwinners. Women, on the other hand, are seen as responsible for childcare and household tasks, as well as the emotional well being of children and the family unit itself. Evidence of such expectations is reflected in practitioners' assumptions about healthy families as well as their treatment behaviors, such as assessment. The woman is the central figure in nearly all forms of family treatment, regardless of presenting problem.

The gender and sex roles of family members are likely to influence the problems they experience and present as agendas for treatment. Women tend to cite more family problems than men and are more likely than men to be dissatisfied with their marriages. Yet women seem more willing to seek family treatment, and practitioners cite fewer problems engaging them in family treatment.

Gender is a clear issue for family practitioners, as well as for clients. As with individual and group treatment, men and women therapists are perceived differently by the families with whom they work. Women are seen as supportive and verbal, while men are seen as competent and "in charge" but not necessarily supportive. Family treatment presents the potential problem of gender-based alliances between the worker and the same-sex spouse. In response to this, male-female co-therapy teams are often advocated; however, co-therapy teams face many problems, some of which are related to societal sex roles. To date, research has not established the merits or effectiveness of co-therapy.

Interventions may be differentially appropriate for families, depending on their sex roles. With respect to treatment effectiveness, very little evidence is available. One study reports that male family practitioners are more effective than females, while another study indicates that they are less effective. Outcome in family treatment does seem to be enhanced by the participation of both spouses, by the wife's commitment to marriage, and by the wife's level of emotional expressiveness. In spite of the clear relevance of gender to family treatment, this topic has been the focus of fewer studies than have individual and group treatment.

9

Gender
and Group Treatment

The influence of gender on group processes and outcomes had received insufficient attention in either the experimental or practice literatures until the 1970s (Cartwright and Zander, 1968; Glasser, Sarri, and Vinter, 1974). Dion (1985) has argued that the omission of gender as a variable of study in small group research can be attributed to the field's focus on situational variables (factors that could be manipulated, such as group size). In addition, men were disproportionately represented as subjects and experimenters in the field.

Gender, as it impacts dynamics, now receives increasing attention by both practitioners and researchers. This is evidenced by recent updates of older group texts that have included content or sections on the influence of gender (Shaw, 1983; Sundel et al., 1985). Moreover, it is now possible to find works that address themselves entirely to gender and group issues (Reed and Garvin, 1983; Dion, 1985). Hence, with the wealth of gender-related information now available in this area, it is clearly within the grasp of practitioners to improve upon the gender-related aspects of their group work services.

GROUP COMPOSITION

Salience to the Client

As is true of most demographic factors, gender is more important to some individuals than to others. This fact has a potentially strong bearing on how clients will respond to a group's gender composition. Consequently, we must use caution in attempting to generalize answers to such questions as, Which gender compositions do males and females prefer? Despite our inability to answer this question unequivocally, there is a great deal of research and practice wisdom to guide group workers in their attempts to compose the best gender balances.

Two of the most frequently cited research studies on the effects of gender composition on small groups are by Aries (1976) and Carlock and Martin (1977). The Aries study was a small group experiment conducted with college students who met for five 1½ hour sessions under the guise of getting to know each other. The Carlock and Martin study was conducted with a noncollege population of men and women who volunteered to participate in intensive weekend group sessions designed to address sex-role issues. Both studies, which varied the gender composition of the groups (e.g., all-male, all-female, and mixed), reported that members in the mixed gender groups found their groups to be more exciting. Additionally, the Carlock and Martin study reported that although women expressed greater satisfaction with the mixed gender group, they actually experienced greater positive outcomes within the all-female groups, a phenomenon that will be addressed later in the discussion on outcomes.

Participants' feelings about group compositions may be influenced by other factors also. For example, Kanter (1977) hypothesized that skewed gender groups (i.e., groups composed predominantly of either males or females) would exhibit greater gender bias than would sexually balanced groups. Taylor and her colleagues (1978) found evidence that supports Kanter's conceptualizations. In a series of small group experiments that employed college subjects, they found that the smaller the sex subgroup, whether male or female, the more members belonging to that subgroup were evaluated as less warm and pleasant. These findings and those of others (Tajfel et al., 1971; Tajfel and Billig, 1974; Ickes, 1984) argue for the creation of groups that contain equal numbers of males and females, as equal gender balances appear to reduce sexual stereotyping. Another study by Marshall and Heshin (1975) attempted to look simultaneously at gender composition, group density, size, and cohesiveness. The study was conducted with college students and resulted in a number of important observations. Group size, for example, was found to vary in its importance for males and females. In mixed groups, males, more so than females, appeared to like the members more in small groups (4 persons) than in large groups (16 persons). The reverse was found for females. That is, females liked the other group members in a mixed group more when the group was larger rather than smaller in size. However, if the group was of the same sex, females preferred the small group. The authors report that male preferences, in contrast to those of females, did not vary significantly as a function of the groups' gender composition.

Also, whether the group was crowded or not crowded (i.e., 4 square feet/person or 18 square feet/person) was found to influence group member attraction. For example, when meeting in mixed-gender groups, both males and females tended to like the other members more when meeting in a crowded group. However, male and female reactions to same-sex group compositions differed. Women liked the other female group members more in the uncrowded groups, while men liked the other men more in the crowded situation. Marshall and Heslin (1975) conclude that males appeared always to prefer mixed-gender groups, and that females preferred mixed-gender groups if they were large, but otherwise preferred small all-female groups. These observations are, however, in contrast to some earlier findings (Freedman et al., 1972; Ross et al., 1973), which have found females to respond more favorably to crowded group conditions than did men. Clearly the area of group density research appears to need further study.

In sum, the gender composition of a group does appear to influence members' attraction to that group. Males and females appear to prefer different sizes of groups depending on whether they are mixed- or single-gender groups. In general it seems that members of both sexes view the other sex more favorably in situations where the gender balances are equitable.

Salience to the Leader

At present, there appears to be a growing acknowledgment on the part of many group practitioners that same-sex groups may offer certain advantages over mixed-sex groups. There has been a particularly strong advocacy for the composition of all-women's groups (Wyckhoff, 1971; Meador, Solomon, and Bowen, 1972; Whiteley, 1973; Joyce and Ha-zelton, 1982; Adolph, 1983; Nayman, 1983). There has also been some advocacy on the behalf of group leaders for increased use of all-male compositions; however, their advocates are noticeably fewer and more recent (Heppner, 1981; Washington, 1982; Stein, 1983).

It is not surprising to find some female group leaders advocating all-female groups, because such groups have been found advantageous for women (Aries, 1976; Carlock and Martin, 1977). That is, they believe female groups afford women greater opportunity to behave in less sex-role stereotyped ways (Halas, 1973; Gottlieb et al., 1983). It is also suggested that all-female groups encourage women to work through gender-related conflicts, encourage greater trust between themselves and other women, and provide support for learning new, more effective behaviors (Joyce and Hazelton, 1982; Sullivan, 1983). In contrast, when in mixed groups, a masculine model tends to prevail; women are reluctant to discuss their feelings about such factors as personal strengths, power, and independence (Halas, 1973; Sullivan, 1983).

Similarly, some leaders advocate all-male groups for similar reasons.

> The men's group provides an alternative process for men to explore so-called masculine appropriate behaviors and roles within a supportive frame-work; to increase their understanding and awareness; and with the influence of peer pressure and support, to evaluate and change old patterns of behavior (Washington, 1982, p. 133; see also Kaufman and Timmers, 1983).

A study by Greene et al. (1980) suggests that client gender is a salient factor influencing workers' assignment of clients to groups. Indeed, Greene et al. (1980) hypothesized that referral to group may be a method whereby practitioners could distance themselves from "least preferred" clients. This hypothesis was based on the conceptualizations of Sarztsky (1977), who posited that referring individuals to group was a way in which practitioners could distance themselves from clients who were anxiety arousing for them or in other ways undesirable. Greene et al. (1980) utilized the case records of 1,920 clients who received either individual or group therapy at a California school of medicine. The findings from their research suggest the following: A greater proportion of female clients were referred to groups than were male clients, and a client was somewhat more likely to be referred to a group by a practitioner of the same sex. Hence, it appears that some clients are more inclined to be "pushed" into group therapy than others. It is also clear that this "push" is apparently influenced by both the gender of the client and that of the therapist.

Salience of the Group Purpose

By far the most common reason offered for a specific group composition is the group's stated purpose. The gender balance of a group may be manipulated because it is believed that a particular gender balance will best facilitate the accomplishment of the group's purpose. There appear to be two broad gender-related group purposes:

1. To facilitate gender or sexual identity of the group members. This first type of group is frequently referred to as a consciousness-raising group (C-R), and generally has a same-sex composition
2. To enhance group members' understanding of, or comfort with, various sex-role dynamics. This second type of group, which deals with gender-oriented topics, generally has a mixed-gender composition (Adolph, 1983; Stein, 1983)

It is suggested that groups which try to help members understand the implications of their own gender should be composed of same-sex members (Carlock and Martin, 1977; Kravetz and Sargent, 1977; Heppner, 1981; Washington, 1982). With respect to all-female group composition, Carlock and Martin suggest that this would be desirable if the leader wishes to help women concentrate on interpersonal issues such as self acceptance or realization of personal power and choice in identification of fears and avoidances. Perhaps the principal underlying assumption for composing groups containing only females is that the absence of men will afford women greater opportunity for disclosure about themselves as women. That is, they will be better able to discuss their vulnerabilities, and at the same time, practice new, less stereotyped role behaviors, often ones involving power and decision making—typically "masculine behaviors."

In some respects, the purposes for composing all-male groups are similar to those for composing all-female groups. For example, men are supposed to behave in "masculine styles," however, an all-male group can provide men with the opportunity to momentarily abandon the macho image. That is, in the absence of women there may be less social pressure to live up to a stereotype of masculine behavior (Washington, 1982). The all-male group may also allow men the opportunity to share their fears and insecurities about such topics as sexual performance (Washington, 1979) and interpersonal relationships (Lewis, 1978). In this sense, all-male groups enable men to get away from expected masculine behaviors. As such, they can practice being "more social emotional" (e.g., less domineering and competitive), and perhaps engage in "feminine behaviors" (e.g., expressing emotion and concern for others). In sum, one of the major advantages of the homogeneous gender group composition is that for both males and females it reduces the often present pressure to behave in gender appropriate ways. Same-gender groups reduce expectations in men and women to play their traditional masculine or feminine roles and afford them the opportunity to try out new ways of behaving that are less restrictive and perhaps less dysfunctional.

Again, depending on the group purpose, there are also some advantages for composing mixed-gender groups. It has been suggested

226 Gender and Group Treatment

that if the group's purpose is to provide members with a focus of the dynamics of sex roles as they manifest themselves in male-female relationships, then the gender composition of the group should be mixed (Carlock and Martin, 1977). However, it is also advocated that such groups first be broken up into same-sex groups so that group members might feel free to make group disclosures. Later these groups could be integrated to afford members an opportunity to practice behaviors and be integrated into mixed-sex groups. This first homogeneous then heterogeneous approach appears to have considerable utility, especially for individuals attempting to learn new ways of behaving with members of the opposite sex.

GROUP DYNAMICS

Intimacy, Numbers, and Balance

The effects of gender on group dynamics have typically received little attention (Cartwright and Zander, 1968; Shaw, 1983). However, there is now considerable research and writing that addresses gender dynamics of groups (Dion, 1985; Reed and Garvin, 1983). In this section we shall review the most salient aspects of this body of knowledge in an effort to provide practitioners with a greater understanding of their groups as affected by gender.

There is a significant body of evidence which suggests that the dynamics of a group are affected by both the gender and numerical composition of the group (Wolman and Frank, 1975; Frank and Katcher, 1977; Kanter, 1977; Patterson and Schaeffer, 1977; Berman, O'Nan, and Floyd, 1981). Among the foremost proponents of the importance of group demographics is Kanter (1977). Perhaps more than any other theorist, she has focused on the importance of gender balance and its potential impact on group interaction. Her "structural numerical-proportions model" argues that the relative proportion of males and females in a group influences the quality of the group experience for the members. It is the central tenet of the structural numerical-proportions model that when females are placed in lopsided male-female gender configurations (i.e., skewed groups that largely outnumber females), the interactions in these groups tend to be less positive for the females.

Specifically, Kanter (1977) contends that skewed groups result in distorted perceptions of the women in them. It is believed that this distortion results from the occurrence of three phenomena: increased visibility (tokens receive disproportionate attention); polarization (differences between men and women are exaggerated); and assimilation (in this case, gender stereotypes about women). Kanter (1977) argues that the greater visibility results in more performance pressures; the polarization effect causes the majority-gender members (men in this case) to heighten group boundaries and engage in behaviors suggestive of "them and us"; and assimilation results in the minority-gender group person being locked into role or behavior descriptions most often ascribed to that gender group. As an intervention against the creation of such scenarios, Kanter argues that proportional representation of both sexes is preferable in small groups.

Hence, in short, the structural numerical-proportions model tends to be a better descriptor of the effects of group gender configurations on females than it is for males. Perhaps because of the statuses associated with being a male or female, mere numbers do not explain all of what is believed to occur under various gender configurations. For example, when a man is outnumbered in a primarily female group, he is likely to be deferred to and respected. However, when a woman is the minority in a similarly male-dominated group, the woman is likely to be isolated and treated as being unimportant. This is an important difference, suggesting that the consequences of an unbalanced gender composition are different for males and females. For example, a 5-to-1 male-to-female group composition is dynamically different from a 5-to-1 female-to-male group. The men in either group composition may be responded to favorably; the consequences for females are less certain.

Findings from empirical studies support Kanter's conceptualizations (Wolman and Frank, 1975; Frank and Katcher, 1977; Berman, O'Nan, and Floyd, 1981). For example, in the small group experiments conducted by Wolman and Frank (1975), lone women in groups composed of helping professionals (e.g., social workers, psychologists, nurses) consistently became deviants, isolates, and fell to low-status membership within the group. The authors state that even though their experimental groups placed high value on the expression of feelings and awareness of group processes, they failed to recognize and constructively address the "solo woman" group dynamics.

Not all research has found support for Kanter's thesis, however. South et al. (1982) found evidence to the contrary. They observed in their study of a federal bureaucracy that as the number of females increased, favorableness of interactions toward them decreased. It is possible that these findings differ with some others due to the differences in situations being assessed (i.e., small groups versus a large bureaucratic setting). Clearly, more research is needed to clarify the discrepancies between these findings.

Not only do the relative numbers of males and females in a group influence how each perceives the other; this ratio also appears to influence how males and females perceive themselves. Ruble and Higgins (1976) report research findings conducted with college students that attempted to determine the effects of gender group compositions on self descriptions. The authors note that gender composition of the group significantly influenced how group members described themselves following the group manipulations. The study employed all-male, all-female, and mixed groups. However, the mixed groups contained only one male or female in an otherwise all-male or female group. Males and females who were in the minority ("solo status") were observed to employ traits typically associated with the opposite sex in describing themselves following the group manipulation. The authors posit that being in a group where everyone else is of the opposite sex may heighten gender awareness and, hence, sensitize that individual to the others' sexual perspective. Ruble and Higgins (1976) also point out the potential value of a dual-gender group in changing the attitudes and perspectives of both sexes.

Finally, it is not surprising to find that the presence of males and females in a group influences the qualitative nature of that group. Groups with both male and female members are observed to be more intimate and expressive in nature than are those groups composed of males alone (Aries, 1976; Piliavin and Martin, 1978). Females, it has been noted, are more inclined to discuss expressive issues when in all-female groups and less inclined to do so in mixed-gender groups. Also, it has been observed that participants sit closer together in mixed-gender groups than in all-male groups (Patterson and Schaeffer, 1977). These findings suggest an unfortunate paradox for those group leaders who wish to lead heterogeneous gender groups: If they include women in a men's group, the quality of expressive conversation goes up, but for those women included in such groups, the expressive conversation for them (relative to that of all-female groups) goes down. Therefore, at least with respect to expressive functions, mixed-gender groups benefit men, while all-female groups are most beneficial to women. Clearly, leaders need to be sensitive to this potentially negative compositional effect on females, and attempt to engage in strategies to sustain the expressive behaviors of both females and males.

Cooperation and Competition

Gender has been consistently noted to affect the dynamics of small groups by influencing the extent to which groups are cooperative or competitive (Aries, 1976; Meeker and Hornung, 1976; McCarrick, Manderscheid, and Silbergeld, 1981). This factor has considerable importance for group practitioners because it dictates the extent to which their skills as leaders are needed to enhance an atmosphere of good will. Some studies have employed subjects in actual treatment or quasi-treatment situations (Carlock and Martin, 1977; McCarrick, Manderscheid, and Silbergeld, 1981). The majority of those who have researched gender effects on cooperation versus competition have concluded that, in general, males are more competitive in groups than are females and that males tend to be more competitive in all-male groups than in mixed-gender groups (Aries, 1976, 1977; Meeker and Weitzer-O'Neill, 1977).

McCarrick, Manderscheid, and Silbergeld (1981) conducted a study with actual clients: clergymen and their wives. The researchers were attempting to inspect the gender differences in competition and dominance during the course of group treatment. The study recorded member interactions over a period of two years. Findings from this study indicate that there is more indiscriminate competition between males than between females. Interestingly, it appeared that females more readily competed with males than males with females. The authors conjecture that because males already assume themselves to be dominant, perhaps they do not need to compete with females. One notable exception was verbal domination, i.e., verbal interruptions. The study suggests that men attempt to verbally dominate each other as well as females. Women, in contrast, respond to each other more symmetrically; that is, they attempted neither to dominate nor be dominated verbally. It was also noted, however, that females resisted being verbally dominated and tended to interrupt back. Females, it was observed, were more submissive to their husbands in this respect than to other males in the group. The authors conclude that attempted dominance, when it does occur, is more likely to occur between two people in an unequal contested relationship. This study, one of the few addressing group couples counseling, may assist practitioner understanding of marital influences on male-female group interactions.

Some authors have offered various rationales for what appear to be differences in competitiveness among males and females in groups. Meeker and Weitzel-O'Neill (1977) argue that men are more competitive and that women are more cooperative because society expects them to be so. Bond and Vinacke (1961) concluded from an experimental study of coalition formation that males and females differ in their basic strategies toward working with others. Their study was conducted with groups of three members—either two males and one female, or two females and one male—all of them introductory psychiatry students.

It was found that males engaged in the group task in a competitive fashion with a strong motivation to win, whereas females appeared to be more concerned with social and ethical considerations. The male style of behavior was referred to as the "exploitative" style and the female style became known as the "accommodative" style. Results from the experiment indicate that the female strategy arrived at more favorable outcomes (e.g., higher rewards) than did the male strategy. Evidence further indicates that the male strategy is self-defeating when it encounters the female strategy. For example, when men were in the majority they tended to compete against each other and invariably the female benefited. When the females were in the majority, the competitive behavior on the part of the male resulted in the two females forming an alliance against this "unduly" competitive group member.

On balance, it would appear that men, whether in actual treatment or experimental situations, tend to behave less cooperatively and more competitively in groups than do females. Moreover, men have a greater variety of ways to express competition than have women—e.g., addressing more comments to the entire group, interrupting others, establishing stricter group hierarchies (Aries, 1977). This often destructive behavioral style on the part of men is moderated by the presence of women; however, it warrants the continual vigilance and sensitivity of group leaders.

Failure to cooperate can be viewed in many respects as failing to do what is expected; that is, failing to conform to group member or leader expectations. Researchers have asked: Do males and females differ in the extent to which they go along with decisions made by the group? In addition, does the gender composition of the group influence the extent to which individuals are likely to conform? In general, the literature in this area suggests that women are more conforming in groups than are men (Maccoby and Jacklin, 1974; Eagly, 1978). It has been posited that because men are more task-oriented and females less so, and because females are more concerned with social emotional concerns of the group, they comply with the wishes of the group, albeit more for the sake of group harmony than out of any personal weakness (Hare, 1962; Dion, 1979; Zander, 1979). There is a basic difference in group orientation between males and females: For males group outcome is most important, while for females the group process is of prime importance (Eagly, 1978; Piliavin and Martin, 1978; Dion, 1979). It has been suggested by Eagly et al. (1981) that it is not that females are conforming, but rather that males are not conforming.

There is also evidence to suggest an association between group conformity and member willingness to take risks. Bauer and Turner (1974) conducted a study that inspected the influence of gender composition on conformity and risk taking. Groups of college students were assigned to either gender homogeneous or heterogeneous four-person groups. Males were found to take more risks in groups than females. However, the gender composition of the group was an important factor to consider in explaining the outcomes. Males in groups containing one female shifted toward greater risk, but males in groups containing three females shifted toward greater caution. Females in all-female groups become slightly more inclined to risk with the introduction of one male and markedly so with the introduction of three males. In summary, it appears that males are greater risk takers in small groups; however, risk taking of group members appears to shift in the direction of the numerically dominant gender group.

Communication, Interaction, and Status

It is now commonly believed by many group practitioners that the ways in which males and females communicate and interact in small groups is substantially a function of status differences attributed to the sexes. This perspective has been supported by considerable research (Berger, Cohen, and Zelditch, 1972; Meeker and Weitzel-O'Neill, 1977; Thune, Manderscheid, and Silbergeld, 1980; Ridgeway, 1982). Status expectation theory argues that differences in behavior between males and females are a function of their ascribed statuses. The theory contends that gender is assigned a social status much like ethnicity or age, and that male gender is accorded a higher social status than female gender. Because gender expectations are believed to be universally known, even if not accepted, being male or female has been referred to as a *diffuse status characteristic* (Lockheed, 1977). This essentially means that we bring the status and accompanying role expectations of our gender into all our social interactions. Hence, group interactions between males and females are, according to status expectation theory, interactions between persons of unequal social statuses.

Meeker and Weitzel-O'Neill (1977) have provided a useful outline for understanding the status expectation model. They suggest that group members ascribed higher performance expectations will receive and take more opportunities to make task contributions, have more influence, and receive more expressions of agreement and approval than those for whom there are lower performance expectations. It is also posited that in the absence of information to the contrary, group members assign performance expectations to self and others on the basis of external status characteristics. As a function of the ascription of unequal status to males and females, women interacting with men can be viewed as having an "interaction disability" (Cohen and Roper, 1972). Moreover, when women do not conform to diffuse status expectations—that is, engaging in behaviors "expected of men"—they may be viewed as attempting to elevate their status, an activity referred to as *competitive status enhancement.*

Despite what appears to be a potentially problematic scenario for male-female small group interactions, there is evidence to suggest that women can act to overcome the effects of this gender-related "interaction disability." For example, Ridgeway (1982) conducted four-person group experiments in which three persons were subjects and one was a confederate. The groups contained either three males and one female or three females and one male. Ridgeway observed that if the confederate female was perceived to be group-oriented, rather than self-oriented, she was able to exert substantial influence in the group. It should be noted, however, that no such apparent concern for the group was required of male group members for them to exert influence over the group. The author concludes that women can overcome interaction disabilities they face in mixed-gender groups by combining reasonably competent task contributions with the explicit communication of group-oriented motivation. Ridgeway also suggests that the "interaction disability" sometimes experienced by females might be reduced substantially by modifying or counterbalancing the expectations of group members prior to the group's initial meeting. Such efforts might include prestigious introductions of female leaders or other statements of their prior successes as leaders.

In view of the above information, it is not surprising to find yet another study which suggests that men are more assertive in groups than women, and that women are less assertive in groups that contain men. However, Kimble, Yoshikawa, and Zehr (1981) not only attempted to determine if males and females differ in their level of assertiveness within groups, but also if the differences were influenced by the sex composition and structure of the group discussions. The subjects in their study were college students. Four-person groups, all-male, all-female, or gender-balanced, were established. Several differences were observed: Women who spoke last in mixed groups were less verbally assertive than women who spoke first. Moreover, women were observed to speak louder when speaking with other women than with men. Also, group structure was found to have effects on communication within the groups for both sexes. Groups with more structure, for example, were found to elevate the volume of speaking of both males and females. The findings from this study are potentially helpful in that they provide group leaders with insight as to the probable development of group leadership, as indicated by the speaking order of the members. Moreover, it seems that by providing greater group structure they may assist all group members to speak more assertively in mixed-gender groups.

Before leaving this general topic, it should be mentioned that gender status effects may be becoming less problematic. In a recent study, Aries (1982) found that experimental groups of males and females are continuing to behave in gender stereotypic ways; however, in mixed-gender groups, females were found to verbally dominate. In short, men did not exert a suppressant effect on female usual behavior. Results from this study strongly support the notion that female gender has become less a disadvantage for females when interacting with men.

LEADERSHIP

One of the most researched areas of gender and group functioning is leadership. Indeed, much of what has been written recently on gender and group dynamics attempts to assess differences in male-female leadership. It has been stated that the problem with all-female groups is that no one wants to lead and the problem with all-male groups is that everyone wants to lead (Meeker and Weitzel-O'Neill, 1977). While this perception is an oversimplification and stereotype of male and female group leadership, it does capture some of the dynamics operative in both groups. In this section we shall inspect topic areas of considerable concern to group practitioners, with hopes of assisting them to better understand the impact of gender on group leadership.

Style and Status

Considerable attention is given to studying and researching factors influencing the leadership of small groups. *Style of leadership* refers to such aspects as active or passive, formal or informal, authoritative or laissez faire, etc. (Cartwright and Zander, 1968). Not surprisingly, group leadership as exhibited by males and females is receiving increased attention. Lockheed and Hall (1976) offer three principal generalizations derived from the research on gender and leadership: Men are more active than women (that is, men tend to initiate more verbal acts than do women); men are more influential than women (that is, the opinions of men carry more weight with the other group members than those of females); and men initiate a higher proportion of their acts in task-oriented categories while women initiate a higher proportion of their acts in social emotional categories. Previously, differences in male-female group leadership have been attributed to gender socialization. For example, Megargee (1969) conducted a very important study in the late sixties which employed sex-role differentiation theory. This laboratory study paired groups of males and females who varied in the attribute of personal dominance. It was observed that when confronted with the need for one of the pair to take a leadership position, the high-dominance person did so 90 percent of the time. However, when a high-dominance female was paired with a low-dominance male, the low-dominance male most often took the position of leadership. The author suggested that the pairing of a high-dominance female with a low-dominance male places the pair in a role conflict, as men are more frequently ascribed leadership roles in society, while females are more frequently ascribed social emotional roles. While this explanation is consistent with sex-role socialization theory, it is also possible that what was in conflict was the roles ascribed to individuals as a function of their gender statuses. Indeed, it is now more generally believed that gender stylistic differences are a function of status expectation differences that exist between males and females more so than differences resulting from gender socialization. (Lockheed, 1977; Meeker and Weitzel-O'Neill, 1977; Fennell et al., 1978). In short, findings from this study suggest that females because of their lower ascribed gender status are "not supposed" to lead males even if they are inclined to do so. The authors note that the leadership of the low-dominance male was not due to his assertiveness, but rather to the reluctance of the high-dominance female to exert leadership over her male partner.

In a conceptually related study, Fenelon and Megargee (1971) also observed that ascribed social status may preempt personal propensities. For example, Fenelon and Megargee reported finding that high-dominance white females failed to take leadership over low-dominance black females. This finding, which appears to be at odds with our expectations based on the salience of personality alone, does, upon closer inspection, appear to be consistent with status expectation theory and with the research findings of others (Brower et al., 1987). Both Brower et al. (1987) and Adams (1980) conducted experiments in which black females were found to exhibit greater levels of assertiveness than their white female counterparts. Their findings are consistent with a commonly-held belief that black females are more competent and "in control" of themselves and others than their white female counterparts (Wallace, 1980; Scanzoni, 1979a). Apparently, the perception of black female competence has its legacy in slavery (Wallace, 1980). In any event, the perception has resulted in black females being ascribed a gender status second only to that of white males.

We know little about the boundaries of this status effect as it pertains to black females. However, it is clear that despite possessing what is referred to as a double whammy (black and female), black females are the recipients of some type of "idiosyncratic" status effect. This little-studied dynamic lowers our ability to predict group member interactions. It should, however, make leading and observing groups more interesting.

There is little evidence which indicates that leadership style differs as a function of gender alone (Eagly, 1970; Schneier, 1978). However, there is some evidence to suggest that gender compositions may influence leadership styles (Chapman, 1975). In two studies of cross-gender leadership, it was found that as the percentage of opposite-sex group members increased, the leader's style appeared to take on more of the characteristics associated with that gender group (Chapman, 1975; Offerman, 1984). For example, females leading a group composed predominantly of males were observed to behave in a more "task-oriented" fashion. Similarly, male leaders with predominantly female groups were reported to behave in a more "social emotional" fashion. Hence it appears that style of group leadership is at least influenced by the gender of those in the group, and that leaders may take on attributes ascribed to the opposite sex if that gender comprises the majority of the group.

There is also evidence to suggest that group members may react differently to similar styles of male and female leadership. For example, Bradley (1980) found female leaders in experimental all-male groups to exert considerable group influence if they were able to demonstrate sufficient expertise. This was in contrast to females who demonstrated low levels of competence (Bradley, 1980). In addition to being influential, those females demonstrating expertise were also treated with greater respect than less competently performing females. Low-competence females were treated with hostility. In contrast, males were treated in a positive fashion regardless of their level of expressed competence. Thus, it appears from the evidence of this study that level of competence exhibited in a group context may have greater implications for females than males. In short, it appears that groups of men may tolerate incompetence in men, but not in women.

Another noteworthy study also attempted to assess the effects of style on gender (Wright, 1976). Students in this study participated in ten-person groups for four 1½ hour sessions. Leaders of the groups were required to vary their leadership style. Some behaved in a formal (nonreciprocating) style in which they maintained impersonal and affectless behavior. In contrast, others were required to behave in what was referred to as an informal (reciprocating) style, where the leaders laughed and expressed themselves emotionally.

Style of leadership appears to have influenced female group members more so than male group members. An informal leader style resulted in female group members speaking less than males, irrespective of the group leader's gender. However, when the leadership was informal and female, females rated their fellow group members more positively. When the leadership was formal and female, female group members perceived their fellow members negatively. Moreover, females talked more in formal leadership situations, but appeared to like the other members less in these formal situations.

Although apparently less influenced by leadership style, males were also affected. They too perceived their fellow group members less positively when the leader's style was formal. However, men appeared to talk more with an informal leadership style. In addition, both male and female members felt most positively toward other group members when led by informal styles of leadership.

Finally, both male and female members were found to be more inclined to talk under male leadership than under female leadership. Noteworthy, and somewhat at odds with the drift of most of the literature in this area, both males and females reported that they perceived female leaders as being stronger leaders than males. The authors suggest that it is possible that female leadership was perceived to be "less in character and hence appeared more forceful."

Personality

Carl Jung (1934) argued that with respect to the treatment process, the personality and attitude of the therapist are more important than therapeutic technique. Hence, it might be asked if certain personality types are more suitable for group leadership than others. Are there certain personality types that are most effective for leading heterogeneous or homogeneous gender group compositions? Answers to these questions have the potential to facilitate the matching of group leaders with the proper groups and gender compositions.

It has also been asserted that the personality of the therapist does not operate in a vacuum, but rather interacts with that of the client's. Parloff, Waskow, and Wolfe suggest that the interaction of these personalities affects the way in which treatment is administered as well as the receptivity of the client to treatment (1978, p. 265). Notably, some researchers have attempted to inspect these dynamics. However, despite the therapeutic community's general consensus with the assertions of Jung and others that personality and attitude of the group leader and members are crucial to the treatment process and outcome, there exists scant evidence to support these assertions (Bednar and Kaul, 1978). However, let us review what little is known about this topic. Spillman et al. (1981) attempted to assess the personality dimensions of masculinity, femininity, and androgyny on group leadership. They employed the Bem Sex Role Inventory for measuring leader personality dimensions. The participants were 38 male and 28 female undergraduate students. As part of the experiment they participated in mixed-gender groups composed of 5 to 8 members. Groups met for four one-hour meetings, during which time they were required to engage in group problem analysis and resolution. Findings from the study were mixed. Clearly, however, the most consistent and important findings were those that addressed personality variables. It was observed that although gender and psychological classification of the group leader (masculine, feminine, or androgynous) had strong implications for the initial stages of the group, these personality differences were mitigated over time. For example, androgynous persons were rated higher on task leadership than masculine persons and masculine persons were rated higher than feminine persons. By the final group sessions, however, these distinctions in group behavior between psychological types became insignificant. It appears that initial personality leadership propensities wash out over the life of the group. Spillman and Reinking concluded that although personality is an important factor in group leadership, those who attempt to study its effects should do so over time so that the influence of sex and personality can be viewed interactively.

As was mentioned above, the personality of the leader does not exist in a vacuum, but, rather, interacts with those of the group members. Thinking along these lines, Yerby (1975) conducted an interesting study in which she posed the research question: How do the attitudes of group members toward female leadership, under conditions of same-, mixed-, and opposite-sex group composition, with the task being either structured or unstructured, affect members and their reactions to the leader? University students employed in the experiment were placed in groups according to their attitudinal scores (i.e., positive or negative toward female leadership). It was observed that groups with equal members of men and women who held positive attitudes toward female leadership were most satisfied with the leaders. Group members with positive attitudes toward female leaders in groups of one female and three males, and group members with negative attitudes in groups of two males and two females, were least satisfied with their leaders. Yerby suggests that the positive attitude group composed of one female and three males may have fostered defensive behavior on the part of the female leader, resulting in negative perceptions of her leadership despite the group members' initial propensity to respond favorably toward her.

It was also found that a one-female negative attitude group resulted in the female leadership being perceived positively. The author suggests that possibly the males' desire to help or protect the lone female may have caused them to also support the female leader, as she may have appeared less threatening and more vulnerable. By the same token, Yerby suggests that in an all-male positive attitude group, the members might have felt less like behaving in a protective fashion and thus reacted negatively to the lone female leader. In any event, it appears that the attitudes of the group members toward female leadership significantly affect their responses to her leadership. Unfortunately, this very useful study by Yerby assessed only the effects of the group member personality attributes on the perception of female leadership. Naturally, it would be of considerable value to investigate the effects of the personality of group members on male leadership.

The dearth of studies in the area of personality and its consequences for group leadership suggest that this area is in need of greater attention. However, the studies by Spillman et al. (1981) and Yerby (1975) suggest that the personalities of the leader and member may have, at least initially, some effects on how leaders respond to and are received by the group.

Performance

Do men perform better as group leaders than women? Most studies of male and female patterns of leadership have not found evidence to support such a claim (Bartol, 1975; Bartol and Wortman, 1975; Petty and Miles, 1976; Rice et al., 1980). However, a number of studies have noted that female leadership performance, even when identical to that of males, is often perceived and responded to less favorably than that of male leadership (Rosen and Jerdee, 1973; Rice et al., 1980; Wiley and Eskilson, 1982). It appears that much of the devaluation of female group leaders is in part a function of the ascription of traditional sex-role behaviors to males and females. Experimental group manipulations by Forsyth et al. (1985) indicated that although both task and socio-emotional functions are equally necessary for good group leadership, task functions are viewed to be more important. Moreover, social emotional skills were both most often attributed to and claimed by women. At the same time, the more valued task skills were more often attributed to and claimed by men.

It has been suggested that women who lead groups have a double deviant status in that they are both status and role incongruent (Laws, 1975; Reed, 1983). Women in leadership positions are in status incongruencies since they occupy a higher-status position than their gender status position would suggest, and they are out of role in that it is not a "woman's place" to lead. These two factors appear to affect perceptions and evaluations of female group leadership negatively. Wiley and Eskilson (1982) contend that gender evokes differential performance expectations, which affect an individual's influence, rewards, and opportunities to act, in addition to his or her performance evaluations. They reported finding that even when identically performing men and women were seen as having equivalent positions, the evaluations of females were still less favorable than those of males. These observations were obtained in a study that employed experienced male and female managers as subjects. The managers were required to respond to a script of a hypothetical management situation in which one person was attempting to influence another. Sex of the influencers and the target of influence were varied.

Wiley and Eskilson (1982) conclude that these findings support the status expectation hypothesis of Meeker and Weitzel-O'Neill (1977). They suggest that a possible means of reducing the negative performance evaluations for female leaders may entail: (1) greater legitimization by appointing them to valued positions and (2) providing their supervisors with positive information about the female's abilities or prior performance before they begin their leadership tasks. Finally, time appears to be on the side of female leaders, as some research found evidence that negative evaluations or attitudes regarding female leadership may be tempered or eliminated by actual working experiences where females serve as supervisors (Bartol and Wortman, 1975).

In a study conducted in Israel (Izraeli, 1983), it was observed that gender composition of the group may have a more powerful effect on perception of leadership for females than for males. In a study of union committee executives it was observed that females viewed women's performance as leaders to be better in groups that contained equal numbers of males and females, and they saw men to perform better as leaders in groups whose composition was predominately male. In contrast, men appeared to be unaffected by the gender balance of the committee and viewed men as performing better than females as leaders, irrespective of the group's ratio of male to female members.

In addition, both the composition and structure of groups have been observed to influence leader performance of males and females. Eskilson and Wiley (1976) investigated leader behavior of males and females through an experimental study. College student subjects were required to work together in three-person problem-solving groups. It was observed that leaders of both sexes concentrated more on the task of leadership in sexually homogeneous groups than in mixed-gender groups. The author suggested that this was due to a hidden agenda effect present in the mixed-gender groups. They argued that in the mixed-gender groups there was a greater desire among members, including the leader, to be more attractive to the opposite sex. Hence, members of homogeneous gender groups may have found it easier to focus on the tasks at hand.

It was also observed that male leaders who led groups containing both male and female members were more frequently challenged by other male group members. The authors dubbed this the "rooster effect." They noted that challenges of male leaders by males in the mixed-gender groups were considerably higher than those in the all-male groups. When females led all-male groups, the female leaders were required to perform minimal leadership tasks. Female leaders received few requests for direction, even though as leaders they were the sole possessors of valuable information. It seems that male followers were reluctant to assume the subordinate role of follower when there was a female leader. Thus, females were least leaderlike when leading groups of men and males were least leaderlike when leading mixed-gender groups. Eskilson and Wiley's (1976) findings indicate these pertinent conclusions:

1. male leaders concentrated on leadership behaviors more than females
2. female leaders concentrated more of their efforts on creating positive affect within the group than did males

3. female leaders were less likely than males to select themselves to be future leaders of the group

The task in which group workers lead their members also appears salient. For example, Rice et al. (1980) constructed a group situation in which three males were led by either a male or a female. Half of the groups were composed of males who held traditional attitudes toward women (as measured by the Attitude Toward Women Scale) and the remaining groups were composed of men who held more liberal attitudes toward women. Rice et al. observed that male followers holding traditional attitudes toward women performed better when the task at hand was "a more masculine one." Conversely, groups composed of male followers with more liberal attitudes toward women performed better on what was perceived to be "a less masculine" task. This finding is consistent with others that have reported that type of group task affects outcome by interacting with the gender composition of the group (Eskilson and Wiley, 1976).

Rice et al. (1980) also noted that male followers with liberal attitudes toward women described the group atmosphere similarly for both male- and female-led groups. However, male followers with more traditional attitudes toward women described the group atmosphere more favorably when it was led by a male. Finally, followers with traditional attitudes toward women were less favorable in their evaluations of both male and female leaders than were followers who held more liberal attitudes toward women. Hence, it appears that both attitudes of members of the group and the nature of the group task interact with gender of the leader, and all have the potential to significantly affect group outcomes.

Finally, it appears that group structure may also influence leadership performance differentially for males and females. Maier (1970) obtained what appear to be interesting findings. Ninety-six four-person groups of two males and two females were required to engage in problem-solving tasks. The groups varied in their degree of structure—the leaders in some groups had the solution to the task, while other groups required the leader to supply the solution. Findings from the study suggest that females appeared to be less confident and performed less well as leaders in the unstructured situation than in the structured situation. Specifically, females were more assertive in the structured group leadership situation. No such structural effects were reported for males. It should be noted, however, that this small group experiment was conducted in the 1960s, and its findings may no longer adequately reflect current leadership dispositions of females. Indeed, as noted earlier, some research has already reported changes in this respect (Aries, 1982).

Co-Leadership

The co-leadership of groups is currently a topic of considerable interest to many helping professionals (Roman and Meltzer, 1977; Papell and Rothman, 1980). There is, however, some debate on this topic, with some authors contending that co-leadership has many virtues (Shilkoff, 1963; Corey and Corey, 1987) while others caution against its use (Yalom, 1975; Kolodny, 1980; Middleman, 1980).

Gender as a factor affecting co-leadership has received some of this attention. It has been argued that group leaders representing both sexes may be essential to provide nonstereotyped role behaviors to gender heterogeneous groups (Folkins et al., 1982). Those advocating this position suggest that male and female co-leaders should behave in an androgynous style to reduce sexist attitudes and behavior within the group. Moreover, even male and female co-leaders who serve as "traditional" male-female role models are argued to have beneficial consequences for certain groups (those composed of older or more conservative members). It is also suggested that male and female co-leaders be used in the treatment of groups of marital couples (Occhetti and Occhetti, 1981). For example, one possible advantage is that the co-leader of one sex can be confrontative while the other is supportive, and vice versa.

Despite many favorable reviews, some have expressed disappointment with the mixed-gender co-leader arrangement. The principal concern for male-female co-leaders of groups appears to revolve around the frequent attribution of unequal status to the male and female practitioners. Indeed, one of the most strongly advocated requirements of co-leaders is that the leaders possess equal status (Yalom, 1975; Kolodny, 1980). However, as it turns out, most research indicates that males are routinely ascribed a higher co-leader status than females (Greene et al., 1981; Thune et al., 1981). For example, Greene et al. (1981) experimentally created a co-leadership situation in which the members, 18 males and 18 females, themselves in training to become psychiatrists, psychologists, social workers, etc., were employed as subjects. These members (subjects) attended a Tavistock conference where they were divided into groups of four (2 males and 2 females). Before interacting as a group, members were *explicitly* informed either that a female would be the dominant co-leader and the male the subordinate, or vice versa.

Results from the Green et al. study (1981) revealed that despite explicit instructions as to who was in authority, the male co-leaders were consistently perceived as more potent, active, instrumental, and insightful than the female co-leaders. The authors conclude that members' attitudes regarding leader competence are influenced more by gender than by any explicit status of ascribed authority. These findings are particularly disturbing in that they suggest that efforts made to reduce gender liabilities may be to a large extent ineffective. These findings indicate that male and female co-leaders may enter groups on an unequal footing, with the males being perceived as the "real leader" and the females as the "helper." At this time, we are unaware of either practice or research efforts that have successfully counteracted this gender-related co-leader bias. It would seem prudent, however, that male and female co-leaders, in their preparation for group, take cognizance of the potentiality of this dynamic to affect their interaction with the group members, as well as their relationship as colleagues.

OUTCOME

By and large, the outcome literature in group work is not well-developed. Hence, the literature pertaining to gender and group outcome is also rudimentary. Even recent discussions of gender issues in group work have paid little attention to outcome per se (Reed and Garvin, 1983). Despite the paucity of empirical outcome data, however, the group practice literature does include numerous sources that attest to the effects of client and leader gender on group outcomes (Carlock and Martin, 1977; Barrett, 1978; Bernardez and Stein, 1979; Heppner, 1981; Joyce and Hazelton, 1982; Hartman, 1983). The discussion that follows will explore the implications of gender for the outcome of group members, group leadership, and the group modality employed.

Salience of the Group Member

Is group treatment more beneficial as a means of intervention for males than females? Are certain group gender compositions more beneficial to clients than others? Although few studies have addressed these questions directly, there is some evidence to suggest that gender may have significant effects on group outcomes and that a group's gender composition may affect the outcomes of members.

It has been suggested that the outcomes for males and females may differ because of their various objectives in seeking group treatment. For example, Noll and Watkins (1974) found that males and females who volunteered for a college encounter group had different reasons for participating. Their findings suggested that females who seek encounter group experiences may be more self-actualized than men who join these groups. The authors speculated that females may be seeking a novel or challenging experience and that encounter groups are the possible outlet for their self-actualizing drives. Men, by contrast, may be seeking a group experience because of some felt personal deficiency. The authors go on to conclude that males, at least those seeking encounter group experiences, may be worse off than females initially and therefore more difficult to work with in a group. Clearly, such initial differences in problem presentation between males and females have a strong potential to affect group outcomes.

It is widely assumed that problems which have to do with sex roles are better treated in homogeneous gender group composition. Although there is scant empirical evidence to support claims that single-gender groups are more effective for the resolution of sex-role problems, anecdotal reports of their success are numerous (Wong, 1978; Bernardez and Stein, 1979; Washington, 1979; Heppner, 1981; Kaufman and Timmers, 1983).

Many articles discuss the beneficial outcomes of "consciousness-raising" groups. Kravetz (1976) suggests from her review of the literature that there appear to be five outcomes unique to women's consciousness-raising groups:

1. women are more likely to perceive themselves as equals in interpersonal relationships
2. women are more likely to develop their own identity independent of men and children
3. women are more likely to trust and respect other women
4. women become aware of social, political, and economic factors that affect their lives
5. social change is defined as a prerequisite for many personal changes

In some respects, the outcome objectives for females in group treatment tend to differ from those of males. Whereas many of the aspired outcomes for females in consciousness-raising groups have to do with social and political liberation, the goals of most all-male consciousness-raising groups focus more on their affective liberation. For example, goals for all-male group members often are to enhance their abilities to share personal information, to express feelings and affinity, and to enhance feelings of trust and noncompetitiveness toward other males (Washington, 1979; Heppner, 1981; Kaufman and Timmers, 1983). It seems that most groups attribute the positive growth of their members to what Yalom (1975) refers to as "universality"—that is, discovering that others also share similar concerns, fears, or limitations. The feeling of universality appears to occur most readily in single-gender groups. This may be due to the fact that in mixed climates, individuals sometimes attempt to maintain or gain masculine roles; such roles, especially for women, seem to elicit hostility, confrontation, and often coalitions rather than the furtherance of exploration (Meador et al., 1972; Halas, 1973; Kirsh, 1974).

Positive outcomes are also reported for single-gender groups other than those focusing on consciousness-raising. Joyce and Hazelton (1982) concluded that alcoholic women are likely to benefit most from treatment in all-female groups. In their view, women in mixed groups, particularly those in early sobriety, are less likely to note their incompetencies in the presence of men. Moreover, they found, during their 18 group sessions with women alcoholics and nonalcoholics, that the alcoholic women benefited significantly from seeing other women as helpers. Consequently, they conclude that groups which provide an opportunity for women to view other women as mentors and helpers are most efficacious for restructuring the social and emotional lives of alcoholic females.

As noted at the beginning of this chapter, the research of Carlock and Martin (1977) indicates that both group and individual outcomes were affected by the group's gender composition. Mixed-gender groups were found more exciting to members and more oriented to "the here and now relationships" within the group than were single-gender groups. However, females who participated in all-female groups experienced more growth, objectively measured, than did those in mixed-gender groups. Yet, paradoxically, these "most helped" females evaluated their group experience less favorably—e.g., less exciting and enjoyable.

The Carlock and Martin findings suggest that group processes and client outcomes may be distinct dimensions of group practice. Hence, group process should not be assumed to also reflect actual client gain. Findings such as these argue strongly for a dual-focused approach to the assessment of group work, in which both process and outcome are independently assessed.

Salience of the Group Leader

This discussion begins with what may be the most frequently asked questions: "Can women lead groups of men? Does male or female group leadership result in differential client outcomes?" Studies that have employed males and females in controlled leadership situations might assist us in answering this question. In general, it appears that whether women have successful outcomes in leading groups containing men is strongly affected by the attitudes of the men they are attempting to lead. That is, studies find that female practitioners whose male group members hold pro-feminist versus "traditional" attitudes toward women experience more favorable outcomes (Follingstad et al., 1976; Rice et al., 1980; Hall et al., 1982).

Follingstad and his colleagues also report that men's gains in female leader groups seem to be influenced by the personality characteristics of the group members. They studied marathon groups co-led by females and composed of male college students. Treatment consisted of a structured personal group experience in which group members discussed alternative ways to handle interpersonal situations and male-female relationships. Each group met for two eight-hour periods. Subjects filled out several personality inventories prior to and after completion of the groups. Findings revealed that males who scored low on authoritarianism before the group experience made the greatest gains in self actualization. Also, those low on authoritarianism and in greater agreement with pro-feminist attitudes prior to treatment rated the group as more effective. As noted by the authors, it was unfortunate that women were not also included as subjects in this study so that it could be determined if female participants would have differentially responded to female leadership as a function of their attitudes.

Hall et al. (1982) offer some clues in answering this question. They studied the dyadic interaction between a male or a female "teacher" and a male or female respondent, using college students as subjects. They found female teachers with more liberal attitudes toward women made a more favorable impression when speaking to women than when speaking to men. However, those female teachers with more traditional attitudes made a better impression when speaking to men. Hence, it appears that gender of the group leader may indeed result in differential treatment outcomes for group members. However, it seems that group member outcomes are significantly influenced by the attitudinal predispositions they bring to the treatment situation. On balance, more liberal, less traditional male group members experience greater positive outcomes than do their conservative male counterparts.

Can male leaders obtain positive outcomes as leaders of all-female groups? Sullivan (1983) answers affirmatively to this question. She states, however, that men need to be trained to do so. They must read, engage in training that will heighten their awareness with respect to sexism, and recognize the impact of male leadership on women's groups. Not all practitioners shared Sullivan's optimism. Bernardez and Stein (1979) observed that male leaders entering an all-female group may receive less than a warm reception. Their reports were based on the observations of three men's and three women's groups conducted over a three-year period. They found that men's and women's groups reacted differently to leaders of the opposite sex. The initial reaction of the men's group to a female leader was generally warm; however, the women's group extended a hostile reception to the male therapist. The appearance of the male therapist may have highlighted already existing gender-related problems in the female groups. Eventually, however, women in the all-female group were able to utilize the male leader to work through issues of transference.

In summary, it is clear that gender of the group leader has the potential to significantly affect the processes and subsequently the outcomes for a group and its members. From the above reviewed studies it also becomes apparent that individual and group outcomes are influenced not only by gender of the leader, but also by the attitudes and values held by the group members. Moreover, it appears that gender of the leader, attitudes of the members, and type of task of the group all interact to influence whether a leader will obtain the desired group outcomes.

Salience of the Modality

Are certain group modalities more effective than others in the treatment of males and/or females? There is little in the treatment literature to suggest that such is the case. However, certain group modalities are advocated for the treatment of gender-related problems. The modalities employed in the treatment of women include: short-term groups (Joyce and Hazelton, 1982); consciousness-raising groups (Kirsh, 1974; Kravetz and Sargent, 1977); brief groups (Killeen and Jacobs, 1976); support groups (Levin, Groves, and Lurie, 1980); and encounter groups (Meador et al., 1972). To a lesser extent, similar groups have been advocated for use with men, especially self-help groups (Wong, 1978) and consciousness-raising groups (Washington, 1979; Solomon, 1982).

Although these group modalities differ in their theoretical tenets, they often share very similar goals. For example, most advocate growth rather than treatment per se. It is noted that consciousness-raising (C-R) groups, in particular, differ from traditional forms of therapy in that the goal is not treatment to bring about intrapsychic change. Instead, the main goals of C-R groups are typically to change group members' perspectives of their roles as males or females in society. These groups can also be characterized as less formal and hierarchical than traditional modalities. They do, however, appear to be slightly larger than most treatment groups, as they are generally composed of 7 to 15 same-sex members (Eastman, 1973; Kirsh, 1974; Kravetz and Sargent, 1977; Wong, 1978).

Few who have employed C-R groups, self-help groups, etc., have measured outcome. Perhaps this is due, in part, to the difficulty of assessing some of their global goals (e.g., increased autonomy, enhanced self confidence and self knowledge). Thus there is little empirical outcome data on the group experience of members who have participated in these groups. However, anecdotal reports indicate positive growth for both males and females, specifically as it pertains to enhancing positive feelings about gender or gender-related issues (Levin et al., 1980).

Barrett (1978) conducted one of the very few group studies providing empirical data on outcomes across group modalities. This study was conducted with 70 urban widows who participated in one of three group treatments: self-help group, confidant group, or consciousness-raising group. In addition, some members were placed in a waiting list control group. Each subject was randomly assigned to one of the group treatment conditions or the waiting list control group. All active groups met for two hours a week over a seven-week period and were led by two nonwidowed female leaders.

The basic assumption in all three treatment groups was that widowed women would be able to help each other cope with the stresses of their situation. The self-help group assumed that people in a similar situation could be of help to each other. The confidant group focused on group sharing to ease the loss of spouse as principal confidant. The consciousness-raising group focused on gender roles.

Although the widows in the control group demonstrated positive change, greater change was experienced by members of treatment groups. The findings noted significant change for all group members, including increased self esteem, a decreased intensity of grief, less negative attitudes toward remarriage, and greater concern with self. The members of the treatment groups also had more positive predictions of their future health status.

With respect to the modalities, the consciousness-raising group was most consistently effective due, perhaps, to the high degree of structure facilitating member participation. By contrast, the self-help format was least effective. The author surmised that the therapist's presence in a self-help group may be counterproductive. A seven month follow up revealed that widows were able to sustain gains made in the treatment groups.

In sum, what little research evidence there is suggests that consciousness-raising groups and self-help groups are most frequently employed as the modalities to address gender-related issues and that they may be among the most effective at doing so.

CONCLUSION

The effects of gender on group work practice have until recently received insufficient attention. In this chapter a variety of gender-related factors that may affect attempts to work successfully with groups were reviewed. We began by inspecting group composition. It appears that males prefer mixed-gender groups while females prefer mixed-gender groups only if they are large. Some leaders prefer to lead all-female groups because females appear to engage in greater trust between themselves and other women and are more able to work through gender-related conflicts. Similar arguments are made on the behalf of male leaders for all-male groups, however, such requests are more recent and less frequent. Group purpose is also influential in determining group composition: Groups that address issues of sexual identity and gender roles tend to be composed of same-gender group members, while groups that have enhanced understanding of gender dynamics as their goal may be mixed in gender composition.

The dynamics of a group may be significantly affected by its gender composition. There is evidence which suggests that gross gender imbalances in group compositions of males or females should be avoided; members of either sex may be responded to most favorably when their numbers are approximately equal. All-female groups tend to be more expressive than groups that contain men, but mixed-gender groups tend to be more expressive than all-male groups. In short, mixed-gender groups tend to retard the expressive behaviors of females but enhance the expressive behaviors of males. Hence, group leaders must attempt to sustain the expressive functions of females in mixed groups and males in all-male groups.

Gender has been observed to influence cooperation and competition in small groups. In general, men tend to be more competitive and women more cooperative. Males are said to have an exploitative behavioral style and females to have an accommodative style; the latter tends to result in more favorable outcomes for group members. Males tend to be less conforming in groups than females and greater risk takers. However, risk taking within a gender-mixed group tends to shift in the direction of the numerically dominant gender group.

Communication in small groups is influenced by gender status effects. Although less true now than before the women's movement, evidence suggests that because of the higher status ascribed to males, males receive and take more opportunities to communicate with other group members. These differential status ascriptions and accompanying behavior expectations may undermine the communication efforts of females in mixed-gender groups. However, this "interaction disability" can be overcome by females who appear to be more concerned with the welfare of the group than with their own self enhancement. Prestigious leader introductions of female group members may also counter this gender bias.

It has been stated that the problem with female groups is that no one wants to lead and the problem with all-male groups is that everyone wants to lead. Here, too, differences in ascribed gender status are believed to result in stereotypic gender perceptions with respect to male and female group leadership. Leadership style does not appear to vary as a function of gender alone. However, it does appear that as the percentage of opposite-sex group members increases, the leader's style takes on more of the characteristics associated with that sex. Moreover, level of competence exhibited in the group may have greater implications for female than male leaders. Male group members are more tolerant of incompetent male group leadership than they are of incompetent female group leadership.

Style of group leadership may have differential influence on male and female group members. There is some evidence that females talk more in formal leadership situations, but men in contrast, talk more in informal leadership situations. Both males and females appear to like their fellow group members more when the leadership is informal.

The personality of the leader (i.e., masculine, feminine, or androgynous) has been noted to affect the perception of the leader's task ability, but the effects are only apparent at the early stages of the group. In addition, the gender attitudes held by the group members (e.g., traditional vs. liberal) may also influence the perception and evaluation of male and female group leadership. Female group leadership may be perceived as being status incongruent, with the consequence that, even when identical to that of males, it is frequently responded to and evaluated less favorably. Both male and female group leaders appear to concentrate more on the task of leadership when the group is gender homogeneous rather than gender-mixed. Moreover, male leaders are most likely to be challenged by other males in groups that are gender-mixed. Male-female co-leadership has received mixed reviews from the field. This co-leadership arrangement may be beneficial for the group members by role modeling nonsexist male-female interactions. However, the effects of gender status may overpower the role expectations of co-leadership, and ascribe to the male the role of leader and the female the role of helper.

There is anecdotal and empirical evidence which suggests that women may experience the most beneficial outcomes in same-gender group compositions. However, they may evaluate their mixed-gender group experiences as more exciting and oriented to the here and now. This noted paradox is important as it suggests that group process and actual client gains should be assessed independently and that one may not be indicative of the other. With respect to leadership, whether women have successful outcomes in leading groups of men is affected by the attitudes of the men they are attempting to lead: More favorable outcomes have been obtained with men who hold less traditional views of women. Anecdotal indications are that men who lead all-female groups may obtain positive client outcomes; however, there are also indications that they may experience, at least initially, resistance to their leadership.

Consciousness-raising groups and self-help groups are those most frequently employed in the treatment of gender-related problems. Furthermore, these groups tend to focus on growth rather than pathology and are typically less formal and hierarchical than traditional group modalities. It also appears that these groups may be the most effective in treating gender-related client concerns.

10

GUIDELINES FOR PRACTICE

When Gender Is Salient

From the previous four chapters, it is clear that gender of worker and client influences the process and outcome of helping. What remains to be identified are the ways in which male and female practitioners can enhance their effectiveness in working with clients of the opposite sex, and the ways in which they need to reduce the effects of sexism in helping.

PREPARING FOR PRACTICE

As with racial and socioeconomic issues, practitioners must ensure that they are prepared to deal with gender issues long before they encounter them face-to-face with clients. Women significantly outnumber men among recipients of social and mental health services, and practitioners must understand the clear role of social sex roles in the development, maintenance, and resolution of their problems. Few agencies deliberately assign clients to workers on the basis of gender. Thus, both male and female practitioners should expect to work with clients of the opposite sex. Even in gender-matched helping, sex roles are likely to influence participants' perceptions of and reactions to each other. In group and family situations, sex roles influence members' communication, expectations, and evaluations of one another.

How can practitioners adequately prepare to respond to gender issues? Knowledge and sensitivity are crucial in such preparation. Important areas of knowledge include human physiology and the relationship between biological and emotional functioning. Special areas of attention should include menstruation, pregnancy, and menopause. It is also critical to understand the pervasiveness of sexism in human relationships, in families, and in society. In particular, practitioners should recognize the impact of sex typing and gender-related norms in reducing individuals' options for work, family, and personal roles. Many client problems stem from such restrictions. Several resources can contribute to such understanding. Texts such as Howell and Bayes' *Women and Mental Health* and Tavris and Wade's *The Longest War* provide theory and research pertinent to gender effects on development and social behavior. In addition, practitioners should recognize the sexism prevalent in many theories of behavior and behavior change. For example, many theories presume limits to women's psychological and moral development, and "blame the mother" for family, interpersonal, and personal problems. Male professionals working with female clients should supplement their preparation for working with female clients by obtaining consultation or supervision from women colleagues.

Self examination of attitudes and assumptions is very important. Given the evidence from research that very few biological differences exist, we are left to conclude that socialization and ideology contribute largely to the vast differences in men's and women's social experiences. As members of society, practitioners have been exposed to and, in all probability, have incorporated the tendency to expect more or less of persons on the basis of their gender. Countering the tendency to ascribe expectations on the basis of gender may be the most important aspect of preparing to work with clients whose gender differs from the practitioners.

MANAGEMENT OF EARLY TREATMENT INTERACTION

There is ample evidence of the importance of the earliest contacts between helper and client. Initial sessions often set the tone for subsequent interaction and, indeed, may determine whether the client will perceive the helping experience as sufficiently beneficial to warrant expenditure of time, energy, and money to continue seeking help.

For women clients it is extremely important for practitioners to provide respect from the beginning, for it is the basis for trust. In many relationships and in many work settings, women are not treated seriously. Women may be treated disrespectfully in treatment as well. For example, practitioners are found to show impatience when women speak and to interrupt them more often than men. Moreover, professionals tend to use first names with women clients sooner and more often than with men. To enhance their demonstration of respect, workers should be diligent to use appropriate titles (e.g., Ms., Mrs.), to ask women (as they routinely ask men) what they do, to refrain from commenting on women's appearance more than men's, and to listen attentively and carefully to what women clients say. Respect is also conveyed by taking women's problems seriously.

A basis for credibility must be established also. Workers must demonstrate their sensitivity to, understanding of, and ability to help resolve client concerns and problems. This issue is complicated by gender, in that women's problems are frequently dismissed as emotional or unreasonable, and men have often encouraged the dependence of women. When the gender of worker and client differs, warmth and interpersonal attraction must be expressed cautiously and within the context of a professional relationship. As noted in Chapter 7, the expression of warmth by male workers may make female clients uncomfortable. The worker's concern and commitment to the client's growth and well being must be clearly conveyed. Thus, attending skills should be carefully and appropriately employed. Sexual innuendos and advances are harmful and unethical. Female workers should also exercise special caution with male clients. Comfort may be maximized with balanced attention to expression of feelings and appeal to logic.

Because gender is an obvious characteristic of which both client and worker will be aware immediately, its salience may need to be acknowledged and discussed. For example, when gender of worker and client differs, workers may need to inquire whether the client sees the gender difference as an impediment to the helping effort. If the client offers a hasty "no," the worker should invite the client to point out any instances in their work together in which the gender difference does seem to impair the worker's understanding. If the client perceives the gender difference as a problem, the worker should be prepared to explore the issue more fully or make a referral to a worker of the client's same sex. Such a conversation will not create a pseudo-issue; that is, the discussion will not make gender an issue when, in fact, it is not. Rather the conversation will demonstrate the worker's sensitivity, skill, and commitment to helping the client.

In some situations, of course, gender differences may create a considerable barrier. Chapter 7 identifies particular client demographics and problems where worker-client gender match seems most important. In addition, some clients will hold preferences regarding worker gender.

When client preference is strong, the worker should be able and willing to refer the client.

ENSURE THE GENDER APPROPRIATENESS
OF THE TREATMENT PROCESS

The treatment process should be gender-appropriate and sex-fair. Crucial to this aim is the reduction of bias in assessment. Practitioners should ensure that they are equally attentive to both men and women. Both men and women should be asked to share feelings and thoughts, and the work and family roles of both sexes should be assessed. In particular, workers should ensure that women's responses are listened to in family and group treatment. Practitioners should avoid instruments and assessment tools that are norm-criterioned only on one sex. Practitioners should ensure that they do not dismiss women's problems as insignificant; in family treatment, for example, the citation of more problems by women than men is normative and does not reflect on the woman as a complainer or hard to please.

Assessment should ensure the exploration of client strengths as well as weaknesses. Male workers, whose assessments tend to be harsher and more negative, should ensure that client strengths are identified.

The role of sex roles in the presenting problems should be explored thoroughly. In addition, the social, economic, and legal aspects of problems should be assessed. Both men and women experience social consequences for their actions; men, for example, are often penalized for expressing the need for professional help, while women may be penalized for assertiveness and independence. Where change needs to be directed to aspects of the social environment, the worker should be prepared to assist the client or provide an appropriate referral.

When treatment goals are explored, a wide range of potential options should be considered and explored. The client's opportunities heretofore may be limited by lack of awareness or gender status restrictions. Workers can assist clients in exploring and possibly pursuing less sex-typed options, such as greater personal independence and autonomy for women and greater emphasis on interpersonal and family relationships for men. Outcome criteria should be gender neutral; in family treatment, they should be acceptable to both husband and wife, or father and mother.

In regard to the helping relationship, some cautions are advised for both male and female clients. With male clients, workers should temper their expectations for immediate and in-depth self disclosure. Men may take longer initially and may ultimately engage in less self disclosure. Men might be engaged more readily when workers emphasize rationality and logic. In family treatment, the participation of men should be assumed and their family roles and emotional investment in family relationships should be acknowledged.

With women clients, the helping relationship should foster independence and autonomy. Such a relationship may offer a new opportunity, quite different from previous and customary patterns of dependency on others. In this regard, female workers may serve as good role models for female clients. Male workers must be diligent to avoid fostering the dependence of female clients.

Available evidence does not support the notion that interventions are differentially appropriate on the basis of gender alone. However, women have been shown to benefit from psychoanalytically-oriented psychotherapy more than men, and to experience gain from feminist therapies. Workers should guard against the apparent tendency to tell women clients what to do; treatment should enhance women's independence and decision-making abilities. Specialized interventions may be needed to help women at vulnerable stages of development, such as new mothers, mothers entering the workplace, and daughters of aging parents. Specialized interventions are also advised for victims of domestic violence and sexual assault.

Worker-client gender match is advised for certain groups of clients with particular presenting problems. On the basis of available evidence, workers may expect women clients to be more responsive to and more satisfied with treatment than men.

Some special guidelines are suggested for male and female practitioners. Male practitioners may have to work harder than female practitioners to be perceived as trustworthy, warm, and friendly. Toward this end, they should refine their communication skills and ability to express empathic understanding. Female workers, on the other hand, need to emphasize their competence and expertise.

Because the sexes so frequently interact in day-to-day activities, workers may overlook the salience of gender in helping. However, the significance of gender and sex roles in the causation and maintenance of problems should not be underestimated. Practitioners should be sensitive to potential gender effects on the treatment process and outcome. Gender will affect most, if not all, helping situations. In some cases, treatment effectiveness may depend on gender matching. More often, success may depend on the worker's sensitivity to sex role and gender status issues and skill in minimizing the effects of sexism on interpersonal helping.

11

Socioeconomic Status as an Issue in Practice

Social class is one of the most potent forces in our society. No other demographic factor has been shown to explain so extensively the differences that exist both within and between groups of people. Indeed, much of what is frequently discussed under the rubric of race or ethnicity may be better explained by social class. Many of the differences believed to exist between various subgroups in the United States disappear when social economic status is controlled for. Some argue that it is class and not race that should be of concern in the United States (Wilson, 1978). While we will not enter into this debate, social class is a potent factor that can profoundly affect helping relationships. Unlike gender and race, social class may not be immediately evident in interpersonal relationships; indeed, if desired, it may be concealed. Yet, there are identifiable consequences to socioeconomic differences.

Social economic status is of importance to those in the helping professions for several reasons. First, the proportion of people in U.S. society who are poor or near poor has been increasing since the late 1970s (Harrington, 1986). Poverty has increased especially among the working poor and, according to a recent study, now affects a surprisingly large proportion of the population. According to Duncan (1984), one-fourth of the total U.S. population lived in poverty for at least one of the ten years from 1969 to 1978; for half of those individuals, poverty did not persist for more than two years. Few people are immune to adverse local or national economic conditions, personal illness, death or departure of a spouse; for many people, these events can lead to a year or two of severe economic hardship. As the ranks of the impoverished swell and as our society, overall, becomes more economically diverse, the likelihood that practitioners will work with clients who differ from them economically also increases.

Second, social work recognizes poverty itself as a major concern and recognizes that socioeconomic problems put people at risk. The poor are more likely than the rest of the population to be either old or members of families with young children (Chilman, 1975; Schiller, 1984; Rogers, 1986). Poor people are also more likely to reside in large central cities and rural areas than in suburban communities (Schiller, 1984). Race is also associated with income differences. Indeed, the single most powerful predictor of persistent poverty is race (Duncan, 1984). It is mostly poor people who are also mental patients, children in foster care and residential treatment, juveniles in custody, adults in prison, the sick, the victims of crime, and the homeless aged (Epstein, 1980). Social work has an historic commitment to serve such vulnerable groups.

Finally, socioeconomic differences are important because they have profound implications for the way individuals interact, communicate, and perceive the world. Socioeconomic status is a pervasive characteristic in our society, with the result that other, secondary differences are assumed as well. Thus, in addition to demographic differences, which are borne out by empirical evidence, other differences are also assumed. The perception of economical dissimilarity appears to suggest not only the possession of more or less money, but other pervasive differences. The manifestation and consequences of such differences is the subject of this chapter. The specific implications for individual, family, and group treatment will be explored in detail in the following three chapters.

PERCEIVING DIFFERENCES IN CLASS

Similarity breeds attraction; this has become a commonly accepted axiom. Research supports the notion that those who are similar in socioeconomic terms are most attracted to each (Byrne et al., 1966). Similarity is believed to enhance attraction because perceived similarities affirm and validate the viewer's own attributes; in short, similarity tends to be reinforcing. Thus, clients and workers who view each other as sharing similar economic levels should, at least initially, be most attracted to one another. Indeed, most research has found that attraction does appear to be enhanced across a variety of attributes, including race, gender, and socioeconomic status. Recently, however, it has been suggested that dissimilarity is the more powerful predictor of whether persons will be attracted to each other (Rosenbaum, 1986). That is, dissimilarity is believed to be a stronger repellant than similarity is an attractant. If so, client-therapist difference may be an even greater cause for concern than originally believed.

Economic similarity and dissimilarity may affect interaction differently than do other characteristics, such as attitudes. The following figure illustrates patterns of attraction under conditions of economic dissimilarity, as observed by Byrne and Nelson (1965).

FIGURE 11.1

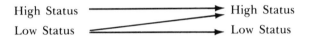

As the figure shows, attraction in the face of economic dissimilarity may be asymmetrical; that is, sometimes persons are attracted to others whose socioeconomic status is different. As predicted by theory, persons of high socioeconomic status were attracted to others with similar (high) status. However, those with low socioeconomic status were more attracted to higher-class persons than predicted; they were attracted to both similar (low-status) persons and to dissimilar (high-status) persons. These findings may suggest that upward economic dissimilarity has a different psychological meaning. That is, having more of a valued quality may be attractive, even to those who possess less of that quality themselves. Thus, attraction sometimes occurs in the face of (economic) dissimilarity.

What are the implications for helpers and clients? These findings suggest that low-income clients and low-income practitioners may be attracted both to economically similar and dissimilar others. However, high-income clients and practitioners may be less attracted to their low-income counterparts. Indeed, this asymmetrical attraction may account for the finding that practitioners who are from lower social class origins appear more willing than their higher SES colleagues to work with a wide range of socioeconomic clients (Kandle, 1966).

PERCEIVING DIFFERENCES IN BELIEFS, ATTITUDES, AND VALUES

Simply put, in our society, the rich, the poor, and the middle class are assumed to think in ways that are distinct. In the language of social scientists, certain beliefs are assumed to be shared by most members of a given socioeconomic group (Merton, 1957; Newcomb, 1963). Hence, when we encounter someone whose economic situation differs from our own, we are likely to assume that their attitudes, beliefs, and values also differ from ours.

To what extent is this assumption borne out by evidence? There is considerable evidence that middle- and lower-income persons differ with respect to their perceptions of causal events (Lerner and Miller, 1978; Lefcourt, 1982). Low-income people are generally more inclined to see life events (e.g., good or bad fortune) as a consequence of factors external to themselves. Such people are described as having an external locus of control. In contrast, middle-income persons are more inclined to believe that events in their lives occur as a function of their own efforts. They are, therefore, described as having an internal locus of control (Rotter, 1966). These differences in beliefs about causation are believed to contribute to lower- and middle-class persons having different world views and orientations toward life (Rotter, 1966). Hence, there has been concern that workers and clients from different social classes may have differing perceptions of problems and events. Recent evidence, however, suggests that such may not be the case. A study by Latting and Zundel (1986) suggests that economically dissimilar therapists and clients did not have significantly different perceptions of problem locus. However, theory and other empirical evidence still point to the likelihood that middle- and low-income persons will differ in their beliefs about factors affecting life events (Sue, 1981; Lefcourt, 1982). The strength of this evidence warrants our continued concern and attention to this issue.

Certainly the values and attitudes of poor people have been assumed to be different from the rest of society; indeed, many have attributed poverty to the values of the poor. Since colonial times, economic problems have been assumed to reflect deficiencies in individuals' values and ambition. Especially when times are good and people are prospering, poverty is suspect and the ambition, motivation, and ability of poor people—especially poor people receiving welfare benefits—is questioned. Indeed, until one of the first major U.S. economic depressions in 1894, the assumption that poverty resulted from sin and laziness was unquestioned (Schiller, 1984). More recently, according to "culture of poverty" notions (Lewis and Lavida, 1968), poverty was assumed to be perpetuated from one generation to the next through the transmission of attitudes and values that differed from those of larger society.

In fact, do the beliefs, attitudes, and values of people vary by socioeconomic status? The evidence suggests not. According to survey data, poor people do not differ from the well-off in terms of aspirations for their children, work orientation, general personality characteristics, and basic life goals (Schiller, 1984). Rather, research on the goals and ambitions of the poor suggests that "they share middle class goals and await improved opportunities to pursue them" (Schiller, 1984, p. 112).

If and where values and beliefs vary by socioeconomic status, it is likely due to different social realities. Poverty, experienced in terms of low wages and unemployment, jeopardizes the most basic needs of food and shelter. In such situations, middle-class values alone do not suffice. As Sue notes, "feelings of helplessness, dependence, and inferiority, are easily fostered under these circumstances" (1981, p. 35). Members of different SES groups experience different conditions of life and, hence, may "come to see the world differently—to develop different conceptions of social reality, different aspirations and hopes and fears, different conceptions of the desirable" (Kohn, 1963, p. 471). In particular, self direction, openmindedness, and trust of others may be possible only when persons have reason to feel in control of fate (Kohn, 1963). Such control, of course, is not a reality for many poor people. These divergent social realities may contribute to value conflicts between worker and client. Social work technology has developed from essentially middle-class conceptions of the universe; moreover, it is generally practiced by those who accept these views. However, the values of low-income individuals are those that are adaptive to poverty. As a result, value conflict may permeate contacts between agencies and low-income people. Indeed, conflicting values may generate "strains between client and worker, leading progressively to dissociation if not to estrangement" (Cloward and Epstein, 1965, p. 629).

This potential is exacerbated with more psychologically-oriented interventions, which increase the intensity of interaction between worker and client. Previously, when concrete services were more routinely offered, any strains arising from value conflicts may have been easily overcome. Currently, however, the more intimate, prolonged, and intensely personal character of therapeutic casework sharply reveals value differences between helpers and low-income clients.

PERCEIVING DIFFERENCES IN COMPETENCE

People generally believe in a "just world" in which individuals receive the outcomes they deserve, given their talents and efforts (Lerner and Miller, 1978; Kluegel and Smith, 1986). Traditional economic theory holds that the ability of each worker determines incomes. Thus we tend to infer the distribution of abilities from the distribution of incomes (Schiller, 1984): people with more money are assumed to be more able. People in the United States assume that all who are able-bodied should provide for themselves and for their family (Toomey, 1980); those who don't work are presumed deficient in some way. This view is consistent with the design of war on poverty programs, which attempted to eliminate poverty by curing the person. The poor were assumed to be marked by psychopathology and family pathology. Currently we evidence this view in our psychologically-oriented treatment, which distinguishes between the psychologically "accessible" and "inaccessible" poor (Cloward and Epstein, 1965) in such terms as the "deserving" and "undeserving" poor.

The view, however, that the poor are less competent is challenged by the data. It appears that income is distributed much less equally than are IQ's or educational attainments (Schiller, 1984). Rather than different competencies and abilities, economic status may reflect opportunity. Schiller has labeled this theory the *restricted opportunity argument*, which basically holds that people are poor because they lack access to good schools, jobs, and income. Thus, many now view poverty as being caused by a deficient demand for labor and hence limited opportunities for persons to enter the job market or to receive high market value for their services. Discrimination plays a crucial role in the distribution of opportunity, as certain groups of persons—such as women and minorities—are more likely than others to lack access to opportunity.

PERCEIVING DIFFERENCES IN STATUS

Individuals in different social economic groups recognize that they possess different social statuses; relative to each other, one receives higher or lower status from society.

According to several theorists, interpersonal interactions are significantly influenced by ascribed status (prestige), a major determinant of which is income (Berger, Cohen, and Zelditch, 1966; Meeker and Weitzel-O'Neill, 1977). Of course, the helping relationship is already role incongruent by virtue of the worker's higher status as helper. It is important to recognize that class differences have the potential to accentuate the client-therapist status differential. In such a situation, the client may assume that, because his or her social situation is so different from that of the worker, the worker's suggestions and advice are suspect. In short, the worker's helpfulness may be seen as socially invalidated. This issue may be the most serious one faced by any cross-class helping relationships. Thus practitioners working with economically different clients should ask themselves, "Does my economic status limit the extent to which I can be helpful?"

A further consequence of economic status incongruence is the apparent devaluation of the client's contribution. Clients who see their socioeconomic status as much lower than that of the practitioner may believe that they can make little contribution to the treatment process.

As a result, they may rely too heavily on the practitioner to carry the treatment process. In the same vein, practitioners who see their status as higher than the client's may overplay their roles as helpers. These problematic tendencies may be reduced by an early discussion of roles and the potential influence of status differentials.

CONCLUSION

It is evident that social economic status is a potent demographic factor with potential to affect client and therapist interaction. The major challenge before practitioners appears to be their ability to minimize the negative effects that often occur when people perceive each other as economically different. Moreover, they need to understand how their particular social economic status may affect the suitability of their interventions. Indeed, the appropriateness of interventions may be challenged by economic dissimilarity between helper and client. According to Cloward and Epstein, "The field may know how to deal differently with various types of small group or various types of personality dysfunction, but it does not know how to deal with people who have not been prepared in advance to use its technology." Indeed they charge that, "Casework technology has become class-bound" (1965, p. 636).

For example, low-income people probably regard as impractical the idea that a person in trouble can improve circumstances through a better understanding of self and the contribution of one's own behavior to problems. Introspection, insight, verbal facility, and capacity to use professional relationships are inherently middle-class, and may not be useful when problems have a socioeconomic basis. The fundamental issue is the appropriateness of casework, group work, or family treatment for problems that are socioeconomic or problems experienced by the poor.

Moreover, workers should not assume that because persons have economic difficulties, they inherently experience or lack other personal or family or interpersonal difficulties. The assumption that one type of intervention will remedy all socioeconomic-related problems should be avoided. Obviously poverty cannot be abolished by individual, group, or family treatment (Chilman, 1975). The problem of poverty requires massive restructuring of social, economic, and political systems. Yet "the problems that poverty inflicts on poor people" can be resolved—or adequately responded to—with the right "series of interlocking policies and programs" (Chilman, 1975, p. 59). The challenge for workers is to match problem and method (Rosen and Connaway, 1969), or to appropriately select social work technology.

These issues are particularly sensitive now. McQuaide notes recent changes in attitudes toward the vulnerable:

> The humanitarianism we value has gone out of fashion. . . . Permission has been given to blame the victim, and helping professionals are no less affected than other people. We may have an additional reason for disappointment because (the) devaluation (of the poor) brings devaluation of our skills (1983, p. 499).

The challenge of helping clients whose socioeconomic status differs from the worker's will be examined in greater detail in the following three chapters, which address socioeconomic status and individual, group, and family treatment.

12

Socioeconomic Status and Individual Treatment

SALIENCE OF SOCIOECONOMIC STATUS

Client Attitude Toward Worker SES

The extent to which worker socioeconomic status is important to clients has received very little attention. Perhaps the very education involved in professional training and the income level provided by worker salary is assumed to make any variation in workers' socioeconomic status less dramatic and, hence, less visible to clients than gender and racial differences. Whatever the reasons, the salience of worker socioeconomic background to clients has not been widely studied.

One study did focus on clients' perceptions of several groups of helpers, who differed considerably in years of training and income (Keith-Spiegel and Spiegel, 1967). When asked to rate the helpfulness of various groups of helpers, more educated clients tended to see psychiatrists and psychologists as helpful; clients with lower levels of education saw nursing aids as most helpful. These findings may suggest a preference among less-educated clients for professionals whose SES is nearer their own.

More attention has focused on the potential merits of using paraprofessional helpers. With paraprofessionals, greater worker-client similarity in education, income, culture, residential location, and similarity of experience are assumed (Cohen, 1976). Paraprofessionals are, indeed, sometimes similar to clients in terms of socioeconomic factors. However, at other times, the SES gap may be increased, as when middle- or upper-class volunteers work with low-income clients.

The use of paraprofessionals, a "long and honorable part of the history of social welfare" (Ginsberg, 1978, p. 8), increased during the 1960s' "war on poverty." Indeed, the Economic Opportunity Act of 1964 called for increased client participation in service delivery and the 1967 Harris Amendments to the Social Security Act required the use of community service aids. The paraprofessional movement served to reduce a person-power shortage (Rioch, 1966; Guerney, 1969). It was assumed also to facilitate client use of services (Pearl and Riessman, 1965; Riessman, 1965; Ginsberg, 1978).

However, implementation of the paraprofessional movement was difficult. Teare (1981) cites such difficulties as the inability of large, bureaucratic social systems to place and supervise paraprofessionals carefully; insufficient development of new service roles or functions; insufficient attention to skill differences among workers; and, finally and perhaps most important, the absence of evidence to support the presumed effectiveness of paraprofessionals.

The effectiveness of paraprofessionals has *not* been clearly established. Social psychological research suggests that although similarity facilitates friendship relationships, it may not have comparable effects in formal helping situations, particularly if the helper is seen as having limited expertise as a helper (Spiegel, 1976). Perception of a helper as an expert significantly influences the chances that the client will refer a close friend to the worker (Dell and Schmidt, 1976), see the worker as competent (Greenberg, 1969; Atkinson and Carskaddon, 1975; Spiegel, 1976), and experience attitude change (Bergin, 1962). These findings are consistent with earlier results in social psychology that credibility enhances ability to influence (Hovland, Janis, and Kelley, 1953). Indeed, Spiegel believes that peer counselors, whose authority derives from "experience in the world," may be disadvantaged without appropriate credentials and extensive training for legitimizing roles and developing skills.

Indeed, Minuchin saw the paraprofessional movement as stemming from "the fantasy that somehow, along with the experience of being poor and black, comes the knowledge of how to treat the poor and black" (1969, p. 725). However, empathy seemed not to overcome lack of training, and "on a practical level . . . problems arose. The paraprofessionals, largely untrained, were given the responsibility for treatment but not the knowledge of how to do it" (1969, p. 725). Current research does not indicate that paraprofessionals are, overall, any more or less effective than professionally trained psychotherapists. However, the findings of Berman and Norton (1985) suggest that professionals may be better for brief treatment and for older clients.

Worker Attitude toward Low-Income Clients

Client socioeconomic status appears to be very important to workers. Schofield (1964) was one of the first to note helpers' apparent preferences for clients who, at the time they seek services, are economically—and otherwise—successful. He described the preferred patient for psychotherapy as YAVIS: young, attractive, verbal, intelligent, and successful (middle- or upper-class).

Non-YAVIS clients seem to evoke negative reactions from workers. Literature over a 25-year period indicates that mental health providers sense a lack of rapport with low-income clients; perceive them as inarticulate and suspicious; find it difficult to be genuinely concerned with them; view them as interested merely in symptomatic relief; view them as resistant, apathetic and passive; see their values as incompatible with the therapeutic endeavor; and see them as unable to benefit from treatment (Schaffer and Myers, 1954; Brill and Storrow, 1960; Affleck and Garfield, 1961; Kaplan, Kurtz, and Clements, 1968; Lorion, 1974; Rabkin, 1977). Recently, Franklin (1985) found that, in responding to an analogue case in which client SES was varied, workers perceived in working-class clients more "acting out," poorer prognosis, less suitability for treatment, and less insight. Workers also saw themselves as less effective with working-class, as compared with middle-class, clients.

Negative attitudes toward poor clients appear to predominate among certain groups of workers. Franklin (1985) found that more experienced workers anticipated work with lower-class clients as less desirable than work with middle-class clients. Similarly, Pratt (1970), who studied social workers and health care professionals, found negative attitudes toward low-income clients more evident among workers with college educations than among paraprofessionals; among those in direct contact with clients than among administrators; and among those more knowledgeable about the impact of social forces on clients.

Main, Bowman, and Peters (1972) studied social service workers in Atlanta model cities programs for a predominately black and low-income population, focusing on workers' perceptions of and relationships with clients. They found that private agency employees, nonprofessionals, and blacks were more likely to perceive clients positively, while public agency employees, professionals, and whites were more likely to perceive tension between themselves and their clients. White and black workers were found to differ in their attitudes toward poor clients in another study. Franklin (1985) found that black workers saw themselves as equally effective with working- and middle-class clients, while three-fourths of white workers saw themselves as more effective with middle-class clients. Similarly, white workers gave working-class clients poor prognoses, were less enthusiastic about working with them, and indicated they would have to alter their treatment approaches for them. The only significant difference in black workers' responses for working-class clients was a poorer prognosis.

What is the basis for some professionals' bias against work with low-income clients? The attitudes of mental health professionals simply may reflect those of the public at large, who have "decidedly more positive attitudes" toward the middle and upper classes (Rabkin, 1977, p. 172; also Bernard, 1965). A related explanation involves the notion of social distance and dissimilarity—and the reduction of attraction between people who differ in important ways. Noting that workers tend to be of middle- or upper-class status, Umbenhauer and DeWitte (1978) suggest that class or cultural differences between workers and clients lead to bias and reduce attraction, consequences that are not overcome by professional training.

Negative attitudes toward low-income clients may be perpetuated by stereotypes within the professional literature itself. For example, Shen and Murray (1981) portray low-income clients as having difficulty verbalizing, as having little faith that talking can help, as tending toward action rather than observation and awareness, as externalizing their problems, and as generally distrustful of others. Moreover, they see in these characteristics "developmental impairments which are manifested in the form of ego deficits, impairments in the capacity for object relations and pathological superego functioning" (p. 270). Judith Lee (1980) reviewed social work literature and found that low-income clients are frequently described as lower-class, apathetic, withdrawn, skeptical, poor therapy patients, deficient, disadvantaged, nonverbal, emotionally unresponsive, lacking self awareness, unable to reason abstractly, emotionally deprived, disorganized, multi-problem, experiencing extreme family pathology, preoccupied with survival issues, inadequate as parents, maladaptive, uneducated, unmotivated, hostile and resistant to any approach, difficult, and forming highly ambivalent relationships with various agencies. It is clear that in addition to being very negative, the literature frequently uses overgeneralizations and euphemisms to describe low-income clients, grouping together many different terms without separating fact from assumption. Lee concludes that the literature has "transmitted an almost totally negative view of the poor" (1980, p. 582). Recently, Sherraden (1984) criticized the use of vague labels, such as "the underclass," which serve to separate and oppress the disadvantaged, and called instead for social workers to use accurate, descriptive labels for the unemployed, hungry, and homeless.

Another possible source of negative attitudes toward the poor is workers' own experiences, suggested by the finding that experienced workers are particularly negative in their attitudes toward working-class clients (Franklin, 1985). Franklin suggests that the optimism for change exhibited by professionals early in their careers may be tempered by the realities of repeated experience with poor and involuntary clients who are not responsive to intervention, or who require resources that agencies cannot supply. Workers, thereby, may experience a diminished expectation of efficacy and a resultant dampening of enthusiasm.

Role conflicts experienced in social service delivery may also contribute to negative attitudes toward the poor. Social workers who resign from public welfare agencies often cite reasons such as overwhelming job demands, poor atmosphere and morale, and perceived inability to help clients (Wills, 1978). Workers in public welfare agencies are charged both with responsibility to serve clients and to follow established administrative procedures. Wills suggests that agency policies often outweigh client needs, resulting in role conflict and disillusionment for workers. Unable to assist clients in the way they would like, workers may become callous, apathetic, bitter, frustrated, and cynical. Main et al. (1972) also see bureaucratic organization in public agencies as contributing to negative attitudes in workers.

Many workers appear to reduce their expectations of significant change. It is widely documented that work with low-income clients seems futile to workers, who perceive clients as unchangeable (Heine and Trosman, 1960), see necessary services and facilities as lacking (Pratt, 1970), see the problems and needs as overwhelming (Cole et al., 1962), and see their own interventive knowledge and efficacy as limited (Pratt, 1970; Franklin, 1985).

Helping professionals also appear to perceive low-income clients inaccurately. For example, the literature repeatedly reflects the notion that low-income clients have less knowledge and more misconceptions about mental illness and psychiatry than middle-class persons, and that they lack interest, motivation, and resources to participate in treatment. Lilienfeld (1969) tested this assumption by comparing clients' answers to questions about mental health and treatment to the predictions of client answers made by professionals who worked at the clinic. Results indicated that professionals' assumptions about the clients' level of information and understanding were quite inaccurate. Although the professionals expected clients to ignore emotional factors and blame physical or unknown causes for mental illness, clients' responses were strikingly like those of the experts themselves. In fact, clients were more likely than professionals to say that treatment should be undertaken for mental illness. The investigator viewed the similarity of the patients' knowledge to that of the experts as "striking." Despite their level of psychological disturbance, the low-income clients answered nearly two-thirds of the questions correctly. Their knowledge was quite contrary to the stereotype of ignorance and misinformation formulated in the early 1950s and reiterated so often in the literature.

Worker Attitudes toward High-Income Clients

In contrast, professional helpers seem to have generally positive attitudes toward and, indeed, prefer clients who demonstrate social and economic success (Rabkin, 1977). However, wealthy and powerful individuals may pose some threat to social workers. In particular, social workers may have difficulty asserting their authority and professional competence with wealthy clients "whose lifestyle connotes a formidable authority . . . in its own right" (McKamy, 1976, p. 257). In such cases, workers need to explore their own feelings, such as envy and resentment, toward the wealthy and powerful; they also should strive to maintain a confident yet sensitive professional style. Powerful and wealthy clients are so atypical at some mental health and social service agencies that workers may alter normal agency routines and procedures for them. According to Soari and Johnson (1975), such alterations reflect workers' failure to respond to the client as an individual and may accentuate some of the client's problems.

CLIENT ENTRY INTO TREATMENT

Access to and Utilization of Services

Socioeconomic status appears to have a major influence on client access to helping services. Although low-income persons are more likely to experience mental health problems (Hollingshead and Redlich, 1958; Cockerham, 1981), those who need the services most seem to have least access to them. Several, but not all, studies of clinic records indicate that low-income clients, including the unemployed, are less likely to be accepted for outpatient mental health services than are higher SES groups (Schaffer and Myers, 1954; Brill and Storrow, 1960; Cole, Branch, and Allison, 1962; Albronda, Dean, Starkweather, 1964; Baker and Wagner, 1966). Low-income status may jeopardize male applicants in particular (Hollingshead and Redlich, 1958; Brown and Kosterlitz, 1964) although bias against accepting low-income women for treatment also has been identified (Rowden, Michel, Dillehay, and Martin, 1970). Rabkin contends that "it often seems that the most basic qualification of a patient regarding both the probability of being accepted for treatment and the type of treatment offered is that of social class" (1977, p. 172), leaving low-income people inadequately served by mental health and social service agencies.

Underutilization may be due to actual rejection of low-income clients from services when intake workers conclude that poor people cannot benefit from services, or to the fact that the available services are not appropriate for their problems (Goin, Yamamoto, and Silverman, 1965). Rowden et al. (1970) found that client socioeconomic status was especially salient in workers' decisions about accepting clients for psychotherapy when low-income applicants were described as having low levels of verbalization and insight. Those with more personal resources—such as high intelligence, insight, and ability to verbalize—and higher socioeconomic status are most likely to gain access to services.

In addition, underutilization may reflect the conclusion of low-income people that agencies and services are not responsive to their needs. Waiting lists, distance from clinics, and loss of work time necessary for appointments may be barriers to low-income clients (Cole et al., 1962). In response to such problems, it has been suggested that agencies tailor services to the needs of low-income clients, rather than viewing them as unwilling to utilize services (Stewart, Lauderdale, and Shuttlesworth, 1972). Agency outreach programs have been successful when low-income clients perceive them as meeting their needs. Weiss (1974) found low-income women willing to seek and utilize services when they were confident a professional could meet their needs; when they needed to act in the face of a confusing situation; and when they perceived the professional as strong and wise. Yet such clients acknowledged the difficulty of seeking help from low-status workers, young workers, or workers too uncertain of their skills.

Over the past two decades, services have probably become more accessible to individuals from varied SES groups (Marsh, 1980). However, recent financial difficulties and pressures toward efficiency have caused many community mental health services to close satellite and neighborhood centers, leading to concerns that services will be even less accessible to low-income clients. Indeed, Weinrich and Steinfeld (1982) found that recentralization produced dramatic changes in the size and demographic composition of agency clients. Clients from neighborhood areas who had been served by satellite sites—particularly women, Hispanics, and blacks—did not continue treatment at the central location after the satellite sites were closed. Loss of clients, and of minority clients in particular, was attributed to confusion from the transfer process, increased travel distance, and removal of services from familiar local communities with cultural supports. Thus, certain groups, such as low-income black women, remain at "double" or even "triple jeopardy." Victims of racism and sexism, and those limited in their ability to attain adequate economic resources as well, seem to remain underserved by helping agencies (Copeland, 1982).

Delay in Service Delivery

Client income also appears to affect the length of time between problem onset and the initiation of services. McDermott, Harrison, Schrager, and Wilson (1965) found that whether problems were identified by teacher, family, or both, the children of unskilled workers experienced a significantly longer delay in referral to mental health services after symptoms first appeared than did children of skilled workers. Thus the problems of low SES children were twice as likely to have persisted for two years or longer by the time treatment was first available. This may explain the fact that more "serious" diagnoses are made for low-income groups (a finding to be explored later) when they finally reach the point of treatment.

Public and Private Agencies

Ozarin and Taube (1974) report that clients with less formal education and fewer financial resources are significantly more likely to be served by public, rather than private, agencies. Two-thirds of the patients in private mental hospitals have at least a high school education, while only 47 percent of community mental health center patients and 38 percent of public mental hospital patients have completed high school. In state hospitals and federally funded mental health centers, 50 percent of patients have less than a 7th grade education.

The routes to services also differ; those with lower socioeconomic status and those in public facilities often are referred by police, correction agencies, community facilities, and schools; those with higher SES using private facilities are more likely to have been referred by family, friends, private psychiatrists, and physicians (Hollingshead and Redlich, 1958; Ozarin and Taube, 1974).

SES and Type of Treatment

Three decades ago, the Hollingshead and Redlich study, "Social Class and Mental Illness" (1958), provided convincing evidence that low-income clients were provided with "less sophisticated" treatment methodologies. Consistently, high SES clients were more likely to be treated as outpatients by private practitioners; if hospitalized, to be placed in private hospitals; to receive classic analytic psychotherapy or directive therapy; and to receive long-term individual treatment of 50 to 60 minute sessions. Lower-income clients, on the other hand, were more likely to be treated in state hospitals; to receive directive psychotherapy, custodial care, or sedation; and to see their workers once or twice a month for brief sessions.

Later studies point to the persistence of these patterns in outpatient services (Schaffer and Myers, 1954; Brill and Storrow, 1960; Soari and Johnson, 1975). In a study of 13,000 clients seen during a 3-year period at 17 community mental health centers in the greater Seattle area, Sue (1976) found that clients with low education were more likely to receive group therapy than individual therapy. However, ethnicity influenced service assignment even more strongly than socioeconomic status.

SES and Assignment of Worker

Several studies indicate that worker assignment also varies with the client's socioeconomic status. Minuchin charged, "the middle class are being treated by the trained, while the poor are being seen by the untrained" (1969, p. 728). According to the findings of several studies, clients of higher SES levels are more likely to be seen by psychiatrists, psychiatric residents, and psychologists, while lower SES clients are more likely to be assigned to social workers and students (Schaffer and Myers, 1954; Hollingshead and Redlich, 1958; Cole, Branch, and Allison, 1962; Baker and Wagner, 1966).

Mitchell and Namenek (1970) found that lower-class clients also were likely to be working with therapists whose parents were of lower socioeconomic status. In their nationwide survey of experienced clinical psychologists and psychiatrists, they found a significant overall relationship between therapist socioeconomic background and the social class of the therapist's "typical client." Such a social class match between worker and client may be a consequence of the fact that decreased social distance enhances comfort and similarity of experience (Pope, 1979).

Dropout

Treatment duration also has been linked to client SES. According to the findings of several studies, clients from low-income groups remained in treatment for a significantly shorter time than did higher income clients (Winder and Herkso, 1955; Hollingshead and Redlich, 1958; Lake and Levinger, 1960; Cole et al., 1962; Yamamoto and Goin, 1966; Beck and Jones, 1975).

Other studies, however, failed to find differences in dropout rate as a function of client SES (Overall and Aronson, 1963; Albronda, Dean, and Starkweather, 1964; Weissman, Geanakoplos, and Prusott, 1973). Safer, Riess, and Klein (1975) compared Medicaid and non-Medicaid patients who were receiving outpatient psychiatric and mental health services. Medicaid patients did not break or miss significantly more appointments than non-Medicaid patients, although there was a trend in that direction. These findings suggest that participation of Medicaid patients may not be "as different from other patients as has been assumed" (Safer, Riess, and Klein, 1975, p. 16).

Other studies identified and explored the complexities in the relationship between SES and dropout. Brown and Kosterlitz (1964) found that SES per se was not significantly related to number of visits, although problem definition—which was related to client SES—was. Clients who defined their problems as intrapersonal or interpersonal (often the more highly educated) stayed in treatment significantly longer than those who were unable to define problems or who stressed somatic symptoms, external situations, or multiple problems (often those with lower levels of education). Nietzel, Hile, and Kondo (1978) report that class IV clients (using Hollingshead and Redlich's scheme), were more likely than class V clients to terminate therapy prior to therapist's recommendation. The very poorest clients either refused service initially or improved at the time of mutually agreed-upon termination.

A number of explanations have been offered for the apparent dropout risk among low-income clients. Some explanations focus on client factors. For example, it has been suggested that attitudes of resignation may contribute to the tendency of low-income clients to drop out (Baum, Felzer, D'Zmura, and Shumaker, 1966). Such clients are frequently seen as unmotivated or incapable of participation in the helping process. Other explanations focus on client expectations about the helping process, suggesting that low-income clients expect to see improvement too soon. Indeed, Goin et al. (1965) found that 61 percent of the middle- and lower-income clients at an outpatient mental health clinic expected less than 10 sessions of treatment. The correspondence of these figures to the average length of stay reported in several studies led the investigators to suggest that low-income clients may not "drop out"; rather they stay in treatment as long as they anticipated.

Siassi and Messer (1976) see the emphasis on client factors as misplaced, and point, instead, to worker factors such as level of experience and training. There is clear evidence that low SES clients are assigned disproportionately to inexperienced therapists and that "almost all studies of low SES patients in therapy have been with relatively inexperienced therapists including psychiatric residents, medical and psychology students, or interns" (Siassi and Messer, 1967, p. 33). Indeed, there is evidence that worker experience is related to dropout among low-income clients. Clients were more likely to drop out with inexperienced workers (Baum et al., 1966). Older workers, with greater clinical experience, were better able to keep both high- and low-income clients. These workers were also more task-oriented, and more giving and less demanding in their treatment styles, suggesting that type of treatment and style of worker-client interaction also may affect dropout. Thus

Baum and Felzer (1964) suggest that low-income clients might be less likely to drop out if initial interviews were handled differently. In particular they stress the importance of establishing a common area of understanding, and suggest that workers discuss client expectations and the nature of the helping process.

Short-term treatment is often seen as more appropriate and sufficient for low-income clients, whose problems are likely to be pressing. In a major study of family service agencies, Beck and Jones (1975) report that low SES clients were more likely than higher SES clients to receive services of only one session. These differences were seen as reflecting the need for brief, practical services for economically disadvantaged clients. Such assumptions and the offer of brief treatment are likely to contribute to the shorter duration of treatment among low-income clients.

SOCIOECONOMIC STATUS AND CONSEQUENCES FOR THE HELPING PROCESS

Communication

Socioeconomic differences between worker and client are seen to impede communication, both when the client is wealthy and when the client is poor. Wealthy clients, according to McKamy (1976), may be reluctant to verbalize factual information about their problems and feelings, and seem to provide fewer nonverbal communication cues. Both the existence of problems and a professional's offer of help may be viewed by wealthy clients as an insult to their capacity. Intellectualization often further impedes therapeutic communication.

Considerably more attention focuses on communication between workers and low-income clients. Social work and social science literature over two decades points to socioeconomic differences in communication; the literature portrays the communication of low-income people as not only different, but also deficient. For example, Bernstein (1960), who studied the vocabularies of English boys, identified social class differences in language code, or schemes for regulating the selection and organization of speech. He found "restricted" and "elaborate codes" to be characteristic of lower and upper socioeconomic groups, respectively. Although he cautioned that a restricted language code is not deprived or deviant (Bernstein, 1970), his findings are often referred to by those who assume the existence of communication barriers in work with low-income clients.

Danziger (1976) concludes from his review of communication studies that socioeconomic status influences the way in which people use various "channels" of communication. For example, middle-class speakers talk more, use more varied vocabulary, and employ more varied grammatical constructions than do blue-collar workers. Nonverbal differences also seem evident, too, as low-income mothers and children engage in more physical contact, while high-income mothers and children engage in more reciprocal eye contact. Low-income children seem more influenced by paralinguistic cues, such as tone of voice.

Within the practice literature, the middle and lower classes have been portrayed as different cultures with different languages (Goldstein, 1973), and class-linked communication barriers between middle-class workers and low-income clients have been assumed. Verbal capacity was identified by Schofield (1964) as one of the characteristics of the preferred (YAVIS) client, a characteristic that low-income clients are assumed to lack. Their language is portrayed as unambiguous and concrete (McMahon, 1964; Gould, 1967), and class-linked differences in self disclosure and content have been assumed (Carkhuff and Pierce, 1967; Pope, 1979). For example, Pierson (1970) sees communication with low-income clients as impeded because they regard feelings as private property, not to be easily shared and explored.

Redlich, Hollingshead, and Bellis studied interviews and rated the communication skills of psychotherapy patients on the basis of "whether or not therapists and patients were relating meaningfully to each other on the verbal level and whether or not the patient understood the principle intent of the therapist" (1955, p. 65). Middle-class patients were found to understand and communicate significantly better than the lowest-class patients, who were seen as not understanding the essential message that their difficulties were attributable to emotional, rather than physical or external, factors. To attempt to bridge the "tangible," "authentic," albeit "permeable" (Pope, 1979) communication barrier between helper and low-income client, workers have been urged to provide information in precise and specific terms (Barr, 1973). They also have been urged to employ specific and concrete helping approaches, which are less dependent on complex and abstract verbalization (Chilman, 1966; Gould, 1967; Fishman and McCormack, 1970; Goldstein, 1973).

More recently, the assumption of class-linked communication difficulties and the findings on which the assumption is based have been strongly challenged. While acknowledging that socioeconomic status may have a stronger influence on communication than either race or gender, Higgins (1976) identifies many problems with these studies. For example, grammar, the focus of Bernstein's work, does not adequately predict communicative function, and laboratory settings may limit the expression and measurement of communication skills. Danziger, while acknowledging some SES differences, cautions against concluding that the language of low-income persons is simpler or more primitive than that of middle-class speakers.

> Lower class language or black language may be different from middle class language but the rules for constructing sentences are of equal difficulty and complexity in all cases. That is why the concept of cultural deprevation acquires rather dubious overtones (Danziger, 1976, p. 164).

Moreover, cultural or socioeconomic groups are not limited to only one style of communication, but instead appear "capable of displaying the full range of linguistic complexity" (Danziger, 1976, pp. 171–72).

Studies focusing on interview and helping situations also indicate that communication with low-income persons is not always problematic. According to Weiss' study (1974), low-income respondents did not differ from the U.S. population at large in their identification of sensitive discussion topics. Income, race, personal relationships, crime, and sex were seen as sensitive, regardless of SES. Moreover, "indigenous" and professional interviewers had similar success interviewing low-income respondents, although indigenous interviewers were better able to establish rapport and locate the hard to reach. However, these advantages appeared attributable to racial/ethnic similarity rather than SES similarity.

Similarly, studies focusing directly on therapy indicate that social class barriers to communication may have been overestimated. Lilienfeld found that clients with little education were still able to evidence a high level of sophistication via their concepts and vocabularies.

> Most of the patients' words were simple, but understanding and empathy were evident. Their sensitivity to suffering, tolerance of others' misbehavior, and appreciation of the possibilities of alleviating or curing mental illness were in direct contradiction to the pessimistic stereotype of the lower class patient's views often found in the literature (1969, p. 275).

Similarly, Weissman et al. (1973), studying female clients who received casework and pharmacological treatment for depression, found no effect of social class on client discussions in the casework sessions. Upper-class clients did not appear to be any more abstract in their discussion than lower-class clients who, in spite of having been discouraged by family and peers from talking about feelings, did not lack verbal skills in the treatment sessions. Some low-income patients answered questions with brief or one-word answers, but by the end of one month in treatment their verbal expressions were indistinguishable from those of higher-income clients.

Hollis concludes that

much has been made of the difficulty of the worker's finding the right words to use with the low income client, particularly in the discussion of feelings. There are, of course, some clients with whom this is truly a problem. Most workers report, however, that if they use simple, everyday English, they have no difficulty. Intellectualization and the use of technical language is helpful with neither lower-class nor middle-class families (1983, p. 637).

Assessment

SES and client presentation of problems.   Considerable attention has focused on the bearing of social class on the problems presented by clients. Several studies have explored the relationship of socioeconomic status to the number and types of problems presented by clients. Although the number of problems presented by clients appears not to vary by socioeconomic status (Beck and Jones, 1975; Safer, Riess, and Klein, 1975), low and high SES clients do seem to present different types of problems. Beck and Jones (1975), who studied the problems of clients at family service agencies, found that upper SES clients were more likely to report problems with personality adjustment and personal relationships, while lower SES clients were more likely to present problems related to economic resources and caretaking of family members. Frequency of family and home management problems did not vary by SES. Other studies suggest that low-income clients and unemployed clients are more likely than higher-income clients to present physical, medical, or somatic complaints (Brill and Storrow, 1960; Brown and Kosterlitz, 1964; Balch and Miller, 1974; Safer et al., 1975; Krystal, Moran-Sacket, Thompson, and Contoni, 1983). High-income clients, on the other hand, appear more likely to present emotional, interpersonal, and personal problems such as tension, anxiety, insecurity, and negative self image (Safer et al., 1975).

Clients' attribution of problems—their identification of causes—also may vary with socioeconomic status. Low-income clients have been found to attribute the cause of their interpersonal problems to another person and to be reluctant to see the contribution of their own behavior to such problems. Clients of higher SES seem more likely to attribute their problems to internal or personal factors (Balch and Miller, 1974; Safer et al., 1975). Of course, these differences in attribution may reflect differences in types of problems; low-income persons, in all likelihood, do experience more problems with social systems and may therefore be accurate when they make more external attributions.

Worker-client agreement on problem priority may also vary with client socioeconomic status. Beck and Jones (1975) found that workers were significantly more likely to agree on problem priority with upper- and middle-income clients than with low-income clients. This difference may be due, in part, to the tendency reported by Balch and Miller (1974) of workers to discount clients' perceptions of problems that are not emotional or social in nature (such as physical or somatic complaints). Low-income clients are more likely to present such problems and, hence, to have a perspective that differs from the workers.

SES and assessment of client functioning.   Worker assessment of client functioning appears to be strongly influenced by social class. Generally, more pathology is seen when low socioeconomic status is ascribed to clients. Levy and Kahn (1970) found SES bias in the test interpretations of both novice and experienced psychologists. When Rorschach test data were accompanied by a description of low socioeconomic status, clients were seen as more pathological and less likely to experience benefit from treatment than when the description was middle-class or when no SES information was provided. Indeed, studies indicate that clients described as middle-class are seen as more self-confident, better liked, more independent, and more assertive than are clients described as identical except of low social class. Lower-class clients, on the other hand, are seen as more conforming, more submissive to authority, significantly more guarded and suspicious, less sophisticated about the therapeutic process, and less intellectually impressive than middle-class clients; as having a less democratic family life, emphasizing somatic complaints, externalizing blame, and having a greater potential to strike their therapists (Briar, 1961; Lerner and Fiske, 1973). Duehn and May-adas (1976) found that social workers with psychoanalytic and ego psychology orientations employed more negative concepts in their assessments when they perceived clients as socioeconomically different from themselves. Behaviorally-oriented workers were not significantly affected by client SES.

Class biases in assessments often belie the facts. For example, McDermott et al. (1965) found that children of the lowest social class were more likely than those at higher class levels to be described as coming from "unstable and conflict ridden homes," when in fact, separation and divorce were more common among the higher SES families. Similarly, class-linked differences in diagnosed psychopathology were not borne out by behavioral measures of the children's adjustment at home.

Not all the evidence on SES and assessment is unanimous. Umbenhauer and DeWitte (1978), who studied the responses of 527 psychiatrists, psychologists, and social workers to a written protocol, found that patients were not seen as significantly more disturbed when the client's SES was identified as low. Moreover, Lerner and Fiske (1973) found that worker perception of client ego strength, verbal fluency, motivation for change, and amount of experienced anxiety did not vary by client SES. Fortunately, they also found that workers' perceptions of clients were not related to treatment outcome. That is, class-linked perceptions did not become "self-fulfilling" prophecies, due, perhaps, to the special desire of the workers studied to work with low-income clients.

SES and diagnosis. Diagnosis, or classification of problems, also has been found to vary by client social class. In general, diagnoses of neurosis are more prevalent among higher SES clients, while diagnoses of psychosis are more prevalent among low-income clients (Hollingshead and Redlich, 1958; Safer et al., 1975; Sue, 1976). Differences in particular diagnoses are evident also. Higher SES clients are more likely to receive such diagnoses as mild behavior disturbance, depression, affective psychoses, psychoneurosis, anxiety reaction, and passive aggressive personality (Hollingshead and Redlich, 1958; Safer et al., 1975). Problems of low-income clients, on the other hand, are more likely to be diagnosed as antisocial personality, acute anxiety neurosis, alcohol- and drug-related psychosis, organic psychosis, mental retardation, and disorders of childhood and adolescence (Hollingshead and Redlich, 1958; Schubert and Miller, 1978). Low-income clients also are significantly more likely than higher-income clients to receive diagnoses of schizophrenia (Dohrenwend and Dohrenwend, 1969; Dohrenwend, 1975; Safer et al., 1975; Nietzel, Hile, and Kondo, 1978).

These trends may occur within, as well as between, social classes; thus the lower the SES, the more likely are certain diagnoses. For example, Nietzel et al. (1978) found that the very lowest SES group (class V) received diagnoses of schizophrenia, personality disorder, or transient situational disturbance significantly more frequently than did clients in class IV. Similarly, personality disorders, including borderline psychoses, were diagnosed significantly more often in children of unskilled workers than in children of skilled blue collar workers (McDermott et al., 1965).

Social class may influence diagnosis even more strongly than the client's presenting problems. In one study, non-Medicaid patients who complained of anxiety were found four times more likely to receive a diagnosis of anxiety reactions than were Medicaid patients with the very same complaints. The Medicaid patients presenting anxiety complaints were five times as likely as non-Medicaid patients to be diagnosed as schizophrenic. Twenty-one percent of Medicaid patients, but only six percent of non-Medicaid patients, complaining of depression were diagnosed as schizophrenic (Safer et al., 1975). The investigators concluded that

> for almost all of the popular presenting complaints, including negative self image, work and school problems, marital and family difficulties, lethargy

and social problems and loneliness, medicaid patients tended to be categorized as schizophrenic and nonmedicaid patients as a variety of less serious—or less pejorative—diagnoses, chiefly as passive-aggressive personality or anxiety reaction . . . Medicaid patients tend to be diagnosed as schizophrenic no matter what problems they report (p. 15).

Why the differential diagnosis? Reasons for persistent findings of more—and more severe—mental illness in persons of lower socioeconomic status should be thoroughly explored. Some explanations focus primarily on workers and their reactions to client socioeconomic status, while others focus on clients and actual differences in the problems they present.

One explanation focusing on workers involves the concept of social distance. Schofield (1964), for example, suggests that workers may more readily identify with and accept clients whose social class is closer to their own. In turn, they may be less understanding of and more ready to reject lower-class clients. Consistent with this hypothesis, Duehn and Proctor (1974) found that social work students perceived and transmitted more information about clients whose socioeconomic status was closer to their own than they did about socioeconomically dissimilar clients.

Another factor involved in explanations of class bias in assessment by workers is attribution. Pollock and Menacken (1971) suggest that when assessing low-income clients, workers may unwittingly attribute consequences of physical and environmental adversity to individual traits of the person. For example, apathy, indifference, and inattentiveness to classroom activities may be attributed to innate personality traits in poor children, when, instead, environmental problems such as hunger, lack of sleep, and overcrowding serve to diminish the child's energy level and motivation. If, indeed, problems of the social environment are attributed to innate personality factors in low-income persons, the data on mental health and diagnoses may be inflated. This hypothesis is consistent with Heider's (1958) attribution formulation, which posits that severe, atypical events are likely to be attributed to internal (within the person) causes, while typical normative events are attributed to external factors. Perhaps the "culture of poverty" notion that socioeconomic difficulties stem from personal deficiency and pathology reflects the more fundamental tendency to attribute severe problems to within the person causes.

On the other hand, rather than revealing bias in assessment, the relationship between social class and diagnosis may reflect the fact that poor people, in fact, do experience more and more severe mental illness than do persons of higher SES levels. Such a conclusion is consistent with the findings of one particular type of study, the study of true prevalence. Studies of mental illness differ in their operational definitions of a "case" or "incidence," and many epidemiological studies, such as that of Hollingshead and Redlich (1958), define disorder in terms of admission to a psychiatric facility, or incidence of treated mental illness. Community surveys, on the other hand, enable the measurement of true prevalance of mental illness, treated or untreated. Such studies are seen as more accurate, since they reflect the actual prevalence of problems free from the potentially biasing effects of diagnosis and admission to a treatment facility.

Community surveys, too, indicate that mental illness appears to vary with social class. Dohrenwend and Dohrenwend (1969) conclude, from their review of 44 community studies, that there is evidence of an inverse relationship between social class and psychological symptoms: the higher the social class, the lower the prevalence of mental illness.

A variety of explanations have been offered. One explanation, the "downward drift" notion, posits that a person's social class is reduced (loss of income, job, or occupational prestige) as a result of mental illness. By the time data are gathered, the mentally ill person is already poor. However, neither geographical mobility nor downward social mobility has been confirmed in studies to date. For example, Hollingshead and Redlich (1958) found the socioeconomic status of schizophrenic patients to be the same as that of their family of origin. Only for the small portion of mental disorders that are genetic in origin is "social class selection processes" (or "downward drift") likely to be operative (Dohrenwend and Dohrenwend, 1969).

Others suggest that higher incidence of mental illness among low-income groups reflects a greater willingness to tolerate abnormal behavior (Hollingshead and Redlich, 1958). Recent data, however, do not support this view. Dohrenwend and Chin-Chong (1967) found that high- and low-status groups may, indeed, have different definitions of deviance, but the low-status groups are less tolerant of deviance than are high-status groups.

A final explanation of the relationship between SES and mental illness focuses on stress and its consequences for mental health. According to this view, low-income persons experience the most stress and, consequently, suffer more mental illness. The findings of Wheaton's (1983) research support the notion that chronic stress adversely influences mental health. Moreover, Dohrenwend and Dohrenwend (1969), who explored the prevalence of stress, found evidence of more stress in low SES groups: Life expectancy is shorter, and job loss or layoff, physical health problems, accidents, and injuries are more frequent. Although some stress, such as that related to achievement, may be more common among higher-income groups, the stresses affecting low SES groups were seen as more severe.

The Dohrenwends view economic instability as "one of the most pervasive and continuous sources of stress in industrialized society" (1969, p. ix), and perceive those threatened by economic instability or insecurity as the major group at psychiatric risk. During periods of economic decline, persons who lose income, prestige, and power are unable to maintain their lifestyle, fulfill personal aspirations, and meet the expectations of others. Greater material and emotional resources may enable higher SES groups to deal more effectively with life problems. Consistent with this view, data indicate that rates of mental hospital admissions fluctuate directly with instabilities in the national economy, a relationship that has been stable for at least 127 years (Dohrenwend and Dohrenwend, 1969). The major diagnostic categories of functional psychosis (including schizophrenia, manic depression, and other psychosis) react more sharply to economic downturns than any other diagnostic group, followed by the category of alcohol psychosis. Catalano, Dooley, and Jackson (1981) report that inpatient admissions of male clients—particularly to public facilities—follow unemployment rates directly, at a two-month lag.

The argument that chronic environmental stress precipitates mental disorder lends support to the notion that more mental illness may actually occur at low SES levels. But the evidence of social class bias in the assessment or diagnostic process is also convincing, particularly the evidence that varying client SES alone influences worker diagnosis.

Goals of helping. The findings of several studies suggest that client goals may vary according to socioeconomic status. In an early study, Hollingshead and Redlich found that the goals of low-income clients included sympathy, support, and "material help in the form of pills, needles, obscure rays, and ritual" (1958, p. 346). More recently, the goals of clients at Family Service Association agencies were found also to vary according to socioeconomic status. The treatment of middle- and upper-income clients, both black and white, was more likely to focus on relationships and issues of individual adjustment; that of lower-income clients, both black and white, was more likely to focus on caretaking services and financial, employment, legal, or environmental goals (Beck and Jones, 1975). Riessman (1966), too, found middle-class clients likely to present such goals as self actualization, growth, and understanding, while those of lower SES clients involved specific vocational, marital, or health changes.

The goals of low-income clients have been characterized as requests for symptomatic relief rather than help for an underlying problem (Brill and Storrow, 1960). However, Marsh views concrete services and tangible resources such as training, transportation, childcare, and health service referrals as perhaps "the most important aid that professionals can provide" (1980, p. 246) to low-income clients, who often experience multiple problems. Similarly, Mayer and Timms (1969, 1970) criticize social work's tendency to become preoccupied with psychological issues, to the neglect of economic problems. Because they fear their problems may appear too simplistic, unemployed clients with employment-related goals may "re-cast" their goals. That is, they may convey to agencies a desire to work on such goals as self growth and improvement in interpersonal relationships, goals that may appear safer, more earnest, and more attainable (Briar, 1980). Too, some clients may "hope that self-change will lead to eventual employment" (Briar, p. 901).

The evidence, then, suggests that the goals presented by clients frequently vary according to socioeconomic status. Some argue that the client's socioeconomic condition makes certain goals particularly important and appropriate. Workers would be cautioned, however, to ensure that the goals of helping are consistent with the problems experienced by clients. Goals should not reflect stereotypic notions of what "poor" or "wealthy" or "middle-class" clients need. Nor should goals reflect primarily the objectives that workers know they or their interventive methods can accomplish most comfortably or easily. What goals should reflect and incorporate is the problem as seen and experienced by the client.

Choice of Intervention

SES and client interventive preferences. It has been widely assumed that client expectations and preferences for the type of intervention vary by social class. According to several studies, low-income clients were found to expect and prefer treatment to be more medically oriented, more active, more concrete, and more directive than it usually is (Overall and Aronson, 1963; Riessman and Frank, 1964; Gould, 1967; Mayer and Timms, 1969; Cobb, 1972; Goldstein, 1973; Balch and Miller, 1974). Such expectations are often assumed to be different from those of middle-class clients, who are seen as less likely to anticipate direction and guidance (Riessman, 1965; Aronson and Overall, 1966). However, in several studies, no differences were found between the treatment expectations of middle- and low-income clients (Balch and Miller, 1974; Lorion, 1974; Frank, Eisenthal, and Lazare, 1978). In particular, clients' expectations for advice, support, and guidance appear not to vary by social class (Balch and Miller, 1974). Indeed, some studies indicate that middle-income clients want and expect more advice and guidance from their workers than they usually get (Heine and Trosman, 1960; Davis, 1974). Moreover, in their study of walk-in psychiatric clients, Frank, Eisenthal, and Lazare (1978) found no social class differences in requests for clarification, ventilation, control, confession, psychodynamic insight, reality contact, advice, and medical help. Although class V clients did want more active help (such as social, community, and administrative help) than other clients, they did want just as much psychodynamic insight and clarification. In summary, Frank et al. (1978) concluded that clients of various social classes tended to be more similar than different; they attributed this similarity among economically diverse clients to changes within the public's perceptions of emotional illness and therapy.

SES and worker interventive preferences.   Several surveys reflect workers' intention or expectation to use different treatment approaches for clients in different social classes. Balch and Miller (1974) found that medication was seen to be appropriate as the primary treatment only for clients at the lowest social class levels; workers expected to use medication with clients from the lowest class three times as often as for those from the highest class, and twice as often as for members of the working class. They expected to provide advice and supportive counseling for two-thirds of their upper- and middle-class clients, and for approximately half of their lower-class clients.

Rice (1963) provided a group of social workers with a description of background information about fictitious clients, varying client social class, and asked workers to indicate their preferred treatment approaches along with a rationale for their choice. They found evidence that workers' choice of treatment methods varied according to client social class. White workers and those whose own social class backgrounds are high have been found particularly likely to vary their interview approaches according to client social class (Rice, 1963; Franklin, 1985).

Data from agency records also reflect differential treatment according to client socioeconomic status. Measuring SES according to five classes, with "I" the highest and "V" the lowest, Hollingshead and Redlich (1958) found a clear class gradient in the provision of individual psychotherapy to "neurotic" clients: "All class I's receive it, 97 percent of the class II's, 84 percent of the class III's, 75 percent of the class IV's, and 59 percent of the class V's. Custodial care is limited largely to class V" (1958, pp. 266–67). Psychoanalysis and analytic psychotherapy were concentrated in the highest classes, and directive therapy was concentrated in middle and working classes.

SES variations in treatment also are reported for clients diagnosed as alcoholic and schizophrenic, but not for those with affective and organic psychotic disorders (Hollingshead and Redlich, 1958). In a recent study of 7,000 clients at a psychiatric clinic, Schubert and Miller (1980) found that the most frequent treatment recommendations for the very poorest clients were "evaluation only" and medication, although poor clients often failed to receive even the medication recommended. The evidence suggests, then, that workers select analytic treatment for higher-income clients (Rabkin, 1977), and medication or referral for lower-income clients. Although the literature does not consistently support the assumption that client preferences for treatment vary according to SES, it is clear that differential treatment is provided as a function of socioeconomic status.

Are interventions differentially appropriate? It is widely assumed that the appropriateness of interventions does, in fact, vary with client socioeconomic status. This assumption seems not to be based on studies of treatment effectiveness (to be reviewed later), but on the belief that clients' values and presenting problems vary by social class, and hence different interventions are appropriate for each social class. For example, traditional insight-oriented psychotherapy has been presumed to be suitable primarily for middle- and upper-class clients and inappropriate for low-income clients. This view has been expressed for over 30 years, although the specifics of the argument vary. For example, the culture of poverty literature of the 1960s assumed particular personality types among those with low income. Specifically, poor people were seen as lacking a future orientation, unable to defer gratification, and as physical rather than intellectual or introspective (Beiser, 1965; Riessman, 1965). Accordingly, low-income clients were seen as lacking in the cognitive and interpersonal skills required for therapy.

More recently, some contend that psychotherapy is inappropriate for the poor because of value incompatibility. The values central to traditional therapy, such as problem solving, future orientation, control of emotions, internal locus of control, adjustment, insight, and verbal and emotional expression, are seen as distinctly middle-class (Gursslin, Hunt, and Roach, 1960; Goldstein, 1973; Sue, 1981), and hence as antagonistic to the poor, whose life experiences teach that external factors prevail over personal effort (Sue, 1981). Thus Riessman and Miller (1964) challenged therapy's "unconscious projection of the values of the middle class" (1964, p. 33).

Finally, the appropriateness of therapy also has been challenged on the grounds that it does not address the problems of low-income individuals. Thus macro level interventions, aimed at social systems rather than at individuals and their interactions with systems, are seen by some as the treatment of choice. As Shapiro argues, the impact of the environment on low-income clients' lives is "so . . . significant that the worker appears compelled to subordinate psychodynamic to environmental intervention" (1983, p. 899).

These criticisms of the appropriateness of individual treatment for low-income clients stimulated a variety of responses. Some advocated the preparation of clients for traditional treatment, so that their expectations for the helping experience and their participation with the worker might be more appropriate. The effectiveness of these preparatory experiences and their impact on client outcome are discussed later in this chapter.

Others argued that workers should modify their interventive approaches or select methods that involve more directive worker roles. Thus, role playing, worker-directed activity, relationship enhancement, role induction, and prescriptive psychotherapy (Goldstein, 1973) were seen as more compatible with the expectations and values of the poor, more comfortable for the clients, and more appropriate for their presenting problems. Similarly, Bernard suggests that psychotherapists abandon traditional attitudes of "benevolent neutrality" (1965, p. 259) and passivity, which may be appropriate only for middle-class neurotics. With low-income clients, for whom nonverbal communication may be salient, workers were encouraged to communicate genuine interest and concern in actions, as well as words. Thus, in the initial phase of helping, workers are urged to be active and attentive to symptoms, and to offer sustainment, suggestions, and advice (Hollis, 1983). Of course, environmental treatment, or obtaining resources on the client's behalf, is advocated as a very important component of the casework method in work with low-income clients (Hollis, 1983).

Discussions of these issues often reflect the assumption that client socioeconomic status critically influences or even determines the appropriate interventive strategy. Some seem to assume that individually-oriented treatment is appropriate, but the particulars of the approach must be modified to enable low-income clients to participate. Others assume that individually-oriented approaches are ineffective for the presenting problems or inappropriate to the social realities of low-income life.

These debates over the appropriateness of individual treatment for low-income clients have served to highlight the potential for value conflicts between helper and client, and between the assumptions inherent in a helping approach and the realities of daily life for some clients. However, they may reflect, too, some confusion over the client's socioeconomic status and the client's presenting problem. Low-income individuals clearly have, among their problems, lack of sufficient economic resources. In this society, insufficient income also is associated with a myriad of other problems, such as inadequate health care, the stress inherent from economic vulnerability, lack of social influence and, often, social stigma. The appropriateness of traditional psychotherapy to such problems could hardly be argued.

However, what may be lost sight of is the vulnerability of low-income individuals to personal and interpersonal problems as well. As Hollis points out, "being poor does not provide immunity to family relationship problems, inner emotional problems, or problems related to illness or other kinds of stress" (1980, p. 10). Thus, low-income clients should not be seen as immune from intrapsychic and interpersonal problems, just as middle- and upper-income clients are not immune from situational, environmental, and economic problems.

Like gender and race, then, it would seem that socioeconomic status itself does not determine the appropriateness or inappropriateness of intervention. Rather the client's presenting problems would seem to dictate the choice of helping method. Socioeconomic status should be considered as only a beginning basis for making decisions about the appropriateness or the necessity of modifying treatment approaches (Goldstein, 1973).

Individual treatment, even psychodynamic casework, is not inherently appropriate for middle- and upper-class clients; nor is it inherently inappropriate for low-income clients. Rather, the array of problems presented by a client should be considered and explored. In many cases, both economic and psychological problems should be attended to, through different interventive approaches. Workers should not assume that because they have responded to problems of economic or environmental resources, emotional or interpersonal problems will be resolved (Siassi and Messer, 1976). Indeed, denying the effects of intrapersonal problems, as well as external stresses, on the poor is akin to inflicting one more form of subtle discrimination (Bernard, 1965, p. 260).

TREATMENT EFFECTIVENESS

The bearing of social class on treatment effectiveness remains the most fundamental issue. Those who provide helping services must consider the extent to which socioeconomic status affects client satisfaction with services and their actual benefit from treatment. It cannot be denied that socioeconomic status significantly affects clients' access to help, the way their problems are perceived and interpreted, their chances of remaining in treatment, the enthusiasm of their helper for working with them, and the type of help they are offered. Indeed, these problems, in and of themselves, have often constituted a basis for concluding that direct helping services are not very effective at meeting the needs of low-income clients. Certainly these problems constitute formidable barriers that preclude some clients from benefiting from services. But evaluation of effectiveness, beyond these mitigating factors, remains an important issue.

Some studies have examined low-income clients' evaluations of their helpseeking experiences. The results are not encouraging. Mayer and Timms (1970) found that low-income clients often saw their workers as uninterested in them or unable to help. Similarly, Weiss (1973) found that helpseeking generally produced considerable distress and difficulty for the low-income women she studied. Clients experienced stress when faced with long waiting lists and when their eligibility for services in one agency depended on referrals or information from another agency. In addition, clients experienced derogation of personal worth, particularly in the most bureaucratized agencies. Even when their relationships with the workers were not adversarial, clients perceived their workers as disapproving their character or condemning their lifestyle. Finally, nearly all respondents receiving public assistance were disappointed by their workers' lack of interest and assistance. Workers were seen as "too young, too harassed, too inexperienced, or too troubled themselves to be of much help" (Weiss, 1973, p. 325). Clients saw workers as failing to provide even the support and guidance that was explicitly requested.

Other studies have explored the bearing of client SES on the outcomes experienced in traditional outpatient mental health services. While a few studies indicate that more positive outcomes occur for higher SES clients than for lower SES clients (Rosenbaum, Friedlander, and Kaplan, 1956; McNair, Lorr, Young, Roth, and Boyd, 1964), most studies failed to find a significant relationship between client social class and treatment effectiveness (Katz, Lorr, and Rubenstein, 1958; Rosenthal and Frank, 1958; Brill and Storrow, 1960; Cole, Branch, and Allison, 1962; Albronda, Dean, and Starkweather, 1964; Brown and Kosterlitz, 1964; Hirt and Genshaft, 1978). Beck and Jones (1975) found race to have a stronger bearing than socioeconomic status on outcome. In evaluating this issue, Lorion concluded that "while socioeconomic status appears to be a significant correlate of acceptance for, and duration of, individual psychotherapy, it does not relate to treatment outcome" (1973, p. 263).

Unfortunately, the practice literature presents numerous accounts of therapy with low-income clients that do not enable clear evaluation of outcome. Some articles simply present the author's clinical impressions (e.g., Gould, 1967). Others, although empirical, limit their focus to dropout rates or client participation in the process, but do not examine actual client change or eventual outcome (e.g., Hacker, Illing, and Bergreen, 1965).

Concern over the problems in retaining clients in treatment prompted extensive efforts at modifying traditional forms of help for low-income clients. During the late 1960s, Goldstein developed an extensive research program to design and evaluate various methods of better "fitting" low-income clients to traditional psychotherapy. The resultant procedures included direct structuring (leading clients to believe they will like their workers); trait structuring (providing clients with information about their workers, such as warmth or experience); modeling (providing clients with models who are highly attracted to their workers); matching (pairing workers and clients on the basis of attitudes or interpersonal needs); leading clients to believe that their therapists have high status; and making the treatment more "effortful" for clients. Evaluation of these efforts revealed that although nearly every procedure was effective at increasing the attraction of middle-class clients to their workers, the attraction of low-income clients was not affected. Goldstein concluded that these efforts failed because they were aimed at fitting low-income persons into the "middle-class technology" (1971, p. 24) of psychotherapy. Noting that workers frequently have been urged to speak in more directive styles, and to try to enter the low-income client's frame of reference, Goldstein concluded that such "minor" modifications of traditional approaches "appear to have yielded rather little therapeutic benefit" (1971, p. 25).

Goldstein's efforts then turned toward the development and evaluation of more extensive modifications to traditional therapy. The resultant "Structured Learning Therapy," involving modeling, role playing, and social reinforcement, was "potentially tailored to lower-class and working-class populations" (1971, p. 201). Goldstein viewed the evidence regarding these methods as "most encouraging," although most of the laboratory and clinical evaluations involved only middle-class clients.

Several studies focused on the effectiveness of pretreatment procedures, often called *role induction procedures,* designed to make the role expectations of workers and low-income clients more congruent. Role induction procedures have involved pretreatment lectures to individual clients or groups of clients (Hoehn-Saric, Frank, Imber, Nash, Stone, and Battle, 1964; Yalom et al., 1967; Orne and Wender, 1968; Strupp and Bloxom, 1971; Jacobs, Charles, Jacobs, Weinstein, and Mann, 1972; Heitler, 1973; Holmes and Urie, 1975); providing reading materials to clients (Heilbrun, 1972; Sauber, 1974); and processes for vicarious or imitative learning through viewing films or modeled behavior (Orne and Wender, 1968; Truax, Wargo, and Volksdorf, 1970; Strupp and Bloxom, 1971).

These procedures have been evaluated in studies of both group and individual treatment and with various client groups. The results, while not unanimous, were generally positive. Some procedures were found to enhance the participation of low-income clients in the helping process (Hoehn-Saric et al., 1964; Heitler, 1973). Moreover, some investigators reported that the outcomes of clients exposed to role induction were more positive than those of control group clients (Hoehn-Saric et al., 1964; Orne and Wender, 1968; Sloane et al., 1970). Of course, the improved client participation in helping and subsequent more positive perception of the client by worker are likely, themselves, to enhance outcome ratings. Other studies, however, failed to find that role induction improved outcomes (Strupp and Bloxom, 1971; Truax et al., 1970).

In an interesting extension of the notion of preparation for treatment, Jacobs, Charles, Jacobs, Weinstein, and Mann (1972) simultaneously studied the effect of preparing not only low-income clients but workers as well. Worker preparation involved an orientation by a supervisor to low-income lifestyles, treatment expectations, and typical problems encountered in the treatment process. Findings revealed that prepared workers, regardless of race and socioeconomic background, were significantly better than nonprepared workers at retaining clients for longer times in treatment, proposing specific treatment plans, and perceiving clients as improved. Similarly, Evans, Acosta, Yamamoto, and Skilbeck (1984) report that as a result of orienting workers, in terms of knowledge about low-income white and minority clients and sensitivity to their problems and requests, client satisfaction and treatment effectiveness were enhanced. Thus, the outcome of treatment with low-income clients may be enhanced by increasing the worker's knowledge and sensitivity.

Other studies have explored the comparative effectiveness of various types of treatment with that of "traditional therapy" for low-income clients. Reid (1977, 1978) reported on effectiveness of task-centered casework with low-income clients in a public school system and a psychiatric outpatient clinic. Most of the clients had very low income levels, lived in inner-city, high-crime neighborhoods, and experienced significant physical and/or mental health problems. Task-centered treatment was found to be significantly more effective than a control procedure (brief, "supportive attention") in addressing clients' specific concerns and their general problem situations. However, a sizable proportion of low-income clients was likely to express reservations about the time limits inherent in the task-centered approach, as was a group of middle-income clients in family treatment (Reid and Shyne, 1969). The findings of other studies indicate that low-income clients responded well to brief or time-limited treatment (Goin, Yamamoto, and Silverman, 1965; Yamamoto and Goin, 1966; Stone and Crowithers, 1972). Mayer and Timms compared the effectiveness of alternative treatment approaches with low-income clients and concluded that low-income clients "profited greatly from a supportive-directive approach but gained little, if anything, from an insight-oriented approach" (1970, p. 143). However, the significance of the differences was not tested.

The bearing of client SES on the effectiveness of behavior therapy and traditional psychotherapy was explored in a well-designed study reported by Sloane, Staples, Cristol, Yorkston, and Whipple (1975). Psychotherapy was found to be significantly more effective with high-income clients than with low-income clients. Behavior therapy, on the other hand, was equally effective for high- and low-income clients, suggesting that behavior therapy may be less class-limited than psychotherapy—that is, it does not put low-income clients at a disadvantage and can better serve diverse groups of clients effectively.

Finally, socioeconomic status appears to have a major impact on the long-term outcome of psychiatric treatment. Gift, Strauss, Ritzeler, Kokes, and Harder (1986) assessed outcome two years after patients had been hospitalized for psychiatric treatment. Socioeconomic status was correlated with outcome, with low-income patients experiencing significantly poorer outcomes. The more specific and relevant question, that of the interaction between SES and treatment effect, was not addressed in the study.

An obvious weakness in even the best studies reviewed is the failure to consider the effectiveness of a particular intervention for clients of a particular SES group, and for various presenting problems. Given the importance of selecting interventions in terms of their appropriateness for the client's problems, such a focus is very important.

In summary, the evidence indicates that socioeconomic status is a powerful, but not necessarily determinant, factor influencing the provision of individual treatment to clients. Socioeconomic status clearly influences workers' attitudes toward and decisions about the help they offer; it also influences the problems that clients experience and bring for help. However, the assumptions that low-income clients cannot participate in the helping encounter, or that they have no problems for which individual treatment is appropriate, appear to be unfounded. Moreover, there is evidence that if their workers are informed about and sensitive to their problems and needs, and the intervention is appropriate for their problems, individual helping can be effective.

CONCLUSION

What conclusions can be drawn about the impact of socioeconomic status on intervention with individuals? First, it is clear that socioeconomic status difference between helper and client may also signal dissimilarity, unfamiliarity, and, perhaps to the client, the worker's inability to understand the presenting problem and pressing social realities. To overcome such barriers, the use of paraprofessionals has been advocated; however, their effectiveness has not been established. Only trained professionals are able to provide expertise and skill.

The extent to which the worker wants to work with a client may be influenced, in large measure, by the client's socioeconomic status. The literature is clear that many workers have negative attitudes toward, and little desire to work with, the poor. With upper-income clients, too, many helping professionals experience inhibitions and estrangement. Such attitudes may become self-fulfilling prophesies if workers harbor negative expectations of treatment efficacy.

Client socioeconomic status clearly affects access to and utilization of services. Low-income clients are less likely to be accepted for outpatient services and more likely to experience longer delays between problem onset and treatment initiation. The well-to-do and the poor also receive their help through different delivery systems; the poor are likely to use public agencies, while those from higher income levels are more likely to use private services. Research over a 30-year period also shows consistent differences in treatment type as a function of client socioeconomic status. Low-income clients are likely to receive brief, drug, or group treatment from student workers and professionals with less status; higher-income clients are more likely to receive individual, more intense forms of help from professionals with higher status and more years of experience.

Not surprisingly, the communication between helper and client is assumed to be affected by socioeconomic distance, although this may be due in large measure to portrayals in the practice literature of the poor as "concrete" in thought and communication. There is considerable evidence that the communication skills of the poor are not limited, and that class differences need not impair the quality of communication in the helping relationship.

Presenting problems and diagnosis vary by client socioeconomic status. Moreover, worker-client agreement about problems and attribution of problems is affected by socioeconomic distance. The problems of low-income clients are more likely to be identified as concrete and due to external factors, and to be more severe with respect to mental health functioning.

Contrary to widespread belief, client treatment expectations do not vary greatly by socioeconomic status. Clients of all income levels express the wish for more guidance and direction than is usually offered; low-income clients, along with the more well-off, understand the role of psychological factors in problem causation and maintenance.

Workers do seem to tailor their interventive approaches according to client SES. To enhance the appropriateness and effectiveness of helping, the literature advises workers to respond flexibly, actively, and directively. With low-income clients, the effectiveness of role induction has been demonstrated. In the final analysis, treatment should be appropriate for the client's presenting problem; socioeconomic status, of course, is likely to be a major influence on such problems.

With respect to treatment effectiveness, the evidence is mixed. While low-income clients often experience negative outcomes, this may be due to the inexperience of their workers, worker pessimism about prognosis, or the "lesser" forms of treatment with which they are often provided. Many studies fail to find a significant relationship between social class and treatment effectiveness. In the final analysis, effectiveness may depend on worker attitude and experience, and on the responsiveness of service delivery systems.

13

Socioeconomic Status and Family Treatment

Family socioeconomic status raises a number of issues for practitioners and agencies. Like the factors of race and gender, socioeconomic status appears to influence worker and agency responsiveness to the family, as well as the worker's perception that the family will be responsive to help. More subtly, a family's socioeconomic success may be viewed as a reflection of their strengths and abilities as a family.

Socioeconomic issues themselves may play a prominent role in the causation or maintenance of the problems experienced by low-income families. Poverty, homelessness, and hunger are problems in their own right, and families experiencing such problems will expect them to be the focus of any treatment they might seek. Their workers should seek to identify and make available the socioeconomic resources the family needs. Thus, resource procurement or systematic efforts toward social change are often the most appropriate interventions for some of the problems of low-income families. Family treatment, as it is usually thought of, is not likely to be as appropriate for the problems of homelessness and unemployment.

That is not to say, however, that family treatment is inappropriate for low-income families. It is appropriate for the personal and interpersonal problems experienced by some or all of the members of a family. Workers should understand that socioeconomic status dictates neither presenting problem nor appropriate treatment approach. Whatever a family's socioeconomic status, problems must be carefully assessed, and the most appropriate helping approaches should be provided.

Of course, socioeconomic status often affects the way treatment is conducted, and the way in which workers perceive and interact with families in particular. Such effects are the focus of this chapter. Thus it explores the effects of socioeconomic factors on worker evaluation of family strengths and weaknesses, the problems on which treatment is focused, and the choice and success of intervention with families at various socioeconomic levels.

THE SALIENCE
OF SOCIOECONOMIC STATUS

Salience to Workers

Family socioeconomic status appears to be very important to workers. For example, according to McKamy (1976), many social workers identify themselves as helpers of the poor and see their professional training as equipping them to deal primarily with those who are economically or socially disadvantaged. Such workers would perceive the treatment of poor families as consistent with their professional mission and objectives. Needless to say, those who do not see working with the poor as part of their professional mission will work with them less readily. They may see their helping approaches as more appropriate for middle- and upper-income families, and might refer low-income families elsewhere.

The employment of paraprofessionals has frequently been advocated for work with low-income families. In particular, they are called upon to deal with problems involving housing, food, jobs, legal issues, and public assistance (Gwyn and Kilpatrick, 1981). There seem to be several reasons for this. Epstein and Shainline (1974) believe that use of paraprofessionals with low-income families reduces the "social and psychological gap" between provider and recipient of service. Moreover, because of their own life experiences, paraprofessionals may be better able to use informal social networks and to communicate without professional jargon. They also may be more willing to visit low-income families in their homes, due perhaps to their comfort level in less affluent communities and to the fact that these tasks are relegated to them by middle-income professionals. However, there may be some disadvantages to their employment. Paraprofessionals may be less skilled at negotiating bureaucratic systems and they may be less skilled as practitioners and hence less able to assess and treat complex problems (see also Chapter 12 for a discussion of this issue).

For some workers, socioeconomic status also influences their comfort in interacting with families. For example, social workers who are not accustomed to wealth and power may experience conflict in working with families who are influential and more successful socioeconomically than themselves (McKamy, 1976). With wealthy families, workers may respond by attempting to defend themselves and their profession.

Salience to Families

Socioeconomic status may be salient to families primarily insofar as it affects their access to treatment. Indeed, concerns have been expressed that socioeconomic factors may limit access to and use of helping services (Bard and Berkowitz, 1969). Especially when agencies limit their focus to particular problems and services, families at certain socioeconomic levels may find themselves unable to obtain the help they need. For example, Cloward and Epstein charge that family agencies have abandoned so-called multiproblem families, leaving them dependent on welfare departments (1965, p. 626). Within the past twenty years, public and private agencies have separated their foci, with public agencies assuming responsibility for environmental and concrete problems such as housing, employment, and medical needs, and private agencies assuming responsibility for interpersonal or psychological problems. However, this division has not been complete; as a result, low-income families are sometimes referred to public agencies when they have problems other than income maintenance. This separation has also accentuated the psychological conception of "family problems" (Cloward and Epstein, 1965).

The data on client SES and use of services indicate that low-income families are less likely to be referred for services (Langner et al., 1974). Once they are in treatment, they often receive fewer treatment sessions than do higher-income families (Cloward and Epstein, 1965). However, according to one study, among those who present marital and parent-child problems at early stages of development, lower-class families are less likely to be placed on waiting lists than are middle- and upper-class families (Beck and Jones, 1975).

SOCIOECONOMIC STATUS
AND FAMILY PROBLEMS

Families at different socioeconomic levels are widely assumed to experience different kinds of problems and, therefore, to present different issues to agencies when they seek help. For example, the practice literature characterizes low-income families as "multiproblem," and indicates that their problems are likely to include crises and emergencies such as suicide attempts, truancy, and runaway adolescent children (Gwyn and Kilpatrick, 1981).

Do families at different income levels in fact present different types of problems for professional help? In one of the very few studies of this question, some SES related differences were found. For example, husband and wife conflict over sex, use of leisure time, and handling of children was somewhat more frequent among upper- than lower-income families; problems involving money, physical abuse, alcoholism, and nonsupport were slightly more prevalent among low-income than high-income families. However, differences over relatives, housekeeping, and infidelity did not differ by socioeconomic status of family. At all socioeconomic levels, communication was the most frequently presented problem (Beck and Jones, 1975). The investigators concluded that "problems . . . varied less by socioeconomic status than might have been predicted" (p. 148), and workers should not assume a priori that the problems presented by families will differ according to their socioeconomic level.

FAMILY DYNAMICS

The perception and assessment of families at various economic levels is complicated by at least three factors. First, in our society, families are seen as responsible for the physical and mental health, economic support, nurturance, and socialization of their members (Sussman, 1977). The inclusion of economic support in these responsibilities signals the role of socioeconomic issues in perceptions of family health and strength. As a consequence, those who are economically disadvantaged also may be seen, even by professionals, as failing to adequately fulfill family responsibilities and roles (Ferree, 1984). In other words, the absence of money may be seen as a reflection of family weakness.

Second, the family functioning typical of middle-class whites in the United States seems to be accepted as the norm, and families that depart from this norm often are seen as problematic. According to Gwyn and Kilpatrick (1981), the family treatment literature appears not to sufficiently recognize and reflect the actual diversity of U.S. families. Geismar (1964) has urged social workers to avoid middle-class biases in their notions of family health and functioning. Toward this end, he suggests that the notion of "inadequate" family functioning be limited to cases in which basic laws are violated, such as situations of extreme stress and physical suffering.

The tendency to define families at certain socioeconomic levels as deficient may be accentuated by the worker's theoretical perspective, or frame of reference. One of the prevailing perspectives on family dynamics, systems theory, may lead workers to view individual or societal problems in terms of pathological family interaction (Bryant, 1980). Thus when individual family members experience problems, the worker may embark on a search for associated problems in the family, such as faulty communication patterns and weak family structures. In particular, members of poor families, though not seen as villainous persons, are seen as agents of a pathological family system. Thus their presenting problems may be seen as resistant to change (Bryant, 1980).

Similarly, family systems theories often focus "almost exclusively on interpersonal transactions," to the neglect of "macrosystem" problems. The result of this perspective is often inappropriate "therapizing." "Family therapists who 'therapize' redefine emotional distress that is environmentally generated as inadequate family or interpersonal functioning" (Johnson, 1986, p. 300).

The third problem evident in perceptions of families is the tendency to generalize and stereotype. In particular, there is the danger of concluding, from the observation that some poor families experience multiple problems, that most low-income families are "disorganized." Minuchin cautioned against such generalizations, making clear that the characteristics of disorganized low SES families are not applicable to all low-income families (Minuchin and Montalvo, 1967). Minuchin himself is careful to differentiate among various types of disorganized families, identifying such different patterns as the disengaged family, the enmeshed family, the family with the peripheral male, the family with noninvolved parents, and the family with juvenile parents.

Unfortunately, the distinctions between disorganized, multiproblem families and low-income families in general have not always been heeded. Minuchin's descriptions of disorganized families are often applied across the board to low-income families. For example, low-income families are often described as angry, aggressive, violent (Wortman, 1981), resigned, and living in hate, hostility, fear, hopelessness, and helplessness. Furthermore, they are perceived as generally "unaware of the society in which they live, what it expects of them, and what they can realistically expect to get" (King, 1967, p. 203). The family unit or structure itself is seen as not only manifesting pathology, but also as serving to transmit problems from one person to another, across situations and generations (Minuchin, 1967). In the words of King, "These people have no concept of a family as a group of individuals related by kinship, marriage, or some systematic regular association, no awareness that parents and children have distinct roles to play, and no sense of the family group with immediate and long-range individual and group goals that require thought and planning" (1967, p. 204). Even recently poor urban families were characterized in terms of the experience of multiple problems; that is, they are perceived to experience chaotic multigenerational patterns with unclear boundaries and roles, inconsistent discipline, family relationships that are too tight or too distant, and parental lack of control (Sherman, 1983). In general, low-income families are seen as differing "markedly from middle class and social structure and cultural norms" (Behrens, Rosenthal, and Chodoff, 1968, p. 689). Thus, the clear impression has been conveyed that socioeconomic status affects family dynamics, beyond its obvious impact on the family's resources.

What the practice literature has not made clear is that what poor families have in common is their economic plight. As Sherman states, "poor families are homogeneous only in their poverty, and even that is relative, based upon family size, age, needs, health, available resources, and the cost of living in a given location" (1983, p. 24). Furthermore, poverty is not necessarily associated with problems in family functioning; some, but not all, low-income families may experience such problems. What follows is a more detailed examination of specific aspects of family dynamics for those at various income levels. It is anticipated that such a review will provide current and accurate information, producing a perspective that may serve to dispel inaccurate assumptions and enable practitioners to approach their work with families from a more informed basis.

Power

Marital interaction is one aspect of family dynamics that is particularly assumed to differ by family socioeconomic level. Indeed, consistent with the culture of poverty assumptions, marital dynamics have been seen as very different, and indeed deficient, for low-income families. Yet patterns of decision making, conflict resolution, and communication might vary less by socioeconomic status than some would expect. In a recent study of primary college education couples, Krausz (1986) found that most decisions were made jointly between husband and wife. This style of decision making is not limited to middle- or upper-class families. Osmond and Martin (1978) found egalitarian decision making not only to occur, but also to be the most important variable for explaining marital intactness among low-income couples. In marriages with egalitarian or democratic decision-making patterns, 72 percent of the marriages were intact; in contrast, where the husband made autocratic decisions, only 27 percent of the marriages were intact. Also important were styles of conflict resolution. Where conflict resolution was democratic, 80 percent of marriages were intact; where one spouse seldom gave in, only 54 percent of marriages were intact. Hawkins, Weisberg, and Ray studied couples' styles of communication and found an identical rank ordering of preferred styles at all educational levels. "Everyone, regardless of class, seems to value talking things over calmly . . . and to detest a pure power orientation . . . The data are even more striking in regard to the degree to which all couples, regardless of class, espouse a modern ideal of intimacy (i.e., respectable confrontation of feelings) in marital communication" (1977, p. 489). Education did seem to affect the style of communication actually engaged in, with more highly educated couples better able to engage in more open, and less closed, communication in emotionally aroused situations. However, all class differences were small and matters of degree, not kind, leading the investigators to conclude that the influence of socioeconomic status on styles of marital communication probably has been overdrawn. Practitioners cognizant of these data would refrain from assuming that a family's income determines their style of decision making or balance of power.

Household Division of Labor

Does division of household labor vary by socioeconomic status? Are low-income families any more or less likely to share such responsibilities? According to some evidence, couples may have similar household divisions of labor, regardless of socioeconomic status. Ferree (1984), who studied couples' working-class marriages, found that they differed less in actual division of labor than they did in norms or beliefs. In working-class marriages, husband were "supposed" to be unwilling participants in housework, although, in fact, family members pooled their efforts and resources to work together. The family was emphasized over individual issues, perhaps because these families together face an oppressive environment. In contrast, middle-class families emphasized the notion of individual opportunity, experiencing family claims on their time as restrictions of individuality and independence.

Family Structure

To what extent does family structure vary by socioeconomic status? Are wealthy or low-income families organized differently or differentially stable?

In terms of family composition, it has been commonly assumed that low-income families would have a different structure than the nuclear family, which is presumed to be the norm for middle- and upper-class families. Multigenerational families have been assumed common at low SES levels. The data, however, suggest that multigenerational, extended families are rare, constituting less than 10 percent of all welfare families, occurring primarily when the mother of children is very young, age 16–17 (Scheirer, 1983). The predominant structure of families receiving Aid to Families with Dependent Children (AFDC) is that of a mother living alone with her children. Scheirer concludes, "the apparent preference of welfare mothers to live apart from other adults when they can afford to, is likely to reflect the values of the American Society as a whole" (1983, p. 770).

Similarly, family stability appears not to vary by social class. Osmond and Martin (1978) found marital stability to be similar among low-income and middle-class families. Contrary to popular assumption, low-income families were quite stable, with more than half either currently married or previously married for a duration of 15 years or longer. Among a clinic population, McDermott et al. (1965) found that separation and divorce were actually more frequent in upper-income or skilled occupational groups. Similarly, Locksley (1982) reports that divorce increases at higher educational levels. Such data should temper the tendency to perceive low-income marriages as unstable. Even when a relationship is evident between low-income status and family breakdown, the direction of causality may differ from that commonly assumed. Chilman cautions that family breakdown should not be seen as the cause of poverty when, in all likelihood, the reverse is true: "Poverty is a leading cause of family instability" (1975, p. 57).

Within two-parent, intact families, family functioning may vary according to amount of time the father is available. Gullotta and Donohue studied higher-income corporate families, and observed a family style in which the wife is generally "in charge" of the family. Husbands were found to exit and re-enter and re-exit the family frequently, both physically and psychologically. Indeed, the husband may himself be seen by other family members as an outsider in the family, although he is not perceived as deserting the family due to the substantial income he provides. The father's time away from family does affect the organizational structure; attempts of husband and wife to share home responsibilities rarely succeed when the father is so frequently absent due to work involvements. Thus practitioners would be cautioned against making assumptions about the structure, stability, and organization of families on the basis of information about their socioeconomic status.

Marital Satisfaction

Does marital satisfaction vary by socioeconomic status? Do the stresses of economic hardship place "ceilings" on the quality of marital relationships? Or, given the evidence that divorce is as likely or more likely at upper educational levels, should we expect a relationship between education and marital satisfaction? Lockley's (1982) research suggests that marital satisfaction varies as a function of education, but not occupation. Data on marital partners with less than a ninth grade education suggest the following:

1. they tended not to spend leisure time with their spouse
2. they did not report having problems with marriages
3. they did not feel inadequate as spouse and parent
4. they tended to view their marital happiness as average

In contrast, those with a college education or more were more likely to

1. acknowledge marital problems
2. feel inadequate at times as a spouse and parent
3. rate their marital happiness as very happy

Locksley assumed that higher levels of education facilitate verbalization and conflict resolution, which over time enhances marital adjustment and furthers marital companionship. However, it also should be noted that divorce increases at higher educational levels. Other studies report that although economic satisfaction is significantly associated with marital satisfaction (Scanzoni, 1977), there is no evidence that socioeconomic level itself affects marital satisfaction (Filsinger and Wilson, 1984). Workers, then, should view marital satisfaction as an issue to be explored and not as a direct function of family socioeconomic status.

Parenting

Most of the literature on socioeconomic status and family treatment focuses not on marital interactions but on parenting issues. Does socioeconomic status bear on parenting, and if so, how? Is the "quality" of parenting affected by economic factors? Does sharing of parenting vary by socioeconomic level? Krausz (1986) reports that high socioeconomic status increased husband's performance of childcare tasks, although the couples she studied were college educated and thus the variability of socioeconomic status was limited.

The practice literature has contributed to the impression that low-income parents are often "poor" parents. Minuchin, one of the major contributors to this literature, focused on multiproblem families with "multiple acting out boys." Seventy percent were welfare, single-parent families. Minuchin described parental relinquishment of responsibility for control, guidance, and protection of the children. Breakdown in communication between parent and child resulted in subsystems within the family, and the sibling subsystem often assumed responsibility for socialization. This was problematic, in that this subgroup drew power-oriented values from the "socially deprived and distorted subculture in which these families lived" (1970, p. 127).

Although Minuchin's descriptions were of disorganized families, it seems to have been a short leap from observations about a particular multiproblem low-income family to conclusions about poor families in general. Indeed, some perceive all low-income families as experiencing severe parenting problems. For example, according to King "the parents must be taught how to rear children; the children have to be taught to think and then how to think in social terms, how to behave in accordance with the basic rule of deportment in social situations" (1967, p. 204). Parental roles such as head of family or provider were seen as unclear or unstable, and parents were assumed to fail to understand age-appropriate roles for children. Low-income fathers were described as "shadowy, transient figures having little strength and . . . stability" (p. 204). Concerns about the quality of parenting in low-income families have led to concerns that the children would suffer. The extent to which this is true remains unclear. Children of AFDC families have been reported more likely than nonwelfare families to be seriously impaired in a variety of ways (Langner et al., 1974). Yet, according to other reports, the social functioning of individuals in poor families is not necessarily more problematic than that of higher-income individuals (Geismar, 1964). These mixed feelings suggest that family socioeconomic status itself does not provide diagnostic information about problems or services required.

Assumptions that poor people are poor parents have been strongly challenged. For example, Chilman (1975) regards such assumptions as "highly fallacious." Moreover, the assumptions are disputed by findings of several studies. For example, Lurie (1974) found that mothers of all income levels were involved with, and expressed concerns about, their children, although the specific nature of the concerns differed by socioeconomic status.

Being poor does increase a person's vulnerability to problems. Crowded inadequate housing, poor sanitation, and inadequate health, educational, vocational, and social services should be recognized as serious environmental stresses. At the same time, they should not be viewed as reflections of either personal or family pathology (Chilman, 1975; Orcutt, 1977). In other words, family pathology does not cause these problems, but practitioners should recognize the contributions of environmental stresses to the problems experienced by poor families.

PRACTITIONER–FAMILY DYNAMICS

Worker assumptions about family dynamics serve as the context in which family problems are perceived. To the extent that workers assume that family mental health and interaction varies by socioeconomic levels, the possibility remains that workers will perceive and incorporate into the treatment agenda problems some class biases. That is, in addition to the problems articulated by the family, the worker may assume certain aspects of family dynamics as problematic as a function of the family's socioeconomic status. This is a particular risk for workers who stereotype, who assume homogeneity among families of particular SES levels, and who adopt middle-class norms as ideal for all families. Such workers may assume that because families are poor, they experience or transmit pathology. In turn, those workers may impose on the family a treatment agenda reflecting problems the worker has stereotypically associated with low-income families.

The tendency to assume certain problems among poor families is reflected in the treatment literature. For example, low-income families are assumed to present problems of underorganization, unhealthy alignment, and diffuse boundaries (Kraft and DeMaio, 1982). Similarly, workers are urged to help poor families clarify subsystems and roles, teach open communication, establish self control (especially for parents), and enhance self esteem (Rabin, Rosenbaum, and Sens, 1982).

Although poor families may experience problems in these areas, workers should not assume that socioeconomic status alone dictates family problems. Hollis (1965) urges workers to avoid stereotyping, pointing to the extensive heterogeneity among low-income families in ethnic background, religion, family structure, educational attainment, values, and aspirations. She also urges workers to recognize that problems of personal and interpersonal adjustment are not the "monopoly" of middle- and upper-income clients. Neither should workers assume that all low-income families necessarily experience problems in family structure, communication, and roles.

Bryant points out that "families do not enter treatment without their own ideas; they often have a rather firmly held belief about the situation that involves at least some psychological theorizing" (1980, p. 631). When workers convey to low-income families that their ideas about problems are invalid, they may experience some puzzlement or anger, and even assume the worker does not understand them.

Thus, workers should first listen carefully to the family's version of the problem, appreciating the problem as it seems to those who experience it. The focus should shift from "what is the hidden problem?" to "how does the family see the problem and what does it mean to them?" Thus, workers need to view the family's perception of the problem as just as accurate as, or more accurate than their own (Bryant, 1980).

ASSESSMENT

In what other ways may the assessment of problems be affected by family socioeconomic status? How is the perceived severity of family problems influenced by socioeconomic status, and to what factors are their problems attributed? Although very little research has focused on these issues, the literature does provide some direction.

Some have suggested that the source and type of information used in family assessment may vary with socioeconomic status. For example, McKamy (1976) sees wealthy families as less likely to convey information about themselves through nonverbal channels. Thus, with these families, workers may rely less on factual information than on clinical observations. With low-income families, home visits—in which families can be observed in the context of their problems—are often suggested as increasing the worker's knowledge about the family and thereby facilitating the assessment of family dynamics (Behrens, 1967; Fleischer, 1975).

Beck and Jones (1975) studied the amount of time workers spent discussing various problems with families, and found that not all problems received the same amount of attention. For example, less time was spent on environmental problems, such as income, employment, and housing, than was spent on problems relating to children, personality adjustment, and home management. Such a finding may make sense, if it is assumed that the resolution of concrete or environmental problems is less complicated and time consuming than is the resolution of interpersonal and intrapersonal problems. Also it should be remembered that direct practitioners are probably more comfortable working on inter- or intrapersonal problems. In this sense they adhere to what is referred to as the "law of the instrument" (Kaplan, 1964). That is, the tools that workers possess determine the types of problems they detect and believe need attention. However, this finding is troublesome if it reflects a tendency of workers to take less seriously or to pay less attention to environmental problems. When such problems are major sources of stress to low-income families, or when these problems exacerbate other problems, their relevance and urgency to clients is not minimized. If, by spending minimal time discussing such problems, workers imply that the importance of these problems is not perceived, the helping process may be seriously impaired.

The attribution of problems, or explanation in terms of various causative or maintaining factors, may be influenced by socioeconomic factors. For most family therapists, problems are seen not only as a function of disturbed intrapsychic reality, but also as a function of family structures that contribute to or maintain problems (Canino and Canino, 1980). The locus of problems, therefore, is often seen within the family rather than within the individual. Such a perspective led Minuchin (1967) to shift his concern from acting out juveniles to the families of the acting out boys. The consequences of this perspective have been critiqued, particularly with respect to low-income families. According to Fleischer, when family therapists perceive the locus of problems within the family rather than within the individual, "they tend to treat the family as if it were an individual and hold it 'responsible' for its problems and for the problems of individuals within the family" (1975, p. 287). Attention thus may be diverted from environmental stresses that contribute to the family's problems (Kraft and DeMaio, 1982). In our view, problems should be viewed not only as a function of interaction within the family, but also in terms of interaction between the family and its environment. This is particularly important for low-income families, who, as noted earlier, often experience extensive problems in their social environments (Cloward and Epstein, 1965).

Indeed, some see nearly all problems of low-income families as a function of social, environmental pressures. In challenging the view that personal problems cause unemployment, Hollis (1965) suggests, instead, that personal and family problems are the end result of unemployment and its resultant poverty. Cloward and Epstein add that economic deprivation compounds the problems of families in an industrial society; "problems related to adolescence, aging, physical disabilities, or other sources are worsened by poverty" (1965).

In summary, the family treatment literature presents a variety of perspectives for the assessment of problems in low-income families. Some perspectives see family problems as residing primarily within the interactions between family members themselves; others see problems in terms of the family's interaction with the larger society; still others see the problem as only an issue of poverty. All of these possibilities have merit, and are supported by the evidence of the varieties of problems experienced by families. Some poor families have difficulties in their interpersonal relationships; others are doing well in spite of their pressing problems of poverty, homelessness, or unemployment. Therefore, workers would be advised to consider all these possibilities, and to assess the range of problems experienced by the particular family they are attempting to help. Low-income families should not be assumed to be immune from, or as necessarily experiencing, any particular problem.

INVOLVING THE FAMILY

Involving the family in the treatment process is always an important and challenging task. The family treatment literature suggests that this task may be complicated by the family's socioeconomic status, both with high- and low-income families. It is often assumed that low-income families are not genuinely motivated for treatment. Although such an assumption is not borne out by higher dropout rates for low-income families, the acceptance of such an assumption by the worker may make the task of involving the family more difficult. Workers who assume families to be unmotivated for change are likely to be less enthusiastic about working with them. Of course, if the assumption is true, such families may be reluctant to form a working alliance with the worker.

It also may be problematic to involve wealthy families in treatment. According to McKamy (1976), wealthy families often insist "we are functioning just fine," when workers attempt to assess their problems and facilitate their participation in treatment. Such resistances, intellectualization, and reluctance to reveal feelings make the task of establishing a working alliance between family and therapist quite difficult. The recommendations offered in Chapter 7 may enhance communication and the establishment of therapeutic relationships.

CHOICE OF TREATMENT APPROACH

When selecting among treatment approaches, is the worker influenced by the socioeconomic status of the family? Although the choice of intervention is important, the attention to this issue in the literature is somewhat one-sided: Much more is said about interventions assumed appropriate for low-income families than is said about those for upper-income families. This may reflect an assumption that while high-income status does not affect the appropriateness of interventive approach, certain approaches are inherently appropriate or inappropriate for low-income families. Such an assumption, however, has not been empirically tested.

For low-income families, the literature conveys a clear impression that the form or structure of helping should be modified. Workers are encouraged to clearly indicate rules about attendance and guidelines for listening and participating in sessions (Sherman, 1983). Furthermore, it is suggested that treatment for low-income families be short-term (Bryant, 1980) and focused on clearly defined goals (Sherman, 1983).

Workers are advised to avoid referrals of low-income families to other agencies or services, since such families have, in all likelihood, already been shuttled around between agencies (Wortman, 1981). Hallowitz (1975) urges workers to see poor families without delay and to attend to immediate, pressing problems. Attention to the family's everyday problems and emergencies, in particular, is advised, not only because such issues are important in their own right, but also because such attention can enhance the family's perception of the worker as trustworthy. Such action also may enhance the worker's ability to enter and influence the family system (Minuchin, 1965). Similarly, Minuchin advocates a focus on "here and now" issues in which family members search for solutions through interaction among themselves.

Workers are encouraged to be directive and assertive with low-income families (Hallowitz, 1975), yet expressive of their feelings and attitudes about the family and what family members say (Minuchin, 1965). Sherman indicates the importance of the worker's modeling and generating acceptance, validation, and respect for the family as a unit and for each family member. Honesty and such common courtesies as hanging a family member's coat are suggested (Wortman, 1981). Respect for the family should be conveyed, and workers should keep in mind the resource limitations of families, be they tangible or emotional, when they make requests of the family. The literature also indicates that the nature of the interventive techniques should vary according to family socioeconomic factors. Several authors have suggested that treatment with low-income families should emphasize demonstration, modeling, and opportunity to practice new behaviors that are learned. Such approaches are seen as more consistent with the action-centered, concrete styles of low-income families (Rabin et al., 1982), whereas verbal, conceptual, or abstract treatment approaches are seen as less appropriate (Levine, 1964). Modeling, particularly within family and group contexts, may provide an opportunity to observe and practice specific new behaviors (Powell and Monahan, 1969; Sherman, 1983). In particular, workers have been encouraged to model parental roles and functions (Minuchin, 1965); sibling and child roles (King, 1967); and husband and wife roles (Rabin et al., 1982) to low-income families. Rabin et al. (1982) suggest that male-female co-therapy teams should model democratic and egalitarian relationships to low-income men and women, and introduce them to patterns compatible with those in the larger culture, such as the inappropriateness of alcoholism and violence against women.

Modeling also may focus on family relationships with agencies and organizations in its environment. Particularly when workers play an advocate role, modeling interaction with agencies can facilitate the family's learning (Hallowitz, 1975; Rabin et al., 1982). Once new patterns have been established, practiced, and learned, workers should provide constant feedback and followup so that family members can evaluate the effects of their new behavior (Sherman, 1983).

According to Nelsen (1983), the appropriateness of "knowledge-oriented" interventions, those in which the practitioner helps the family understand their problems and their options for action, may vary according to family socioeconomic status. She suggests that working-class and lower-class family members may be less interested in knowing the reasons for things, and may be more willing to simply be given new knowledge of what they might try in order to change things.

The importance of creativity, innovation, and outreach in work with low-income families is widely noted. King (1967) suggests that two therapists may be needed for family therapy with low-income clients, in order to better diagnose observations and provide demonstrations for the family. Often, treatment should take place in the home (Levine, 1964; Bryant, 1980). Interventions should make frequent use of the extended family network with which the low-income family is involved (Canino and Canino, 1980). Similarly, Kraft and DeMaio (1982) suggest that treatment should create a supportive network between the family and other professional resources, noting that frequently there is a lack of coordination and cooperation between schools, courts, and welfare departments.

Agencies' usual efforts to strengthen poor families through such activities as counseling and family life education programs may be seriously limited. For example, Chilman sees such programs as ineffective at eliminating the problems of poor families without larger efforts to first alter "the destructive conditions of poverty" (1975, p. 58). Minuchin even characterizes some responses of social service agencies to low-income families as destructive. For example, when families are unable to meet the needs of children, the children are placed in residential treatment or foster care, in spite of the lack of evidence supporting the effectiveness of these measures at strengthening the family. Minuchin states, "There still has not been an organized, overall conceptualization of the delivery of services to families in this country. The family is studied and respected as a viable socialization unit when it is working; when trouble arises, the response is to split it" (1965, p. 129–30). In summary, the literature is clear in recommending certain interventive approaches as particularly appropriate for low-income families. Fewer recommendations are forthcoming regarding the treatment of high-income families. In our view, the critical determinant of an intervention's appropriateness is not a demographic characteristic per se, such as socioeconomic status. Rather, it is the appropriateness of the intervention for the presenting problem. Of course, as presenting problems vary, as they might according to socioeconomic status, then interventions should also vary. But we would urge workers to avoid stereotypes and the provision of different—and potentially inferior—forms of help to families solely on the basis of socioeconomic status.

FAMILY SOCIOECONOMIC STATUS
AND TREATMENT OUTCOME

Within the larger issue of treatment effectiveness, the relevance of the intervention of the family's presenting problem is an important issue. A treatment approach cannot be considered effective unless it can address the relevant problems. The relevance of various approaches to family treatment to families of different social classes has been widely discussed.

Some contend that traditional forms of family treatment are irrelevant to the needs of poor people. For example, Fleischer (1975) views the usual focus of family therapy as irrelevant to the needs of disorganized families. The irrelevance of some therapies to the needs of the poor may be due to efforts of professionals to enhance their professional prestige and image. Cloward and Epstein (1965) charge that social workers have "upgraded" their clients in terms of socioeconomic level, leaving the poor behind, and "upgraded" their helping process to "talking," an approach that may not be relevant to poor clients or their problems.

Wortman (1981) cautions against assuming that poor families cannot benefit from insight-oriented therapy. Family therapy, and in particular, the structural model of family treatment, is widely seen as quite appropriate for low-income families. The structural model, which emerged in the mid-1970s, and for which Minuchin remains the dominant force, emphasizes looking at family interaction patterns or rules, at the family's environment, and at its life cycle stage. This approach, perhaps more than most others, recognizes the importance of the physical, social, and sociocultural environment of the family. According to Gwyn and Kilpatrick (1981), this approach can strengthen the family's ability to handle its problems in concrete terms and can solidify the way in which the family carries out its basic tasks.

While the exchange of opinions about appropriate interventions flourishes, the more specific questions of effectiveness have received less attention. Although his conclusions are not based on empirical research, King (1967) sees family therapy as more successful with certain kinds of low-income families than others. Specifically, he sees family therapy as less successful in families where key members are absent, families with intrapsychic stress, and families with weak controls. Similarly, Hallowitz (1975) predicts poor outcomes in disorganized families where there are conditions for disturbed emotional development in children. In contrast, family therapy is seen as successful with intact families, families in which one parent is overcontrolling (family therapy is seen as able to help that parent relax excessive controls), and families needing guidance, teaching, and support.

In one of the very few studies of outcomes at a family service agency, Pardeck, Wolf, Killion, and Silverstein (1983) report that for low-income families, family treatment was less successful than individual or joint (couple) treatment. For middle-income clients, joint treatment was slightly more effective than individual or family treatment; and for higher-income families, family treatment was more successful than individual or joint treatment.

Comparing the effectiveness of each type of treatment across income level of client, individual treatment was somewhat more effective with low-income clients than with medium- and higher-income groups; family treatment was considerably more effective with higher-income than with lower- and medium-income clients; and joint treatment was slightly more effective with lower- than medium- and higher-income clients. However, the significance of these differences was not tested (Pardeck et al., 1983).

Another study (Cline, Mejia, Coles, Klein, and Cline, 1984) focused on the relationship between worker interventions and outcomes, exploring differences with middle- and lower-class couples in marital therapy. Different relationships between worker behaviors and outcome were observed for middle- and lower-class couples. The most significant relationships were found when focusing on husband rather than wife behavior. In general, directive therapy did not produce positive outcomes for middle-class couples. Rather, directive therapy seemed to produce negative social behavior, decreased expression of personal feelings, and low levels of self-reported marital satisfaction. Unfortunately, there was no clear trend as to what did work with middle-class couples. Their expression of personal feeling, especially that of husbands, seemed to be facilitated by worker relationship skills, such as reflectiveness. Reflectiveness, however, was not effective for lower-class couples; indeed, it was correlated negatively with positive social behavior between husband and wife. However, directive questions by the worker, exploring affect and reflecting statements related to affect, seemed to correlate positively with outcome among lower-class couples. As the researchers concluded,

> It appears that the therapist must walk a fine line with the lower-class husband, in which he helps him understand the workings of his marriage without changing the communication style in the marriage . . . As the lower-class husband understands the cause-and-effect relationships going on in his marriage, he is able to make sense of his marriage, and his negative social interactions decreases (Cline et al., 1984, p. 702).

For lower-class wives, it appeared that the most effective worker style was that of "an authority figure who directively resolves role conflict issues and feelings" (p. 703).

These findings suggest that different styles of worker behavior may be effective with couples (or even one partner of a couple) of varying socioeconomic levels. They further indicate that successful workers must be skilled in various techniques, and be able to adapt them to the needs and responses of clients (Cline et al., 1984). However, one or two studies is a limited basis for conclusions, and the importance of more studies, which systematically examine the impact of socioeconomic factors on the outcome of family therapy, is apparent.

Socioeconomic variables seem to be an important consideration in making decisions about appropriate and effective interventions. However, they should be only a beginning, and the importance of selecting interventions primarily in terms of their relevance to the presenting problems should not be overlooked.

CONCLUSION

What conclusions can be drawn about the impact of socioeconomic status on family treatment? First, it is clear that socioeconomic issues may play a prominent role in the causation, maintenance, or exacerbation of many family problems. For families lacking food, money, and shelter, workers may need to provide basic resources or intervene in the social environment. Family treatment, however, is important for those facing family and interpersonal problems, whatever the family's socioeconomic status.

How different are families at various socioeconomic levels? With respect to the dynamics of marital interaction, household division of labor, family structure, marital satisfaction, and parenting, the evidence suggests that generalizations should not be drawn on the basis of socioeconomic status. Although the social science and practice literatures contribute to the widespread assumptions that poor families are different from the middle and upper classes in these respects, there is little evidence that low-income families aspire to less or are less capable in accomplishing familial roles. In many respects low-, middle-, and upper-income families are more alike than different. Moreover, on the basis of available evidence, workers should not assume the presenting problems of families to vary significantly by socioeconomic status. Although the frequency of some problems varies by socioeconomic status, communication seems to be the most frequently presented problem of families, regardless of SES. Poverty, of course, does cause stress and increase vulnerability to other problems. But socioeconomic status itself reflects neither family pathology nor health.

The practice literature does indicate, however, that family treatment varies in several respects according to socioeconomic factors. Families' access to and use of helping services may be affected. Low-income families are less likely to be referred for services, and once they are in treatment, they receive fewer sessions. Studies of family treatment indicate that workers spend less time discussing environmental problems than parenting and personal problems with families. This finding may be discrepant with suggestions in the practice literature that treatment for low-income families should be short-term, directive, and focused on clearly defined goals and pressing, immediate problems. Such interventive approaches as modeling, advocacy, feedback, and followup are advocated for low-income families. Fewer specific treatment recommendations are found for high-income families.

Few studies have tested the comparative effectiveness of interventions for families at various socioeconomic levels. There is some evidence that low- and middle-income families respond differently to individual, couple, and family treatment and to directive and reflective treatment styles. Pending more conclusive and extensive findings, family therapists should view socioeconomic status as only a preliminary basis for making decisions about appropriate and effective interventions. Treatment success depends primarily on an accurate and thorough assessment and on selecting an intervention appropriate for the identified problems.

14

Socioeconomic Status
and Group Treatment

Group work has a long and well-established history of service delivery
to the poor and other social economic classes (Jaggard, 1950; Middleman,
1959; McManus, 1962; Ortoff, 1962; Trecker, 1964; Youngman, 1965;
Kevin, 1967; Schwartz, 1968; Barclay, 1969; Feldman, 1969; Garvin,
1985). Despite this legacy, few writers have specifically addressed class
factors as they act independently on group treatment. Most often, articles
that address class focus on group work with low-income minorities;
articles that have income as the primary focus are less frequent. In the
pages to follow, we will pull together the group work practice, theory,
and research findings that have socioeconomic status as their focus of
attention.

GROUP COMPOSITION

Given that individuals who seek therapeutic assistance are from varied
socioeconomic groups, the question as to whether groups should be
heterogeneous or homogeneous with respect to SES is an important
one. Indeed, one of the most salient and frequently asked questions is
whether it is more beneficial to construct groups that contain both lower-

and middle-income individuals, or whether it is better to treat low- and middle-income clients separately. Both group practitioners and researchers have provided guidelines to assist us in making such decisions.

Salience to the Group Member

In contrast to the wealth of research data on race and gender preferences for group inclusion, data on class preferences are notably fewer. This is probably due largely to the fact that most small group research is conducted with college students, and that most college students are middle-class. Despite this fact, some small group research has provided us with valuable insights into SES group preferences. For example, Byrne and his colleagues (1966) found significant evidence of SES preferences. Their findings indicated that degree of economic similarity significantly affected individuals' attraction to others. That is, similar individuals were most attracted to each other. These authors found within-class self selection to occur for both low- and high-income groups. Such findings argue that it is not only members of higher status who wish to maintain group distinctions, but members of lower-status groups as well. Moreover, they posit that both low- and high-income groups may choose this separation in an attempt to ignore what may be unfavorable comparisons between themselves and others.

It should be noted that findings from the Byrne et al. (1966) study indicated that there existed greater attraction of low SES individuals to high SES individuals than was expected. Similar observations have been noted elsewhere, in that high-status individuals are noted to be attracted to other high-status individuals, but that low-status persons are also attracted to high-status individuals (Byrne and Nelson, 1965). Byrne et al. (1966) suggest that upward economic dissimilarity has a different psychological meaning than downward economic dissimilarity. It appears that favorable differences (that is, having more of a desirable quality) are more acceptable than unfavorable differences (having less of a desirable quality or attribute). Simons, Berkowitz, and Moyer (1970) have noted from their review of studies that certain dissimilarities do have positive effects on attraction. Specifically, they suggest that various types of similarity-dissimilarity may have differential effects on various credibility factors. As an example, individuals may be influenced most by a person more esteemed than themselves. In pointing this out we are made aware of the frequent association between respect and attraction. For example, a low-status member might be attracted to a dissimilar high-status person whom he or she could admire. Clearly, these findings have important implications for both members and leaders of groups.

It appears that both similar and different status levels and presumably class levels may be tolerated by group members. Some may prefer group members who are similar with respect to their SES levels, perhaps so as to feel comfortable (Bloch, 1968), but prefer leaders or even perhaps other members who by virtue of their higher SES positions are viewed with admiration and attraction. These findings suggest that heterogeneous SES compositions may be acceptable to low SES individuals. That is, they may enjoy groups composed of individuals who are of both the same and different social economic status as themselves. With respect to the perspective of high-income individuals, there are also reports that they have benefited and enjoyed group experiences that have included low-income group members (Navarre, Glasser, and Costabile, 1985). Indeed, there are indications that they may find the mixed SES group beneficial to their own understanding of social and personal problems.

Moreover, some have argued that another salient criterion for group inclusion is employment. Wold and Steger (1976) contend that whether a group member is capable of holding employment, and not his SES level per se, may be most important as an inclusion criterion. Those authors suggest that clients whose coping capacity is too impaired to sustain employment may not make good candidates for "talking therapies" and presumably not good candidates for inclusion into groups that include higher functioning individuals (in this instance, those capable of holding employment). Certainly we do not wish to imply that low-income persons are also low functioning. However, when a low income is a function of mental incapabilities, this fact should be weighted into the decision to include or not to include an individual in a group.

Finally, in agreement with others (Yalom, 1975; Garvin, 1987), we, too, advocate against the inclusion of only one low- or middle-income person in an otherwise homogeneous SES group. Such a solo status places that single individual in a deviant status and requires him or her to become a representative of his or her income group, an ominous task.

Salience to the Group Leader

Do group leaders prefer to lead groups composed of middle- or lower-income individuals? There is a wealth of data which indicate that workers have strong class biases. By and large, workers appear to prefer to work with clients who are from the same socioeconomic class as themselves. Hence, given that most therapists are middle-class, their biases are slanted toward working with clients from the middle and upper classes (MacLennan, 1968). Evidence suggests that mental health practitioners in general feel more comfortable, work better with, and are more accepting of clients from the middle classes (Schaffer and Meyers, 1954; Brill and Storrow, 1960; Srole, Langer, Michael, Opler, and Rennie, 1962; Schofield, 1964; Gould, 1967; Jones, 1980). Interestingly, however, clients from low-income background are more likely than middle-class clients to be referred to group therapy (Sue, 1976). It has been suggested that referring clients to groups rather than seeing them individually is one way in which therapists distance themselves from clients whom they least prefer (Green et al., 1980). Thus, group therapy with respect to low-income clients has been employed in some instances not as a modality of therapeutic choice, but rather as one that facilitated practitioner avoidance of low-income clients. At the same time, when group is the preferred treatment modality of the practitioner, low-income clients are frequently excluded from group composition because of various class-related factors (e.g., low social effectiveness, IQ, or environmental problems) (Yalom, 1975). Thus, it would appear that low-income clients are at risk of experiencing a double whammy with respect to group practice: They are sometimes assigned to groups composed of individuals whom practitioners do not wish to see and excluded from those groups that practitioners most want to lead.

Despite this disturbing scenario, all is not lost for clients of low SES status who either seek or are referred to group treatment. Mitchell and Namenek (1970) found that lower-class clients are more likely to be selected for treatment by therapists whose parents are from lower-income groups. This finding was similar to that of Kandel (1966), in that he also observed that therapists whose own social class origins were lower (e.g., class 3 and 4 according to Hollingshead's 1957 classification), tended to select and to treat equal numbers of middle- and low-income clients. By contrast, therapists with higher-class origins (e.g., classes 1 and 2 according to Hollingshead), chose to undertake therapy only with clients from their own SES class. These findings are both disturbing and encouraging. It is disturbing that even trained practitioners appear to have difficulty discarding their biases, and appear to fall victim to classist effects. On the brighter side, practitioners from lower economic origins do appear to be accepting of the lower-class client. This latter fact argues strongly for the recruiting and training of practitioners who are from lower SES origins.

Despite the fact that it has been noted that middle-income group leaders may exhibit some group bias, it has also been noted that the group therapy context may be the best context in which a practitioner may gain an understanding of working with low-income populations (Allgeyer, 1970). For example, Allgeyer suggests that "therapists in a crisis group can learn rapidly from the peers of the poor whites how to understand and empathize with the hardships of their world" (1970, p. 237). Indeed, some have argued that both the poor who are served, and the practitioner who helps them, benefit from working with groups of low-income clients (Beck et al., 1968).

Salience to the Group Purpose

How important is the group purpose? To what extent does the group purpose influence how a group might best be composed with respect to the social class of its members? This issue has received scant attention in the group literature. However, from what we have learned from the literature, it appears plausible that some class compositions might be more suitable for certain group purposes than for others.

There is some evidence which suggests that, in general, task groups may be less affected by a heterogeneous composition than growth groups (Hartford, 1972; Davis, 1979). It may be that class differences are more important in those group situations where individuals, in order to benefit from the group experience, must share information of a more intimate nature. For example, class differences among members may be more important to a group of persons who are attempting to learn parenting skills than to a group of persons who are attempting to lose weight. The former group would require that members have some a priori understanding of the values and customs of the other group members. The weight loss group would probably not require knowledge about the values and customs of the other members.

Thus, on balance, it is probably wiser to compose class homogeneous groups when the group purpose is of an intimate nature. Class differences may imply differences in the life experiences of those individuals involved. Hence, group members belonging to different social classes may feel that these past differences may invalidate the "different class other" as an appropriate advice giver, and advice coming from such persons may be viewed as class inappropriate. By the same token, less intimate groups, such as task-focused groups, may be affected less by class heterogeneity among members, as they require less of an understanding of members' past and present social realities.

GROUP DYNAMICS

Social status appears to have extensive consequences for both individual members and the group. Namely, an individual's status has consequences for the person's behavior toward others, their behavior toward him or her, evaluations of their behavior, and the communication between themselves and other group members (Shaw, 1981). We have elected to discuss what both the practice and research literature indicate to be the most important social class factors affecting group dynamics.

Intimacy, Numbers, and Balance

There is very little known about the dynamics of groups as they are affected by the membership ratio of middle- and low-income individuals. This is due largely to the fact that most experimental studies have been conducted employing middle-class college students. Despite this state of affairs, some of the small group research that has employed status as a variable may prove useful in our better understanding of the effects of social class on group behavior. It has been suggested by Shaw (1981), and we strongly agree, that the social status associated with individuals has extensive consequences for both the person and the other group members.

Generally we would assume that the law of attraction is operative for social class as it is for other personal attributes, e.g., race and gender. That is, persons who are most similar to one another should be most attracted to each other. However, as we noted earlier, some of the research on social class suggests that social class may operate differently (Byrne, 1971). Specifically, attraction toward persons of higher income levels may occur irrespective of the social class of the other person. Hence, while we feel relatively confident that a homogeneous group of either all middle- or lower-income people is likely to be a cohesive group, we are less certain about the dynamics of a group with a mixed social class composition.

In short, we know little about the effects on group attraction of varying the numbers of individuals of different social classes. However, Kanter's (1977) schema as it pertains to the ratio of males to females in groups may be helpful in our understanding of social class effects on group composition. Following her paradigm, it could be expected that if a group included "too few" (e.g., only a small minority of) low-income individuals then

1. the behavior of these few would be highly visible and subject to greater scrutiny than other group members
2. actual differences in their behaviors would be exaggerated beyond their real degree of difference
3. perceptions of the lower-class member would be distorted to fit whatever class stereotypes middle-class group members have of them

Employing the conceptualizations of Davis (1981) may also prove useful in understanding social class and group dynamics. His work suggests that if there are "too many" low-income clients relative to the number of middle-income, the middle-income group members may feel threatened and leave the group. We would presume that the reverse is also true: Too many middle-income members may cause the low-income members to terminate. Davis' work also suggests that to the extent that a group is an intimate one, the social class of the other members will be of more importance to all members. Specifically, as the intimacy of the group increases, group members would prefer to be in groups that include greater numbers of members from their own social class. Hence, as was true of race, class might be expected to influence both "how many" low- and middle-income group members appear to be acceptable to one another and also "how closely" they might feel comfortable working together. In short, differences in social class may influence both the acceptable class mixture and the level of intimacy with which members are comfortable.

Cooperation, Competition, and Behavior

Is it possible to compose groups of high- and low-income individuals who can work well together? Will heterogeneous groups of low- and middle-income individuals be cooperative? That is, will they attempt to assist each other within the group? If social class operates like race, the answer is probably yes (see Chapter 4). However, there is some evidence that perceived differences in status have the potential to negatively affect the probability of helping behavior. For example, Roman, Bontemps, Flynn, McGuire, and Gruder (1977) found that persons were most likely to assist a person who asked for help if the person had similar status to themselves and if there was a likelihood that the person might return the favor in the future. Thus, it might happen that helping behavior within a class heterogeneous group would occur most readily between group members of the same social class, or with low SES members helping high SES members because they are perceived to be more capable of returning the favor in the future. There is potentially a positive side to class heterogeneous groupings, however, as there exists evidence to suggest that cross-group attractions are enhanced if members help each other (Blanchard and Cook, 1976).

Among the most important factors operative in class heterogeneous groups are status effects—specifically, the differential behavioral expectations accorded members of low- and high-status groups (Berger, Cohen, and Zelditch, 1966; Berger, Fisek, Norman, and Zelditch, 1977; Meeker, 1981; Berger and Zelditch, 1983; Tuzlak and Moore, 1984). For example, there is an abundance of evidence which suggests that initial status differences between members of informal task groups result in their being ascribed power, prestige, and performance expectations that are consistent with their status outside the group. Research supporting this position has come from a variety of settings: street corner gangs (Whyte, 1943), mental health personnel (Caudill, 1958), conference participants (Hurwitz et al., 1953), bomber crews (Torrance, 1954), family groupings (Strodtbeck and Mann, 1956), and biracial groupings (Katz et al., 1958;

Katz, Goldston, and Benjamin, 1960; Katz and Cohen, 1962). In general, high-status persons are ascribed more power and prestige and expected to be more competent and influential in performing individual or group tasks.

Moreover, it is reasonable to expect that interactions among low- and middle-income group members will be significantly influenced by the differentials in status ascribed to them in small groups. Initially, at least, low-income individuals can be expected to come to the group with less power to influence other members, and to have lower expectations of their performance behaviors (Berger, Cohen, and Zelditch, 1966). These status expectations may become self-fulfilling prophesies, in that the high-income (and presumably higher status) persons in such groups are more confident and may subsequently take more initiative from the group's onset. Correspondingly, low-income (and presumably lower status) clients may be less confident than the higher-income group members and initiate lower levels of activity at the group's onset. Some have suggested that low-status group members be introduced to the other members as having high competence, as a potential means to lessen this effect (Cohen and Roper, 1972). Certainly some effort to equalize statuses of group members is worthwhile. Failure to counteract the imbalance of power and expectations ascribed to low- and high-status income members could result in low-income members participating minimally and maybe only tangentially in group activities.

It has been suggested that persons to whom society ascribes a low status are expected to be compliant and nonassertive (Garvin, 1985). As one possible intervention, Garvin advocated that low-income individuals be provided with assertiveness training as an aid to counter their low-status role ascriptions. Certainly pre-group training could benefit low-income members in their efforts to be received as full-fledged group members. In addition, it has been wisely suggested that to treat the expectations of the low-status individuals only will be less effective than also altering the behavioral expectations of the high-status persons. Both income groups should be made aware of class dynamics that have the potential to be influenced by group behavior (Berger, Cohen, and Zelditch, 1966).

The idea of pre-group coaching of both low- and middle-income group members may have an additional benefit. Some research has observed that low-income clients are more susceptible to aggressive behavior from the group than higher-status members (Worchel, 1957). For example, low-status persons who are viewed as a source of frustration are more likely to be targets of aggression than are high-status persons who are viewed in this manner. Consequently, the low-status person who advocates unpopular positions or ideas within the group may be more harshly dealt with than a high-status person who does so. Hence, a discussion sensitizing group members to the stereotypic behavioral expectations associated with different economic statuses might lessen the probability of low-income members being treated inequitably.

Communication, Interaction, and Status

Communication between therapists and clients is at the very heart of the helping relationship (Hunt, 1960). At the same time, social economic differences between therapists and clients may make viable communication between them difficult, if not impossible (Rapoport, 1959; Garfield, 1978). Hunt (1960) has viewed the cross-class communication process to be so impeded that he questions whether therapists would not do better, (that is, the greatest good) to limit their treatment efforts to clients who are from their own social class. Indeed, there is support in both the practice and small group research literature which attests to the fact that groups composed of individuals from different social economic levels are at great risk of experiencing communication problems.

By and large the bases for cross-class communication problems spring from two sources: the lack of a common experiential background and differences in social status. The first, lack of a common experiential background upon which to base understanding of one another, has been well documented (Hunt, 1960; Haase, 1964; Meyers and Roberts, 1959; Vontress, 1981). On this point, Haase (1964) has put the dilemma quite well in pointing to the lack of common background when the therapist often fails to understand what in the client's story or behavior is really important to the patient, and the patient, in turn, frequently fails to comprehend the nature of the question. Meyers and Roberts (1959) contend that lower-income clients use restrictive forms of communication that further hamper the practitioner's efforts to follow and to understand the clients' experiences. Others, too, have noted this potential risk to communication when working with "socially disadvantaged" clients (MacLennan, 1968; Smith, 1975). It is important to acknowledge that this lack of common experiential base is not limited to contact between minorities and whites, but occurs also between same-race individuals who, however, belong to different social economic groups (Vontress, 1981). Finally, communication problems between clients and therapists are not limited to middle-class therapists and lower-income clients. Indeed, communication problems between middle-class therapists and upper-class clients have been noted also (McKamy, 1976); here the problems in communication again spring from a lack of a common experimental base and a difference in social status.

What about communication problems caused by status effects? Such problems have been frequently noted by small group researchers. Shaw

(1981) posits that one of the pervasive effects of status differences is on the pattern and content of communication in small groups. It appears that the societal statuses of group members significantly influence the amount of communication they receive from others and with whom they are most likely to communicate. By and large, high-status persons both initiate and receive more communication from others and such communication is generally more central to the topic under discussion. Moreover, communication is more likely to occur between individuals of equal statuses (Kelley, 1951; Barnlund and Harland, 1963). These factors are apt to have significant, if not profound, effects on the communication between persons who differ in social class. For example, low-income members who are ascribed lower status in the group are less likely to participate as full-fledged members. They are less likely to initiate communication or be the recipients of communication from either low- or high-status members. Thus groups composed of both low- and middle-income individuals are at risk of the middle-income individuals communicating mostly among themselves and the lower-income individuals communicating to a more limited degree, and then largely about information not central to the group's discussion.

It thus appears that balanced group communication can be difficult to achieve in groups composed of individuals from different status groups. There are no apparent easy solutions to the problems of group communication caused by differences in social economic statuses of the group members and leaders. For example, even "artificially" structuring equal statuses of group participants may be problematic—e.g., assigning status to group members. Norvel and Worchel (1981) have noted that equal status at the structural level does not necessarily correspond to equal status at the psychological level. For example, both historical and immediate status differences between members may influence intergroup processes. Moreover, despite the fact that members possess equal statuses within the group, their statuses outside the group may overpower those inside. Some status characteristics appear to act as master traits (e.g., race or sex) and essentially overpower other statuses (e.g., job titles or degrees). Thus it may be easier to change a person's status sociologically or organizationally than psychologically. Hence, efforts to reduce status differences between low- and middle-income persons must also take into account pre-group status differences (Riordan and Ruggiero, 1980).

This discussion is not intended to dissuade group leaders from composing groups of heterogeneous class members. However, it is intended to caution leaders on the possibility of group communication being truncated due to status differences between high- and low-income individuals. Given that all groups may engage in some forms of oneupsmanship, safeguards must be taken to ensure that low-income group members are not discouraged from participating in the group process.

In conclusion, it may prove useful to attempt to "deintimidate" the low-income members with respect to the status and verbiage of the high-income members, and explore with high-income members the potential for them to dominate group discussion and ways to prevent this. These steps might well be taken in a pre-group interview with group members.

LEADERSHIP

Social class has important implications for the leadership of small groups. We have all heard numerous reports of the difficulties middle-income therapists experience with low-income clients. Similarly, there is evidence to support the fact that low-income clients experience difficulties in working with middle-class therapists. However, thus far, as indicated by the literature, the preponderance of attention in this area has focused on preparing the lower-income client for group work with middle-class practitioners. While we do not advocate that these efforts be discontinued, there is also a need for middle-class therapists to be better prepared to lead groups of clients whose social economic status may be lower than their own. This is not a new suggestion (Baum and Felzer, 1964; Bernard, 1965). Unfortunately, however, as it pertains to group work, it appears to be one to which little attention has been given. In the discussion to follow we have identified some major areas that are influenced by class and should be of concern to group leadership.

Style and Status

Kadushin (1983) assists us in better understanding leadership difficulties with low-income clients. He posits that class status differences reinforce role status differences between clients and therapists. It is suggested that because of these differences in status and hence expected roles, low-income clients tend to feel "inordinately subordinate" to middle-income therapists. Such perceived or felt social distance has potentially negative effects for leaders attempting to lead groups composed of low-income clients (MacLennan, 1968). The most obvious consequence is that members who perceive their group leaders as being too distant are less likely to engage in open and candid group discussions. In other words, the leader, because of his status as a middle-class person and his position as a group leader, will be perceived as being too different and hence lacking sufficient approachability. In response to this problematic scenario, Kadushin (1983) advocates that the practitioner must engage in efforts to reduce his or her distance. For example, practitioners must engage in greater self disclosure of mutual problems with clients— e.g., problems in childrearing, etc. They must make themselves more personable, which may be facilitated by decreasing their professional anonymity. Typically, it has been in the effort to reduce the effects of status and social distance that the use of paraprofessionals has been advocated. Christmas and Davis (1965) conclude from their practice experiences that the familiar indigenous nonprofessional group worker significantly facilitates the treatment process. However, not all evidence has supported the assumption that paraprofessionals can provide effective group work services (Feldman and Caplinger, 1977; Feldman, Caplinger, and Wodarski, 1983).

Problems of status are not limited to lower-class clients and middle-class workers. Practitioners leading groups of clients whose status is higher than their own may also experience difficulties related to differentials in status. For example, upper-class clients may pose problems for the therapist in that the client may view life experiences of the therapist to be dissimilar from his or her own (Saari and Johnson, 1975). It may also pose a leader-member status incongruency for the group—that is, high-income members may feel that the leader's lower social status is at odds with his or her group position as leader. They may subsequently resist the worker's efforts to lead the group as the worker's lower social status suggests that the high-income group member should theoretically be in the position of leadership (McKamy, 1976).

Finally, we might ask, does style of group leadership have implications for the social class of the group members? While there appears to be no clear answer to this question, style of group leadership does appear to affect different social economic groups of clients differently. Most notably, evidence suggests that low-income clients may prefer directive styles of leadership, while higher-income clients may prefer more nondirective styles (Abramowitz et al., 1974; Acosta et al., 1982). Thus, when leading groups composed primarily of high-income individuals, those leadership behaviors that are less authoritative, more reflective, and offer members a greater stake in the management and direction of the group may be most beneficial. In contrast, leaders of groups composed of low-income individuals might do better to provide members with greater direction and advice giving. Moreover, advice giving and the sharing of personal information are both in line with the expectations of many low-income clients (Kadushin, 1983), and thus should facilitate the group treatment process. It has also been suggested that activities which aid in the establishment of a positive therapeutic relationship should take place early in the group's history (Baum and Felzer, 1964).

Personality and Attitudes

Are certain leader personality attributes more suitable for working with groups of different SES populations than others? There is some evidence that therapists who differ on the dimension of Type A and

Type B personality may respond differently to clients on the basis of their social economic status. It seems that Type A therapists may tend to rate the prognosis of upper-class clients higher than lower-class clients, while Type B therapists have been shown to rate lower-class clients as having a better prognosis than upper-class clients (Anzel, 1970). We might conjecture from the findings of Anzel that such personality differences might further manifest themselves in the willingness of therapists to lead groups of clients who differ from themselves in their social economic statuses.

Moreover, researchers have observed that group leadership styles which are directive rather than nondirective are most effective in working with clients who are externally oriented (Abramowitz et al., 1974). This observation has potentially important implications in that the personality trait of being either internally or externally focused (I-E) has been observed to be class linked: Individuals from low SES categories are more inclined to be external in their orientation than are higher SES individuals. Hence, group leaders who are more inclined toward the use of direct treatment methods may better serve clients who are more external with respect to their locus of control. Conversely, clients whose personality with respect to I-E is more internal may be better served by therapists who are more nondirective.

Performance

Does the social economic status of the leader have implications for his or her performance as group leader? Does performance appear to be best when the leader and members share a common social economic status? Is it better to have the leader from one social economic group and the members from another? Unlike the topic areas of race and gender, little research has been conducted on the salience of social class to group leadership. However, there are indications that performance evaluations of practitioners may be influenced by their social class. For example, an individual's social status may enhance the appearance of his or her performance (McKamy, 1976; Bumagin and Smith, 1985).

This factor was outlined in our earlier discussion of client preferences for group composition. Intuitively, at least, this makes sense, as in general, higher-income individuals, in addition to being ascribed higher levels of expertise, are also most attractive to the other group members. Thus, group members are inclined to view the performance behaviors of persons from higher economic groups more favorably.

Also operative is the factor of social role. By this, we mean persons of higher social status are expected to be in role positions consistent with their statuses. Thus, situations where low-status persons lead high-status persons are said to be role incongruent (Adams, 1953). In other words, it is role congruent for high-status persons to lead lower-status persons, but the reverse violates a social expectation. In her discussions of working with the wealthy, McKamy (1976) provides insights into this dynamic. She notes that wealthy clients may be reluctant to follow the lead of a practitioner whom they perceive to have a lower achieved social status (income). Although McKamy addresses this issue in a dyadic context, it has applicability for group workers as well. Leaders who find themselves in such status incongruencies may anticipate more resistance to their leadership efforts than leaders who, in their roles as leaders, are status consistent. Both the experimental and practice literature suggest that perceptions of the leader's performance will be influenced by perceptions of his or her social class relative to that of the members. It should also be noted that social status in this scenario would be based on both achieved status (income) and status ascribed to him or her as a professional. Hence, the potentially negative affect of the group leader's low income status could be offset by an enhanced perception of his or her professional expertise or exceptional commitment to the group (Reed and Garvin, 1983).

Co-Leadership

Are there any benefits or liabilities for group co-leaders having different social economic statuses? There is little empirical evidence or practice wisdom to guide us in answering this question. Yet, from what we know of both class and co-leadership, we can offer some suggestions. The employment of co-leaders who differ in their social economic status would seem to be potentially beneficial for group compositions of two types. First, those where the group membership was also mixed with respect to social economic status. Members here would each have a co-leader whom they felt understood them. The second potentially beneficial composition is one where the group membership consists of low-income clients. In this situation the members theoretically would have the best of both worlds. They would have a leader whose high-income status and hence high esteem they perhaps admired and a co-leader who, although of low-income status, they could identify and feel comfortable with.

However, as is true for mixed race and gender co-leadership teams, co-class group leadership may violate what is viewed by some as one of the essential ingredients for co-leadership—equal status among the leaders (Yalom, 1975). Indeed, the risk to a mixed-class co-leadership team is that members may view one or the other of the co-leaders as being the "real leader" and the other as a "helper." Which leader would be perceived as which would depend on the group members. It is quite possible that the higher-income/status co-leader may be perceived as the "real leader" by the members, irrespective of their identification with the low-income co-therapist. On the other hand, the low-income group leader might be seen by low-income clients as the "real leader" if not the "real helper," with the higher-income/status leader there only to legitimize the treatment process. This topic has received almost no attention in the group work literature and clearly deserves greater notice.

OUTCOME

What are the consequences of social class on group treatment outcomes? Have some low-income clients responded more favorably to treatment than others? Are there means by which low-income clients can be assisted to obtain greater benefits from group treatment?

Group work has been employed extensively with clients from different SES backgrounds, and practitioners have repeatedly reported the gains in group practice with low-income clients: Bowery men (Brooks, 1978); women on AFDC (Green, 1970; Bumagin and Smith, 1985; Navarre, Glasser, and Costabile, 1985); low-income mental patients (Gonzales, Doring, and Demathmann, 1979); and youth (Scheidlinger, 1965; Levitt, 1968; Barclay, 1969). Clearly, the low-income client is no stranger to group work.

Although there are frequent claims of successful treatment, most accounts of group work practice with the poor have not done a good job of documenting those outcomes. Two factors unique to working with the poor may contribute to the lack of systematic evaluation: the unfavorable conditions under which much of the work with low-income clients often takes place; and the frequently unpredictable and unstable environments faced by low-income clients, which make monitoring their actual change more difficult. However, despite the low numbers of empirical studies, the literature does point to several factors that impact on the outcome of low-income clients' group treatment. Those factors are: client preparation for group treatment; various worker factors such as experience, attitude, and socioeconomic status; and modality of group treatment.

Salience of the Group Member

Practitioners may expect less positive outcomes of their low-income clients. In a study by Vail (1979), social class was found to be a powerful influence on workers' expectations of treatment outcome. The study called for practitioners (140) and students (140) to respond to a therapeutic analogue. Both groups evaluated lower-class clients as having less favorable chances of therapeutic success.

There is evidence that low-income clients have shorter treatment durations than do higher-income clients (Rubenstein and Lorr, 1956; Rogers, 1960). It has been observed that 30 to 60 percent of psychotherapy with low-income clients terminates within six sessions (Rogers, 1960). However, this finding may be less an indicator of poor rapport between practitioner and client, as is often assumed, and more an indication of the type of problems low-income clients bring to treatment, such as situational crises (Rubenstein and Lorr, 1956). Such problems may require more immediate, but briefer, attention than do many other problems. Moreover, Goin, Yamamoto, and Silverman (1965) found that their low-income clients expected treatment to be of briefer duration. Thus, time of client termination may be a function both of presenting problem and of client expectations regarding the time needed for problem amelioration.

Moreover, several studies demonstrate the benefits of preparing clients for group treatment. For example, Heitler (1973) studied 48 white lower-income hospital psychiatric clients as subjects over a five-week period. They were divided into two groups; those who were "prepared" for group treatment versus those who were not. Preparation consisted of individualized anticipatory socialization into the roles and expectations of group clients prior to their participation in group. Those clients who were prepared benefited more from group treatment than those who did not receive the anticipatory socialization. For example, the "prepared" group members participated sooner, more frequently, and for longer periods of time in their groups. In addition, they engaged in these behaviors with less prompting. These are important findings, as evidence suggests that group members who participate most are also the recipients of greater benefits from group treatment (Yalom, 1975). Noteworthy, too, the prepared group members were viewed by the leader as being closer to their ideal of a group therapy client. Overall, it appears that low-income clients who are instructed as to their roles and duties as group members may, in fact, engage more fully in the treatment process. Further, we may assume that they receive some additional benefit from such participation. However, prepared clients found the therapeutic relationship no more gratifying than did the unprepared clients, nor did they report being any less anxious.

Salience of the Group Leader

Worker factors also appear to bear on treatment outcome in work with low-income clients. One such factor is level of worker experience. Although the Vail (1979) study found SES to be more significant than therapist level of experience, another study has found worker experience to be the most salient factor. Findings of Baum et al. (1966) indicated that those therapists who were most secure and clinically experienced established the best relationships with lower-income clients and had lower dropout rates.

Another influence on group outcome with low-income clients may be worker attitude. Lerner (1972, 1973) noted that, under individual treatment condition, therapists with more democratic attitudes have greater client improvement. For example, low-income black clients experienced greater psychological gains when they worked with a therapist who had democratic attitudes. Although assessed under individual treatment conditions, there is nothing to suggest that similar dynamics would not occur for group clients. Indeed, attitudes of the practitioner may be even more salient for leaders of small groups, where competition for the time among the group members increases the tendency, if not also the opportunity, to be autocratic.

The social distance between group leader and low-income clients appears to influence outcome (Bernard, 1965; Gould, 1967; Lorin, 1978; Garvin, 1985). Social distance, which is largely a function of status differences (Shaw, 1981), inhibits the establishment of rapport and a viable therapeutic relationship. However, the effect of therapist rapport on client outcome may vary with different group modalities. For example, Sloane et al. (1975) found that therapist attraction for the client affected outcomes in psychodynamically-oriented treatment but not in behavioral treatment. This is noteworthy, in that it suggests that group leaders who are less attracted to low-income clients might work better with them from a behavioral, rather than a psychodynamic orientation.

Finally, some group leaders of low-income clients (Bumagin and Smith, 1985) have noted that level of leader effort is a salient factor in obtaining positive treatment outcomes. Bumagin and Smith report favorable client outcomes as a consequence of increased practitioner's effort. They report that eleven of sixteen mothers made significant positive change. Thus, it may be necessary for group leaders to exert considerably more activity than is customary in order to produce positive outcome for low-income clients. The necessity for greater group leader efforts may further reduce workers' desire to work with these clients.

Salience of the Modality

There is widespread acceptance of the notion that group outcome for low-income clients is influenced by treatment modality. Although some have argued for use of classical insight approaches with the poor (Gould, 1967; MacLennan, 1968; Lerner, 1972), it is generally concluded by most that such psychotherapies are ineffective with this population

(Garfield, 1978; Jones, 1980). Hence, group practitioners intending to work with low-income clients must ask themselves which types of group modalities appear to be most effective. There does appear to be solid support for the use of groups with the poor, as it is believed that they (clients) benefit from the presence of others who are in similar situations (Allgeyer, 1970; Washington, 1977; Garvin, 1985). There appears to be considerable consensus that low-income clients are served best by short-term groups that are active and more responsive to client environmental needs (Rubenstein and Lorr, 1956). Let us consider these factors.

In further support of the employment of short-term groups with the poor, Allgeyer (1970) advocates the crisis group. He suggests that the crisis group is well-suited for low-income clients because they often do not seek assistance until a crisis is upon them. This pattern of attempted problem resolution is in part a function of the difficulty low-income clients experience in efforts to control significant life events. The crisis group, Allgeyer contends, is subsequently an ideal modality for the treatment of low-income clients. The crisis group is also believed to be important because low-income clients can enlist the support of their peers, thereby countering their frequent social isolation (Garvin, 1985). Allgeyer (1970) also suggests the employment of pre-group interviews for low-income group members. As was noted earlier, it was found that low-income clients benefit from a brief period of therapeutic role induction in which the expectations of the client and therapist are clearly spelled out (Overall and Aronson, 1963; Strupp and Bloxom, 1973). This process can be carried out either by employing a film or by interview. The process has these major purposes:

1. to establish a rational basis for the patients to accept psychotherapy as a means of helping them deal with their problems
2. to clarify the role of the patient and the therapist in the course of treatment
3. to provide a general outline of the course of psychotherapy and its vicissitudes

Secondly, there is also considerable support in the literature for the theory that a successful group modality for working with the poor should be active and goal-directed (Bernard, 1965; Howard, Rickels et al., 1970; Abramowitz et al., 1974; Navarre et al., 1985). Bernard (1965) has urged that therapists who work with the poor come out from behind the facade of neutrality and passivity. He advocates also that they adapt their techniques to maintain a more active role than is customary in psychotherapy. Such efforts should minimize social distance between the practitioner and client, thereby advancing active, informal, goal-focused groups. This notion is consistent with the findings of Abramowitz et al. (1974), who found that a direct style of group modality appears to be more effective with clients who perceive events in their lives to be controlled by factors residing in the environment. This is noteworthy in that low-income clients are at greater risk from the environment and, not surprisingly, have a greater environmental focus than middle-income clients (Lefcourt, 1973).

Finally, Allgeyer (1970) advocates the employment of open-ended groups where patients rotate in and out of the group. The rationale put forth for the use of open-ended groups with low-income clients is that their problems have a propensity to be resolved one way or another within five or six weeks. Hence, having the group open-ended would allow the leader to sustain the group structure and momentum rather than starting a series of brief groups that suffer from poor and sporadic attendance.

CONCLUSION

In this chapter we have pulled together theory, practice, and research findings that address socioeconomic status and group work. This area of group work literature is considerably less developed than are the areas of race and gender. This is largely due to the fact that most group research is conducted with college students and most college students are middle-class. Consequently, it was often necessary to extrapolate from the class literature that pertained more directly to individual practice.

Both low- and high-income individuals may elect to be in class homogeneous groups in an attempt to ignore comparisons between themselves and others. However, it appears that low-income individuals may have a greater acceptance of class heterogeneous groups than do middle-income persons. Group leaders, it appears, also exhibit class biases in that they prefer to lead groups composed of group members of the same class as themselves. Class seems to be more important to the group composition when the purpose of the group requires that members have some a priori understanding of the values and customs of the other members. Class of the group members may be less important when the group is task-focused. Employing the conceptual frameworks used to explain race and gender dynamics, it is suggested that grossly imbalanced class group compositions of either the poor or middle-class be avoided.

Group interactions between low- and middle-income group members may be influenced by the differentials in status that are ascribed to each. Hence, when in class heterogeneous groups, low-income persons may behave less assertively or in ways consistent with their lower socially ascribed status. Communication within class heterogeneous groups is characterized by the higher-status person initiating and receiving more of the group discussion. Consequently, class heterogeneous groups are at risk of underparticipation by low-income members.

The perceptions of leader performance will be influenced by the perceptions of his or her social class relative to that of the members; higher-income leaders are viewed most positively. Generally directive styles of group leadership appear most beneficial in working with lower-income members, while reflective and nondirective styles appear better suited for work with middle-income members. Group practitioners who are high on external locus of control may be best at leading groups of low-income members. Similarly, those practitioners high on internal locus of control may be better at leading groups composed of middle-income group members. Co-class group leadership may be useful in working with low-income clients. This co-leadership arrangement has the potential advantage of offering low-income group members both someone with whom they can identify and someone whom they may wish to emulate.

Outcome literature on group work with low-income clients is sparse. Practitioners may expect lower levels of outcomes with low-income clients and subsequently get them. However, clients who are prepared for group, by way of a brief role introduction, appear to participate more fully in the group experience than those clients who do not undergo such preparation. Even with preparation, it does seem that leading groups of poor persons may require more effort than leading groups composed of nonpoor persons. Also, level of group leader experience and the possession of a democratic attitude appear beneficial in working with low-income clients. There is no empirical evidence to suggest that any particular group modality is superior to others in working with the poor. However, because of the frequent crisis nature of the problems faced by the poor, short-term, open-ended, directive groups are most commonly advocated.

15

GUIDELINES FOR PRACTICE

When Socioeconomic Status Is Salient

The previous four chapters have explored the impact of social economic status on work with individuals, families, and groups. The best of research and practice wisdom was reviewed in this task. Clearly, further research is needed. One of the most difficult tasks was to separate the dynamics of social class from race. Much of what is written on the poor is confounded by race or ethnicity, making it difficult to determine what factors cause which effects. Indeed, it is probable that much of what has been written about whites has focused on the middle class, while most of what has been written about the poor has focused on minorities. Nonetheless, we can derive some implications—some guidelines—for practice when socioeconomic status is salient. Although a variety of cross-class worker-client combinations occur, we have focused primarily on the most typical situation, that of middle-class practitioners working with lower-income clients or families.

PREPARING FOR PRACTICE

As we noted in chapter 11, the number of poor persons in our society is increasing. Hence, helping professionals, most of whom are middle-class, must better prepare themselves to work with low-income persons.

Such preparation should begin with at least a general understanding of the distribution of economic resources in our society. That is, practitioners should be cognizant of the fact that poverty is not an isolated event experienced by only a small group of persons in our society. Rather, poverty is widespread, affecting as many as 1 in 4 people in the United States. Moreover, helping professionals should be aware that poverty is not confined to minority groups; indeed, there are greater numbers of poor whites in the United States than nonwhites. This reality is sometimes obscured by the fact that the percentage of nonwhites who are poor is larger than that of whites.

Practitioners must also eradicate their own classist notions of the causes of poverty. If they are to work successfully with the poor, they must not assume that the poor have elected poverty. Studies indicate that the poor hold aspirations and values similar to those of middle-class persons. The "culture of poverty" notions are inaccurate at best and classist at worse. What most clearly differentiates the poor from the nonpoor is money. "To start where the client is," when the client is poor, is to start with an understanding of their limited resources and opportunities (Schneiderman, 1965). Practitioners should further understand the influence of status expectations on interpersonal interactions. In general, low-income individuals are expected to behave less assertively and competently in their interactions with higher-income persons. When they do not behave in this manner they may be viewed as rude and uppity. Practitioners should recognize the classist nature of such expectations, and seek to overcome such perceptions.

One way to reduce class biases is to understand that behavior is purposive: People by and large do not engage in nonsensical behavior. Most often, misunderstandings occur between practitioners and clients when they share different social realities (world views) and, hence, do not understand the purposiveness of each other's actions. The behavior of one appears, to the other, to reflect poor judgment, lack of wisdom, or "inappropriate values."

Finally, those attempting to help the poor should seek exposure to them. They should make some efforts to obtain other than "book" knowledge of the poor. For some, this might be accomplished through volunteer work in low-income neighborhoods, agencies, or community projects. For students, this might best be accomplished in a practicum setting or such experiences as Vista. If at all possible, when assessing an individual's or family's presenting problems, workers should attempt to determine the extent to which inadequate economic resources play a contributing role. We are not suggesting that persons who are poor do not experience emotional problems, nor that all their problems are attributable to financial causes. However, we are suggesting that practitioners should look carefully at the impact that economic factors have on a client's presenting problems before deciding that the person is in some way deficient.

MANAGEMENT OF EARLY TREATMENT INTERACTION

As we have noted earlier, the beginning phase of treatment may be the most important, especially with the poor. Low-income clients generally are seen for fewer sessions than are higher-income clients. Although some contend that the brevity of contact is a function of the concrete, pressing nature of their problems, the poor reception they receive from helping professionals likely plays a role also. In either event, it is imperative for practitioners to enhance their effectiveness in the very beginning of the helping process. Practitioners who do not establish a positive rapport with their clients are not likely to keep them even if long-term treatment is needed. Even when only short-term assistance is needed, failure to establish a positive rapport will impair the accomplishment of goals.

Practitioners must appear attractive to their low-income clients. Persons are attracted to others whom they believe like them. Thus clients must view the worker as friendly and wanting to help them with their problems. As we have noted elsewhere, attraction is also enhanced by perceived similarity. Hence, class differences, where they are apparent, must be subordinated and worker-client similarities should be emphasized. Such attempts to enhance attraction are always important in the establishment of rapport; however, these efforts are especially critical when important differences, such as social economic status, are overtly apparent.

The establishment of trust is also imperative. Toward this end, workers must demonstrate their goodwill; that is, they must convey that they are well-meaning individuals who have elected to work with people whom they value. In particular they must be as free as possible of socioeconomic bias. Trust is also enhanced by the worker's demonstration of the skills necessary to address the client's problems. To low-income clients, the worker should not only appear to be sufficiently educated but also knowledgeable about resources in the community upon which the client might rely.

Practitioners also must convey an understanding of the client's social reality, including the problems and resource limitations experienced by low-income clients. When appropriate, and without exaggeration, workers should inform clients of prior personal and or practice experiences that enhance their understanding of the social realities of various income levels. Most importantly, the worker must convey to the client a willingness to learn more about the situations faced by the client. Yet workers should never assume that they will understand the social realities of the client as well as the client does. Practitioners should make every attempt to convey respect for the client or family. Respect is especially important to the poor, to whom society shows little, if any, respect on a day-to-day basis. Hence, early in the helping relationship, workers should demonstrate full professional courtesy. For example, clients should always be referred to by their last names (e.g., Mr. or Mrs. Jones) and never seen hurriedly, in an effort to get to another appointment.

Finally, low-income clients may be completely unfamiliar with the roles and tasks associated with treatment relationships. Hence, workers may find it beneficial to engage in a brief role introduction with low-income clients, to whom the professional helping relationship may be foreign. Role introductions should include descriptions of the expectations, roles, and tasks of both the worker and client. For example, it might be explained to the client that the helping relationship is a talking- or action-oriented one and not a medical one. Also, the worker should inform the client that he or she "does not have all the answers" and that the client will be expected to work on problems with the assistance of the worker. The clarification of the roles and responsibilities of the helping relationship will reduce confusion and the probability of client disappointment resulting from unrealistic treatment expectations.

ENSURE CLASS APPROPRIATENESS OF TREATMENT PROCESS

Clearly, any assessment of low-income clients is at considerable risk of underestimating the influence of the environment. Hence, in addition to intra-psychic or interpersonal assessments, attention should be given to environmental factors such as the social and economic resources in the neighborhood, and the availability of employment.

The identification of economic constraints and environmental limitations may leave some practitioners pessimistic about the likelihood of change. Indeed, helping professionals typically have expected low levels of treatment gain with low-income clients (Pratt, 1970), at times engaging in self-fulfilling prophecies. Yet many who have worked extensively with poor individuals and families have often been impressed with both their resiliency and resourcefulness to make ends meet and not only survive but grow under adverse conditions. Thus, we advocate the expectation of success.

At the same time, the goals established for low-income clients must be realistic. Practitioners must recognize that clients may not have the means or resources to eliminate all of their problems. Failure to establish realistic goals, and hence the failure to reach expected outcomes, is likely to result in both worker and client dissatisfaction with treatment.

Treatment must also be appropriate in terms of its consistency with the lifestyles, attitudes, and values of the client's socioeconomic status. Furthermore, interventive efforts with low-income clients should attempt to place the client in an active position, that is, one in which the client gains a sense of problem mastery and resolution (Solomon, 1976).

While it is impossible to identify specific interventions suitable for all low-income clients, some basic ingredients seem most appropriate. Due to the crisis nature of many problems experienced by low-income clients and their frequent limited control over external events, such as employment and availability of transportation, practitioners should be flexible in their intervention efforts. For example, practitioners should be flexible with respect to the time, place, duration, and frequency of treatment. Moreover, active and concrete interventions are consistently reported to be most satisfying to low-income clients. The preference for such interventions is again probably a function of the immediacy of problems experienced by low-income clients, rather than of their inability to benefit from introspective approaches.

Practitioners should not assume, simplistically, that low-income clients prefer direction and advice while middle- and upper-income clients prefer nondirective insight, introspection, and support. Low-income clients often desire insight, and many middle-income clients desire direction and guidance. For clients of all income levels, interventions should be selected in terms of their correspondence to client preferences, and their appropriateness for the presenting problems.

RECOGNIZE AND ANTICIPATE
THE POTENTIAL FOR EFFECTIVENESS

Again, the importance of the worker's anticipation of success should be emphasized. The treatment literature consistently shows worker experience to be the most salient factor in success with clients of different socioeconomic status (Baum et al., 1966). Practitioners who have worked most frequently with low-income clients make the most positive prognoses and obtain the best outcomes. Indeed, much of the reported failure to obtain positive outcomes with low-income clients may be due to the inexperience of the practitioner in working with this client population (Weiss, 1973; Siassi and Messer, 1976).

We recognize, of course, that all workers are not suited to work with all clients. Some workers elect to work with economically different populations; other practitioners are assigned to such clients. Workers must know when it is best to refer clients with whom they are uncomfortable or cannot provide appropriate help. This, of course, requires familiarity with other service providers or agencies that can better meet the needs of these clients. However, we do not advocate the quick abandonment of clients who differ economically from their workers. Furthermore, there are indications that middle-income workers may benefit from their experiences with low-income clients. Moreover, there is evidence to suggest that repeated exposure to individuals enhances not only understanding of, but also attraction to them. In short, obvious worker-client class differences should not immediately signal the need to refer, or the unlikelihood of success. Indeed, practitioner skills and comfort levels are likely to develop as exposure to and experience with diverse client populations increase.

Bibliography

ABAD, V., AND BOYCE, E. (1979). Issues in pychiatric evaluations of Puerto Ricans: A sociocultural perspective. *Journal of Operation Psychiatry, 10*(1), 28–30.

ABRAMOWITZ, C. V. (1977). Blaming the mother: An experimental investigation of sex-role bias in countertransference. *Psychology of Women Quarterly, 2,* 24–34.

ABRAMOWITZ, C., ABRAMOWITZ, S., ROBACK, H. B., AND JACKSON, C. (1974). Differential effectiveness of directive and non-directive group therapies as a function of client internal-external control. *Journal of Consulting and Clinical Psychology, 42*(6), 849–853.

ABRAMOWITZ, C. V., ABRAMOWITZ, S. I., AND WEITZ, L. J. (1976). Are men therapists soft on empathy? Two studies in feminine understanding. *Journal of Clinical Psychology, 36*(2), 434–437.

ABRAMOWITZ, C. V., AND DOKECKI, P. R. (1977). The politics of clinical judgment: Early empirical returns. *Psychological Bulletin, 84*(3), 460–476.

ABRAMOWITZ, S. I., AND ABRAMOWITZ, C. V. (1977). Sex-biased researchers of sex-bias in psychotherapy and impartial reviewers. *American Psychologist, 32,* 893–894.

ABRAMOWITZ, S. I., ABRAMOWITZ, C. V., JACKSON, C., AND GIMES, B. (1973). The politics of clinical judgment: What nonliberal examiners infer about women who do not stifle themselves. *Journal of Consulting and Clinical Psychology, 41*(3), 385–391.

ABRAMOWITZ, S. I., ABRAMOWITZ, C. V., ROBACK, H. B., CORNEY, R. T., AND McKEE, E. (1976b). Sex-role related countertransference in psychotherapy. *Archives of General Psychiatry, 33*(1), 71–73.

ABRAMOWITZ, S. I., AND HERRERA, H. R. (1981). On controlling for patient psychopathology in naturalistic studies of sex bias: A methodological demonstration. *Journal of Consulting and Clinical Psychology, 49*(4), 597–603.

ABRAMOWITZ, S. I., ROBACK, H. B., SCHWARTZ, J. M., YASUNA, A., ABRAMOWITZ, C. V., AND GOMES, B. (1976a). Sex bias in psychiatry: A failure to confirm. *American Journal of Psychiatry, 133*(6), 706–709.

ACOSTA, F., AND YAMAMOTO, J. (1984). The utility of group work practice for Hispanics. In L. Davis (Ed.), *Ethnicity in social group work practice.* New York: Haworth Press, Inc.

ACOSTA, F., YAMAMOTA, J., AND EVANS, L. (1982). *Effective psychotherapy for low income and minority patients.* New York: Plenum Press.

ADAMS, E. F. (1978). A multivariate study of subordinate perceptions of and attitudes toward minority and majority managers. *Journal of Applied Psychology, 63,* 277–288.

ADAMS, J. (1953). Status congruency as a variable in small group performance. *Social Forces, 32,* 16–22.

ADAMS, K. A. (1980). Who has the final word? Sex, race, and dominance behavior. *Journal of Personality and Social Psychology, 38*(1), 1–8.

ADAMS, R. L., BOAKE, C., AND CRAIN, C. (1982). Bias in a neuropsychological test classification related to education, age, and ethnicity. *Journal of Consulting and Clinical Psychology, 50*(1), 143–145.

ADEBIMPE, V. R. (1981). Overview: white norms and psychiatric diagnosis of black patients. *American Journal of Psychiatry, 138,* 279–285.

ADEBIMPE, V. R. (1982). Psychiatric symptoms in black patients. In S. M. Turner and R. T. Jones (Eds.), *Behavior modification in black populations: Psychosocial issues and empirical findings.* New York: Plenum Press.

ADEBIMPE, V. R., GIGANDET, J., AND HARRIS, E. (1979). MMPI diagnosis of black psychiatric patients. *American Journal of Psychiatry, 136*(1), 85–87.

ADOLPH, M. (1983). The all-women's consciousness raising group as a component of treatment for mental illness. *Social Work with Groups, 6,* 117–131.

AFFLECK, D. C., AND GARFIELD, S. L. (1961). Predictive judgments of therapists and duration of stay in psychotherapy. *Journal of Clinical Psychology, 17*(2), 134–137.

AGUILAR, I. (1972). Initial contact with Mexican-American families. *Social Work, 17,* 66–70.

ALBRONDA, H. F., DEAN, R. L., AND STARKWEATHER, J. A. (1964). Social class and psychotherapy. *Archives of General Psychiatry, 10,* 276–283.

ALLEN, W. R. (1981). Moms, dads, and boys—race and sex differences in the socialization of male children. In G. Lawrence (Ed.), *Black men.* Beverly Hills: Sage Publications, pp. 99–114.

ALLGEYER, J. M. (1970). The crisis group: Its unique usefulness to the disadvantaged. *International Journal of Group Psychotherapy, 20*(2), 235–239.

ALLPORT, G. (1954). *The nature of prejudice.* Boston: Addison-Wesley.

ALONSO, A., AND RUTAN, J. S. (1978). Cross-sex supervision for cross-sex therapy. *American Journal of Psychiatry, 135*(8), 928–931.

ALONSO, A., AND RUTAN, J. S. (1981). Couples therapy and the new sexual politics. *Family Therapy, 8,* 149–157.

ALSDORT, S., AND GRUNEBAUM, H. (1969). Group psychotherapy on alien turf. *Psychiatry Quant, 43,* 156.

ALVIREZ, D., AND BEAN, F. D. (1976). The Mexican American family. In C. H. Mindel and R. W. Habenstein (Eds.), *Ethnic families in America.* New York: Elsevier, 269–292.

ALYN, J. H., AND BECKER, A. L. (1984). Feminist therapy with chronically and profoundly disturbed women. *Journal of Counseling Psychology, 31*(2), 202–208.

AMERICAN PSYCHOLOGICAL ASSOCIATION. (1975). Report of the task force on sex bias and sex-role stereotyping in psychotherapeutic practice. *American Psychologist, 30*(12), 1169–1175.

AMIR, Y. (1969). Contact hypothesis in ethnic relations. *Psychol. Bull., 71,* 319–342.

ANDERSON, J. (1983). The effects of culture and social class on client preference for counseling methods. *Journal of Non-White Concerns, 11,* 84–88.

ANTILL, J. K., AND CUNNINGHAM, J. D. (1979). Self-esteem as a function of masculinity in both sexes. *Journal of Consulting and Clinical Psychology, 47*(4), 783–785.

ANZEL, A. S. (1970). A-B typing and patient socioeconomic and personality characteristics in a quasi-therapeutic situation. *Journal of Consulting and Clinical Psychology, 35*(1), 102–115.

ARCHES, J. (1984). Women and mental health: One step forward, one step back? *Catalyst, 4*(4), 43–58.

ARIES, E. (1976). Interaction patterns and themes of male, female, and mixed groups. *Small Group Behavior, 7*(1), 7–18.

ARIES, E. J. (1977). Male-female interpersonal styles in all male, all female and mixed groups. In A. G. Sargent (Ed.), *Beyond sex roles*. St. Paul, Minn.: West Publishing Co.

ARIES, E. J. (1982). Verbal and nonverbal behavior in single-sex and mixed-sex groups: Are traditional sex-roles changing? *Psychological Reports, 51*(1), 127–134.

ARONSON, E., BLANEY, H., SIKES, J., STEPHAN, C., AND SNAPP, M. (1975). Busing and racial tensions: The jigsaw route to learning and liking. *Psychology Today, 8*, 43–50.

ARONSON, H., AND OVERALL, B. (1966). Treatment expectations of patients in two social classes. *Social Work, 11*(1), 35–42.

ASHMORE, R. D. (1970). Solving the problems of prejudice. In B. E. Collins (Ed.), *Social psychology reading*. Boston: Addison-Wesley.

ASLIN, A. L. (1977). Feminist and community mental health center psychotherapists' expectations of mental health for women. *Sex Roles, 3*(6), 537–544.

ATKINSON, D. R. (1983). Ethnic similarity in counseling psychology: A review of research. *The Counseling Psychologist, 11*(3), 79–92.

ATKINSON, D. R., AND CARSKADDON, G. (1975). A prestigious introduction, psychological jargon, and perceived counselor credibility. *Journal of Counseling Psychology, 22*, 180–186.

ATKINSON, D. R., FURLONG, M. J., AND POSTON, W. C. (1986). Afro-American preferences for counselor characteristics. *Journal of Counseling Psychology, 33*(3), 326–330.

ATKINSON, D. R., MARUYAMA, M., AND MATSUI, S. (1978). Effects of counselor race and counseling approach on Asian Americans' perceptions of counselor credibility and utility. *Journal of Counseling Psychology, 25*, 76–83.

ATKINSON, D. R., MARUYAMA, M., AND MATSUI, S. (1981). The effects of counselor race and communication style on Indian perceptions of counselor effectiveness. *Counselor Education and Supervision, 21*, 72–80.

ATKINSON, D. R., PONTEROTTO, J. G., AND SANCHEZ, A. R. (1984). Attitudes of Vietnamese and Anglo-American students toward counseling. *Journal of College Student Personnel*, pp. 448–452.

ATTNEAVE, C. (1982). American Indians and Alaskan native families: Immigrants in their own homeland. In M. McGoldrick et al., *Ethnicity and family therapy*. New York: Guilford Press, 55–83.

BAGAROZZI, D. A. (1980). Family therapy and the black and middle class: A neglected area of study. *Journal of Marital and Family Therapy, 6*, 159–166.

BAHN, A. K., CONWELL, M., AND HURLEY, P. (1965). Survey of psychiatric practice. *Archives of General Psychiatry, 12*(3), 295–302.

BAKER, J., AND WAGNER, N. N. (1966). Social class and treatment in a child psychiatry clinic. *Archives of General Psychiatry, 14*, 129–133.

BAKER, R. (1964). *Following the color line*. New York: Harper and Row.

BALCH, P., AND MILLER, K. (1974). Social class and the community mental health center: Client and therapist perceptions of presenting problems and treatment expectations. *American Journal Community Psychology, 2*(3), 243–253.

BALL, R. E., AND ROBBINS, L. (1986). Black husbands' satisfaction with their family life. *Journal of Marriage and the Family, 48*(4), 849–856.

BANIKIOTES, P. G., AND MERLUZZI, T. V. (1981). Impact of counselor gender and counselor sex role orientation on perceived counselor characteristics. *Journal of Counseling Psychology, 28*(4), 342–348.

BANIKIOTES, P. G., RUSSELL, J. M., AND LINDEN, J. H. (1972). Interpersonal attraction in simulated and real interactions. *Journal of Personality and Social Psychology, 23*(1), 1–7.

BANKS, G., BERENSON, B., AND CARKHUFF, R. (1967). The effects of counselor race and training upon Negro clients in initial interviews. *Journal of Clinical Psychology. 23*, 70–72.

BANKS, H. C. (1975). The black person as client and as therapist. *Professional Psychology*, pp. 470–474.

BANKS, W. M. (1972). The black client and the helping professionals. In R. L. Jones (Ed.), *Black psychology*. New York: Harper and Row, pp. 205–212.

BAPTISTE, D. A., JR. (1984). Marital and family therapy with racially/culturally intermarried step-families: Issues and guidelines. *Family Relations, 33*(3), 373–380.

BARATZ, S. (1967). Effects of race of experimenter, interactions, and comparison population upon level of reported anxiety in negro subjects. *Journal of Personality and Social Psychology, 7,* 194–196.

BARCLAY, L. E. (1969). A group approach to young unwed mothers. *Social Casework, 50,* 379–384.

BARD, M., AND BERKOWITZ, B. (1969). A community psychology consultation program in police family crisis intervention: Preliminary impressions. *International Journal of Social Psychiatry, 15,* 209–215.

BARLING, J. (1984). Effects of husband's work experiences on wives marital satisfaction. *The Journal of Social Psychology, 124,* 219–225.

BARNES, E. J. (1980). The Black community as the source of positive self-concept for Black children: A theoretical perspective. In R. Jones (Ed.), *Black psychology.* New York: Harper and Row, pp. 106–130.

BARNLUND, D. C., AND HARLAND, C. (1963). Propinquity and prestige as determinants of communication networks. *Sociometry, 26,* 467–479.

BAROCAS, R., AND VANCE, F. I. (1974). Physical appearance and personal adjustment counseling. *Journal of Counseling Psychology, 21,* 96–100.

BARR, S. (1973). The social agency as a dissemination of information. In J. Fischer (Ed.), *Interpersonal emergent approaches for social work practice.* Springfield, Ill.: Charles C Thomas.

BARRETT, C. J. (1978). Effectiveness of widows' groups in facilitating change. *Journal of Consulting and Clinical Psychology, 46*(1), 20–31.

BARRETT, Q. T., AND PERLMUTTER, Q. (1972). Black clients and white workers: A report from the field. *Child Welfare, 51,* 19–24.

BARTOL, K. (1975). The effect of male versus female leaders on follower satisfaction and performance. *Journal of Business Research, 3,* 33–42.

BARTOL, K. M., AND WORTMAN, M. S. (1975). Male versus female leaders: Effects on perceived leader behavior and satisfaction in a hospital. *Personnel Psychology, 28,* 533–547.

BARTZ, K. W., AND LEVINE, S. (1978). Childbearing by black parents: A description and comparison to Anglo-Chicano parents. *Journal of Marriage and Family, 40*(4), 709–718.

BASKIN, D., BLUESTONE, H., AND NELSON, M. (1981). Ethnicity and psychiatric diagnosis. *Journal of Clinical Psychology, 37,* 529–538.

BASKIN, D., BLUESTONE, H., AND NELSON, M. (1981). Mental illness in minority women. *Journal of Clinical Psychology, 37*(3), 491–498.

BASS, B. A., ACOSTA, F. X., AND EVANS, L. A. (1982). The Black American patient. In F. X. Acosta, J. Yamamoto, and L. A. Evans (Eds.), *Effective psychotherapy for low-income and minority patients.* New York: Plenum Press.

BATTLE, E. S., AND ROTTER, J. B. (1963). Children's feeling of personal control as related to social class and ethnic group. *Journal of Personality, 31,* 482–490.

BAUCOM, D. H., AND AIKEN, P. A. (1984). Sex role identity, marital satisfaction and response to behavioral marital therapy. *Journal of Consulting and Clinical Psychology, 3*(52), 438–444.

BAUER, R. H., AND TURNER, J. H. (1974). Betting behavior in sexually homogeneous and heterogeneous groups. *Psychological Reports, 34*(1), 251–258.

BAUM, M. C., AND LAMB, D. H. (1983). A comparison of the concerns presented by black and white students to a university counseling center. *Journal of College-Student Personnel,* pp. 127–131.

BAUM, O. E., AND FELZER, S. B. (1964). Activity in initial interviews with lower-class patients. *Archives General Psychiatry, 10,* 345–353.

BAUM, O. E., FELZER, S. B., D'ZMURA, T. L., AND SHUMAKER, E. (1966). Psychotherapy, dropouts and lower socioeconomic patients. *American Journal of Orthopsychiatry, 36*(4), 629–635.

BEACH, S. R., AND BRODERICK, J. E. (1983). Commitment: A variable in women's response to marital therapy. *American Journal of Family Therapy, 11*(4), 16–24.

BEAN, F., CURTIS, R., AND MARCUM, J. (1977). Familism and marital satisfaction among Mexican Americans: The effects of family size, wife's labor force participation, and conjugal power. *Journal of Marriage and the Family, 39*(4), 759–767.

BECK, A. T. (1967). *Depression: Clinical, experimental, and theoretical aspects.* New York: Harper and Row.

BECK, D. F., AND JONES, M. A. (1975). *Progress on family problems.* New York: Family Service Association of America.

BECK, J. C., BUTTENWIESER, P., AND GRUNEBAUM, H. (1968). Learning to treat the poor: A group experience. *International Journal of Group Psychotherapy, 18*(3), 325–336.

BECKETT, D., JR., AND SMITH, A. D. (1981). Work and family roles: Egalitarian marriage in black and white families. *Social Service Review, 55*(2), 314–326.

BEDNAR, R. L., AND KAUL, T. (1978). Experiential group research current perspectives. In S. L. Garfield and A. E. Bergin (Eds.), *Handbook of psychotherapy and behavior change.* New York: John Wiley and Sons, Inc.

BEHRENS, M. (1967). Brief home visits by the clinic therapist in the treatment of lower-class patients. *American Journal of Psychiatry, 124*(3), 371–375.

BEHRENS, M., ROSENTHAL, A., AND CHODOFF, P. (1968). Communication in lower class families of schizophrenics. *Archives of General Psychiatry, 18*(6), 689–696.

BEISER, M. (1965). Poverty, social disintegration, and personality. *Journal of Social Issues, 21*, 56–78.

BELL, J. E. (1975). *Family therapy.* New York: Jason Aronson.

BELL, L., AND BELL, D. (1982). Family climate and the role of the family adolescent: Determinates of adolescent functioning. *Family Relations, 31*, 519–527.

BEM, S. L. (1974). The measurement of psychological androgyny. *Journal of Consulting and Clinical Psychology, 42*, 155–162.

BEM, S. L. (1981). Gender schema theory: A cognitive account of sex typing. *Psychological Review, 88*(4), 354–364.

BENEDEK, E. P. (1981). Women's issues: A new beginning. *The American Journal of Psychiatry, 138*(10), 1317–1318.

BERGER, J., COHEN, B. P., AND ZELDITCH, M., JR. (1966). Status characteristics and expectation states. In J. Berger et al. (Eds.), *Sociological Theories in Progress,* Vol. 1. Boston: Houghton Mifflin Company, pp. 29–46.

BERGER, J., COHEN, B. P., AND ZELDITCH, M. (1972). Status characteristics and social interaction. *American Sociological Review, 32*, 241–255.

BERGER, J., CONNER, T. L., AND FISEK, M. H. (Eds.). (1974). *Expectation states theory: A theoretical research program.* Washington, D.C.: University Press of America, Inc.

BERGER, J., FISEK, M. H., NORMAN, R. Z., AND ZELDITCH, M., JR. (1977). *Status characteristics and social interaction: An expectation states approach.* New York: Elsevier.

BERGER, J., AND ZELDITCH, M., JR. (1983). Artifacts and challenges: A comment on Lee and Ofshe. *Social Psychology Quarterly, 46*, 59–62.

BERGER, M., AND WRIGHT, L. (1978). Divided allegiance: Men, work and family life. *The Counseling Psychologist, 8*(4), 50–52.

BERGIN, A. E. (1962). The effect of dissonant persuasive communications upon changes in a self-referring attitude. *Journal of Personality, 30*, 423–438.

BERGIN, A. E. AND SILVERMAN, H. L. (1986). Working with religious issues in therapy. *Contemporary Psychology, 31*(2), 85–88.

BERKUN, M., AND MEELAND, T. (1958). Sociometric effects of race and of combat performance. *Sociometry, 21*, 145–149.

BERLIN, S. B. (1976). Better work with women clients. *Social Work, 21*(6), 492–497.

BERMAN, J. S., AND NORTON, N. C. (1985). Does professional training make a therapist more effective: Review. *Psychological Bulletin, 98*(2), 401–407.

BERMAN, P., O'NAN, B., AND FLOYD, W. (1981). The double standard of aging and the social situation: Judgments of attractiveness of the middle-aged woman. *Sex Roles, 7*, 87–95.

BERNAL, M., AND PADILLA, A. (1982). Status of minority curricula and training in clinical psychology. *American Psychology, 37*(7), 780–787.

BERNARD, J. (1972). *The future of marriage.* New York: Bantam.

BERNARD, J. (1981). The good-provider role: Its rise and fall. *American Psychologist, 36*(1), 1–12.

BERNARD, V. W. (1965). Some principles of dynamic psychiatry in relation to poverty. *American Journal of Psychiatry, 122*(3), 254–267.

BERNARDEZ, T., AND STEIN, T. S. (1979). Separating the sexes in group therapy: An experiment with men's and women's groups. *International Journal of Group Psychotherapy*, 29(4), 493–502.

BERNSTEIN, B. (1960). Language and social class. *British Journal of Sociology*, 11, 271–276.

BERNSTEIN, B. (1970). A sociolinguistic approach to socialization: With some reference to educability. In F. Williams (Ed.), *Language and poverty*. Chicago: Rand McNally College Publishing Co.

BERNSTEIN, B. L., AND FIGIOLI, S. W. (1983). Gender and credibility introduction effects on perceived counselor characteristics. *Journal of Counseling Psychology*, 30(4), 506–513.

BERNSTEIN, B. L., AND LECOMTE, C. (1982). Therapist expectancies: Client gender, and therapist gender, profession, and level of training. *Journal of Clinical Psychology*, 38, 744–754.

BERTCHER, H., AND MAPLE, F. (1974). Elements and issues in group composition. In M. Sunder, P. Glasser, R. Sarri, and R. Vinter (Eds.), *Individual change through small groups*. New York: Free Press, pp. 180–202.

BETZ, N. E., AND SHULLMAN, S. L. (1979). Factors related to client return rate following intake. *Journal of Counseling Psychology*, 26(6), 542–545.

BIDDLE, B., AND THOMAS, E. (1966). *Role theory: Concepts and research*. New York: John Wiley and Sons, Inc.

BILLINGSLEY, A. (1968). *Black families in white America*. Englewood Cliffs, N.J.: Prentice-Hall.

BILLINGSLEY, D. (1977). Sex bias in psychotherapy: An examination of the effects of client sex, client pathology, and therapist sex on treatment planning. *Journal of Consulting and Clinical Psychology*, 45(2), 250–256.

BIRK, J. M. (1981). Relevance and alliance: Cornerstones in training counselors of men. *The Personnel and Guidance Journal*, 60(4), 259–262.

BLANCHARD, F., ADELMAN, L., AND COOK, S. W. (1975). Effect of group success and failure upon interpersonal attraction in cooperating interracial groups. *Journal of Personality & Social Psychology*, 31(6), 1020–1030.

BLANCHARD, F. A., AND COOK, W. (1976). Effects of helping a less competent member of a cooperating interracial group on the development of interpersonal attraction. *Journal of Personality & Social Psychology*, 34(6), 1245–1255.

BLANCHARD, F., WEIGEL, R., AND COOK, S. (1975). The effect of relative competence of group members upon interpersonal attraction in cooperating interracial groups. *Journal of Personality & Social Psychology*, 32(3), 519–530.

BLECKMAN, E. (1982). Are children with one parent at psychological risk? A methodological review. *Journal of Marriage and the Family*, 44(1), 179–195.

BLOCH, H. S. (1968). An open-ended crisis-oriented group for the poor who are sick. *Archives of General Psychiatry*, 18(2), 178–185.

BLOOD, R. O., AND WOLFE, D. M. (1960). *Husbands and wives*. New York: Free Press.

BLOOM, L. J., WEIGEL, R. G., AND TRAUTT, G. M. (1977). "Therapeugenic" factors in psychotherapy: Effects of office decor and subject-therapist sex pairing on the perception of credibility. *Journal of Consulting and Clinical Psychology*, 45(5), 867–873.

BLOOMBAUM, M., YAMAMOTO, J., AND JAMES, Q. (February, 1968). Cultural stereotyping among psychotherapists. *Journal of Consulting & Clinical Psychology*, 32,(1), 99.

BLUMSTEIN, P., AND SCHWARTZ, P. (1983). *American couples*. New York: Morrow.

BOGARDUS, E. J. (1925a). Social distance and its origins. *Journal of Applied Sociology*, 9, 216–226.

BOGARDUS, E. J. (1925b). Measuring social distance. *Journal of Applied Sociology*, 9, 299–308.

BOGARDUS, E. J. (1926a). The group interview. *Journal of Applied Sociology*, 10, 372–382.

BOGARDUS, E. J. (1926b). Social distances between groups. *Journal of Applied Sociology*, 10, 423–430.

BOGARDUS, E. J. (1932–1933). A social distance scale. *Sociology and Social Research*, 17, 265–271.

BOND, J. R., AND VINACKE, W. E. (1961). Coalitions in mixed sex triads. *Sociometry*, 24, 61–75.

BOND, T. T. (1982). Identity development of the traditional female client. *The Personnel and Guidance Journal*, 60(9), 532–534.

BOOTH, A. (1979). Does wives' employment cause stress for husbands? *The Family Coordinator, 28*(4), 445–449.

BOULETTE, T. R. (1975). Group therapy with low income Mexican Americans. *Social Work, 20,* 403–404.

BOULWARE, D. W., AND HOLMES, D. S. (1970). Preferences for therapists and related expectancies. *Journal of Consulting and Clinical Psychology, 35*(2), 269–277.

BOYD, N. (1982). Family therapy with black families. In L. E. Jones and S. Korchin (Eds.), *Minority mental health.* New York: Praeger.

BRADLEY, P. H. (1980). Sex, competence and opinion deviation: An expectation states approach. *Communication Monographs, 47*(2), 101–110.

BRADSHAW, W. (1978). Training psychiatrists for working with Blacks in basic residency programs. *American Journal of Psychiatry, 135*(17), 1520–1524.

BRAVERMAN, L. (1986). Reframing the female clients profile. *Affila, 1*(2), 30–40.

BRAYBOY, T. (1971). The Black patient in group therapy. *International Journal of Group Psychotherapy, 21,* 288–293.

BREISINGER, G. D. (1976). Sex and empathy, re-examined. *Journal of Counseling Psychology, 23*(3), 289–290.

BRIAR, K. H. (1980). Helping the unemployed client. *Journal of Sociology and Social Welfare, 7*(6), 895–906.

BRIAR, S. (1961). Use of theory in studying effects of client social class on students' judgments. *Social Work, 6*(3), 91–97.

BRIELAND, D. (1969). Black identity and the helping person. *Children, 16,* 170–176.

BRILL, N. Q., AND STORROW, H. A. (1960). Social class and psychiatric treatment. *Archives of General Psychiatry, 3*(4), 340–344.

BRISCHETTO, C. M., AND MERLUZZI, T. B. (1981). Client perceptions in an initial interview as a function of therapist sex and expertness. *Journal of Clinical Psychology, 37*(1), 82–87.

BRODEY, J. F., AND DETRE, T. (1972). Criteria used by clinicians in referring patients to individual or group therapy. *American Journal of Psychotherapy, 26*(2), 176–184.

BRODSKY, A. M. (1980). A decade of feminist influence on psychotherapy. *Psychology of Women Quarterly, 4*(3), 331–345.

BRODSKY, A. M., AND HOLROYD, J. (1981). Report of the task force on sex bias and sex-role stereotyping in psychotherapeutic practice. In E. Howell and M. Bayes (Eds.), *Women and mental health.* New York: Basic Books.

BROOKS, A. (1978). Group work on the "Bowery." *Social Work with Groups, 1,* 53–63.

BROOKS, L. (1974). Interactive effects of sex and status on self-disclosure. *Journal of Counseling Psychology, 21*(6), 469–474.

BROOKS, V. R. (1981). Sex and sexual orientation as variables in therapists' biases and therapy outcomes. *Clinical Social Work Journal, 9*(3), 198–210.

BROVERMAN, I. K., BROVERMAN, D. M., CLARKSON, F. E., ROSENKRANTZ, P. S., AND VOGEL, S. R. (1970). Sex role stereotypes and clinical judgments of mental health. *Journal of Consulting Psychology, 34*(1), 1–7.

BROVERMAN, I. K., VOGEL, S. R., BROVERMAN, D. M., CLARKSON, F. E., AND ROSENKRANTZ, P. S. (1972). Sex-role stereotypes: A current appraisal. *Journal of Social Issues, 28*(2), 59–78.

BROWER, A., GARVIN, C., HOBSON, J., REED, B., AND REED, H. (1987). Exploring the effects of leader gender and race on group behavior. In J. Lassner, K. Powell, and E. Finnegan (Eds.), *Social groupwork: Competence and values in practice.* New York: Haworth Press, pp. 129–148.

BROWN, C. R., AND HELLINGER, M. L. (1975). Therapists' attitudes toward women. *Social Work, 20*(4), 266–270.

BROWN, J. A., AND AREVALO, R. (1979). Chicanos and social group work models: Some implications for group work practice. *Social Work with Groups, 2*(4), 331–342.

BROWN, J. A. (1981). Parent education groups for Mexican-Americans. *Social Work in Education, 3*(4), 22–31.

BROWN, J. S., AND KOSTERLITZ, N. (1964). Selection and treatment of psychiatric outpatients. *Archives of General Psychiatry, 11*(4), 425–438.

BROWNMILLER, S. (1975). *Against our will: Men, women, and rape.* New York: Bantam Books.

BRUCH, M. A. (1978). Holland's typology applied to client-counselor interaction: Implications for counseling with men. *Counseling Psychologist, 7*(4), 26–32.

BRYANT, C. (1980). Introducing students to the treatment of inner-city families. *Social Casework, 61*(10), 629–636.

BRYSON, S., AND CODY, J. (1973). Relationship of race and level of understanding between counselor and client. *Journal of Counseling Psychology, 20,* 495–498.

BUCZEK, T. A. (1981). Sex biases in counseling: Counselor retention of the concerns of a female and male client. *Journal of Counseling Psychology, 28*(1), 13–21.

BUMAGIN, S., AND SMITH, J. (1985). Beyond support: Group psychotherapy with low-income mothers. *International Journal of Group Psychotherapy, 35*(2), 279–294.

BURGER, A. L., AND JACOBSON, N. S. (1979). The relationship between sex role characteristics, couple satisfaction and couple problem-solving skills. *American Journal of Family Therapy, 7*(4), 52–60.

BURKE, J. L. (1982). Suggestions for a sex-fair curriculum in family treatment. *Journal of Education for Social Work, 18*(2), 98–102.

BURLIN, F., AND PEARSON, R. (1978). Counselor-in-training response to a male and female client: An analogue study exploring sex-role stereotyping. *Counselor Education and Supervision, 17*(3), 213–221.

BURNSTEIN, E., AND MCRAE, A. D. (1962). Some effects of shared threat and prejudice in racially mixed groups. *Journal of Abnormal Social Psychology, 64,* 257–263.

BURRELL, L., AND RAYDER, N. (1971). Black and white students' attitudes towards counselors. *Journal of Negro Education, 40,* 48–52.

BURT, M. R., GLYNN, T. S., AND SOWDER, B. J. (1979). Psychosocial characteristics of drug-abusing women. DHEW Publication No. ADM 80–917. Washington, D. C.: U. S. Government Printing Office.

BYRNE, D. (1971). *The attraction paradigm.* New York: Academic Press, Inc.

BYRNE, D., CLORE, G. L., AND WORCHEL, P. (1966). Effect of economic similarity-dissimilarity on interpersonal attraction. Journal of Personality and Social Psychology, 4, 220–224.

BYRNE, D., AND CLORE, G. L. (1967). Effectance arousal and attraction. *Journal of Personality and Social Psychology, 6,* 1–18.

BYRNE, D., AND NELSON, D. (1965). Attraction as a linear function of proportion of positive reinforcements. *Journal of Personality and Social Psychology, 1,* 659–667.

BYRNE, D., AND RHAMEY, R. (1965). Magnitude of positive and negative reinforcements as a determinant of attraction. *Journal of Personality and Social Psychology, 2,* 884–889.

BRYNE, D., AND WONG, T. (1962). Racial prejudice, interpersonal attraction, and assumed dissimilarity of attitudes. *Journal of Abnormal and Social Psychology, 65,* 246–253.

CALHOUN, L., CHENEY, T., AND DAWES, A. S. (1974). Locus of control, self-reported depression, and perceived causes of depression. *Journal of Consulting Psychology, 42,* 736.

CAMPBELL, F. A., BREITMAYER, B., AND RAMER, C. T. (1986). Disadvantaged single teenage mothers and their children: Consequences of free educational day care. *Family Relations, 35*(1), 63–68.

CANINO, I. A., AND CANINO, G. (1980). Impact of stress on the Puerto Rican family: Treatment consideration. *American Journal of Orthopsychiatry, 50*(3), 535–541.

CANNON, M. S., AND REDICK, R. W. (1973). Differential utilization of psychiatric facilities by men and women. Statistical note 81. Washington, D.C.: Biometry Branch, National Institute of Mental Health.

CARKHUFF, R. R., AND PIERCE, R. (1967). Differential effects of therapist race and social class upon patient depth of self-exploration in the initial clinical interview. *Journal of Consulting Psychology, 31,* 632–634.

CARLOCK, C. J., AND MARTIN, P. Y. (1977). Sex composition and the intensive group experience. *Social Work, 22*(1), 27–32.

CARLSON, N. L. (1981). Male client–female therapist. *The Personnel and Guidance Journal, 60*(4), 228–231.

CARMEN, E. H., RUSSO, N. F., AND MILLER, J. B. (1981). Inequality and women's mental health: An overview. *The American Journal of Psychiatry, 138*(10), 1319–1330.

CARPENTER, P. J., AND RANGE, L. M. (1982). Predicting psychotherapy duration from therapists' sex, professional affiliation, democratic values, and community mental health ideology. *Journal of Clinical Psychology, 38*(1), 90–91.

CARTER, C. A. (1971). Advantages of being a woman therapist. *Psychotherapy: Theory, research and practice, 8*(4), 297–300.

CARTER, J. A. (1978). Impressions of counselors as a function of counselor or physical attractiveness. *Journal of Counseling Psychology, 25*(1), 28–34.

CARTWRIGHT, D. S. (1955). Success in psychotherapy as a function of certain actuarial variables. *Journal of Consulting Psychology, 19*(5), 357–363.

CARTWRIGHT, D., AND ZANDER, A. (1968). *Group dynamics*, 3rd ed. New York: Harper and Row.

CASCIANI, J. M. (1975). Influence of model's race and sex on interviewees' self disclosure. *Journal of Counseling Psychology, 25*(5), 435–440.

CASHION, B. G. (1982). Female-headed families: Effects on children and clinical implications. *Journal of Marital and Family Therapy, 8*(2), 77–85.

CATALANO, R., DOOLEY, D., AND JACKSON, R. (1981). Economic predictors of admissions to mental health facilities in a nonmetropolitan community. *Health and Social Behavior, 22*(3), 284–297.

CAUDILL, W. (1958). *The psychiatric hospital as a small society*. Cambridge: Harvard University Press.

CAUST, B. L., LIBOW, J. A., AND RASKIN, P. A. (1981). Challenges and promises of training women as family systems therapists. *Family Process, 20*(4), 439–447.

CAVENAR, J. O., JR., AND SPAULDING, J. G. (1978). When the psychotherapist is black. *American Journal of Psychiatry, 134*(1), 1084–1087.

CHANDLER, S. (1980). Self perceived competency in cross cultural counseling. *Social Casework, 61*, 347–353.

CHANG, C. C. (1972). Experiences with group psychotherapy in Taiwan. *International Journal of Group Psychotherapy, 22*, 210–227.

CHAPMAN, J. B. (1975). Comparison of male and female leadership styles. *Academy of Management Journal, 18*, 645–650.

CHAVETZ, J. S. (1972). Women in social work. *Social Work, 17*(5), 12–19.

CHEEK, D. K. (1976). *Assertive black . . . puzzled white*. San Luis Obispo, Cal.: Impact Publishers, Inc.

CHERLIN, A., AND WALTERS, P. B. (1981). Trends in U.S. men's and women's sex role attitudes: 1972 to 1978. *American Sociological Review, 46*(4), 453–460.

CHESLER, P. (1971a). Patient and patriarch: Women in the psychotherapeutic relationship. In V. Gornick and B. Moran (Eds.), *Women in sexist society*. New York: Basic Books, pp. 251–275.

CHESLER, P. (1971b). Women as psychiatric and psychotherapeutic patients. *Journal of Marriage and the Family, 33*(4), 746–759.

CHESSICK, R. D. (1984). Was Freud wrong about female psychology? *The American Journal of Psychoanalysis, 44*(4), 355.

CHESTANG, L. (1980). Character development in a hostile environment. In M. Bloom (Ed.), *Life span development: Bases for preventive and interventive helping*. New York: Macmillan Publishers, pp. 40–50.

CHIEN, C., AND YAMAMOTO, J. (1982). Asian-American and Pacific-islander patients. In F. X. Acosta, J. Yamamoto, and L. A. Evans (Eds.), *Effective psychotherapy for low-income and minority patients*. New York: Plenum Press.

CHILMAN, C. S. (1966). Social work practice with very poor families. *Welfare in Review, 4*, 13–21.

CHILMAN, C. S. (1975). Families in poverty in the early 1970's: Rates, associated factors, some implications. *Journal of Marriage and the Family, 37*(1), 49–60.

CHING, W., AND PROSEN, S. (1980). Asian-Americans in group counseling: A case of cultural dissonance. *Journal for Specialists in Group Work*, pp. 229–233.

CHODOFF, P. (1982). Hysteria and women. *The American Journal of Psychiatry, 139*(5), 545–551.

CHRISTMAS, J. J., AND DAVIS, E. B. (1965). Group therapy programs with the socially deprived in community psychiatry. *Initial Journal of Group Psychotherapy, 15*, 464–476.

CHU, J., AND SUE, S. (1984). Asian/Pacific-Americans and group practice. In L. Davis (Ed.), *Ethnicity in social group work practice.* New York: Haworth Press, Inc.

CICONE, M. V., AND RUBLE, D. N. (1978). Beliefs about males. *Journal of Social Issues, 34*(1), 5–16.

CIMBOLIC, P. (1972). Counselor race and experience effects on black clients. *Journal of Consulting and Clinical Psychology, 39,* 328–332.

CLARK, K. B., AND CLARK, M. P. (1947). Racial identification and preference in Negro children. In T. Newcomb and E. Hartley (Eds.), *Readings in social psychology.* New York: Holt, Rinehart and Winston.

CLEARY, P. D., MECHANIC, D., AND GREENLEY, J. R. (1982). Sex differences in medical care utilization: An empirical investigation. *Journal of Health and Social Behavior, 23*(2), 106–119.

CLINE, V. B., MEJIA, J., COLES, J., KLEIN, N., AND CLINE, R. A. (1984). The relationship between therapists' behaviors and outcome for middle- and lower-class couples in marital therapy. *Journal of Clinical Psychology, 40*(3), 691–704.

CLOPTON, J. R., AND HAYDEL, J. (1982). Psychotherapy referral patterns as influenced by sex of referring therapist and sex and age of the client. *Journal of Consulting and Clinical Psychology, 50*(1), 156–157.

CLOWARD, R. A., AND EPSTEIN, I. (1965). Private social welfare's disengagement from the poor: The case of family adjustment agencies. In M. N. Zald (Ed.), *Social welfare institutions: A sociological reader.* New York: John Wiley and Sons, Inc.

COBB, C. W. (1972). Community mental health services and the lower socioeconomic classes: A summary of research literature on out patient treatment. *American Journal of Orthopsychiatry, 42*(3), 404–414.

COBBS, P. M. (1972a). Ethnotherapy. *Intellectual Digest, 2,* 26–28.

COBBS, P. M. (1972b). Ethnotherapy in Groups. In L. N. Solomon and B. Berzon (Eds.), *New perspectives on encounter groups.* San Francisco: Jossey-Bass, Inc.

COCHRANE, R., AND STOPES-ROE, M. (1981). Women, marriage, employment and mental health. *British Journal of Psychiatry, 139*(5), 373–381.

COCKERHAM, W. C. (1981). *Sociology of mental disorder.* Englewood Cliffs, N.J.: Prentice-Hall.

COHEN, E. G., AND ROPER, S. S. (1972). Modification of interracial interaction disability: An application of status characteristic theory. *American Sociological Review, 37,* 643–657.

COHEN, J. F. (1979). Male roles in mid-life, *The Family Coordinator, 28*(4), 465–471.

COHEN, R. (1976). *New careers grows older.* Baltimore: The Johns Hopkins University Press.

COIE, J. D., PENNINGTON, B. F., AND BUCKLEY, H. H. (1974). Effects of situational stress and sex roles on the attribution of psychological disorder. *Journal of Consulting and Clinical Psychology, 42*(4), 559–568.

COLE, N. T., BRANCH, C. H., AND ALLISON, R. B. (1962). Some relationships between social class and practice of dynamic psychotherapy. *American Journal of Psychiatry, 118*(11), 1004–1012.

COLEMAN, J. S., CAMPBELL, E. Q., HOBSON, C. J., MCPARTLAND, J., MOOD, A. M., WEINFELD, F. D., AND YORK, R. L. (1966). *Equality of educational opportunity.* Washington: U.S. Government Printing Office.

COLLISON, B. B. (1981). Counseling adult males. *The Personnel and Guidance Journal, 60*(4), 219–222.

COMAS-DÍAZ, L. (1981). Effects of cognitive and behavioral group treatment on the depressive symptomatology of Puerto Rican women. *Journal of Consulting and Clinical Psychology, 49*(5), 627–632.

COMAS-DÍAZ, L. (1984). Content themes in group treatment with Puerto Rican women. In L. Davis (Ed.), *Ethnicity in social group work practice.* New York: Haworth Press Inc.

COMPAS, B. E., AND ADELMEN, H. T. (1981). Clinicians' judgements of female clients casual attributions. *Journal of Clinical Psychology, 37*(2), 456–60.

CONDRY, J., AND DYER, S. (1976). Fear of success: Attribution of the cause to the victim. *Journal of Social Issues, 32*(3), 63–83.

COOK, S. W. (1957). Desegregation: A psychological analysis. *American Psychologist, 12,* 1–13.

COOK, S. W. (1969). Motives in conceptual analysis of attitude related behavior. In W. Arnold and D. Levine (Eds.), *Nebraska symposium on motivation*, Vol. 17. Lincoln: University of Nebraska Press.

COOK, S. W., AND SELLITZ, C. (1955). Some factors which influence the attitudinal outcomes of personal contacts. *International Sociological Bulletin, 7*, 51–58.

COOKE, M., AND KIPNIS, D. (1986). Influence tactics in psychotherapy. *Journal of Consulting and Clinical Psychology, 54*(1), 22–26.

COOPER, E. J., AND CENTO, M. H. (1977). Group and the Hispanic prenatal patient. *American Journal of Orthopsychiatry, 47*(4), 689–700.

COOPER, S. (1973). A look at the effect of racism on clinical work. *Social Casework, 54*(2), 76–84.

COPELAND, E. J. (1982). Oppressive conditions and the mental health needs of low income black women: Barriers to services, strategies for change. *Women and Therapy, 1*(1), 13–26.

COREY, H., AND COREY, M. S. (1987). *Groups: Process and practice.* Monterey, Cal.: Brooks/Cole Publishing Company.

CORMIER, W. H., AND L. S. C. (1979). *Interviewing strategies for helpers: A guide to assessment, treatment and evaluation.* Monterey, Cal.: Brooks/Cole Publishing Company.

COTLER, S. B. (1970). Sex differences and generalization of anxiety reduction with automated desensitization and minimal therapist interaction. *Behavior Research and Therapy, 8*(3), 273–285.

COZBY, P. C. (1973). Self-disclosure: A literature review. *Psychological Bulletin, 79*(2), 73–91.

CRISWELL, J. H. (1937). Racial cleavage in Negro-white groups. *Sociometry, 1*, 81–89.

CROMWELL, R. E., CORRALES, G., AND TORSIELLO, P. M. (1973). Normative patterns of marital decision making and influence in Mexico and the United States: A partial list test of resource and ideology theory. *Journal of Comparative Family Studies, 4*, 177–196.

CROSBY, F. (1982). *Relative deprivation and working women.* New York: Oxford.

CROSS, W. (1978). Models of psychological Nigrosence: A literature review. *Journal of Black Psychology, 5*, 13–31.

CRUSE, H. (1967). *Crisis of the negro intellectual.* New York: Morrow & Co.

CULLEN, J. B., AND PERREWE, P. L. (1981). Superiors' and subordinates' gender: Does it really matter? *Psychological Reports, 48*(2), 435–438.

CURRANT, E. F., DICKSON, A. L., ANDERSON, H. N., AND FAULKENDER, P. J. (1979). Sex-role stereotyping and assertive behavior. *The Journal of Psychology, 101*(2), 223–228.

CURRY, A. (1964). Myth, transference and the black psychotherapist. *Psychoanalytic Review, 51*, 7–14.

CYRUS, A. A. (1967). Group treatment of ten disadvantaged mothers. *Social Casework, 48*, 81–84.

DAILEY, D. M. (1980). Are social workers sexists? A replication. *Social Work, 25*(1), 46–50.

DALTON, J. E., AND DUBNICKI, C. (1981). Sex, race, age, and education variables in Shipley-Hartford scores of alcoholic inpatients. *Journal of Clinical Psychology, 37*(4), 885–888.

DANZIGER, K. (1976). *Interpersonal communication.* New York: Pergamon.

DAUPHINAIS, P., DAUPHINAIS, L., AND ROWE, W. (1981). Effects of race and communication style on Indian perceptions of counselor effectiveness. *Counselor Education and Supervision, 21*(1), 72–80.

DAUPHINAIS, P., LA FROMBOISE, T., AND ROWE, W. (1980). Perceived problems and sources of help for American Indian students. *Counselor Education and Supervision, 20*, 37–46.

DAVENPORT, J., AND REIMS, N. (1978). Theoretical orientation and attitudes toward women. *Social Work, 23*(4), 306–309.

DAVIDSON, C. V., AND ABRAMOWITZ, S. I. (1980). Sex bias and clinical judgment: Later empirical returns. *Psychology of Women Quarterly, 43*(3), 377–395.

DAVIS, C., HAUB, A., AND WILLETTE, J. (1983). U.S. Hispanics—Changing the race of America. *Population Bulletin, 38*,(3), 38–41.

DAVIS, I. P. (1975). Advice-giving in parent counseling, *Social Casework, 56*, 343–347.

DAVIS, L. (June, 1975). Dynamics of race in therapeutic practice. A preliminary examination in social work.

DAVIS, L. (1979). Racial composition of groups. *Social Work, 24*, 208–213.

DAVIS, L. (1980). When the majority is the psychological minority. *Group Psychotherapy, Psychodrama and Sociometry, 33,* 179–184.

DAVIS, L. (1981). Racial issues in the training of group workers. *Journal for Specialists in Group Work,* pp. 155–160.

DAVIS, L. (1984). *Ethnicity in social group work practice.* New York: Haworth Press, Inc.

DAVIS, L., AND BURNSTEIN, E. (1981). Preference for racial composition of groups. *The Journal of Psychology, 109,* 293–301.

DAVIS, L. E., AND PROCTOR, E. K. (February 29–March 6, 1981). Student racial attitudes and perceptions of causal events at entry to graduate social work education. Paper presented at the Annual Program Meeting, Council on Social Work Education, Louisville, Kentucky.

DAVIS, M. (1974). Separate and together, all black therapist group in the white hospital. *American Journal of Orthopsychiatry, 44,* 19–25.

DAWKINS, M. P., AND DAWKINS, M. P. (1978). A program for the treatment of post-hospitalized mental patients in a low-income Black community. *Journal of Community Psychology, 6*(3), 257–262.

DEAUX, K. (1985). Sex and gender. *Annual Review of Psychology, 36,* 49–81.

DEAUX, K., AND LEWIS, L. L. (1984). Structure of gender stereotypes: Interrelationships among components and gender label. *Journal of Personality and Social Psychology, 46,* 991–1004.

DEFOREST, C., AND STONE, G. L. (1980). Effects of sex and intimacy level of self-disclosure. *Journal of Counseling Psychology, 27*(1), 93–96.

DEGEYNDT, W. (1973). Health behavior and health needs in urban Indians in Minneapolis. *Health Service Reports, 88,* 749–758.

DE HOYOS, A., AND DE HOYOS, G. (1965). Symptomatology differentials between Negro and white schizophrenics. *International Journal of Social Psychiatry, 11,* 245–255.

DELGADO, M. (1977). Puerto Rican spiritualism and the social work profession. *Social Casework, 58*(8), 451–458.

DELGADO, M. (1987). Puerto Ricans. *Encyclopedia of Social Work, 2,* 426–434.

DELGADO, M., AND HUMN-DELGADO, D. (1982). Natural support systems: Source of strength in Hispanic communities. *Social Work, 27,* 83–89.

DELGADO, M., AND SIFF, S. (1980). A Hispanic adolescent group in a public school setting: An inter-agency approach. *Social Work with Groups, 27,* 83–89.

DEL GAUDIO, A. C., CARPENTER, P. J., AND MORROW, G. R. (1978). Male and female treatment differences: Can they be generalized? *Journal of Consulting and Clinical Psychology, 46*(6), 1577–1578.

DELK, J. L., AND RYAN, T. T. (1975). Sex role stereotyping and A-B therapist status: Who is more chauvanistic? *Journal of Consulting and Clinical Psychology, 43*(4), 589.

DELL, D. M., AND SCHMIDT, L. D. (1976). Behavioral cues to counselor expertness. *Journal of Counseling Psychology, 23,* 197–201.

DERLEGA, V. J., AND CHAIKIN, A. L. (1976). Norms affecting self-disclosure in men and women. *Journal of Consulting and Clinical Psychology, 44*(3), 376–380.

DIANGSON, P., KRAVETZ, D., AND LIPTON, J. (1975). Sex-role stereotyping and social work education. *Journal of Education for Social Work, 11*(3), 44–49.

DIBBLE, U., AND STRAUS, M. A. (1980). Some social-structure determinants of inconsistency between attitudes and behavior—case of family violence. *Journal of Marriage and the Family, 42*(1), 71–80.

DIENSTBIER, R. A. (1972). A modified belief theory of prejudice emphazing the mutual causality of racial prejudice and anticipated belief differences. *Psychological Review, 79,* 146–160.

DIETRICH, K. T. (1975). A re-examination of the myth of Black matriarchy. *Journal of Marriage and Family, 37,* 367–374.

DIMOND, R. E., AND MUNZ, D. C. (1967). Ordinal position of birth and self-disclosure in high school students. *Psychological Reports, 21,* 829–833.

DINGLES, N. G., TRIMBLE, J. E., MANSON, S. M., AND PASQUALE, F. L. (1981). Counseling and psychotherapy with American Indians and Alaska natives. In A. J. Marsella and P. B. Pedersen (Eds.), *Cross-cultural counseling and psychotherapy.* New York: Pergamon Press, pp. 243–276.

DION, K. L. (1979). Status equity, sex composition of group, and intergroup bias. *Personality & Social Psychology Bulletin, 5*(2), 240–244.

DION, K. (1985). Sex, gender, and groups: Selected issues. In V. E. O'Leary, R. K. Unger, and B. A. Wallston (Eds.), *Women, gender, and social psychology.* Hillsdale, N.J.: Lawrence Erlbaum Associates.

DOHERTY, W. (1981). Involving the reluctant father in family therapy. In A. S. Gurman (Ed.), *Questions and answers in the practice of family therapy.* New York: Brunner/Mazel Publishers.

DOHRENWEND, B. (1975). Problems in defining and sampling the relevant population of stressful life events. In B. J. Dohrenwend and B. P. Dohrenwend (Eds.), *Stressful life events: Their nature and effects.* New York: John Wiley and Sons, pp. 275–310.

DOHRENWEND, B. P., AND CHIN-SHONG, E. (1967). Social status and attitudes toward psychological disorder: The problem of tolerance of deviance. *American Sociological Review, 32*(32), 417–433.

DOHRENWEND, B. P., AND DOHRENWEND, B. S. (1969). *Social status and psychological disorder: A causal inquiry.* New York: John Wiley and Sons.

DOHRENWEND, B., AND DOHRENWEND, B. (1976). Sex differences and psychiatric disorders. *American Journal of Sociology, 81*(6), 1447–1454.

DONAHUE, T. J. (1979). Counselor discrimination against women: Additional information. *Journal of Counseling Psychology, 26*(3), 276–278.

DORFMAN, E., AND KLEINER, R. J. (1962). Race of examiner and patient in psychiatric diagnosis and recommendations. *Journal of Consulting Psychology, 26,* 393.

DOSTER, J. A. (1976). Sex role learning and interview communication. *Journal of Counseling Psychology, 23*(5), 482–485.

DOSTER, J. A., AND STRICKLAND, B. R. (1969). Perceived childrearing practices and self-disclosure patterns. *Journal of Clinical and Consulting Psychology, 33,* 382.

DRAGUNS, J. G. (1981). Counseling across cultures: Common themes and distinct approaches. In P. P. Pedersen, J. G. Draguns, W. J. Lonner, and J. E. Trible (Eds.), *Counseling across cultures.* Honolulu, Hi.: The University of Hawaii Press.

DUBEY, S. (1970). Blacks' preference for black professionals, businessmen, and religious leaders. *Public Opinion Quarterly, 34,* 113–116.

DUEHN, W. D., AND MAYADAS, N. S. (1976). The effect of practice orientations on clinical assessment. *American Journal of Orthopsychiatry, 46*(4), 629–636.

DUEHN, W. D., AND PROCTOR, E. K. (1974). A study of cognitive complexity in the education for social work practice. *Journal of Education for Social Work, 10,* 20–26.

DUNBAR, P. L. (1970). We wear the mask. In *The complete works of Paul Lawrence Dunbar.* New York: Dodd, Mead and Company.

DUNCAN, G. (1984). *Years of poverty, years of plenty.* Ann Arbor, Mich.: Institute for Social Research, The University of Michigan.

DURRETT, M. E., O'BRYANT, S., AND PENNEBAKER, J. W. (1975). Child-rearing reports of white, black and Mexican-American families. *Developmental Psychology, 11,* 871.

DUVALL, E. M. (1971). *Family development,* 4th ed. New York: J. B. Lippincott.

DWECK, C. S., DAVIDSON, W., NELSON, S., AND ENNA, B. (1978). Sex differences in learned helplessness: The contingencies of evaluated feedback in the classroom and experimental analysis. *Developmental Psychology, 14,* 268–276.

EAGLY, A. H. (1970). Leadership style and role differentiation as determinates of group effectiveness. *Journal of Personality, 38,* 509–524.

EAGLY, A. H. (1978). Sex differences in influenceability. *Psychological Bulletin, 85*(1), 86–116.

EAGLY, A. H. (1983). Gender and social influence: A social psychological analysis. *American Psychologist, 38*(9), 971–981.

EAGLY, A., AND CROWLEY, M. (1986). Gender and helping behavior: A meta-analytic review of the social psychological literature. *Psychological Bulletin, 100*(3), 283–308.

EAGLY, A. H., AND STEFFEN, V. J. (1984). Gender stereotypes stem from the distribution of women and men into social roles. *Journal of Personality and Social Psychology, 46*(4), 735–754.

EAGLY, A. H., AND WOOD, W. (1982). Inferred sex differences in status as a determinant of gender stereotypes about social influence. *Journal of Personality and Social Psychology, 43*(5), 915–928.

EAGLY, A. H., AND WOOD, W. (1985). Gender and influenceability: Stereotype versus behavior. In V. E. O'Leary, R. K. Unger, and B. A. Wallston, (Eds.), *Women, gender, and social psychology*. Hillsdale, N.J.: Lawrence Erlbaum Associates, Publishers.

EAGLY, A. H., et al. (1981). Sex differences in conformity: Surveillance by the group as a determinant of male nonconformity. *Journal of Personality and Social Psychology, 40*(2), 384–394.

EASTMAN, P. C. (1973). Consciousness-raising as a resocialization process for women. *Smith College Studies in Social Work, 43*, 153–183.

EDLESON, J. J., AND BRYGGER, M. P. (1986). Gender differences in reporting of battering incidences. *Family Relations, 35*, 377–382.

EDWARDS, E. D., AND EDWARDS, M. E. (1984). Group work practice with American Indians. In L. Davis (Ed.), *Ethnicity in social group work practice*. New York: Haworth Press Inc.

EDWARDS, E. D., EDWARDS, M. E., DAINES, G., AND EDDY, F. (1978). Enhancing self-concept and identification with "Indianness" of American Indian girls. *Social Work with Groups, 1*(3), 309–18.

EISENMAN, (1965). Reducing prejudice by Negro, white contacts. *Journal of Negro Education, 34*, 461–467.

ENDO, R. (1984). Use of informal social networks for service-related information. *Psychological Reports, 54*, 354.

EPPERSON, D. L. (1981). Counselor gender and early premature terminations from counseling: A replication and extension. *Journal of Counseling Psychology, 28*(4), 349–356.

EPPERSON, D. L., BUSHWAY, D. J., AND WARMAN, R. E. (1983). Client self-terminations after one counseling session: Effects of problem recognition, counselor gender and counselor experience. *Journal of Counseling Psychology, 30*(3), 307–315.

EPSTEIN, C. F. (1981). *Women in law*. New York: Basic Books.

EPSTEIN, L. (1980). *Helping people: The task-centered approach*. St. Louis: C. V. Mosby Co.

EPSTEIN, N., AND JAYNE, C. (1981). Perceptions of cotherapists as a function of therapist sex roles and observer sex roles. *Sex Roles, 7*(5), 497–509.

EPSTEIN, N., JAYNE-LAZARUS, C., AND DeGIOVANNI, I. S. (1979). Cotrainers as models of relationships: Effects on the outcome of couples therapy. *Journal of Marriage and Family Therapy, 5*(4), 53–60.

EPSTEIN, N., AND SHAINLINE, A. (1974). Paraprofessional parent-aides and disadvantaged families. *Social Casework, 55*(4), 230–236.

ESKILSON, A., AND WILEY, M. G. (1976). Sex composition and leadership in small groups. *Sociometry, 39*(3), 183–194.

ESPIN, O. M. (1982). Woman as client, woman as counselor: Some old and new thoughts. *The Personnel and Guidance Journal, 60*(5), 334–336.

ESTRADA, L. F. (1985). Understanding demographics: The case of Hispanics in the United States. In L. B. Brown, J. Otevir, and J. J. Klor de Alva, (Eds.), *A resource guide for human service professionals: Sociocultural and service issues in working with Hispanic American clients*. New York: Rockefeller College Press, 1–17.

ESTRADA, L. F. (1987). Hispanics. *Encyclopedia of social work, 1*, 732–739.

EVANS, L. A., ACOSTA, F. X., YAMAMOTO, J., AND HURWICZ, M. (1986). Patient requests: Correlates and therapeutic implications for hispanic, black, and caucasian patients. *Journal of Clinical Psychology, 42*(1), 213–221.

EVANS, L. A., ACOSTA, F. X., YAMAMOTO, J., AND SKILBECK, W. M. (1984). Orienting psychotherapists to better serve low income and minority patients. *Journal of Clinical Psychology, 40*, 90–96.

EWING, T. N. (1974). Racial similarity of client and counselor and client satisfaction with counseling. *Journal of Counseling Psychology, 21*, 446–449.

EXLINE, R., GRAY, D., AND SCHUETTE, D. (1965). Visual behavior in a dyad as affected by interview content and sex of respondent. *Journal of Personality and Social Psychology, 1*(3), 201–209.

EZELL, H. F., ODEWAHN, C. A., AND SHERMAN, J. D. (1981). The effects of having been supervised by a woman on perceptions of female managerial competence. *Personnel Psychology, 34*, 291–300.

FABRIKANT, B. (1974). The psychotherapist and the female patient: Perceptions, misperceptions and change. In V. Franks and V. Burtle (Eds.), *Women in therapy.* New York: Brunner/Mazel, pp. 83–109.

FALICOV, C. J. (1982). Mexican families. In M. McGoldrick, et al. (Eds.), *Ethnicity and family therapy.* New York: Guilford Press, 134–163.

FARINA, A., AND HAGELAUER, H. D. (1975). Sex and mental illness: The generosity of females. *Journal of Consulting and Clinical Psychology, 43*(1), 122.

FARINA, A., MURRAY, P. J., GROH, T. (1978). Sex and worker acceptance of a former mental patient. *Journal of Consulting and Clinical Psychology, 46*(5), 887–891.

FARLEY, R., SCHUMAN, H., BIANCHI, S., COLASANTO, D., AND HATCHETT, S. (1978). Chocolate city, vanilla suburbs: Will the trend toward racially separate communities continue? *Social Science Research, 7*(4), 319–344.

FELD, S., AND N. RADIN. (1982). *Social psychology for social work and the mental health professions.* New York: Columbia University Press.

FELDMAN, R. A. (1969). Group service programs in public welfare: Patterns and perspectives. *Public Welfare, 27*(3), 266–271.

FELDMAN, R., AND CAPLINGER, T. (1977). Social work experience and client behavioral change: A multivariate analysis of process and outcome. *Journal of Social Service Research, 1*(1), 5–34.

FELDMAN, R., CAPLINGER, T., AND WODARSKI, J. (1983). *The St. Louis conundrum: The effective treatment of antisocial youths.* Englewood Cliffs, N.J.: Prentice-Hall.

FELDSTEIN, J. C. (1979). Effects of counselor sex and sex role and client sex on clients' perceptions and self-disclosure in a counseling analogue study. *Journal of Counseling Psychology, 26*(5), 437–443.

FELDSTEIN, J. C. (1982). Counselor and client sex pairing: The effects of counseling problem and counselor sex role orientation. *Journal of Counseling Psychology, 29*(4), 418–420.

FELTON, G. S., AND BIGGS, B. E. (1973). Psychotherapy and responsibility: Teaching internalization behavior to black low achievers through group therapy. *Small Group Behavior, 4*(2), 147–155.

FEMINIST COUNSELING COLLECTIVE, Washington, D.C. (1975). Feminist psychotherapy. *Social Policy, 6*(2), 54–62.

FENELON, J. R., AND MEGARGEE, E. I. (1971). Influence of race in the manifestation of leadership. *Journal of Applied Psychology, 55,* 353–358.

FENNELL, M. L., et al. (1978). An alternative perspective on sex differences in organizational settings: One process of legitimation. *Sex Roles, 4*(4), 589–604.

FERREE, M. M. (1984). The view from below: Women's employment and gender equality in working class families. *Marriage and Family Review, 7,* 57–75.

FICHER, I. V., AND LINSENBERG, M. (1976). Problems confronting the female therapist doing couple therapy. *Journal of Marital and Family Therapy, 2,* 331–340.

FIDELL, L. S. (1981). Sex differences in psychotropic drug use. *Professional Psychology, 12*(1), 156–162.

FIEDLER, F. (1951). A method of objective quantification of certain counter transference attitudes. *Journal of Clinical Psychology.*

FIEDLER, F. E. (1962). The effect of leadership and cultural heterogeneity on group performance: A test of contingency model. *Journal of Experimental Social Psychology, 65,* 308–318.

FILSINGER, E. E., AND WILSON, M. R. (1984). Religiosity, socioeconomic rewards, and family development: Predictors of marital adjustment. *Journal of Marriage and the Family, 46*(3), 663–670.

FINKELHOR, D. (1983). Common features of family abuse. In D. Finkelhor, R. J. Gilles, G. T. Hotaling, and M. A. Straus (Eds.), *The dark side of families.* Beverly Hills: Sage, 17–24.

FISCHER, J., DULANEY, D. D., FAZIO, R. T., HUDAK, M. T., AND ZIVOTOFSKY, E. (1976). Are social workers sexists? *Social Work, 21*(6), 428–433.

FISCHER, J., AND MILLER, H. (1973). The effect of client race and social class on clinical judgments. *Clinical Social Work Journal, 1*(2), 100–109.

FISHMAN, J. R., AND McCORMACK, J. (1970). Mental health without walls: Community mental health in the ghetto. *American Journal of Psychiatry, 26,* 1461–1467.

FLAHERTY, J. A., AND MEAGHER, R. (1980). Measuring racial bias in inpatient treatment. *American Journal of Psychiatry, 137*(6), 679–682.

FLEISCHER, G. (1975). Producing effective change in impoverished, disorganized families: Is family therapy enough? *Family Therapy, 2*(3), 277–289.

FOLEY, V. (1975). Family therapy with black disadvantaged families: Some observations on roles, communication and techniques. *Journal of Marriage and Family Counseling, 1,* 57–65.

FOLEY, V. (1983). Can a white therapist deal with Black families? In C. Obudho (Ed.), *Black marriage and family therapy.* Westport, Conn.: Greenwood Press.

FOLKINS, C., ROCKWELL, F., VANDO, R., VANDO, A., SPENSLEY, J., AND ROCKWELL, D. (1982). A leaderless couples group postmortem. *International Journal of Group Psychotherapy, 32*(3), 367–373.

FOLLINGSTAD, D. R., KILMANN, P. R., AND ROBINSON, E. (1976). Prediction of self-actualization in male participants in a group conducted by female leaders. *Journal of Clinical Psychology, 32*(3), 706–712.

FONG, M. T., AND BORDERS, L. D. (1985). Effect of sex role orientation and gender in counseling skills training. *Journal of Counseling Psychology, 32*(1), 104–110.

FORREST, T. (1969). Treatment of the father in family therapy. *Family Process, 8,* 106–117.

FORSYTH, P., SCHLENKER, B., LEARY, M., AND McCOWN, N. (1985). Self-presentational determinants of sex differences in leadership behavior. *Small Group Behavior, 16*(2), 197–210.

FOSTER, S. W. (1981). The female therapist as symbolic father in family therapy. *American Journal of Family Therapy, 9,* 88–89.

FRANK, A., EISENTHAL, S., AND LAZARE, A. (1978). Are there social class differences in patient's treatment conceptions? *Archives of General Psychiatry, 35,* 61–69.

FRANK, H. H., AND KATCHER, A. H. (1977). The qualities of leadership: How male medical students evaluate their female peers. *Human Relations, 30,* 403–416.

FRANK, J. D. (1961). *Persuasion and healing.* Baltimore: The Johns Hopkins Press.

FRANK, J. D., GLIEDMAN, L. H., IMBER, S. D., NASH, E. H., AND STONE, A. R. (1957). Why patients leave psychotherapy. *A.M.A. Archives of Neurological Psychiatry, 77,* 283–299.

FRANKLIN, D. L. (1985). Differential clinical assessments: The influence of class and race. *Social Service Review, 59,* 44–61.

FRANKLIN, G. S., AND KAUFMAN, K. S. (1982). Group psychotherapy for elderly female Hispanic outpatients. *Hospital and Community Psychiatry, 33*(5), 385–387.

FRANKLIN, J. H. (1968). Introduction: Color and race in the modern world. In J. H. Franklin (Ed.), *Color and Race,* p. vii. Boston Academy of Arts and Sciences, Houghton Mifflin.

FRANKLIN, J. H. (1969). *From Slavery to Freedom: A history of Negro Americans.* New York: Vintage House.

FRAZIER, E. F. (1964). *The Negro church in America.* New York: Schocker Books.

FRAZIER, F. E. (1968). *On race relations: Selected papers.* G. F. Edwards (Ed.), Chicago: University of Chicago, 1968.

FREEDMAN, J. T., LEVY, A., BUCHANAN, R., AND PRICE, J. (1972). Crowding and human aggressiveness. *Journal of Experimental Social Psychology, 8,* 549–557.

FREEMAN, J. (1980). Women and urban policy. *Signs, 5*(3), 54–521.

FRIEDMAN, H. J. (1977). Special problems of women in psychotherapy. *American Journal of Psychotherapy, 31*(3), 405–416.

FRY, P. S., KROPF, G., AND COE, K. J. (1980). Effects of counselor and client racial similarity on the counselors response patterns and skills. *Journal of Counseling, 27,* 130–137.

FUGITA, S. S., WEXLEY, K. N., AND HILLERY, J. M. (1974). Black-white differences in nonverbal behavior in an interview setting. *Journal of Applied Social Psychology, 4,* 343–350.

FULLER, F. F. (1963). Influence of sex of counselor and of client on client expression of feeling. *Journal of Counseling Psychology, 10*(1), 34–40.

FULLER, F. F. (1964). Preference for female and male counselors. *Personnel and Guidance Journal, 42*(5), 463–467.

FURLONG, M. J., ATKINSON, D. R., AND CASAS, J. M. (1979). Effects of counselor ethnicity and attitudinal similarity on chicano students' perceptions of counselor credibility and attractiveness. *Hispanic Journal of Behavioral Sciences, 1,* 41–53.

GALE, M. S., BECK, S., AND SPRINGER, K. (1978). Effects of therapists' biases on diagnosis and disposition of emergency services patients. *Hospital and Community Psychiatry, 29*(11), 705–708.

GARCIA-PRETO, N. (1982). Puerto Rican families. In M. McGoldrick, et al. (Eds.), *Ethnicity and family therapy.* New York: The Guilford Press, 164–186.

GARDNER, J. (1971). Sexist counseling must stop. *The Personnel and Guidance Journal, 49*(9), 705–714.

GARDNER, W. E. (1972). The differential effects of race, education and experience in helping. *Journal of Clinical Psychology, 28,* 87–89.

GARFIELD, S. L. (1978). Research on client variables in psychotherapy. In A. E. Bergin and S. L. Garfield (Eds.), *Handbook of psychotherapy and behavior change: An empirical analysis.* New York: John Wiley and Sons.

GARVIN, C. (1987). *Contemporary group work.* Englewood Cliffs, N.J.: Prentice-Hall.

GARVIN, C. D. (1985). Work with disadvantaged and oppressed groups. In M. Sundel, P. Glasser, R. Sarri, R. Vinter (Eds.), *Individual change through small groups.* New York: The Free Press.

GARVIN, C. D., AND REED, B. G. (1983). Gender issues in social group work: An overview. In B. G. Reed and C. D. Garvin (Eds.), *Groupwork with women/groupwork with men: An overview of gender issues in social group work practice.* New York: Haworth Press, pp. 5–18.

GARZA, R., ROMERO, G., COX, B., AND RAMIREZ, M. (1982). Biculturalism, locus of control and leader behavior in ethnically mixed small groups. *Journal of Applied Social Psychology, 12*(3), 237–253.

GASSER, R. D., AND TAYLOR, C. M. (1976). Role adjustment of single parent fathers with dependent children. *The Family Coordinator, 25*(4), 397–400.

GATZ, M., TYLER, F., PARAGAMENT, K. (1978). Goal attainment, locus of control, and coping style in adolescent group counseling. *Journal of Counseling Psychology, 25,* 310–319.

GEER, C. A., AND HURST, J. C. (1976). Counselor-subject sex variables in systematic desensitization. *Journal of Counseling Psychology, 23*(4), 296–301.

GEISMAR, L. (1964). Family functioning as an index of need for welfare services. *Family Process, 3*(1), 99–113.

GELLER, J. A., AND WALLERSTROM, J. (1984). Conjoint therapy for the treatment of domestic violence. In A. R. Roberts (Ed.), *Battered women and their families.* New York: Springer, pp. 33–48.

GEORGE, V., AND WILDING, P. (1972). *Motherless families.* London: Routledge and Kegan Paul.

GHALI, S. B. (1977). Culture sensitivity and the Puerto Rican client. *Social Casework, 58*(8), 459–468.

GIBBS, J. T. (1975). Use of mental health services by black students at a predominantly white university: A three-year study. *American Journal of Orthopsychiatry, 45,* 430–445.

GIBBS, J. T. (1984). Black adolescents and youth: An endangered species. *American Journal of Orthopsychiatry, 54*(1), 6–21.

GIFT, T. E., STRAUSS, J. S., RITZELER, B. A., KOKES, R. F., AND HARDER, D. W. (1986). Social class and psychiatric outcome. *American Journal of Psychiatry, 143*(2), 222–225.

GILBERT, L. A., AND WALDROOP, J. (1978). Evaluation of a procedure for increasing sex-fair counseling. *Journal of Counseling Psychology, 25*(5), 410–418.

GILES, M., CATALDO, E., AND GATLIN, D. (1975). White flight and percent black: The tipping point reexamined. *Social Science Quarterly, 56,* 85–92.

GILLIGAN, C. (1979). Woman's place in man's life cycle. *Harvard Educational Review, 49,* 431–446.

GILLIGAN, C. (1982). *In a different voice: Psychological theory and women's development.* Cambridge, Mass.: Harvard University Press.

GINN, R. O. (1975). Male and female estimates of personal problems of men and women. *Journal of Counseling Psychology, 22*(6), 518–522.

GINSBERG, L. H. (1978). Forward. In M. J. Austin (Ed.), *Professionals and paraprofessionals.* New York: Human Science Press.

GINZBURG, R. (1962). *One hundred years of lynchings.* New York: Lancer Books.

GLADOW, N. W., AND RAY, M. P. (1986). The impact of information support systems on the well-being of low-income single parents. *Family Relations, 35,* 113–123.

GLASSER, P. H., SARRI, R. C., AND VINTER, R. D. (Eds). (1974). *Individual change through small groups.* New York: Free Press.

GLENWICK, D. S., AND MOWREY, J. D. (1986). When parent becomes peer: Loss of intergenerational boundaries in single parent families. *Family Relations, 35*(1), 57–62.

GOEBEL, J. B., AND COLE, S. G. (1975). Mexican-American and white reactions to stimulus persons of same and different race: Similarity and attraction as a function of prejudice. *Psychological Reports, 36,* 827–833.

GOIN, M. K., YAMAMOTO, J., AND SILVERMAN, J. (1965). Therapy congruent with class-linked expectations. *Archives of General Psychiatry, 13*(2), 133–137.

GOLDBERG, I. D., REGIER, D. A., AND BURNS, B. J. (1980). *Use of health and mental health outpatient services in four organized health care settings.* Rockville, Md.: National Institute of Mental Health.

GOLDSTEIN, A. P. (1962). *Therapist-patient expectancies in psychotherapy.* New York: Pergamon Press.

GOLDSTEIN, A. (1971). *Psychotherapeutic attraction.* New York: Pergamon Press.

GOLDSTEIN, A. (1973). *Structured learning therapy: Toward a psychotherapy for the poor.* New York: Academic Press.

GOLDSTEIN, A., HELLER, K., AND SECHREST, L. (1966). *Psychotherapy and the psychology of behavior change.* New York: John Wiley and Sons.

GOMES, B., AND ABRAMOWITZ, S. I. (1976). Sex-related patient and therapist effects on clinical judgment. *Sex Roles, 2*(1), 1–13.

GOMES-SCHWARTZ, B. (1981). Gender in psychotherapy research. *Contemporary Psychology, 26*(11), 864–866.

GOMEZ, E., ZURCHER, L. A., FARRIS, B. E., AND BECKER, R. E. (1985). A study of psychosocial casework with Chicanos. *Social Work, 30*(6), 477–482.

GONZALES, J. L., DORING, R., AND DEMATHMANN, C. D. (1979). Co-therapy in a group of lower class psychosomatic patients. *Dynamic Psychiatry, 12,* 73.

GOODMAN, M. (1952). *Race consciousness in young children.* Cambridge, Mass.: Addison-Wesley.

GORE, S., AND MANGIONE, T. W. (1983). Social roles, sex roles and psychological distress: Additive and interactive models of sex differences. *Journal of Health and Social Behavior, 24,* 300–312.

GOTTLIEB, N., BURDEN, D., McCORMICK, R., AND NICARTHY, G. (1983). The distinctive attributes of feminist groups. *Social Work with Groups, 6*(3/4), 149–161.

GOULD, L. J., AND KLEIN, E. B. (1971). Performance of Black and white adolescents on intellectual and attitudinal measures as a function of the race of the tester. *Journal of Consulting and Clinical Psychology, 37,* 195–200.

GOULD, R. E. (1967). Dr. Strangeclass: Or how I stopped worrying about the theory and began treating the blue-collar worker. *American Journal of Orthopsychiatry, 37,* 78–86.

GOVE, W. (1972). The relationship between sex roles, mental illness, and marital status. *Social Forces, 51,* 34–44.

GOVE, W. R. (1980). Mental illness and psychiatric treatment among women. *Psychology of Women Quarterly, 4*(3), 345–362.

GOVE, W. R., AND TUDOR, J. F. (1973). Adult sex roles and mental illness. *American Journal of Sociology, 78*(4), 812–835.

GRANTHAM, R. J. (1973). Effects of counselor sex, race and language style on black students in initial interviews. *Journal of Counseling Psychology, 20*(6), 553–559.

GREEN, C. F., CUNNINGHAM, J., AND YANICO, B. J. (1986). Effects of counselor and subject race and counselor physical attractiveness on impressions and expectations of a female counselor. *Journal of Counseling Psychology, 33*(3), 349–352.

GREEN, P. (1970). Group work with welfare recipients. *Social Work, 15,* 3–4.

GREEN, R. (1974). *Sexual identity conflict in children and adults.* New York: Basic Books.

GREENBERG, R. P. (1969). Effects of presession information on perception of the therapist and receptivity to influence in a psychotherapy analogue. *Journal of Consulting and Clinical Psychology, 33,* 425–429.

GREENBERG, R. P., FISHER, S., AND SHAPIRO, J. (1973). Sex-role development and response to medication by psychiatric in-patients. *Psychological Reports, 33*(2), 675–677.

GREENBERG, R. P., AND ZELDOW, P. B. (1980). Sex differences in preferences for an ideal therapist. *Journal of Personality Assessment, 44*(5), 474–478.

GREENE, L. R. (1980). On terminating psychotherapy: More evidence of sex-role related countertransference, *Psychology of Women Quarterly, 4*(4), 548–557.

GREENE, L. R., ABRAMOWITZ, S. I., DAVIDSON, C. V., AND EDWARDS, D. W. (1980). Gender, race and referral to group psychotherapy: Further empirical evidence of countertransference. *The International Journal of Group Psychotherapy, 30*(3), 357–363.

GREENE, L. R., MORRISON, T. L., AND TISCHLER, N. G. (1981). Gender and authority: Effects on perceptions of small group co-leaders. *Small Group Behavior, 12*(4), 401–413.

GREVIOUS, C. (1985). The role of the family therapist with low-income Black families. *Family Therapy, 12*(2), 115–122.

GRIER, W., AND COBBS, P. (1968). *Black Page.* New York: Bantam Books.

GRIFFITH, M. S. (1977). The influences of race on the psychotherapeutic relationship. *Psychiatry, 40*(1), 27–40.

GRIFFITH, M. S., AND JONES, E. E. (1979). Race and psychotherapy: Changing perspectives. *Current Psychiatric Therapies, 18,* 225–232.

GROSS, H. S., HERBERT, M. R., KNATTERUD, G. L., AND DONNER, L. (1969). The effect of race and sex on the variation of diagnosis and disposition in a psychiatric emergency room. *Journal of Nervous and Mental Disease, 148*(6), 638–642.

GUERNEY, B. G. (Ed.) (1969). *Psychotherapeutic agents: New roles for nonprofessionals, patients, and teachers.* New York: Holt, Rinehart, and Winston.

GUILLEBEAUX, F., STORM, C. L., AND DEMARIS, A. (1986). Luring the reluctant male: A study of males participating in marriage and family therapy. *Family Therapy, 13*(2), 215–225.

GULLOTTA, T. P., AND DONOHUE, K. C. (1981). Corporate families: Implications for preventive intervention. *Social Casework, 62,* 109–114.

GUMP, J. P. (1975). Comparitive analysis of black women's and white women's sex-role attitudes. *Journal of Consulting and Clinical Psychology, 43*(6), 858–863.

GURIN, G., GURIN, L. R., AND BEATTIE, M. (1969). Internal-external control in the motivational dynamic of negro youths. *Journal of Social Issues, 25,* 29–53.

GURMAN, A. D., AND KNISKERN, D. P. (1978). Research on marital and family therapy: Progress, perspective, and prospect. In S. L. Garfield and A. E. Bergin (Eds.), *Handbook of psychotherapy and behavior change.* New York: John Wiley and Sons.

GURMAN, A. S. (1975). The effects and effectiveness of marital therapy. In A. S. Gurman and D. G. Rice (Eds.), *Couples in conflict.* New York: Jason Aronson.

GURMAN, A. S., AND KLEIN, M. H. (1980). Marital and family conflicts. In A. M. Brodsky and R. T. Hare-Mustin (Eds.), *Women in psychotherapy: An assessment of research and practice.* New York: Guilford Press.

GURSSLIN, O. R., HUNT, R. G., AND ROACH, J. L. (1959–1960). Social class and the mental health movement. *Social Problems, 7,* 210–218.

GUTTENTAG, M., AND SECORD, P. (1983). *Too many women: The sex ratio question.* Beverly Hills, Cal.: Sage.

GWYN, F. S., AND KILPATRICK, A. C. (1981). Family therapy with low-income blacks: Tool or turn-off. *Social Casework, 62*(5), 259–266.

HAAN, N., AND LIVSON, N. (1973). Sex differences in the eyes of expert personality assessors: Blind spots? *Journal of Personality Assessment, 37*(5), 486–492.

HAAS, A. (1979). Male and female spoken language differences: Stereotypes and evidence. *Psychological Bulletin, 86*(3), 616–626.

HAASE, W. (1964). The role of socioeconomic class in examiner bias. In F. Riessinan et al. (Eds.), *Mental health of the poor.* New York: Free Press.

HACKER, F. J., ILLING, H., AND BERGREEN, S. W. (1965). Impact of different social settings on type and effectiveness of psychotherapy. *Psychoanalytic Review, 52*(3), 38–49.

HACKER, H. M. (1981). Blabbermouths and clams: sex differences in self-disclosure in same-sex and cross-sex friendship dyads. *Psychology of Women Quarterly, 5*(3), 385–401.

HADLEY, R. G., AND HADLEY, P. A. (1976). Response to task force report. *American Psychologist, 31,* 613–614.

HAFNER, J. R. (1986). *Marriage and Mental Illness.* New York: Guilford Press.

HALAS, C. (1973). All women's groups: A view from inside. *Personnel and Guidance Journal, 52*(2), 91–95.

HALEY, J. (1976). *Problem-solving therapy: New strategies for effective family therapy.* San Francisco: Jossey-Bass.

HALL, J. A. (1978). Gender effects in decoding nonverbal cues. *Psychological Bulletin, 85*(4), 845–857.

HALL, J. A., AND BRAUNWALD, K. G. (1981). Gender cues in conversations. *Journal of Personality and Social Psychology, 40*(1), 99–110.

HALL, J. A., BRAUNWALD, K. G., AND MROZ, B. J. (1982). Gender, affect, and influence in a teaching situation, *Journal of Personality and Social Psychology, 43*(2), 270–280.

HALL, W. S., CROSS, W. E., AND FREEDLE, R. (1972). Stages in the development of black awareness: An exploratory investigation. In R. Jones (Ed.), *Black psychology.* New York: Harper and Row, pp. 156–165.

HALLOWITZ, D. (1975). Counseling and treatment of the poor black family. *Social Casework, 56*(8), 451–569.

HAMMEN, C. L., AND PADESKY, C. A. (1977). Sex differences in the expression of depressive responses on the Beck Depression Inventory. *Journal of Abnormal Psychology, 86,* 609–614.

HAMMEN, C. L., AND PETERS, S. D. (1977). Differential responses to male and female depressive reactions. *Journal of Consulting and Clinical Psychology, 45*(6), 994–1001.

HAMPTON, B., LAMBERT, F., B., AND SNELL, W. E., JR. (1986). Therapists' judgments of mentally healthy beliefs for men and women. *Journal of Rational-Emotive Therapy, 4*(2), 169–179.

HAMPTON, R. (1980). Institutional decimation, marital exchange and disruption in Black families. *Western Journal of Black Studies, 4,* 132–139.

HANKINS-MCNARY, L. D. (1979). The effect of institutional racism on the therapeutic relationship. *Perspectives In Psychiatric Care, 17*(1), 25–54.

HANSON, R. D., AND O'LEARY, V. (1985). Sex-determined attributions. In V. E. O'Leary, R. K. Unger, and B. S. Wallston (Eds.), *Women, gender and social psychology.* Hillsdale, N.J.: Lawrence Erlbaum Associates, Publishers.

HANSON, S. M. H. (1986). Healthy single parent families. *Family Relations, 35*(1), 125–132.

HANSON, W. (1980). The urban Indian woman and her family. *Social Casework, 61*(8), 476–483.

HARDIN, S. I., AND YANICO, B. J. (1981). A comparison of modes of presentation in vicarious participation counseling analogues. *Journal of Counseling Psychology, 28*(6), 540–543.

HARDIN, S. I., AND YANICO, B. J. (1983). Counselor gender, type of problem, and expectations about counseling. *Journal of Counseling Psychology, 30*(2), 294–297.

HARDING, J., PROSHANSKY, H., KUTNER, B., AND CHEIN, J. (1969). Prejudice and ethnic relations. In G. Lindsey and B. Arouson (Eds.), *Handbook of social psychology,* Vol. 5. Reading, Mass.: Addison-Wesley.

HARDY-FANTA, C., AND MACMAHON-HERRERA, E. (1981). Adapting family therapy to the Hispanic family. *Social Casework, 62*(3), 138–148.

HARDY-FANTA, C., AND MONTANA, P. (1982). The Hispanic female adolescent: A group therapy model. *International Journal of Group Psychotherapy, 32*(3), 351–366.

HARE, A. P. (1962). *Handbook of small group research.* New York: Free Press.

HARE-MUSTIN, R. T. (1978). Feminist approach to family therapy. *Family Procedure Process, 17,* 181–194.

HARE-MUSTIN, R. T. (1979a). Family therapy and sex role stereotypes. *Counseling Psychologist, 8,* 31–32.

HARE-MUSTIN, R. T. (1979b). Sexism in family therapy. *American Journal of Family Therapy, 7,* 81–83.

HARE-MUSTIN, R. T., AND LAMB, S. (1984). Family counselors' attitudes toward women and motherhood: A new cohort. *Journal of Marital and Family Therapy, 10*(4), 419–421.

HARRINGTON, M. (1986). Willful shortsightedness on poverty. *Dissent, 31*(1), 19.

HARRIS, L. H., AND LUCAS, M. E. (1976). Sex-role stereotyping. *Social Work, 21*(5), 390–395.

HARRIS, O., AND BALGOPAL, P. (1980). Intervening with the black family. In C. Janzen and O. Harris, (Eds.), *Family treatment in social work.* Peacock, Ill.: C. Janzen and O. Harris, 168–184.

HARRISON, D. K. (1975). Race as a counselor client variable in counseling and psychotherapy: A review of the research. *The Counseling Psychologist,* 5(1), 124–133.

HARTFORD, M. (1972). *Groups in social work.* New York: Columbia University Press, pp. 111–112.

HARTLEY, E. L., AND MINTZ, A. (1946). A technique in the study of the dynamics of the racial saturation point. *Sociometry,* 9, 14–21.

HARTMAN, L. M. (1983). Effects of sex and marital therapy on sexual interaction and marital happiness. *Journal of Sex and Marital Therapy,* 9(2), 137–151.

HARTMAN, S. (1983). A self-help group for women in abusive relationships. *Social Work with Groups,* 6, 133–146.

HARVEY, O. J. (1953). An experimental approach to the study of status relations in informal groups. *American Sociological Review,* 18, 357–367.

HAVILAND, M. G., HORSWILL, R. K., O'CONNELL, J. J., AND DYNNESON, V. V. (1983). Native American college student's preference for counselor race and sex and the likelihood of their use of a counseling center. *Journal of Counseling Psychology,* 30(2), 267–270.

HAWKES, G. R., AND TAYLOR, M. (1975). Power structure in Mexican and Mexican American farm labor families. *Journal of Marriage and the Family,* 37(4), 807–811.

HAWKINS, J. L., WEISBERG, C., AND RAY, D. L. (1977). Marital communication style and social class. *Journal of Marriage and the Family,* 39(3), 479–490.

HAYES, K. E., AND WOLLEAT, P. L. (1978). Effects of sex in judgments of a simulated counseling interview. *Journal of Counseling Psychology,* 25(2), 164–168.

HAYES, W. A. (1976). Radical black behaviorism. In R. L. Jones (Ed.), *Black psychology,* (2nd ed.). New York: Harper and Row.

HEATHERINGTON, L., AND ALLEN, G. J. (1984). Sex and relational communication patterns in counseling. *Journal of Counseling Psychology,* 31(3), 287–294.

HECKEL, R. V. (1966). Effects of northern and southern therapists on racially mixed psychotherapy groups. *Mental Hygiene,* 50, 304.

HEFFERNON, A., AND BRUEHL, D. (1971). Some effects of race of inexperienced lay counselors on black junior high school students. *Journal of School Psychology,* 9, 35–37.

HEIDER, F. (1958). *The psychology of interpersonal relations.* New York: John Wiley and Sons.

HEILBRUN, A. B. (1970). Toward resolution of the dependency-premature termination paradox for females in psychotherapy. *Journal of Consulting and Clinical Psychology,* 34(3), 382–386.

HEILBRUN, A. B. (1972). Effects of briefing upon client satisfaction with the initial counseling contact. *Journal of Consulting and Clinical Psychology,* 38, 50–56.

HEILBRUN, A. B., JR. (1961). Male and female personality correlates of early termination in counseling. *Journal of Counseling Psychology,* 8(1), 31–36.

HEILBRUN, A. B., JR. (1971). Female preference for therapist interview style as a function of "client" and therapist social role variables. *Journal of Counseling Psychology,* 18(4), 285–291.

HEILBRUN, A. B., JR. (1982). Tolerance for ambiguity in female clients: A further test of the catharsis model for predicting early counseling dropout. *Journal of Counseling Psychology,* 29(6), 567–571.

HEINE, R. W., AND TROSMAN, H. (1960). Initial expectations of the doctor-patient interaction as a factor in continuance in psychotherapy. *Psychiatry,* 23, 275–278.

HEITLER, J. B. (1973). Preparation of lower-class patients for expressive group psychotherapy. *Journal of Consulting and Clinical Psychology,* 41(2), 251–260.

HEITLER, J. B. (1976). Preparatory techniques in initiating expressive psychotherapy with lower-class, unsophisticated patients. *Psychological Bulletin,* 83, 339–352.

HELLER, K., AND GOLDSTEIN, A. P. (1961). Client dependency and therapist expectancy as relationship maintaining variables in psychotherapy. *Journal of Consulting Psychology,* 25, 371–375.

HELMS, J. E. (1978). Counselor reactions to female client: Generalizing from analogue research to a counseling setting. *Journal of Counseling Psychology,* 25(3), 193–199.

HELMS, J. E. (1979). Perceptions of a sex-fair counselor and her client. *Journal of Counseling Psychology, 26*(6) 504–513.
HENDRICK, C., BIXENSTINE, V. E., AND HAWKINS, G. (1971). Race versus belief similarity as determinants of attraction: A search for a fair test. *Journal of Personality and Social Psychology, 17,* 250–258.
HENDRICK, C., STIKES, C., AND MURRAY, B. (1972). Race versus belief similarity as determinants of attraction in a live interaction setting. *Journal of Experimental Research in Personality, 6,* 162–168.
HEPPNER, P. P. (1981). Counseling men in groups. *The Personnel and Guidance Journal, 60*(4), 249–252.
HEPPNER, P. P., AND PEW, S. (1977). Effects of diplomas, awards, and counselor sex on perceived expertness. *Journal of Counseling Psychology, 24*(2), 147–149.
HERZ, F. M., AND ROSEN, E. J. (1982). Jewish families. In M. McGoldrick, et al. (Eds.), *Ethnicity and family therapy.* New York: Guilford Press, 364–392.
HETHERINGTON, E. M., COX, M., AND COX, R. (1976). Divorced fathers. *The Family Coordinator, 25,* 417–428.
HIGGINBOTHAM, H. N., AND TANAKA-MATSUMI, J. (1981). Behavioral approaches to counseling across cultures. In P. P. Pedersen, J. G. Draguns, W. J. Lonner, and J. E. Trimble (Eds.), *Counseling across cultures.* Honolulu, Hi.: The University of Hawaii Press.
HIGGINS, E. T. (1976). Social class differences in verbal communicative accuracy. A question of "which question?" *Psychological Bulletin, 83*(4), 695–714.
HIGHLEN, P. S., AND GILLIS, S. F. (1978). Effects of situational factors, sex and attitude on affective self-disclosure and anxiety. *Journal of Counseling Psychology, 25*(4), 270–276.
HIGHLEN, P. S., AND RUSSELL, B. (1980). Effects of counselor gender and counselor and client sex role on female's counselor preference. *Journal of Counseling Psychology, 27*(2), 157–165.
HIGHTOWER, N. A., RODRIGUEZ, S., AND ADAMS, J. (1983). Ethnically mixed co-therapy with families. *Family Therapy, 10*(2), 105–110.
HILER, E. W. (1959). Initial complaints as predictors of continuation of psychotherapy. *Journal of Clinical Psychology, 15*(3), 344–345.
HILL, C. E. (1975). Sex of client and sex and experience level of counselor. *Journal of Counseling Psychology, 22*(1), 6–11.
HILL, C. E., TANNEY, M. F., LEONARD, M. M., AND REISS, J. (1977). Counselor reactions to female clients: Type of problem, age of client, and sex of counselor. *Journal of Counseling Psychology, 24*(1), 60–65.
HILL, R. (1971). *The strength of black families.* New York: Emerson Hall.
HILL, R. (1986). Life cycle stages for types of single parent families: Of family development theory. *Family Relations, 35,* 113–123.
HILL, W. A., AND FOX, W. M. (1973). Black and white marine squad leaders' perceptions of racially mixed squads. *Academy of Management Journal,* p. 16.
HILL, W. A., AND RUHE, J. A. (1974). Attitudes and behaviors of black and white supervisors in problem solving groups. *Academy of Management Journal, 17,* 563–569.
HILLARD, J. R., HOLLAND, J. M., AND RAMM, D. (1981). Christmas and psychopathology: Data from a psychiatric emergency room population. *Archives of General Psychiatry, 38*(12), 1377–1381.
HINES, P. M., AND BOYD-FRANKLIN, N. (1982). In M. McGoldrick, J. K, Pearce, and J. Giordano (Eds.), *Ethnicity and family therapy.* New York: The Guilford Press.
HINRICHSEN, J. J., FOLLANSBEE, D. J., AND GANELLEN, R. (1981). Sex-role-related differences in self-concept and mental health. *Journal of Personality Assessment, 45*(6), 584–592.
HIPGRAVE, T. (1981). Child rearing by lone fathers. In R. Chester, P. Diggony, and M. B. Sutherland (Eds.), *Changing patterns of child-bearing and child rearing.* London: Academic Press, 149–166.
HIPPLE, J. L., AND HIPPLE, L. (1980). Concepts of ideal woman and ideal man. *Social Work, 25,* 147–149.
HIRT, M., AND GENSHAFT, J. (1978). Factor related to patient dispositions for psychiatric hospitals. *Journal of Community Psychology, 6*(3), 253–256.

Ho, M. K. (1983). Social work with Asian Americans. In F. Turner (Ed.), *Differential diagnosis and treatment in social work.* New York: Free Press.

Ho, M. K. (1984). Social group work with Asian/Pacific-Americans. In L. Davis (Ed.), *Ethnicity in social group work practice.* New York: Haworth Press, Inc.

HOEHN-SARIC, R., FRANK, J. D., IMBER, S. D., NASH, E. H., STONE, A. R., AND BATTLE, C. C. (1964). Systematic preparation of patients for psychotherapy: Effects of therapy behavior and outcomes. *Journal of Psychiatric Research, 2,* 267–281.

HOFFMAN, N. T. (1977). Sex differences in empathy and related behaviors. *Psychological Bulletin, 84,* 712–722.

HOLLINGSHEAD, A. B. (1957). *Two-factor index of social position.* New Haven, Conn.: Author.

HOLLINGSHEAD, A. B., AND REDLICH, R. C. (1958). *Social class and mental illness.* New York: John Wiley and Sons.

HOLLINGSHEAD, A. B., ELLIS, R. A., AND KIRBY, E. C. (1954). Social mobility and mental illness. *American Sociological Review, 19,* 577–584.

HOLLIS, F. (1964). *A typology of casework treatment.* New York: Family Service Association of America.

HOLLIS, F. (1965). Casework and social class. *Social Casework, 46,* 463–471.

HOLLIS, F. (1983). Casework and social class. In F. J. Turner (Ed.), *Differential diagnosis and treatment in social work,* (3rd ed.). New York: The Free Press.

HOLMES, C. M., SHOLLEY, B. K. et al. (1980). Leader, follower, and isolate personality patterns in black and white emergent leadership groups. *Journal of Psychology, 105*(1), 41–46.

HOLMES, D. S., AND URIE, R. G. (1975). Effects of preparing children for psychotherapy. *Journal of Consulting and Clinical Psychology, 43,* 311–318.

HOPPS, J. (1982). Oppression based on color. *Social Work, 27*(1), 1–5.

HORNER, M. S. (1969). Fail: Bright women. *Psychology Today, 3*(6), 36–38.

HORNER, M. S. (1972). Toward an understanding of achievement-related conflicts in women. *Journal of Social Issues, 28*(2), 157–175.

HOUSEKNECHT, S. K., AND MACKE, A. S. (1981). Combining marriage and career: The marital adjustment of professional women. *Journal of Marriage and the Family, 43,* 651–661.

HOVLAND, C. I., JANIS, I. L., AND KELLEY, H. H. (1953). *Communication and persuasion: Psychological studies of opinion change.* New Haven: Yale University Press.

HOWARD, K. I., ORLINSKY, D. E., AND HILL, J. A. (1969). The therapist's feelings in the therapeutic process. *Journal of Clinical Psychology, 25*(1), 83–93.

HOWARD, K. I., ORLINSKY, D. E., AND HILL, J. A. (1970). Patients' satisfactions in psychotherapy as a function of patient-therapist pairing. *Psychotherapy: Theory, Research and Practice, 7*(3), 130–134.

HOWARD, K., RICKELS, K., MOCK, J. E., LIPMAN, R. S., CORI, L., AND BAUMAN, N. C. (1970). Therapeutic style and attrition rate from psychiatric drug treatment. *Journal of Nervous and Mental Diseases, 150,* 102–110.

HOWELL, E. (1981). The influence of gender on diagnosis and psychopathology. In E. Howell and M. Bayes (Eds.), *Women and mental health.* New York: Basic Books, pp. 153–159.

HOWELL, E., AND BAYES, M. (1981). *Women and mental health.* New York: Basic Books.

HRABA, J., AND GRANT, G. (1970). Black is beautiful: A re-examination of racial preference and identification. *Journal of Personality and Social Psychology, 3,* 398–402.

HSU, J., TSENG, W. S., ASHTON, G., McDERMOTT, J., AND CHAR, W. (1985). Family interaction patterns among Japanese-American and caucasian families in Hawaii. *American Journal of Psychiatry, 142*(5), 577–581.

HUNT, R. G. (1960). Social class and mental illness: Some implications for clinical theory and practice. *American Journal of Psychiatry, 116,* 1065–1069.

HURST, C. E. (1972). Race, class, and consciousness. *American Sociological Review, 37,* 658–670.

HURWITZ, J. I., ZANDER, A. F., AND HYMOVITCH, B. (1953). Some effects of power on the relations among group members. In D. Cartwright and A. Zander (Eds.), *Group dynamics: Research and theory.* Evanston: Row, Peterson and Co., pp. 483–492.

ICKES, W. (1984). Compositions in black and white: Determinants of interaction in interracial dyads. *Journal of Personality and Social Psychology, 47*(2), 330–341.

IGLEHART, A. P. (1982). Wives, husbands and social change: The role of social work. *Social Work Review, 56*(1), 27–38.

IZRAELI, D. N. (1983–1984). Sex effects or structural effects? An empirical test of Kanter's theory of proportions. *Social Forces, 62,* 153–165.

JACKSON, A. M. (1983). Treatment issues for black patients. *Psychotherapy: Theory, Research, and Practice, 20*(2), 143–151.

JACKSON, A. M., BERKOWITZ, H., AND FARLEY, G. K. (1974). Race as a variable affecting the treatment involvement of children. *Journal of the American Academy of Child Psychiatry, 13,* 20–31.

JACKSON, A. M., FARLEY, G. K., ZIMET, S. G., AND WATERMAN, J. M. (1978). Race and sex as variables for children involved in treatment. *Psychological Reports, 43,* 883–886.

JACKSON, G. G., AND KIRSCHNER, S. A. (1973). Racial self designation and preference for a counselor. *Journal of Counseling Psychology, 20*(6), 560–564.

JACOBS, D., CHARLES, E., JACOBS, T., WEINSTEIN, H., AND MANN, D. (1972). Preparation of treatment of the disadvantaged patient: Effects on disposition and outcome. *American Journal of Orthopsychiatry, 42,* 666–674.

JAGGARD, N. (1950). The role of groupwork consultant in a casework agency. *Child Welfare, 29*(11), 14–17.

JAYARATNE, S., AND IVEY, K. V. (1981). Gender differences in the perceptions of social workers. *Social Casework, 62*(7), 405–412.

JOHNSON, B. H. (1986). Single mothers following separation and divorce: Making it on your own. *Family Relations, 35*(1), 189–197.

JOHNSON, D. H. (1978). Students' sex preferences and sex role expectancies for counselors. *Journal of Counseling Psychology, 25*(6), 557–562.

JOHNSON, H. C. (1986). Emerging concerns in family therapy. *Social Work, 31*(4), 299–306.

JOHNSON, M. (1978). Influence of counselor gender on reactivity to clients. *Journal of Counseling Psychology, 25*(5), 359–365.

JONES, B. E., AND GRAY, B. A. (1985). Black and white psychiatrists: Therapy with blacks. *Journal of the National Medical Association, 77*(1), 19–25.

JONES, B. E., GRAY, B., PEARSON, E. B. (1981). Manic depressive illness among poor urban blacks. *American Journal of Psychiatry, 138,* 654–657.

JONES, D. L. (1979). African American clients: Clinical practice issues. *Social Work, 24,* 112–118.

JONES, E. E., AND ZOPPEL, C. L. (1982). Impact of client and therapist gender on psychotherapy process and outcome. *Journal of Consulting and Clinical Psychology, 50*(2), 259–272.

JONES, J. (1972). *Prejudice and racism.* Reading, Mass.: Addison-Wesley Co.

JONES, R. (Ed.). (1980). *Black psychology.* New York: Harper and Row Publishers.

JONES, W. H., CHERNOVETZ, M. E., AND HANSSON, R. O. (1978). The enigma of androgyny: Differential implications for males and females. *Journal of Consulting and Clinical Psychology, 46,* 298–313.

JOURARD, S. M., AND LASAKOW, P. (1958). Some factors in self-disclosure. *Journal of Abnormal and Social Psychology, 56,* 91–98.

JOYCE, C., AND HAZELTON, P. (1982). Women in groups: A pre-group experience for women in recovery from alcoholism and other addictions. *Social Work with Groups, 5*(1), 57–63.

JUNG, C. G. (1934). The state of psychotherapy today. *Collected Works,* Vol. 10. Princeton, N.J.: Princeton University Press, pp. 157–173.

KADUSHIN, A. (1972). The racial factor in the interview. *Social Work, 17,* 88–98.

KADUSHIN, A. (1972). *The social work interview.* New York: Columbia University Press, pp. 219–244.

KADUSHIN, A. (1976). Men in a woman's profession. *Social Work, 21*(6), 440–447.

KADUSHIN, A. (1983). *The Social Work Interview,* 2nd ed. New York: Columbia University Press.

KAHN, A. S., AND GAEDDERT, W. P. (1985). From theories of equity to theories of justice: The liberating consequences of studying women. In V. E. O'Leary, R. K. Unger, and B. S. Wallston, (Eds.), *Women, gender, and social psychology.* Hillsdale, N.J.: Lawrence Erlbaum Associates, Publishers.

KAHN, M. W., LEWIS, J., AND GALVEZ, E. (1974). An evaluation study of a group therapy procedure with reservation adolescent Indians. *Psychotherapy: Theory, Research and Practice, 11*(3), 239–242.

KANDEL, D. B. (1966). Status homophily, social context and participation in psychotherapy. *American Journal of Sociology, 71*, 640–650.

KANESHIGE, E. (1973). Cultural factors in group counseling and interaction. *Personnel and Guidance Journal, 51*, 407–412.

KANTER, R. M. (1977a). Some effects of proportions on group life: Skewed sex ratios and responses to token women. *American Journal of Sociology, 82*, 965–990.

KANTER, R. M. (1977b). Women in organizations: Sex roles, group dynamics and change strategies. In A. Sargent (Ed.), *Beyond sex roles.* St. Paul, Minn.: West Publishing Co.

KAPLAN, A. (1964). *The conduct of inquiry.* San Francisco: Chandler.

KAPLAN, A. G. (1979a). Clarifying the concept of androgyny: Implications for therapy. *Psychology of Women Quarterly, 3*(3), 223–230.

KAPLAN, A. G. (1979b). Toward an analysis of sex-role related issues in the therapeutic relationship. *Psychiatry, 42*(2), 112–120.

KAPLAN, M. L., KURTZ, R. M., AND CLEMENTS, W. H. (1968). Psychiatric residents and lower class patients: Conflict in training. *Community Mental Health Journal, 4*, 91–97.

KARDINER, A., AND OVESEY, L. (1962). *The mark of oppression.* New York: World Publishing.

KASCHAK, E. (1978). Therapist and client: Two views of the process and outcome of psychotherapy. *Professional Psychology, 9*(2), 271–277.

KASLOW, F. W. (1981). Involving the peripheral father in family therapy. In A. S. Gurman (Ed). *Questions and answers in the practice of family therapy.* New York: Brunner/Mazel, Publishers.

KATZ, A. J. (1979). Lone fathers: Perspectives and implications for family policy. *The Family Coordinator, 28*(4), 521–528.

KATZ, I. (1955). *Conflict and harmony in an adolescent interracial group.* New York: New York University Press.

KATZ, I., AND BENJAMIN, L. (1960). Effects of white authoritarianism in biracial work groups. *Journal of Abnormal and Social Psychology, 61*, 448–456.

KATZ, I., AND COHEN, M. (1962). The effects of training Negroes upon cooperative problem solving in biracial terms. *Journal of Abnormal and Social Psychology, 64*, 319–325.

KATZ, I., GOLDSTON, J., AND BENJAMIN, L. (1958). Behavior and productivity and biracial work groups. *Human Relations, 11*, 123–141.

KATZ, I., GOLDSTON, J., AND BENJAMIN, L. (1960). Effects of white authoritarianism in biracial work groups. *Journal of Abnormal and Social Psychology, 61*, 448–456.

KATZ, I., ROBERTS, S. O., AND ROBINSON, J. M. (1965). Effects of difficulty, race of administration, and instructions on Negro digit-symbol performance. *Journal of Personality and Social Psychology, 2*, 53–59.

KATZ, M. M., LORR, M., AND RUBENSTEIN, E. A. (1958). Remainer patient attributes and their reaction to subsequent improvement in psychotherapy. *Journal of Consulting Psychology, 22*, 411–413.

KAUFMAN, J., AND TIMMERS, R. L. (1983). Searching for the hairy man. *Social Work with Groups, 6*(3/4), 163–175.

KEITH-SPIEGEL, P., AND SPIEGEL, D. (1967). Perceived helpfulness of others as a function of compatible intelligence levels. *Journal of Counseling Psychology, 14*, 61–62.

KELLERMAN, J. (1975). Sex role stereotypes and attitudes toward parental blame for the psychological problems of children. *Journal of Consulting and Clinical Psychology, 42*, 153–154.

KELLEY, H. H. (1951). Communications in experimentally controlled hierarchies. *Human Relations, 4*, 39–56.

KERR, B. (1985). *Smart girls, gifted women.* Columbus: Ohio Psychological Publishing Co.

KESSLER, R. C., AND MCRAE, J. A., JR. (1981). Trends in the relationship between sex and psychological distress: 1957–1976. *American Sociological Review, 46*(4), 443–452.

KESSLER, R., AND MCRAE, J. (1982). The effect of wives' employment on the mental health of married and women. *American Sociological Review, 47*, 216–227.

KESSLER, R. C., AND NEIGHBORS, H. W. (1986). A new perspective on the relationships among race, social class, and psychological distress. *Journal of Health and Social Behavior, 27*(2), 107–115.

KEVIN, D. (1967). Group counseling of mothers in an AFDC Program. *Children, 14,* 69–74.

KIESLER, S. (1972). *Racial choice among children in realistic situations.* In J. Jones (Ed.), *Prejudice and racism.* Reading, Mass.: Addison-Wesley.

KIESLER, S. B. (1975). Actuarial prejudice toward women and its implications. *Journal of Applied Social Psychology, 5*(3), 201–216.

KILLEEN, M. R., AND JACOBS, C. C. (1976). Brief group therapy for women students. *Social Work, 21*(6), 521–522.

KIM, S. C. (1985). Family therapy for Asian Americans—A strategic—structural framework. *Psychotherapy, 22*(2), 342–348.

KIMBLE, C. E., YOSHIKAWA, J. C., AND ZEHR, H. D. (1981). Vocal and verbal assertiveness in same-sex and mixed-sex groups. *Journal of Personality and Social Psychology, 40*(6), 1047–1054.

KING, C. (1967). Family therapy with the deprived family. *Social Casework, 48*(4), 203–208.

KIRKPATRICK, M. (1982). Lesbian mother families. *Psychiatric Annals, 12*(9), 842–848.

KIRSCHNER, L. A. (1978). Effects of gender on psychotherapy. *Comprehensive Psychiatry, 19*(2), 79–82.

KIRSCHNER, L. A., GENACK, A., AND HAUSER, S. (1978). Effects of gender on short-term psychotherapy. *Psychotherapy: Theory, Research, and Practice, 15*(2), 158–167.

KIRSH, B. (1974). Consciousness raising groups as therapy for women. In V. Frauks and V. Burtle (Eds.), *Women in therapy: New psychotherapies for a changing society.* New York: Brunner/Mazel.

KITANO, H. H. (1987). Asian Americans. *Encyclopedia of social work, 1,* 156–171.

KITANO, H. L. (1969). *Japanese Americans: The evolution of a subculture.* Englewood Cliffs, N.J.: Prentice-Hall.

KLEIN, M. (1976). Feminist concepts of therapy outcome. *Psychotherapy: Theory, Research and Practice, 13*(1), 89–95.

KLINE, F., ADRIAN, A., AND SPIVAK, M. (1974). Patients' evaluate therapists. *Archives of General Psychiatry, 31,* 113–116.

KLOR DE ALVA, J. J. (1985). The Hispanic subculture of the United States. In L. B. Brown, J. Oliner, and J. J. Klor de Alva (Eds.), *A resource guide for human service professionals: Sociocultural and service issues in working with Hispanic American clients.* New York: Rockefeller College Press, pp. 38–79.

KLUEGEL, J. R., AND SMITH, E. R. (1986). *Beliefs about inequality: Americans' views of what is and what ought to be.* New York: Aldine De Gruyter.

KNESPER, D. J., PAGNUCCO, D. J., AND WHEELER, J. R. C. (1985). Similarities and differences across mental health service providers and practice settings in the United States. *American Psychologist, 40*(12), 1352–1369.

KO, H. (1986). Minuchin's structural therapy for Vietnamese-Chinese families: A systems perspective. *Contemporary Family Therapy: An International Journal, 8*(1), 20–32.

KOCHMAN, T. (1981). *Black and white styles of conflict.* Chicago: The University of Chicago Press.

KOHEN, J. A. S. (1975). The development of reciprocal self-disclosure in opposite sex interaction. *Journal of Counseling Psychology, 22*(5), 404–410.

KOHN, M. L. (1963). Social class and parent-child relationships: An interpretation. *American Journal of Sociology, 68,* 471–480.

KOLODNY, R. (1980). The dilemma of co-leadership. *Social Work with Groups, 3,* 31–38.

KOMAROVSKY, M. (1973). Cultural contradictions and sex roles: The masculine case. *American Journal of Sociology, 78*(4), 873–884.

KOSCHERAK, S., AND MASLING, J. (1972). Noblesse oblige effect: The interpretation of Rorschach as a function of ascribed social class. *Journal of Consulting and Clinical Psychology, 39*(3), 415–419.

KRAFT, S. P., AND DeMAIO, T. J. (1982). An ecological intervention with adolescents in low-income families. *American Journal of Orthopsychiatry, 52*(1), 131–140.

KRAUSKOPF, C. J., BAUMGARDNER, A., AND MANDRACCHIA, S. (1981). Return rate following intake revisited. *Journal of Counseling Psychology, 28*(6), 519–521.

KRAUSZ, S. L. (1986). Sex roles within marriage. *Social Work, 31*(6), 457–464.

KRAVETZ, D. F. (1976). Consciousness-raising groups and group psychotherapy: Alternative mental health resources for women. *Psychotherapy: Theory, Research and Practice, 13,* 66–71.

KRAVETZ, D. (1976). Sexism in a woman's profession. *Social Work, 21,* 421–426.

KRAVETZ, D. (1976). Sex role concepts of women. *Journal of Consulting and Clinical Psychology, 44*(3), 437–443.

KRAVETZ, D. (1982). An overview of content on women for the social work curriculum. *Journal of Education for Social Work, 18*(2), 42–49.

KRAVETZ, D., AND JONES, L. E. (1981). Androgyny as a standard of mental health. *American Journal of Orthopsychiatry, 51*(3), 502–509.

KRAVETZ, D. F., AND SARGENT, A. G. (1977). Consciousness-raising groups: A resocialization process for personal and social change. In A. G. Sargent (Ed.), *Beyond sex roles.* St. Paul, Minn.: West.

KREBS, R. L. (1971). Some effects of a white institution on black psychiatric outpatients. *American Journal of Orthopsychiatry, 41,* 589–597.

KREISMAN, J. (1975). The curandero's apprentice: A therapeutic integration of folk and medicinal healing. *American Journal of Psychiatry, 132*(1), 81–83.

KREMSDORF, R. B., PALLADINO, L. J., POLENZ, D. D., AND ANTISTA, B. J. (1978). Effects of the sex of both interviewer and subject on reported manifest dream content. *Journal of Consulting and Clinical Psychology, 46*(5), 1166–1167.

KRISTEN, S. (1982). Sex bias in therapy: Are counselors immune? *The Personnel and Guidance Journal, 61*(2), 81–83.

KRYSTAL, E., MORAN-SACKET, M., THOMPSON, S. V., AND CONTONI, L. (1983). Serving the unemployed. *Social Casework, 64*(2), 67–76.

KUNIN, C. C., AND RODIN, M. J. (1982). The interactive effects of counselor gender, physical attractiveness and status on client self-disclosure. *Journal of Clinical Psychology, 38*(1), 84–90.

LA FRAMBOISE, T. D., AND DIXON, D. N. (1981). American Indian perception of trustworthiness in a counseling interview. *Journal of Counseling Psychology, 28,* 135–139.

LAFRANCE, M., AND MAYO, C. (1976). Racial differences in gaze behavior during conversations: Two systematic observational studies. *Journal of Personality and Social Psychology, 33,* 547–552.

LAKE, M., AND LEVINGER, G. (1960). Continuance beyond application interviews at a child guidance clinic. *Social Casework, 41,* 303–309.

LANE, E. A. (1968). The influence of sex and race on process reactive ratings of schizophrenics. *Journal of Psychology, 68,* 15–20.

LANGNER, T. S., BERSTEN, J. C., GREENE, E. L., EISENBERG, J. G., HERSON, J. H., AND MCCARTHY, E. D. (1974). Treatment of psychological disorders among urban children. *Journal of Consulting and Clinical Psychology, 42,* 170–179.

LATORRE, R. A. (1975). Gender and age as factors in the attitudes toward those stigmatized as mentally ill. *Journal of Consulting and Clinical Psychology, 43*(1), 97–98.

LATTING, J., AND ZUNDEL, C. (1986). World view differences between clients and counselors. *Social Casework, 67*(9), 533–541.

LAWS, J. L. (1975). The psychology of tokenism: An analysis. *Sex Roles, 1,* 51–67.

LEE, D. Y., HALLBERG, E. T., JONES, L., AND HAASE, R. F. (1980). Effects of counselor gender on perceived credibility. *Journal of Counseling Psychology, 27*(1), 71–75.

LEE, D. Y., SUTTON, R., FRANCE, H., AND UHLEMANN, M. (1983). Effects of counselor race on perceived counseling effectiveness. *Journal of Counseling Psychology, 30*(3), 447–450.

LEE, E. (1982). A social systems approach to assessment and treatment for Chinese American families. In M. McGoldrick, J. K. Pearce, and J. Giordano (Eds.), *Ethnicity and family therapy.* New York: The Guilford Press, pp. 527–551.

LEE, J. A. B. (1980). The helping professionals use of language in describing the poor. *American Journal of Orthopsychiatry, 50*(4), 580–584.

LEFCOURT, H. M. (1973). The function of the illusions of control and freedom. *American Psychologist, 28,* 417–425.

LEFCOURT, H. (1982). *Locus of control.* Hillsdale, N.J.: Lawrence Erlbaum Associates.

LEFCOURT, H. M., AND LADWIG, G. W. (1965). The effect of reference groups upon Negroes' task persistence in a biracial competitive game. *Journal of Personality and Social Psychology*, 668–671.

LEICHNER, P., AND KALIN, R. (1981). Sex-role ideology among practicing psychiatrists and psychiatric residents. *The American Journal of Psychiatry, 138*(10), 1342–1345.

LEONG, F. T. L. (1986). Counseling and psychotherapy with Asian-Americans: Review of the literature. *Journal of Counseling Psychology, 33*(2), 196–206.

LERMAN, H. (1978). Some thoughts on cross-gender psychotherapy. *Psychotherapy: Theory, Research, and Practice, 15*(3), 248–250.

LERNER, B. (1972). *Therapy in the ghetto: Political impotence and personal disintegration.* Baltimore: Johns Hopkins University Press.

LERNER, B. (1973). Democratic values and therapeutic efficacy: A construct validity study. *Journal of Abnormal Psychology, 82*, 491–498.

LERNER, B., AND FISKE, D. W. (1973). Client attributes and the eye of the beholder. *Journal of Consulting and Clinical Psychology, 40*(2), 272–277.

LERNER, H. E. (1981). The hysterical personality: A "woman's disease." In E. Howell and M. Bayes (Eds.), *Women and mental health.* New York: Basic Books, pp. 196–206.

LERNER, M. J., AND MILLER, D. T. (1978). Just world research and the attribution process: Looking back and ahead. *Psychological Bulletin, 85*, 1030–1051.

LEVIN, S. S., GROVES, A. C., AND LURIE, J. D. (1980). Sharing the move—support groups for relocated women. *Social Work, 25*(4), 323–325.

LEVINE, E., AND FRANCO, J. N. (1981). A reassessment of self disclosure patterns among Anglo-Americans and Hispanics. *Journal of Counseling Psychology, 28*(6), 522–524.

LEVINE, R. (1964). Treatment in the home. *Social Work, 9*(1), 19–28.

LEVINE, S. V., KAMIN, L. E., AND LEVINE, E. L. (1974). Sexism and psychiatry. *American Journal of Orthopsychiatry, 44*(3), 327–336.

LEVINSON, D. A., AND JENSEN, S. M. (1967). Assertive versus passive group therapist behavior with southern white and Negro schizophrenic hospital patients. *International Journal of Group Psychotherapy, 17,* 328–335.

LEVITT, L. (1968). Rehabilitation of narcotics addicts among lower-class teenagers. *American Journal of Orthopsychiatry, 38*(1), 56–62.

LEVY, M., AND KAHN, M. (1970). Interpreter bias on the Rorschach test as a function of patients' socioeconomic status. *Journal of Projective Techniques and Personality Assessment, 34,* 106–112.

LEWIN, K. (1948). Self hatred among Jews. In *Resolving social conflicts.* New York: Harper and Row, pp. 186–200.

LEWINE, R. R. J. (1980). Sex differences in age of symptom onset and first hospitalization in schizophrenia. *American Journal of Orthopsychiatry, 50*(2), 316–322.

LEWINE, R. R. J. (1981). Sex differences in schizophrenia: Timing or subtypes? *Psychological Bulletin, 90*(3), 432–444.

LEWIS, D. O., BALLA, D., AND SHANOK, S. (1979). Race bias in the diagnosis and treatment of the juvenile offender. *American Journal of Orthopsychiatry, 49*(10), 53–61.

LEWIS, G. H. (1978). Role differentiation. *American Sociological Review, 37,* 424–434.

LEWIS, H. B. (1981). Madness in women. In E. Howell and M. Bayes (Eds.), *Women and mental health.* New York: Basic Books, pp. 207–227.

LEWIS, O. (1961). *The children of Sanchez.* New York: Random House.

LEWIS, O. (1966). La vida: A Puerto Rican family. In *The culture of poverty—San Juan and New York.* New York: Random House.

LEWIS, R. A. (1978). Emotional intimacy among men. *Journal of Social Issues, 34*(1), 108–121.

LEWIS, R. A. (1981). Men's liberation and the men's movement: Implications for counselors. *The Personnel and Guidance Journal, 60*(4), 256–259.

LEWIS, R. A., AND PLECK, J. H. (Eds.). (1979). Men's roles in the family. *The Family Coordinator, 28*(4), 428–432.

LEWIS, R. G., AND HO, M. K. (1975). Social work with native Americans. *Social Work, 20*(5), 379–382.

LIBOW, J. A., RASKIN, P. A., AND CAUST, B. L. (1982). Feminist and family systems therapy: Are they irreconcilable? *American Journal of Family Therapy, 10*(3), 3–12.

LICHTENBERG, J. W., AND HECK, E. J. (1981). Much ado about nothing? *Personnel and Guidance Journal, 59*(5), 317–320.

LIEBERMAN, M. A., YALOM, I. D., AND MILES, B. M. (1973). Interracial encounter. In *Encounter groups: First facts.* New York: Basic Books, pp. 379–393.

LILIENFELD, D. M. (1969). Mental health information and moral values of lower class psychiatric clinic patients. *International Journal of Social Psychiatry, 15*(4), 264–278.

LITJESTRAND, P., GERLING, E., AND SALIBA, P. (1978). The effects of social sex-role stereotypes and sexual orientation on psychotherapeutic outcomes. *Journal of Homosexuality, 3*(4), 361–372.

LINN, M. W., HUNTER, K. I., AND PERRY, P. R. (1979). Differences by sex and ethnicity in the psychosocial adjustment of the elderly. *Journal of Health and Social Behavior, 20*(3), 273–281.

LISS, J. S., WELNER, A., ROBINS, E., AND RICHARDSON, M. (1973). Psychiatric symptoms in black and white inpatients. I: Record study. *Comprehensive Psychiatry, 14,* 457–482.

LITTRELL, J. M., AND LITTRELL, M. A. (1982). American Indian and caucasian student's preferences for counselors: Effects of counselor dress and sex. *Journal of Counseling Psychology, 29*(1), 48–57.

LOPICCOLO, J., HEIMAN, J. R., HOGAN, D. R., AND ROBERTS, C. W. (1985). Effectiveness of single therapists versus cotherapy teams in sex therapy. *Journal of Consulting and Clinical Psychology, 53,* 287–294.

LOPICCOLO, J., AND STOCK, W. E. (1986). Treatment of sexual dysfunction. *Journal of Consulting and Clinical Psychology, 54*(2), 158–167.

LOCKHEED, M. E. (1977). Cognitive style effects on sex status in student work groups. *Journal of Educational Psychology, 69*(2), 158–165.

LOCKHEED, M. E., AND HALL, K. P. (1976). Conceptualizing sex as a status characteristic: Applications to leadership training strategies. *Journal of Social Issues, 32*(3), 111–124.

LOCKSLEY, A. (1982). Social class and marital attitudes and behavior. *Journal of Marriage and the Family, 44*(2), 427–440.

LOFARO, G. A., AND REEDER, C. (1978). Male competition: An issue in counselor training. *Counseling Psychologist, 7*(4), 20–22.

LORANGER, A. W., AND LEVINE, P. M. (1978). Age at onset of bipolar affective illness. *Archives of General Psychiatry, 35*(11), 1345–1348.

LORENZO, M. K., AND ADLER, D. A. (1984). Mental health services for Chinese in a community health center. *Social Casework, 65*(10), 600–609.

LORION, R. P. (1973). Socioeconomic status and traditional treatment approaches reconsidered. *Psychological Bulletin, 79*(4), 263–270.

LORION, R. P. (1974). Patient and therapist variables in the treatment of low income patients. *Psychological Bulletin, 81*(6), 344–354.

LORION, R. P. (1978). Research on psychotherapy and behavior change with the disadvantaged: Past, present and future directions. In S. L. Garfield and A. E. Bergin (Eds.), *Handbook of psychotherapy and behavior change* (2nd ed.). New York: John Wiley and Sons.

LOWE, G. D., AND ALSTON, J. P. (1974). Hospital structure and racial discrimination. *Journal of Alcohol and Drug Education, 19,* 29–37.

LOWERY, C. R., AND HIGGINS, R. L. (1979). Analogue investigation of the relationship between clients' sex and treatment recommendations. *Journal of Consulting and Clinical Psychology, 47*(4), 792–794.

LUBORSKY, L., CHANDLER, M., AUERBACH, A. H., COHEN, J., AND BACHRACH, H. M. (1971). Factors influencing the outcome of psychotherapy: A review of quantitative research. *Psychological Bulletin, 75*(3), 145–185.

LURIE, O. R. (1974). Parents' attitudes toward children's problems and toward use of mental health services: Socio-economic differences. *American Journal of Orthopsychiatry, 44*(1), 109–120.

MCADOO, H. (1977). Family therapy in the Black community. *Journal of Orthopsychiatry, 47*(1), 75–79.

MCADOO, H. (1978). Factors related to stability in upwardly mobile Black families. *Journal of Marriage and the Family, 40*(4), 761–776.

MCADOO, J. (1979). A study of father-child interaction patterns and self-esteem in Black pre-school children. *Young Children, 34*(1), 46–53.

MCADOO, J. (1981). Black fathers and child interaction. In L. Gray (Ed.), *Black men.* Beverly Hills: Sage, pp. 115–130.

MACCOBY, E., AND JACKLIN, C. N. (1974). *The psychology of sex differences*. Stanford, Cal.: Stanford University Press.

MCCARRICK, A. K., MANDERSCHEID, R. W., AND SILBERGELD, S. (1981). Gender differences in competition and dominance during married-couples group therapy. *Social Psychology Quarterly, 44*(3), 164–177.

MCCARTHY, P. R. (1979). Differential effects of self-disclosing versus self-involving counselor statements across counselor-client gender pairings. *Journal of Counseling Psychology, 26*(6), 538–541.

MCDERMOTT, J., HARRISON, S. I., SCHRAGER, J., AND WILSON, P. (1965). Social class and mental illness in children: Observations of blue-collar families. *American Journal of Orthopsychiatry, 35*(3), 500–508.

MCDONALD, T. (1975). Group process and the Chicano: Clinical issues. *International Journal of Group Psychotherapy, 25*(4), 410–420.

MCFEE, M. (1968). The 150% man, a product of Blackfeet acculturation. *American Anthropologist, 70*, 1096–1103.

MCGINNIES, E., NORDHOLM, L. A., WARD, C. D., AND BHANTHUMNAVIN, D. L. (1974). Sex and cultural differences in perceived locus of control among students in five countries. *Journal of Consulting and Clinical Psychology, 42*(3), 451–455.

MCINTOSH, J. L., AND JEWELL, B. L. (1986). Sex difference trends in completed suicide. *Suicide and Life-Threatening Behavior, 16*(1), 16–27.

MCKAMY, E. H. (1976). Social work with the wealthy. *Social Casework, 57*(4), 254–258.

MCKINLEY, C. K., RITCHIE, A. M., GRIFFIN, D., AND BONDES, W. (1970). The upward mobile Negro family in therapy. *Diseases of the Nervous System, 31*(10), 710–775.

MCKISSICK, F. (1969). *Three-fifths of a man*. New York: Macmillan.

MACLENNAN, B. W. (1968). Group approaches to the problems of socially deprived youth: The classical psychotherapeutic model. *International Journal of Group Psychotherapy, 18*(4), 481–494.

MCMAHON, J. T. (1964). The working class psychiatric patient: A clinical review. In F. Riessman, J. Cohen, and A. Pearl (Eds.), *Mental health and the poor*. New York: Free Press.

MCMANUS, J. E. (1962). Group techniques in a child welfare agency. *Group Psychotherapy, 15*(1), 63–68.

MCNAIR, D. M., LORR, M., YOUNG, H. H., ROTH, I., AND BOYD, R. W. (1964). A three-year follow-up of psychotherapy patients. *Journal of Clinical Psychology, 20*, 258–264.

MCNEELY, R., AND BADAMI, M. (1984). Interracial communication in schools of social work. *Social Work, 29*(1), 22–26.

MCQUAIDE, S. (1983). Human service cutbacks and the mental-health of the poor. *Social Casework, 64*(8), 497–499.

MCROY, R., AND OGLESBY, Z. (1984). Group work with black adoptive applicants. *Social Work with Groups, 7*, 125–134.

MCWHIRTER, R. M., AND JECKER, J. D. (1967). Attitudinal similarity and inferred attraction. *Psychonomic Science, 327*, 327–337.

MAIER, N. R. F. (1970). Male versus female discussion leaders. *Personnel Psychology, 23*, 455–461.

MAIN, E. C., BOWMAN, L., AND PETERS, B. G. (1972). Model cities workers' perceptions of clients. *Urban Affairs Quarterly, 7*(3), 309–313.

MAKOSKY, V. P. (1980). Stress and the mental health of women: A discussion of research and issues. In M. Guttentag, S. Salasin, D. Beele (Eds.), *The mental health of women*. New York: Academic Press.

MALCHON, M. J., AND PENNER, L. A. (1981). The effects of sex and sex-role identity on the attribution of maladjustment. *Sex Roles, 7*(4), 363–378.

MALDONADO-SIERRA, E., AND TRENT, R. (1960). The sibling relationship in group psychotherapy with Puerto Rican schizophrenics. *American Journal of Psychiatry, 117*(3), 239–244.

MALGADY, R. G., ROGLER, L. H., AND COSTANTINO, G. (1987). Ethnocultural and linguistic bias in mental health evaluation of hispanics. *American Psychologist, 42*(3), 228–234.

MALLOY, T. E. (1981). The relationship between therapist-client interpersonal compatibility, sex of therapist, and therapeutic outcome. *Journal of Clinical Psychology, 37*(2), 316–322.

MANN, J. (1958). The influence of racial prejudice on sociometric choices and perceptions. *Sociometry, 21*, 150–158.

MARECEK, J., AND BALLOU, D. J. (1981). Family roles and women's mental health. *Professional Psychology, 12*(1), 39–46.

MARECEK, J., AND KRAVETZ, D. (1977). Women and mental health: A review of feminist change efforts. *Psychiatry, 40*(4), 323–329.

MARECEK, J., AND JOHNSON, M. (1980). Gender and the process of therapy. In A. M. Brodsky and R. T. Hare-Mustin (Eds.), *Women and psychotherapy: An assessment of research and practice.* New York: The Guilford Press.

MARECEK, J., KRAVETZ, D., AND FINN, S. (1979). Comparison of women who enter feminist therapy and women who enter traditional therapy. *Journal of Consulting and Clinical Psychology, 47*(4), 734–742.

MARGOLIN, G., TALOVIC, S., FERNANDEZ, V., AND ONORATO, R. (1983). Sex role considerations and behavioral marital therapy: Equal does not mean identical. *Journal of Marital and Family Therapy, 9*(2), 131–145.

MARKUS, H., CRANE, M., BERNSTEIN, S., AND SILADI, M. (1982). Self-schemas and gender. *Journal of Personality and Social Psychology, 42*(1), 38–50.

MARKWARD, M. S. (1979). Group process and black adolescent identity crisis. *School, Social Work Journal, 3*(2), 78–84.

MARSH, J. C. (1980). Help seeking among addicted and nonaddicted women of low socioeconomic status. *Social Service Review, 54*(2), 239–248.

MARSHALL, J. E., AND HESLIN, R. (1975). Boys and girls together: Sexual composition and the effect of density and group core on cohesiveness. *Journal of Personality and Social Psychology, 31*(5), 952–961.

MARSHALL, M. (1983). Can a marriage survive when the wife earns more? *Ebony, 38*, 44–48.

MARTIN, P., AND SHANAHAN, K. A. (1983). Transcending the effects of sex composition in small groups. *Social Work with Groups, 6*(3/4), 19–32.

MARTINEZ, C. (1977). Group process and the Chicano: Clinical issues. *International Journal of Group Psychotherapy, 27*(2), 225–231.

MARWIT, S. J. (1981). Assessment of sex-role stereotyping among male and female psychologist practitioners. *Journal of Personality Assessment, 45*(6), 593–599.

MASLIN, A., AND DAVIS, J. L. (1975). Sex-role stereotyping as a factor in mental health standards among counselors-in-training. *Journal of Counseling Psychology, 22*(2), 87–91.

MASLING, J., AND HARRIS, S. (1969). Sexual aspects of TAT administration. *Journal of Consulting and Clinical Psychology, 33*(2), 166–169.

MASON, K. O., CZAJKA, J. T., AND ARBER, S. (1976). Change in U.S. women's sex role attitudes, 1964–1974. *American Sociological Review, 41*(4), 573–596.

MAULTSBY, M. C., JR. (1982). A historical view of blacks' distrust of psychiatry. In S. M. Turner and R. T. Jones (Eds.), *Behavior modification in black populations: Psychosocial issues and empirical findings.* New York: Plenum Press.

MAYER, J., AND TIMMS, N. (1969). Clash in perspective between worker and client. *Social Casework, 50*(1), 32–40.

MAYER, J. E., AND TIMMS, N. (1970). *The client speaks: Working class impressions of casework.* New York: Atherton Press.

MAYO, J. A. (1974). Utilization of a community mental health center by blacks: Admission to inpatient status. *Journal of Nervous and Mental Disease, 158*, 202–207.

MAYO, J. A. (1981). The concept of masked anxiety in young adult black males. In D. F. Klein and J. Rabkin (Eds.), *Anxiety: New research and changing concepts.* New York: Raven Press, pp. 381–398.

MEADOR, B., SOLOMON, E., AND BOWEN, M. (1972). Encounter groups for women only. In L. N. Solomon and B. Berzon (Eds.), *New perspectives on encounter groups.* San Francisco: Jossey-Bass.

MEEKER, B. F. (1981). Expectation states and interpersonal behavior. In M. Rosenberg and R. H. Turner (Eds.), *Social psychology: Sociological perspectives.* New York: Basic Books, pp. 290–319.

MEEKER, B. F., AND HORNUNG, C. A. (1976). Strategies of interaction. *Social Science Research, 5*, 153–172.

MEEKER, B. F., AND WEITZEL-O'NEILL, P. A. (1977). Sex roles and interpersonal behavior in task oriented groups. *American Sociological Review, 42,* 91–105.

MEGARGEE, E. I. (1969). Influence of sex roles on the manifestation of leadership. *Journal of Applied Psychology, 53,* 377–382.

MEHRABIAN, A. (1972). *Nonverbal communication.* Chicago, Ill.: Aldine-Alherton.

MELTZOFF, J., AND KORNREICH, M. (1970). *Research in psychotherapy.* New York: Atherton.

MERLUZZI, B. (1981). Androgyny, stereotype and the perception of female therapists. *Journal of Clinical Psychology, 37*(2), 280–284.

MERLUZZI, B. H., AND MERLUZZI, T. V. (1978). Influence of client race on counselor's assessment of case materials. *Journal of Counseling Psychology, 25,* 399–404.

MERLUZZI, T. V., BANIKIOTES, P. G., AND MISSBACH, J. W. (1978). Perceptions of counselor characteristics: Contributions of counselor sex, experience, and disclosure level. *Journal of Counseling Psychology, 25*(5), 479–482.

MERLUZZI, T. V., MERLUZZI, B. H., AND KAUL, T. J. (1977). Counselor race and power base: Effects on attitudes and behavior. *Journal of Counseling Psychology, 24*(5), 430–436.

MERTON, R. K. (1957). *Social theory and social structure.* New York: Free Press.

MEYERS, J. K., AND ROBERTS, B. H. (1959). *Family and class dynamics in mental illness.* New York: John Wiley and Sons.

MICHELINI, R. L., EISEN, D., AND SNODGRASS, S. R. (1981). Success orientation and the attractiveness of competent males and females. *Sex Roles, 7*(4), 391–401.

MIDDLEMAN, R. R. (1959). Social group work in a maternity home. *Child Welfare, 38*(2), 13–18.

MIDDLEMAN, R. R. (1980). Co-leadership and solo-leadership in education for social work with groups. *Social Work with Groups, 3*(4), 39–50.

MILLER, D., (1974). The influence of the patient's sex on clinical judgment. *Smith College Studies in Social Work, 44*(2), 89–100.

MILLER, D. et al. (1975). *Native American families in the city.* San Francisco: Scientific Analysis.

MINTZER, E., AND HALPERN, J. (1980). Effect of sex of therapist and client on therapists' attitudes toward assertiveness problems. *Journal of Clinical Psychology, 36*(3), 704–708.

MINUCHIN, S. (1965). Conflict resolution family therapy. *Psychiatry, 28*(3), 278–286.

MINUCHIN, S. (1967). The disorganized and disadvantaged family. In S. Minuchin, et al. (Eds.), *Families of the slums.* New York: Basic Books.

 MINUCHIN, S. (1969). The paraprofessional and the use of confrontation in the mental health field. *American Journal of Orthopsychiatry, 39,* 722–729.

MINUCHIN, S. (1970). The plight of the poverty-stricken family in the United States. *Child Welfare, 49*(3), 124–130, summarized.

MINUCHIN, S. (1974). *Families and family therapy.* Cambridge: Harvard University Press.

MINUCHIN, S., AND MONTALVO, B. (1967). Techniques for working with disorganized, low-socioeconomic families. *American Journal of Orthopsychiatry, 37*(5), 880–887.

MINUCHIN, S., MONTALVO, B., GUERNEY, B. C., JR., ROSMAN, B. L., AND SCHUMER, F. (1967). *Families of the slums: An exploration of their structure and treatment.* New York: Basic Books, Inc.

MIRANDE, A. (1977). The Chicano family: A re-analysis of conflicting views. *Journal of Marriage and the Family, 39,* 747–756.

MITCHELL, C. (1969). The uses and abuses of co-therapy as a technique in family unit therapy. *Bulletin of the Family Mental Health Clinic of Jewish Family Services, 1,* 8–10.

MITCHELL, K. M., AND NAMENEK, T. M. (1970). A comparison of therapist and client social class. *Professional Psychology, 1,* 225–230.

MIZIO, E. (1972). White worker—minority client. *Social Work, 17,* 82–86.

MIZIO, E. (1979). *Puerto Rican Task Report—Project on ethnicity.* New York: Family Service Association.

MOGUL, K. M. (1982). Overview: The sex of the therapist. *The American Journal of Psychiatry, 139*(1), 1–10.

MOLINA, R. A., AND FRANCO, J. N. (1986). Effects of administrator and participant sex and ethnicity on self-disclosure. *Journal of Counseling and Development, 63*(3), 160–162.

MONAGAN, A. P. (1985). Rethinking "matrifocality." *Phylon, 46*(4), 353–362.

MONTIEL, M. (1970). The social science myth of the Mexican American family. *El Grito, 3*(4), 56–63.

MONTIEL, M. (1973). The Chicano family: A review of research. *Social Work, 18*(2), 22–23.

MORELAND, J., AND SCHWEBEL, A. I. (1981). A gender role transcendent perspective on fathering. *The Counseling Psychologist, 9*(4), 45–53.

MORENO, J. L. (1934). *Who shall survive?* Washington, D.C.: Nervous and Mental Disorders, No. 58.

MOSKOL, M. D. (1976). Feminist theory and casework practice. In B. Ross and S. K. Khinduka (Eds.), *Social work in practice: Fourth NASW symposium.* Washington, D.C.: NASW, pp. 181–190.

MOYNIHAN, D. (1965). *The Negro family: The case for national action.* Washington, D.C.: Office of Policy Planning and Research, U.S. Department of Labor.

MULOZZI, A. D. (1972). Interracial counseling: Clients' ratings and counselors' ratings in a first session. (Doctoral dissertation, Southern Illinois University, 1972.) *Dissertation Abstracts International, 33,* 2175A (University Microfilms NO. 72-28, 546).

MUMMAH, H. R. (1975). Group work with the aged blind Japanese in the nursing home and in the community. *New Outlook for the Blind, 69*(4), 160–167.

MURRAY, D. C., BROWN, J., AND KNOX, W. (1964). Verbal participation of Negro psychotics in combined as contrasted to all-Negro groups. *International Journal of Group Psychotherapy, 14,* 221–223.

MURRAY, S. R., AND MEDNICK, M. T. S. (1975). Perceiving the causes of success and failure in achievement: Sex, race and motivational comparisons. *Journal of Consulting and Clinical Psychology, 43*(6), 881–885.

MYERSON, M., AND BANFIELD, E. (1955). *Politic, planning and public interest.* Glencoe, Ill.: The Free Press.

NADELSON, C. C., NOTMAN, M. T., AND BENNETT, M. B. (1978). Success or failure: Psychotherapeutic considerations for women in conflict. *American Journal of Psychiatry, 135*(9), 1092–1096.

NATIONAL CENTER FOR HEALTH STATISTICS. (1976). *Hypertension: United States, 1974 advance data, No. 2.* (Washington, D.C.: U. S. Government Printing Office, DHEW Publication No. HRA 77-1250, Health Resources Administration.

National Commission on Working Women. (1986). Washington, D.C.

NAVARRE, E., GLASSER, P., AND COSTABILE, J. (1985). An evaluation of group work practice with AFDC mothers. In Sundel, Glasser, Sarri, and Vinter (Eds.), *Individual change through small groups* (2nd ed.). New York: The Free Press, pp. 391–407.

NAYMAN, R. (1983). Group work with Black women: Some issues and guidelines. *Journal for Specialists in Group Work, 8*(1), 31–38.

NEIGHBORS, H. W., AND JACKSON, J. S. (1984). The use of informal and formal help: Four patterns of illness behavior in the black community. *American Journal of Community Psychology, 12*(6), 629–644.

NEIMEYER, G. J., AND GONZALES, M. (1983). Duration, satisfaction and perceived effectiveness of cross-cultural counseling. *Journal of Counseling Psychology, 30*(1), 91–95.

NELSEN, J. C. (1983). *Family treatment: An integrative approach.* Englewood Cliffs, N.J.: Prentice-Hall.

NEULINGER, J., STEIN, M. I., SCHILLINGER, M., AND WELKOWITZ, J. (1979). Perceptions of the optimally integrated person as a function of therapists' characteristics. *Perceptual and Motor Skills, 30*(2), 375–384.

NEWCOMB, T. (1947). Autistic hostility and social reality. *Human Relations, 1,* 69–87.

NEWCOMB, T. M. (1961). *The acquaintance process.* New York: Holt, Rinehart and Winston, Inc.

NEWCOMB, T. M. (1963). Resistance and regression of changed attitudes: Long range studies. *Journal of Social Issues, 19*(14), 3–14.

NICHOLS, W. C. (1986). Understanding family violence: An orientation for family therapists. *Contemporary Family Therapy, 8*(3), 188–207.

NICHOLS-CASEBOLT, A. M. (1988). Black families headed by single mothers: Growing numbers and increasing poverty. *Social Work, 33*(4), 306–313.

NIETZEL, M. T., HILE, M. G., AND KONDO, C. Y. (1978). Diversity among lower-class therapy clients: A comparison of class IV and class V psychotherapy recipients. *Journal of Consulting and Clinical Psychology, 46*(2), 377–378.

NIEVA, V. F., AND GUTEK, B. A. (1980). Sex effects and evaluation. *The Academy of Management Review, 5*(2), 267–276.

NOLL, G. A., AND WATKINS, J. T. (1974). Differences between persons seeking encounter group experiences and others on the personal orientation inventory. *Journal of Counseling Psychology, 21*(3), 206–209.

NORDHOLM, L. A., WARD, C. D., AND BHANTHURNAVIN, D. (1974). Sex and cultural differences in perceived locus of control among students in five countries. *Journal of Consulting and Clinical Psychology, 42*(3), 451–455.

NORMAND, W., IGLESIAS, J., AND PAYN, S. (1974). Brief group therapy to facilitate utilization of mental health services by Spanish-speaking patients. *American Journal of Orthopsychiatry, 44*(1), 37–42.

NORTON, A. J., AND GLICK, P. C. (1986). One parent families: A social and economic profile. *Family Relations, 35*(1), 9–17.

NOVAK, D., AND LERNER, M. (1968). Rejection as a consequence of perceived similarity. *Journal of Personality and Social Psychology, 9*, 147–152.

NORVELL, N., AND WORCHEL, P. (1981). A re-examination of the relation between equal status contact and intergroup attraction. *Journal of Personality and Social Psychology, 41*(5), 902–908.

NOWACKI, C. M., AND POE, C. A. (1973). The concept of mental health as related to sex of person perceived. *Journal of Consulting and Clinical Psychology, 40*(1), 160.

OCCHETTI, A. E., AND OCCHETTI, D. B. (1981). Group therapy with married couples. *Social Casework, 62*(2), 74–79.

O'CONNOR, K., MANN, D. W., AND BARDWICK, J. M. (1978). Androgyny and self-esteem in the upper-middle class: A replication of Spence. *Journal of Consulting and Clinical Psychology, 46*(5), 1168–1169.

OFFERMAN, L. R. (1984). Short-term supervisory experience and LPC score: Effects of leaders' sex and group sex composition. *The Journal of Social Psychology, 123*, 115–121.

O'KELLEY, F. R., AND SCHULDT, W. J. (1981). Self-disclosure as a function of experimenter's self-disclosure, experimenter's sex and subject's sex. *Perceptual and Motor Skills, 52*, 557–558.

O'LEARY, K. D., CURLEY, A., ROSENBAUM, A., AND CLARKE, C. (1985). Assertion training for abused wives: A potentially hazardous treatment. *Journal of Marital and Family Therapy, 11*, 319–322.

OLESKER, W., AND BALTER, L. (1972). Sex and empathy. *Journal of Counseling Psychology, 19*(6), 559–562.

OLIVER, L. W. (1975). Counseling implications of recent research on women. *The Personnel and Guidance Journal, 53*(6), 430–437.

OLMEDO, E., AND PARRON, D. L. (1981). Mental health of minority women: Some special issues. *Professional Psychology, 12*(1), 103–111.

O'NEIL, J. M. (1981). Patterns of gender role conflict and strain: Sexism and fear of femininity in men's lives. *The Personnel and Guidance Journal, 60*(4), 203–210.

O'NEIL, J. M. (1981). Male sex role conflicts, sexism and masculinity: Psychological implications for men, women and the counseling psychologist. *The Counseling Psychologist, 9*(2), 61–80.

OPPENHEIMER, V. K. (1977). The sociology of women's economic role in the family. *American Sociological Review, 42*, 387–406.

ORCUTT, B. A. (1977). Family treatment of poverty level families. *Social Casework, 58*, 92–100.

ORLINSKY, D. E., AND HOWARD, K. I. (1976). The effects of sex of therapist on the therapeutic experiences of women. *Psychotherapy: Theory, Research, and Practice, 13*(1), 82–88.

ORLINSKY, D. E., AND HOWARD, K. I. (1980). Gender and therapeutic outcome. In A. M. Brodsky and R. T. Hare-Mustin (Eds.), *Women and psychotherapy: An assessment of research and practice.* New York: The Guilford Press.

ORNE, M. I., AND WENDER, P. H. (1968). Anticipatory socialization for psychotherapy: Method and rationale. *American Journal of Psychiatry, 124*, 1202–1212.

ORTHNER, D. K., BROWN, T., AND FERGUSON, D. (1976). Single-parent fatherhood: An emerging lifestyle. *The Family Coordinator, 25*(4), 429–437.

ORTOFF, M. (1962). Group services to families receiving ADC. *Child Welfare*, (March), pp. 118–122.

O'SHEA, C. (1972). Two gray cats learn how it is in a group of black teenagers. In I. H. Berkovitz (Ed.), *Adolescents grow in groups.* New York: Brunner/Mazel.
OSMOND, M. W., AND MARTIN, P. Y. (1978). A contingency model of marital organization in low income families. *Journal of Marriage and the Family, 40*(2), 315–329.
OVERALL, B., AND ARONSON, H. (1963). Expectations of psychotherapy in patients of lower socioeconomic class. *American Journal of Orthopsychiatry, 33,* 421–430.
Overview of minority women in the work force. (February, 1986). Washington, D.C.: National Commission on Working Women.
OWEN, I. (1970). Adlerian counseling in racially mixed groups of elementary school children. *Individual Psychologist, 7,* 53–58.
OZARIN, L. D., AND TAUBE, C. A. (1974). Psychiatric inpatients: Who, where and the future. *American Journal of Psychiatry, 131*(1), 98–101.
PADESKY, C. A., AND HAMMEN, C. L. (1981). Sex differences in depressive symptom expression and help-seeking among college students. *Sex Roles, 7*(3), 309–320.
PADILLA, A. M., RUIZ, R. A., AND ALVAREZ, R. (1975). Community mental-health services for Spanish-speaking surnamed population. *American Psychologist, 30*(9), 892–905.
PAPELL, C., AND ROTHMAN, B. (1980). Relating the mainstream model of social work with groups to group psychotherapy and the structured group approach. *Social Work with Groups, 3,* 5–23.
PAPELL, C., AND ROTHMAN, B. (Eds.) (1980). Co-leadership in social work with groups. *Social Work with Groups,* Special Issue, *3*(4), 1–78.
PARADISE, L. V., CONWAY, B. S., AND ZWEIG, J. (1986). Effects of expert and referent influence, physical attractiveness, and gender on perceptions of counselor attributes. *Journal of Counseling Psychology, 33*(1), 16–22.
PARDECK, J. T., WOLF, V., KILLION, S., AND SILVERSTEIN, G. (1983). Individual therapy vs. family therapy: Which is more effective? *Family Therapy, 10*(2), 173–181.
Parents without partners. (1983). Bethesda, Md.: Parents without Partners.
PARKER, G. V. C. (1967). Some concomitants of therapist dominance in the psychotherapy interview. *Journal of Consulting Psychology, 31,* 313–318.
PARKER, S., AND KLEINER, R. (1970). Status position, mobility and ethnic identification of the Negro. In N. Smelser and W. Smelser (Eds.), *Personality and Social Systems.* New York: John Wiley and Sons, pp. 353–367.
PARKER, W. M., AND MCDAVIS, R. J. (1983). Attitudes of blacks toward mental health agencies and counselors. *Journal of Non-White Concerns, 11*(3), 89–98.
PARKER, W. S. (1976). Black-white differences in leaders behavior related to subordinates reaction. *Journal of Applied Psychology, 61,* 140–147.
PARLOFF, M. B. (1961). Therapist-patient relationships and outcome of psychotherapy. *Journal of Consulting Psychology, 25,* 29–38.
PARLOFF, M. B., WASKOW, E., AND WOLKE, B. F. (1978). Research on therapist variables in relation to process and outcomes. In S. L. Garfield and A. E. Bergin (Eds.), *Handbook on psychotherapy and behavioral change.* New York: John Wiley and Sons.
PARRY, G. (1986). Paid employment, life events, social support, and mental health in working-class mothers. *Journal of Health and Social Behavior, 27*(2), 193–208.
PATTERSON, M. L., AND SCHAEFFER, R. E. (1977). Effects of size and sex composition on interaction distance, participation and satisfaction in small groups. *Small Group Behavior, 8*(4), 433–442.
PAZ, O. (1961). *The labyrinth of solitude: Life and thought in Mexico.* New York: Grove Press.
PEARL, A., AND RIESSMAN, F. (1965). *New careers for the poor.* New York: Free Press.
PEOPLES, V. Y., AND DELL, D. M. (November, 1975). Black and white student preferences for counselor roles. *Journal of Counseling Psychology, 22*(6) 529–534.
PERES, Y. (1971). Ethnic relations in Israel. *American Journal of Sociology, 76,* 1021–1047.
PERSONS, R. W., PERSONS, M. K., AND NEWMARK, I. (1974). Perceived helpful therapists' characteristics, client improvements, and sex of therapist and client. *Psychotherapy: Theory, Research and Practice, 11*(1), 63–65.
PETERS, M. F. (1981). Parenting in black families with young children. In H. McAdoo (Ed.), *Back Families.* Beverly Hills, Cal.: Sage, 211–224.
PETRO, C. S., and HANSEN, J. C. (1977). Counselor sex and empathic judgement. *Journal of Counseling Psychology, 24*(4), 373–376.

PETTIGREW, T. (1967). Social evaluation theory: Convergences and applications. *Nebraska symposium on motivation.* Lincoln: University of Nebraska Press.

PETTIT, I. B., PETTIT, T. F., AND WELKOWITZ, J. (1974). Relationship between values and social class, and duration of psychotherapy. *Journal of Consulting and Clinical Psychology, 42*(4), 482–490.

PETTY, M. M., AND MILES, R. H. (1976). Leader sex-role stereotyping in a female-dominated work culture. *Personnel Psychology, 29*, 393–404.

PHILLIPS, D. L. (1964). Rejection of the mentally ill: The influence of behavior and sex. *American Sociological Review, 29*(5), 679–687.

PHILLIPS, D. L., AND SEGAL, B. E. (1969). Sexual status and psychiatic symptoms. *American Sociological Review, 34*(1), 58–72.

PHILLIPS, W. (1960). Counseling Negro pupils: An educational dilemma. *Journal of Negro Education, 29,* 504–507.

PIERSON, A. (1970). Social work techniques with the poor. *Social Casework, 51*(8), 481–485.

PILIAVIN, J. A., AND MARTIN, R. R. (1978). The effect of sex composition of groups on style of social interaction. *Sex Roles, 4*(2), 281–296.

PINDERHUGHES, E. (1982a) Afro-American families and the victim system. In M. Mc-Goldrick, J. K. Pearce, and J. Giordano, *Ethnicity and family therapy.* New York: The Guilford Press, pp. 108–122.

PINDERHUGHES, E. B. (1982b). Family functions of Afro-Americans. *Social Work, 27*(1), 91–97.

PIPES, W. H. (1981). Old time religion: Benches can't say amen. In H. P. McAdoo (Ed.), *Black families,* Beverly Hills, Cal.: Sage, pp. 54–76.

PLECK, J. H. (1976). Male threat from female competence. *Journal of Consulting and Clinical Psychology, 44*(4), 608–613.

PLECK, J. H. (1976). Sex role issues in clinical training. *Psychotherapy: Therapy, Research and Practice, 13*(1), 17–19.

Pleck, J. H. (1983). Husband's paid work and family roles: Current research issues. In H. J. Lopata and J. H. Pleck (Eds.), *Research on the interwave of social roles,* Vol. 3. Greenwich: JAI Press.

PLECK, J. H. (1985). *Working wives/working husbands.* Beverly Hills: Sage.

PLECK, J., STAINES, H., AND LANG, L. (1978). Work and family life. In the 1977 *Quality of employment survey.* Wellesley, Mass.: Wellesley College Center for Research on Women, Working Papers.

POLLACK, D., AND SHORE, J. H. (1980). Validity of the MMPI with Native Americans. *American Journal of Psychiatry, 137*(8), 946–950.

POLLACK, E., AND MENACKEN, J. (1971). *Spanish-speaking students and guidance.* Boston: Houghton Mifflin.

POMALES, J., CLAIBORN, C. D., AND LaFROMBOISE, T. D. (1986). Effects of black sutdents' racial identity on perceptions of white counselors varying in cultural sensitivity. *Journal of Counseling Psychology, 33*(1), 57–61.

POPE, B. (1979). *The mental health interview: Research and application.* New York: Pergamon Press.

PORCHE, L. M., AND BANIKIOTES, P. G. (1982). Racial and attitudinal factors affecting the perceptions of counselors by Black adolescents. *Journal of Counseling Psychology, 29*(2), 169–174.

POUSSAINT, A. (1972). *Why Blacks kill Blacks.* New York: Emerson Hall Publisher.

POWELL, B., AND REZNIKOFF, M. (1976). Role conflict and symptoms of psychological distress in college-educated women. *Journal of Consulting and Clinical Psychology, 44*(3), 473–479.

POWELL, M., AND MONAHAN, J. (1969). Reaching the rejects through multifamily group therapy. *International Journal of Group Psychotherapy, 19*(1), 35–43.

PRATT, L. (1970). Optimism-pessimism about helping the poor with health problems. *Social Work, 15*(2), 29–33.

PROCTOR, E. K. (1982). Defining the worker client relationship. *Social Work, 27*(5), 430–435.

PROCTOR, E. K. (May 15–16, 1985). Social work with women: Perspectives and realities. Paper presented at the 60th Anniversary of the George Warren Brown School of Social Work, Washington University, St. Louis, Mo.

PROCTOR, E. K., AND ROSEN, A. (1983). Problem formulation and its relation to treatment planning. *Social Work Research and Abstracts, 19*(3), 22–28.

PROCTOR, E. P., AND ROSEN, A. (1981). Expectations and preferences for counselor race and their relation to intermediate treatment outcome. *Journal of Counseling Psychology, 28,* 40–46.

PUCEL, J. C., AND NAWAS, M. M. (1970). The effects of sex pairings of experimenter and subject on the outcome of systematic desensitization. *Journal of Behavioral Therapy and Experimental Psychiatry, 1*(2), 103–107.

PURSELL, S., BANIKIOTES, P. O., AND SEBASTIAN, R. J. (1981). Androgyny and the perception of marital roles. *Sex Roles, 7*(2), 201–215.

RABIN, C., ROSENBAUM, H., AND SENS, M. (1982). Home-based marital therapy for multi-problem families. *Journal of Marital and Family Therapy, 8*(4), 451–461.

RABKIN, J. (1977). Therapists' attitudes toward mental illness and health. In A. S. Gurman and A. M. Razin (Eds.), *Effective psychotherapy: A handbook of research.* Oxford: Pergamon Press.

RACHLIN, V. C., AND HANSEN, J. C. (1985). The impact of equity or egalitarianism on dual-career couples. *Family Therapy, 12*(2), 151–164.

RADIN, N. (1982). Primary caregiving and role-sharing fathers. In M. E. Lamb (Ed.), *Nontraditional families: Parenting and child development.* Hillsdale, N.J.: Lawrence Erlbaum, pp. 173–204.

RADIN, N., AND KAMII, C. (1965). The child-rearing attitudes of disadvantaged Negro mothers and some educational implications. *Journal of Negro Education, 34*(2), 138–146.

RADOV, C. G., MASNICK, B. R., AND HAUSER. B. B. (1977). Issues in feminist therapy: The work of a women's study group. *Social Work, 22*(6), 507–509.

RANSOHOFF, R. (1981). An analysis of male attitudes toward women's cognitive functions: A life-cycle approach. *American Journal of Orthopsychiatry, 51*(4), 724–729.

RAPOPORT, A. (1954). *Operational philosophy.* New York: Harper.

RAUBOLT, R. R., AND RACHMAN, A. W. (1980). A therapeutic group experience for fathers. *The International Journal of Group Psychotherapy, 30*(2), 229–239.

RAUCH, J. B. (1978). Gender as a factor in practice. *Social Work, 23*(5), 388–395.

RAYNES, A. E., AND WARREN, G. (1971). Some distinguishing features of patients failing to attend a psychiatric clinic after referral. *American Journal of Orthopsychiatry, 41,* 581–588.

REDFERING, D. L. (1975). Differential effects of group counseling with Black and white female delinquents: One year later. *Journal of Negro Education, 44*(4), 530–537.

REDHORSE, J. G. (1980). American Indian elders: Unifiers of Indian families. *Social casework: The journal of contemporary social work,* pp. 490–493.

REDHORSE, J., LEWIS, R., AND DECKER, J. (1978). Family behavior of urban American Indians. *Social Casework, 59*(2), 67–72.

REDLICH, F. C., HOLLINGSHEAD, A. B., AND BELLIS, E. (1955). Social class difference in attitudes towards psychiatry. *American Journal of Orthopsychiatry, 25,* 65–70.

REED, B. (1983). Women leaders in small groups: Social-psychological perspectives and strategies. In B. Reed and C. Garvin (Eds.), *Groupwork with women/groupwork with men: An overview of gender issues in social group work practice.* New York: Haworth Press, pp. 35–42.

REED, R. (1988). Education and achievement of young black males. In J. T. Gibbs, (Ed.), *Young, Black, and male in America: An endangered species.* Dover, Mass.: Auburn House.

REESE-DUKES, J. L., AND REESE-DUKES, C. (1983). Pairs for pairs: A theoretical base for cotherapy as a nonsexist process in couple counseling. *Personnel and Guidance Journal, 62*(2), 99–101.

REID, W. J. (1977). A study of the characteristics and effectiveness of task-centered methods. Chicago: The School of Social Service Administration, The University of Chicago.

REID, W. J. (1978). *The task-centered system.* New York: Columbia University Press.

REID, W. J., AND SHYNE, A. (1969). Brief and extended casework. New York: Columbia University Press.

REPORT FROM THE DIRECTOR, NATIONAL INSTITUTE OF MENTAL HEALTH. (1976). *How women see their roles: A change in attitudes.* Rockville, Md.: Dept. of Health, Education, and Welfare, National Institute of Mental Health.

REYNOLDS, F. (1983). *Catching up: Recent changes in the social and economic status of Blacks.* Cambridge: Harvard University Press.

RHYNE, D. (1981). Bases of marital satisfaction among men and women. *Journal of Marriage and the Family, 43,* 941–955.

RICCIO, A. C., AND BARNES, K. D. (1973). Counselor preferences of senior high school students. *Counselor Education and Supervision, 13,* 36–40.

RICE, D. G. (1969). Patient sex differences and selection for individual psychotherapy. *The Journal of Nervous and Mental Disease, 148*(2), 124–133.

RICE, D. G. (1978). The male spouse in marital and family therapy. *The Counseling Psychologist, 7*(4), 64–66.

RICE, D. G., AND RICE, J. K. (1977). Non-sexist "marital" therapy. *Journal of Marriage and Family Counseling, 3*(1), 3–10.

RICE, J. D., AND RICE, D. G. (1975). Status and sex-role issues in co-therapy. In A. S. Gurman and D. G. Rice (Eds.), *Couples in conflict: New directions in marital therapy.* New York: Aronson, pp. 145–150.

RICE, R. W., BENDER, L. R., AND VITTERS, A. G. (1980). Leader sex, follower attitudes toward women, and leadership effectiveness: A laboratory experiment. *Organizational Behavior & Human Performance, 25*(1), 46–78.

RICE, V. (1963). Social class as a dimension in casework judgment. *Smith College Studies in Social Work, 34*(1), 30–48.

RICHARDS, S. A., AND JAFFEE, C. L. (1972). Blacks supervising whites: A study of interracial difficulties in working together in a simulated organization. *Journal of Applied Psychology, 56,* 234–240.

RICHARDSON, H. U. (1966). The Negro in American religious life. In J. P. Davis (Ed.), *The American Negro reference book.* Englewood Cliffs, N.J.: Prentice-Hall.

RIDGEWAY, C. L. (1982). Status in groups: The importance of motivation. *American Sociological Review, 47,* 76–88.

RIDLEY, C. (1984). Clinical tx. of the nondisclosing black client—a therapeutic paradox. *American Psychologist, 39*(11), 1234–1244.

RIESSMAN, F. (1965). The helper therapy principle. *Social Work, 10,* 27–32.

RIESSMAN, F. (1966). New approaches to mental health treatment for low-income people. In *Social work practice, 1965.* New York: Columbia University Press, pp. 174–187.

RIESSMAN, F., AND MILLER, S. M. (1964). Social change versus the "psychiatric world view." *American Journal of Orthopsychiatry, 34,* 29–38.

RIOCH, M. J. (1966). Changing concepts in the training of the therapist. *Journal of Consulting Psychology, 30,* 290–292.

RIORDAN, C., AND RUGGIERO, J. (1980). Producing equal-status inter-racial interaction— A replication. *Social Psychology Quarterly, 43*(1), 131–136.

RISMAN, B. J. (1986). Can men "mother"? Life as a single father. *Family Relations, 35*(1), 125–132.

RIVERO, E. M., AND BORDIN, E. S. (1980). Initiative behavior of male and female therapists in first interviews with females. *Journal of Consulting and Clinical Psychology, 48*(1), 124–125.

ROBERTS, R. E., AND ATTKINSON, C. C. (1983). Assessing client satisfaction among Hispanics. *Evaluation and Program Planning, 6,* 401–413.

ROBINOWITZ, C. B., NADELSON, C. C., AND NOTMAN, M. T. (1981). Women in academic psychiatry—politics and progress. *American Journal of Psychiatry, 138*(10), 1357–1361.

ROBYAK, J. E. (1981). Effects of gender on the counselor's preferences for methods of influence. *Journal of Counseling Psychology, 28*(1), 7–12.

ROBYAK, J. E., GOODYEAR, R. K., PRANGE, M. E., AND DONHAM, G. (1986). Effects of gender, supervision, and presenting problems on practicum students' preference for interpersonal power bases. *Journal of Counseling Psychology, 33*(2), 159–163.

RODGERS, H. R., JR. (1982). *The cost of human neglect: America's welfare failure.* Armonk, N.Y.: E. M. Sharpe, Inc.

RODGERS, H. R., JR. (1986). *Poor women, poor families.* New York: M. E. Sharpe, Inc.

ROGERS, C. R. (1962). The interpersonal relationship: the core of guidance. *Harvard Educational Review, 32,* 416–429.

ROGERS, L. S. (1960). Drop-out rates and results of psychotherapy in government aided mental hygiene clinics. *Journal of Clinical Psychology, 16,* 89–92.

ROGLER, L. H., MALGADY, R. G., COSTANTINO, G., AND BLUMENTHAL, R. (1987). What do culturally sensitive mental health services mean? The case of Hispanics. *American Psychologist, 42*(6), 565–570.

ROKEACH, M., AND MEZEL, L. (1966). Race and shared belief as factors in social choice. *Science, 151,* 167–172.

ROKEACH, M., SMITH, W., AND EVANS, R. I. (1960). Two kinds of prejudice or one? In *The open and closed mind.* New York: Basic Books, Inc.

ROMAN, D., BONTEMPS, M., FLYNN, M., MCGUIRE, T., AND GRUDER, C. L. (1977). The effects of status similarity and expectation of reciprocation upon altruistic behavior. *Personality and Social Psychology Bulletin, 3,* 103–106.

ROMAN, M., AND MELTZER, B. (1977). Cotherapy: A review of current literature (with special reference to therapeutic outcomes). *Joy of Sex and Marital Therapy, 3,* 501–514.

ROOT, M. P. (1985). Guidelines for facilitating therapy with Asian American clients. *Psychotherapy, 22,* 349–356.

ROSEN, A. (1967). Client preferences: An overview of the literature. *Personnel and Guidance Journal, 46,* 785–789.

ROSEN, A., AND CONNAWAY, R. S. (1969). Public welfare, social work, and social work education. *Social Work, 14*(2), 87–94.

ROSEN, A., AND PROCTOR, E. P. (1978). Specifying the treatment process: The basis for effectiveness research. *Journal of Social Service Research, 2,* 25–43.

ROSEN, A., AND PROCTOR, E. (1981). Distinctions between treatment outcome and their implications for treatment evaluation. *Journal of Consulting and Clinical Psychology, 49,* 418–425.

ROSEN, A., PROCTOR, E., AND LIVNE, S. (1985). Planning and direct practice. *Social Service Review, 59,* 161–177.

ROSEN, B., AND JERDEE, T. H. (1973). Influence of sex-role stereotypes on evaluations of male and female supervisory behavior. *Journal of Applied Psychology, 57,* 44–48.

ROSENBAUM, J., FRIEDLANDER, J., AND KAPLAN, S. (1956). Evaluation of results of psychotherapy. *Psychosomatic Medicine, 18,* 113–132.

ROSENBAUM, M. (1986). The repulsion hypothesis: On the nondevelopment of relationships. *Journal of Personality and Social Psychology, 51*(6), 1156–1166.

ROSENBAUM, M., AND HARTLEY, Z. (1966). Group psychotherapy and the integration of the Negro. *International Journal of Group Psychotherapy, 16,* 86–90.

ROSENKRANTZ, P., VOGEL, S., BEE, H., BROVERMAN, I., AND BROVERMAN, D. M. (1968). Sex role stereotypes and self-concepts in college students. *Journal of Consulting and Clinical Psychology, 32,* 287–295.

ROSENTHAL, D., AND FRANK, J. D. (1958). The fate of psychiatric clinic outpatients assigned to psychotherapy. *Journal of Nervous and Mental Disorders, 127,* 330–343.

ROSS, C. E., AND DUFF, R. S. (1982). Returning to the doctor: The effect of client characteristics, type of practice, and experiences with care. *Journal of Health and Social Behavior, 23*(2), 119–131.

ROSS, M., LAYTON, B., ERICSON, B. M., AND SCHOPLER, J. (1973). Affect, facial regard, and reactions to crowding. *Journal of Personality and Social Psychology, 28,* 69–76.

ROSSI, A. S. (1980). Life-span theories and women's lives. *Signs, 6*(1), 4–32.

ROSSI, A. S. (1984). Gender and parenthood. *American Sociological Review, 49*(1), 1–19.

ROSSMAN, J. E., AND KIRK, B. A. (1970). Comparison of counseling seekers and nonseekers. *Journal of Counseling Psychology, 17,* 184–188.

ROTHMAN, J., GANT, L. M., AND STEPHEN, A. H. (1985). Mexican-American family culture. *Social Service Review, 59*(2), 195–215.

ROTTER, J. B. (1966). Generalized expectancies for internal versus external control of reinforcement. *Psychological Monographs, 80,* (609).

ROWDEN, D. W., MICHEL, J. B., DILLEHAY, R. C., AND MARTIN, H. W. (1970). Judgments about candidates for psychotherapy: The influence of social class and insight-verbal ability. *Journal of Health and Social Behavior, 11*(1), 51–58.

RUBENSTEIN, E. A., AND LORR, M. A. (1956). A comparison terminators and remainers in outpatient psychotherapy. *Journal of Clinical Psychology, 12,* 345–349.

RUBIN, I. (1967). The reduction of prejudice through laboratory training. *Journal of Applied Behavioral Science, 3,* 29–51.

RUBLE, D., AND HIGGINS, E. T. (1976). Effects of group sex composition on self presentation and sex typing. *Journal of Social Issues, 32,* 125–132.

RUHE, J., AND EATMAN, J. (1977). Effects of racial composition on small work groups. *Small Group Behavior, 8*(4), 479–486.

RUIZ, R. (1981). Cultural and historic perspectives in counseling Hispanics. In D. Sue (Ed.), *Counseling the culturally different.* New York: John Wiley and Sons, pp. 186–215.

RUSSO, N. F., AND SOBEL, S. (1981). Sex differences in the ulilization of mental health services. *Professional Psychology, 12*(1), 7–19.

RUSSO, N. F., AND VANDENBOS, G. R. (1981). Women in the mental health delivery system. In W. H. Silverman (Ed.), *A community mental health sourcebook for board and professional action.* New York: Praeger.

SAARI, C. AND JOHNSON, S. R. (1975). Problems in the treatment of VIP clients. *Social Casework, 56,* 599–604.

SAFER, J., RIESS, B. F., AND KLEIN, K. (1975). Demographic and psychological characteristics of psychotherapy outpatients receiving medicaid. *International Mental Health Research Newsletter, 17*(4), 14–16.

SAFILIOS-ROTHSCHILD, C. (1969). Family sociology or wives' family sociology? A cross-cultural examination of decision-making. *Journal of Marriage and the Family, 31,* 290–301.

SAGER, C., et al. (1970). *Black ghetto family in therapy.* New York: Grove Press.

SALTZMAN, C., LUETGART, M. J., ROTH, C. H., CREASER, J., AND HOWARD, L. (1976). Formation of a therapeutic relationship: Experiences during the initial phase of psychotherapy as predictors of treatment duration and outcome. *Journal of Consulting and Clinical Psychology, 44,* 546–555.

SALZMAN, C., SHADER, R. I., SCOTT, D. A., AND BINSTOCK, W. (1970). Interviewer anger and patient dropout in walk-in clinic. *Comprehensive Psychiatry, 11,* 267–273.

SAMUELS, A. S. (1972). The reduction of interracial prejudice and tension through group therapy. In H. I. Kaplan and B. J. Sadock (Eds.), *New models for group therapy.* New York: E. P. Dutton, pp. 214–243.

SANCHEZ, A. R., AND ATKINSON, D. R. (1983). Mexican-American cultural commitment, preference for counselor ethnicity, and willingness to use counseling. *Journal of Counseling Psychology, 30*(2), 215–220.

SANIK, M. M., AND MAULDIN, T. (1986). Single versus two parent families: A comparison of mothers' time. *Family Relations, 35*(1), 53–56.

SAPOLSKY, A. (1965). Relationship between patient-doctor compatibility, mutual perception and outcome of treatment. *Journal of Abnormal Psychology, 70*(1), 70–76.

SARETSKY, T. (1977). *Active techniques and group psychotherapy.* New York: Aronson.

SATTLER, J. M. (1970). Racial "experimenter effects" in experimentation, testing interviewing, and psychotherapy. *Psychological Bulletin, 73*(2), 137–160.

SATTLER, J. M. (1977). The effects of therapist-client racial similarity. In A. S. Gurman and A. M. Razin (Eds.), *Effective psychotherapy: A handbook of research.* New York: Pergamon Press.

SAUBER, S. R. (1974). Approaches to pretherapy training. *Journal of Contemporary Psychotherapy, 6,* 190–197.

SCANZONI, J. (1975). Sex roles, economic factors, and marital solidarity in Black and white marriages. *Journal of Marriage and the Family, 37,* 130–144.

SCANZONI, J. (1977). *The Black family in modern society: Patterns of stability and security.* Chicago: University of Chicago Press.

SCANZONI, J. (1978). *Sex roles, women's work, and marital conflict.* Lexington, Mass.: Heath.

SCANZONI, J. (1979a). Sex-role influences on married women's status attainments. *Journal of Marriage and the Family, 41*(4), 793–800.

SCANZONI, J. (1979b). Strategies for changing male family roles: Research and practice implications. *The Family Coordinator, 28*(4), 435–442.

SCHAFFER, L., AND MYERS, J. K. (1954). Psychotherapy and social stratification: An empirical study of practice in a psychiatric outpatient clinic. *Psychiatry, 17,* 83–93.

SCHEIDLINGER, S. (1965). Three group approaches with socially deprived latency-age children. *International Journal of Group Psychotherapy, 15,* 434–445.

SCHEIRER, M. A. (1983). Household structure among welfare families: Correlates and consequences. *Journal of Marriage and the Family, 45*(4), 761–771.

SCHER, M. (1975). Verbal activity, sex, counselor experience, and success in counseling. *Journal of Counseling Psychology, 22*(2), 97–101.

SCHER, M. (1981). Counseling males: Introduction. *The Personnel and Guidance Journal, 60*(4), 198.

SCHER, M. (1981). Men in hiding: A challenge for the counselor. *The Personnel and Guidance Journal, 60*(4), 199–202.

SCHILLER, B. R. (1984). *The economics of poverty and discrimination* (4th ed.). Englewood Cliffs, N.J.: Prentice-Hall.

SCHNEIDERMAN, L. (1965). A social action model for the social work practitioner. *Social Casework, 46*(8), 490–493.

SCHNEIER, C. E. (1978). The contingency model of leadership: An extension to emergent leadership and leader's sex. *Organizational Behavior and Human Performance, 21*(2), 220–239.

SCHOFIELD, W. (1964). *Psychotherapy, the purchase of friendship.* Englewood Cliffs, N.J.: Prentice-Hall.

SCHOVER, L. R., AND LOPICCOLO, J. (1982). Treatment effectiveness for dysfunctions of sexual desire. *Journal of Sex and Marital Therapy, 8*(3), 179–197.

SCHUBERT, D., AND MILLER, S. I. (1978). Social class and psychiatric diagnosis: Differential findings in a lower-class sample. *The International Journal of Social Psychiatry, 24*(2), 117–124.

SCHUBERT, D., AND MILLER, S. I. (1980). Differences between the lower social classes: Some new trends. *American Journal of Orthopsychiatry, 50*(4), 712–717.

SCHUMACHER, L. C., BANIKIOTES, P. G., AND BANIKIOTES, F. G. (1972). Language compatibility and minority group counseling. *Journal of Counseling Psychology, 19,* 255–256.

SCHWARTZ, G. S., FRIEDLANDER, M. L., AND TEDESCHI, J. T. (1986). Effects of clients' attributional explanations and reasons for seeking help on counselors' impressions. *Journal of Counseling Psychology, 33*(1), 90–93.

SCHWARTZ, J. M., AND ABRAMOWITZ, S. I. (1975). Value-related effects on psychiatric judgment. *Archives of General Psychiatry, 32*(12), 1525–1529.

SCHWARTZ, J. M., AND ABRAMOWITZ, S. I. (1978). Effects of female client physical attractiveness on clinical judgement. *Psychotherapy: Theory, Research and Practice, 15*(3), 251–257.

SCHWARTZ, M. C. (1973). Sexism in the social work curriculum. *Journal of Education for Social Work, 9*(3), 65–70.

SCHWARTZ, M. C. (1974). Importance of the sex of worker and client. *Social Work, 19*(2), 177–185.

SCHWARTZ, W. (1968). Group work in public welfare. *Public Welfare, 26*(4), 322–370.

SCONTRINO, M. P., LARSEN, J. R., AND FIEDLER, F. E. (1977). Racial similarity as a moderator variable in perception of leader behavior and control. *International Journal of Intercultural Relations, 1,* 111–117.

SEARS, D. O., AND ABELES, R. P. (1969). Attitudes and opinions. *Annual Review of Psychology, 20,* 253–288.

SEARS, R. R., RAU, L., AND ALPERT, R. (1965). *Identification and child rearing.* Stanford, Cal.: Stanford University Press.

SEDLACEK, W. E., TROY, W., AND CHAPMAN, T. (1976). An evaluation of three methods of racism—Sexism training. *Personnel & Guidance Journal, 55*(4), 196–198.

SEGAL, J., AND YAHRAES, H. (1978). *A child's journey.* New York: McGraw-Hill.

SEGALMAN, R., AND BASU, A. (1981). *Poverty in America: The welfare dilemma.* Westport, Conn.: Greenwood Press.

SELLS, L. W. (1978). Mathematics—A critical filter. *The Science Teacher, 45*(2), 28–29.

SELLS, L. W. (1980). The mathematics filter and the education of women and minorities. In L. H. Fox, L. Brody, and D. Tobin (Eds.), *Women and the mathematical mystique.* Baltimore: Johns Hopkins Press, pp. 60–75.

SETTIN, J. M., AND BRAMEL, D. (1981). Interaction of client class and gender in biasing clinical judgment. *American Journal of Orthopsychiatry, 51*(3), 510–520.

SEYMOUR, P., AND KLEINER, R. (1964). Status position, mobility, and ethnic identification of the Negro. *Journal of Social Issues, 20*(2), 85–102.

SHAPIRO, A. K. (1971). Placebo effects in medicine, psychotherapy, and psychoanalysis. In A. E. Bergin and S. L. Garfield (Eds.), *Handbook of psychotherapy and behavior change: An empirical analysis.* New York: John Wiley and Sons.

SHAPIRO, J. (1983). Commitment to disenfranchised clients. In A. Rosenblatt and D. Waldfogel (Eds.), *Handbook of clinical social work.* San Francisco: Jossey-Bass Publishers.

SHAPIRO, R. J., AND BUDMAN, S. H. (1973). Defection termination and continuation in family and individual therapy. *Family Process, 12,* 55–67.

SHAW, M. (1983). *Group dynamics: The psychology of small group behavior.* New York: McGraw Hill.

SHEN, J., AND MURRAY, J. (1981). Psychotherapy with the disadvantaged. *American Journal of Psychotherapy, 35*(2), 268–275.

SHERIDAN, K. (1982). Sex bias in therapy: Are counselors immune? *The Personnel and Guidance Journal, 61*(2), 81–83.

SHERMAN, J., KOUFACOS, C., AND KENWORTHY, J. A. (1978). Therapists: Their attitudes and information about women. *Psychology of Women Quarterly, 2*(4), 299–313.

SHERMAN, R. (1983). Counseling the urban economically disadvantaged family: The action counseling method. *American Journal of Family Therapy, 11,* 22–30.

SHERMAN, S. N. (1976). The therapist and changing sex roles. *Social Casework, 57*(2), 93–96.

SHERRADEN, M. W. (1984). Working over the "underclass." *Social Work, 29*(4), 391–392.

SHILKOFF, D. (1983). The use of male-female co-leadership in an early adolescent girl's activity group. *Social Work with Groups, 6*(2), 67–80.

SHOEMAKER, L. O. (1963). Social group work in the ADC program. *Social Work, 8,* 30–36.

SHON, S. P., AND JA, D. Y. (1982). Asian families. In M. McGoldrick, K. Pearce, and J. Giordano (Eds.), *Ethnicity and family therapy.* New York: The Guilford Press.

SHOSTECK, H. (1977). Respondent militancy as a control variable for interviewer effect. *Journal of Social Issues, 33*(4), 36–45.

SHULLMAN, S. L., AND BETZ, N. E. (1979). An investigation of the effects of client sex and presenting problem in referral from intake. *Journal of Counseling Psychology, 26*(2), 140–145.

SHULMAN, S., AND KLEIN, M. M. (1984). Resolution of transference problems in structural therapy of single-parent families by a male therapist. *The American Journal of Family Therapy, 12*(2), 38–44.

SIASSI, I., AND MESSER, S. B. (1976). Psychotherapy with patients from lower socioeconomic groups. *American Journal of Psychotherapy, 30*(1), 29–40.

SIEGEL, J. M. (1974). A brief review of the effects of race in clinical service interactions. *American Journal of Orthopsychiatry, 44*(4), 555–562.

SIEGMAN, A. W. (August, 1977). Effects of cross-gender pairing on vocal behavior. Paper presented at the meeting of the American Psychological Association, San Francisco, Cal.

SIMONS, H. W., BERKOWITZ, N. N., AND MOYER, R. J. (1970). Similarity, credibility and attitude change: A review and a theory. *Psychological Bulletin, 73*(1), 1–16.

SIMONS, J. A., AND HELMS, J. E. (1976). Influence of counselors' marital status, sex, and age on college and noncollege women's counselor preferences. *Journal of Counseling Psychology, 23*(4), 380–386.

SINGER, B. D. (1967). Some implications of differential psychiatric treatment of Negro and white patients. *Social Science and Medicine, 1,* 77–83.

SIPPS, G. J., AND JANECZEK, R. G. (1986). Expectancies for counselors in relation to subject gender traits. *Journal of Counseling Psychology, 33*(2), 214–216.

SKILBECK, W. M., ACOSTA, F. X., YAMAMOTO, J., AND EVANS, L. A. (1984). Self-reported psychiatric symptoms among black, hispanic and white outpatients. *Journal of Clinical Psychology, 40*(5), 1184–1189.

SLADEN, B. J. (1982). Effects of race and socioeconomic status on the perception of process variables in counseling. *Journal of Counseling Psychology, 29*(6), 560–566.

SLOANE, R. B., STAPLES, F. R., CRISTOL, A. H., YORKSTON, N. J., AND WHIPPLE, K. (1975). *Short-term analytically oriented psychotherapy vs. behavior therapy.* Cambridge, Mass.: Harvard University Press.

SLOANE, R. B., STAPLES, F. R., CRISTOL, A. H., YORKSTON, N. J., AND WHIPPLE, K. (1976). Patient characteristics and outcome in psychotherapy and behavior therapy. *Journal of Consulting and Clinical Psychology, 44*(3), 330–339.

SLOANE, R., CRISTOL, A., PEPERNICK, M., AND STAPLES, F. (1970). Role preparation and expectancy of improvement in psychotherapy. *Journal of Nervous and Mental Diseases, 150*, 18–26.

SLOANE, R. B., STAPLES, F. R., CRISTOL, A. H., YORKSTON, N. J., AND WHIPPLE, K. (1975). *Short-term analytically oriented psychotherapy vs. behavior therapy.* Cambridge, Mass.: Harvard University Press.

SMITH, A. W. (1981). Racial tolerance as a function of group position. *American Sociological Review, 46*(5), 558–573.

SMITH, D. S. (1985). Wife employment and marital adjustment: A cumulation of results. *Family Relations, 34*(4), 483–490.

SMITH, E. (1977). Counseling black individuals: Some stereotypes. *Personnel & Guidance Journal, 55*(7), 390–396.

SMITH, E. J. (1981). Cultural and historical perspectives in counseling blacks. In D. W. Sue (Ed.), *Counseling the culturally different: Theory and practice.* New York: John Wiley and Sons.

SMITH, M. L. (1974). Influence of client sex and ethnic group on counselor judgments. *Journal of Counseling Psychology, 21*(6), 516–521.

SMITH, M. L. (1979). Counselor "discrimination" based on client sex: Reply to Donahue and Costar. *Journal of Counseling Psychology, 26*(3), 270–272.

SMITH, M. L. (1980). Sex bias in counseling and psychotherapy. *Psychological Bulletin, 81*(2), 392–407.

SMITH, O. S., AND GUNDLACH, R. H. (1974). Group therapy for blacks in a therapeutic community. *American Journal of Orthopsychiatry, 44*(1), 26–36.

SMITH, W. P., AND BORDNAND, F. (1975). Self-esteem and satisfaction as affected by unexpected social status placement. *Sociometry, 30*, 223–246.

SOARI, C., AND JOHNSON, S. R. (1975). Problems in the treatment of VIP clients. *Social Casework, 56*(10), 599–604.

SOBEL, S. B., AND RUSSO, N. F. (1981). Sex roles, equality, and mental health: An introduction. *Professional Psychology, 12*(1), 1–5.

SOLE, K., MARTON, J., AND HORNSTEIN, H. A. (1975). Opinion similarity and helping: Three field experiments investigating the bases of promotive tension. *Journal of Experimental Social Psychology, 11*, 1–13.

SOLOMON, B. (1976). *Black empowerment: Social work in oppressed communities.* New York: Columbia University Press.

SOLOMON, K. (1982.) Individual psychotherapy and changing masculine roles: Dimensions of gender role psychotherapy. In K. Solomon and N. B. Levy (Eds.), *Men in transition: Changing male roles, theory and therapy.* New York: Plenum Press.

SOMMERS, U. (1953). An experiment in group psychotherapy with members of mixed minority groups. *International Journal of Group Psychotherapy, 3*, 254–269.

SOTOMAYOR, M. (1971). Mexican-American interaction with social systems. *Social Casework, 52*(5), 316–322.

SOUTH, S. J., et al. (1982). Social structure and intergroup interaction: Men and women of the federal bureaucracy. *Sociological Review, 47*, 587–599.

SPANIER, G., AND GLICK, P. (1980). Married and unmarried cohabitation in the U. S. *Journal of Marriage and the Family, 42*(1), 19–130.

SPANIER, G., AND GLICK, P. (1980). Mate selection differentials between blacks and whites. *U.S. Social Forces, 58*, 707–725.

SPANIER, G., AND GLICK, P. (1980). Paths to remarriage. *Journal of Divorce, 3*, 293–298.

SPANIER, G., AND GLICK, P. (1980). The life cycle of American families: An expanded analysis. *Journal of Family History,* (Spring), pp. 98–112.

SPENCE, J. T., AND SAWIN, L. W. (1985). Images of masculinity and feminity: A reconceptualization. In V. E. O'Leary, R. K. Unger, and B. S. Wallston (Eds.), *Women, gender and social psychology.* Hillsdale, N.J.: Lawrence Erlbaum Associates, Publisher.

SPIEGEL, S. B. (1976). Expertness, similarity and perceived counselor competence. *Journal of Counselor Psychology, 23*, 432–441.

SPILLMAN, B., et al. (1981). Leadership emergence: Dynamic analysis of the effects of sex and androgyny. *Small Group Behavior, 12*(2), 139–157.

SROLE, L., LANGER, T. S., MICHAEL, S. T., OPLER, M. K., AND RENNIE, T. A. C. (1962). *Mental health in the metropolis: The midtown Manhattan study.* New York: McGraw-Hill.

STACK, C. (1974). *All our kin—Strategies for survival in a Black community.* New York: Harper and Row.

STAINES, G. I., PLECK, J. H., SHEPARD, L., AND O'CONNOR, P. (1978). Wives' employment status and marital adjustment: Yet another look. *Psychology of Women Quarterly,* pp. 90–120.

STAMM, A. M. (1969). NASW membership: Characteristics, deployment, and salaries. *Personnel Information, 12*(3), 1, 34–45.

STAPLES, R. (1971). Toward a sociology of the Black family. *Journal of Marriage and the Family, 33,* 119–138.

STAPLES, R. (1971). *The Black family: Essays and studies* (2nd ed.). Belmont, Cal.: Wadsworth.

STAPLES, R. (1981). Changes in Black family structures, the conflict between family ideology and structural conditions. *Journal of Marriage and the Family, 47*(4), 1005–1013.

STAPLES, R., AND MIRANDE, A. (1980). Racial and cultural variations among American families: A decennial review of the literature on minority families. *Journal of Marriage and the Family, 42*(3), 887–899.

STEBBING, D. B. (1972). "Playing it by ear" in answering the needs of a group of Black teenagers. In I. H. Berkowitz (Ed.), *Adolescents grow in groups.* New York: Brunner/Mazel.

STEIN, D. D., HARDYCK, J. A., AND SMITH, M. B. (1965). Race and belief: An open and shut case. *Journal of Personality and Social Psychology, 1,* 281–289.

STEIN, L. S., DEL GAUDIO, A. C., CARPENTER, P. J., AND ANSLEY, M. Y. (1978). Influence of professional background and sex of therapist on attitudes toward patients. *Perceptual and Motor Skills, 46*(3, pt. 1), 901–902.

STEIN, P. J. (1984). Men in families. *Marriage and Family Review, 7*(3/4), 143–162.

STEIN, T. (1983). An overview of men's groups. *Social Work with Groups, 6*(3/4), 149–161.

STEPHENSON, P. S., AND WALKER, G. A. (1981). The psychiatrist–woman patient relationship. In E. Howell and M. Bayes (Eds.), *Women and mental health.* New York: Basic Books, Inc.

STEVENS, B. (1971). The psychotherapist and women's liberation. *Social Work, 16*(3), 12–18.

STEWART, E. C. (1981). Cultural sensitivities in counseling. In P. P. Pedersen, J. G. Draguns, W. J. Loner, and J. E. Trimble (Eds.), *Counseling across cultures.* Honolulu: The University of Hawaii Press.

STEWART, J. C., JR., LAUDERDALE, M. AND SHUTTLESWORTH, G. E. (1972). The poor and the motivation fallacy. *Social Work, 17*(6), 34–37.

STOKES, J., FUEHRER, A., AND CHILDS, L. (1980). Gender differences in self-disclosure to various target persons. *Journal of Counseling Psychology, 27*(2), 192–198.

STOKES, J., CHILDS, L., AND FUEHRER, A. (1981). Gender and sex roles as predictors of self-disclosure. *Journal of Counseling Psychology, 28*(6), 510–514.

STONE, J. L., AND CROWITHERS, V. (1972). Innovations in program and funding of mental health services for blue-collar families. *American Journal of Psychiatry, 128,* 1375–1380.

STRANGES, R., AND RICCIO, A. (1970). Counselee preference for counselors: Some implications for counselor education. *Counselor Education and Supervision, 10,* 39–46.

STRASSBERG, D. S., AND ANCHOR, K. N. (1977). Ratings of client self-disclosure and improvement as a function of sex of client and therapist. *Journal of Clinical Psychology, 33*(1), 239–241.

STRAUS, M., GELLES, R., AND STEINMETZ, S. (1980). *Behind closed doors: Violence in the American family.* Garden City, N.Y.: Anchor/Doubleday.

STRICKER, G. (1977). Implications of research for psychotherapeutic treatment of women. *American Psychologist, 32*(1), 14–22.

STRODTBECK, F. L., AND MANN, R. D. (1956). Sex role differentiation in jury deliberations. *Sociometry, 19,* 3–11.

STRONG, S. R. (1968). Counseling: An interpersonal influence process. *Journal of Counseling Psychology, 15,* 215–224.

STRONG, S. R., AND SCHMIDT, L. D. (1970). Expertness and influence in counseling. *Journal of Counseling Psychology, 15,* 31–35.

STRUPP, H., AND BLOXOM, A. (1973). Preparing lower-class patients for group psychotherapy patients for group evaluation of a role induction film. *Journal of Consulting and Clinical Psychology, 41*(3), 373–384.

STRUPP, H. H., AND BLOXOM, A. L. (1971). Preparing the lower-class patient for psychotherapy: Development and evaluation of a role induction procedure. (Final Report Research and Demonstration Grant No. 15-P-55164, Social and Rehabilitation Service of U.S. Department, HEW). Nashville: Vanderbilt University.

SUBICH, L. M. (1983). Expectancies for counselors as a function of counselor gender specification and subject sex. *Journal of Counseling Psychology, 30*(3), 421–424.

SUE, D. W. (1981). *Counseling the culturally different: Theory and practice.* New York: John Wiley and Sons.

SUE, S. (1976). Clients' demographic characteristics and therapeutic treatment: Differences that make a difference. *Journal of Consulting and Clinical Psychology, 44*(5), 864.

X SUE, S. (1977). Community mental health services to minority groups. *American Psychologist, 32,* 616–624.

SUE, S., AND MCKINNEY, H. (1975). Asian Americans in the community mental health care system. *American Journal of Orthopsychiatry, 45*(1), 111–118.

✗SUE, S., MCKINNEY, H., ALLEN, D., AND HALL, J. (1974). Delivery of community mental health services to black and white clients. *Journal of Consulting and Clinical Psychology, 42*(6), 794–801.

SUE, S., AND ZANE, N. (1987). The role of culture and cultural techniques in psychotherapy. *American Psychologist, 42*(1), 37–45.

SULLIVAN, M. (1983). Introduction to women emerging: Group approaches. *The Journal for Specialists in Group Work, 8,* 3–8.

SUNDEL, M., GLASSER, P., SARRI, R., AND VINTER, R. (1985). *Individual change through small groups.* New York: The Free Press.

SUSSMAN, M. B. (1977). Family. In *Encyclopedia of social work.* Washington, D.C.: National Association of Social Workers.

SZAPOCZNIK, J., SCOPETTA, M., AND KING, O. (1978). Theory and practice in matching treatment to the special characteristics and problems of Cuban immigrants. *Journal of Community Psychology, 6,* 112–122.

SZINOVACZ, M. (1984). Changing family roles and interactions. *Marriage and Family Review, 7,* 163–201.

TAJFEL, H., AND BILLIG, M. (1974). Familiarity and categorization in intergroup behavior. *Journal of Experimental Social Psychology, 10,* 159–170.

TAJFEL, H., BILLIG, M., BUNDY, R. P., AND FLAMENT, C. (1971). Social categorization and intergroup behavior. *European Journal of Social Psychology, 1,* 149–178.

TANNEY, M. F., AND BIRK, J. M. (1976). Women counselors for women clients? A review of the research. *The Counseling Psychologist, 6*(2), 28–31.

TAUBE, C. A., BURNS, B. J., AND KESSLER, L. (1984). Patients of psychiatrists and psychologists in office-based practice: 1980. *American Psychologist, 39*(12), 1435–1447.

TAUSSIG, I. M. (1987). Comparative responses of Mexican Americans and Anglo-Americans to early goal setting in a public mental health clinic. *Journal of Counseling Psychology, 34*(2), 214–217.

TAVRIS, C., AND WADE, C. (1984). *The longest war: Sex differences in perspective (2nd Ed.).* San Diego: Harcourt, Brace Jovanovich.

TAYLOR, R. G., JR. (1966). Racial stereotypes in young children. *Journal of Psychology, 64,* 137–142.

TAYLOR, S. E., FISKE, S. T., ETCOFF, N. L., AND RUDERMAN, A. J. (1978). Categorical and contextual basis of person memory and stereotyping. *Journal of Personality and Social Psychology, 36,* 778–793.

TEARE, R. J. (1981). *Social work practice in a public welfare setting: An empirical analysis.* New York: Praeger Publications.

THOMAS, A., AND SILLEN, S. (1976). *Racism and psychiatry.* Secaucus, N.J.: The Citad' Press.

THOMAS, A. H., AND STEWART, N. R. (1971). Counselor response to female clients with deviate and conforming career goals. *Journal of Counseling Psychology, 18*(4), 352–357.

THOMAS, S. A. (1977). Theory and practice in feminist therapy. *Social Work, 22*(6), 447–454.

THOMPSON, M. E. (1981). Sex differences: Differential access to power or sex-role socialization? *Sex Roles, 7*(4), 413–424.

THUNE, E. S., MANDERSCHEID, R. W., AND SILBERGELD, S. (1980). Status of sex roles as determinants of interaction patterns in small mixed groups. *The Journal of Social Psychology, 112,* 51–65.

THUNE, E. S., MANDERSCHEID, R. W., AND SILBERGELD, S. (1981). Sex, status and cotherapy. *Small Group Behavior, 12,* 415–442.

Time Magazine (November 11, 1985). Education: Dramatic drops for minorities.

TOBIAS, S. (1982). Sexist equations. *Psychology Today, 16*(1), 14.

TOLDSON, I. L., AND PASTEUR, A. B. (1975). Developmental stages of Black self-discovery: Implications for using Black art forms in group interaction. *Journal of Negro Education, 44*(2), 130–138.

TOLDSON, I. L., AND PASTEUR, A. B. (1976). Beyond rhetoric: Techniques for using the Black aesthetic in group counseling and guidance. *Journal of Non-White Concerns in Personnel & Guidance, 4*(3), 142–151.

TOOMEY, B. G. (1980). Work ethic and work incentives: Values and income maintenance reform. *Journal of Sociology and Social Welfare, 7,* 148–160.

TORRANCE, E. R. (1954). Some consequences of power differences on decision making in permanent and temporary three-man groups. *Research Studies,* State College of Washington, *22,* pp. 130–140.

TRACEY, T. J., SHERRY, P., BAUER, G. P., ROBINS, T. H., TODARO, L., AND BRIGGS, S. (1984). Help seeking as a function of student characteristics and program description: A logit-loglinear analysis. *Journal of Counseling Psychology, 31*(1), 54–62.

TRECKER, H. B. (1964). *Group services in public welfare.* Washington, D.C.: U.S. Government Printing Office.

TRIANDIS, H. (1961). A note on RoKeach's theory of prejudice. *Journal of Abnormal and Social Psychology, 62,* 184–186.

TRIANDIS, H. C. (1976). Interpersonal behavior across cultures. In H. C. Triandis (Ed.), *Variations in black and white perceptions of the social environment.* Chicago: University of Illinois Press.

TRIANDIS, H., AND DAVIS, E. (1965). Race and belief as determinants of behavioral intentions. *Journal of Personality and Social Psychology, 2,* 715–725.

TRIANDIS, H., AND TRIANDIS, L. (1960). Race, social class, religion and nationality as determinants of social distance. *Journal of Abnormal and Social Psychology, 61,* 110–118.

TRIANDIS, H., AND TRIANDIS, L. (1965). Some studies of social distance. In I. D. Steiner and M. Fishbein (Eds.), *Current studies in social psychology.* New York: Holt, Rinehart, and Winston, 207–217.

TRUAX, C. B., WARGO, D. G., AND VOLKSDORF, N. R. (1970). Antecedents to outcome in group counseling with institutionalized juvenile delinquents: Effects of therapeutic conditions, patient self-exploration, alternate sessions and vicarious therapy pretraining. *Journal of Abnormal Psychology, 76,* 235–242.

TSUI, P., AND SCHULTZ, G. L. (1985). Failure of rapport: Why psychotherapeutic engagement fails in the treatment of Asian clients. *American Journal of Orthopsychiatry, 55*(4), 561–569.

TURKAT, D. (1980). Demographics of hospital recidivists. *Psychological Reports, 47*(2), 566.

TURKEL, A. R. (1976). The impact of feminism on the practice of a women analyst. *The American Journal of Psychoanalysis, 36*(2), 119–126.

TURNER, S. L. (1982). Behavior modification and black populations. In S. M. Turner and R. T. Jones (Eds.), *Behavior modification in Black populations: Psychosocial issues and empirical findings.* New York: Plenum Press.

TURNER, S., AND ARMSTRONG, S. (1981). Cross-racial psychotherapy. What the therapists say. *Psychotherapy: Theory, Research and Practice, 18*(3), 375–378.

TUZLAK, A., AND MOORE, J. C. (1984). Status, demeanor and influence: An empirical reassessment. *Social Psychology Quarterly, 47*(2), 178–183.

TWENTYMAN, C. T., AND McFALL, R. M. (1975). Behavioral training of social skills in shy males. *Journal of Consulting and Clinical Psychology, 43*(3), 384–395.

TYLIM, I. (1982). Group psychotherapy with Hispanic patients: The psychodynamics of idealization. *International Journal of Group Psychotherapy, 32*(3), 339–350.

UMBENHAUER, S. L., AND DEWITTE, L. L. (1978). Patient race and social class: Attitudes and decisions among three groups of mental health professionals. *Comprehensive Psychiatry, 19*(6), 509–515.

U.S. BUREAU OF THE CENSUS. (1982). *Money income of households, families and persons in the United States, 1980.* Washington, D.C.: U.S. Government Printing Office, Current Population Reports, Series P-60, No. 132.

U.S. BUREAU OF THE CENSUS. (1983). *America's Black population, 1970–1982: A statistical view.* Washington, D.C.: U.S. Government Printing Office, Series P 10/Pop 83.

U. S. BUREAU OF THE CENSUS. (1984). *Fertility of American women: June 1983.* Washington, D.C.: U.S. Government Printing Office, Series P-20, No. 386.

U.S. BUREAU OF THE CENSUS. (1985a). *Money income of households, families, and persons in the United States: 1983.* Washington, D.C.: U.S. Government Printing Office, Current Population Reports, P-60, No. 146.

U.S. BUREAU OF CENSUS. (1985b). *Household and family characteristics, March 1984.* Washington, D.C.: U.S. Government Printing Office, Current Population Reports, Series P-20, No. 398.

U.S. DEPARTMENT OF COMMERCE, BUREAU OF THE CENSUS. (1976). *1976 Survey of institutionalized persons: A study of persons receiving long-term care.*

U.S. DEPARTMENT OF HEALTH, EDUCATION, AND WELFARE. (1970). *Selected symptoms of psychological distress.* Washington, D.C.: U.S. Department of Health, Education, and Welfare, Public Health Services, and Mental Health Administration.

U.S. DEPARTMENT OF LABOR, BUREAU OF LABOR STATISTICS. (August, 1988). *Employment and earnings, 35*(8).

VAIL, A. (1978). Factors influencing lower-class black patients remaining in treatment. *Journal of Consulting and Clinical Psychology, 46*(2), 341.

VAIL, S. (1979). The effects of socio-economic class, race, and level of experience on social workers' judgments of clients. *Smith College Studies in Social Work, 14*(4).

VALENTINE, C. A. (1971). Deficit, difference, and bicultural models of Afro-American behavior. *Harvard Educational Review, 41,* 137–157.

VAN HOOK, M. (1979). Female clients, female counselors: Combating learned helplessness. *Social Work, 24*(1), 63–65.

VEGA, W. A., et al. (1986). Cohesion and adaptability in Mexican-American and Anglo families. *Journal of Marriage and the Family, 48*(4), 857–868.

VERBRUGGE, L. M. (1985). Gender and health: An update on hypotheses and evidence. *Journal of Health and Social Behavior, 26*(3), 156–182.

VEROFF, J. B. (1981). The dynamics of help-seeking in men and women: A national survey study. *Psychiatry, 44*(3), 189–200.

VONTRESS, C. E. (1970). Counseling blacks. *Personnel and Guidance Journal, 48*(9). 713–719.

VONTRESS, C. E. (1971). Racial differences: Impediments to rapport. *Journal of Counseling Psychology, 18*(1), 7–13.

VONTRESS, C. E. (1981). Racial and ethnic barriers in counseling. In P. P. Pedersen, J. G. Draguns, W. J. Lonner, and J. E. Trimble (Eds.), *Counseling across cultures.* Honolulu: The University of Hawaii Press.

WALKER, A. (1982). Embracing the dark and the light. *Essence, 13.*

WALKER, E. F., AND STAKE, J. E. (1978). Changes in preferences for male and female counselors. *Journal of Consulting and Clinical Psychology, 46*(5), 1153–1154.

WALKER, J. R., AND HAMILTON, L. S. (1973). A Chicano/Black/white encounter. *Personnel and Guidance Journal, 51*(7), 471–477.

WALKER, L. E. (1981). Battered women: Sex roles and clinical issues. *Professional Psychology, 12*(1), 81–91.

WALLACE, J. L. D. (1977). Race and the diagnostic prognostic, and treatment orientations of social work students. *Smith College Studies in Social Work, 48,* 60–61.

WALLACE, M. (1980). *Black macho and the myth of the super-woman.* New York: Warner Books, Inc.

WALTERS, J., AND STINNETT, N. (1971). Parent-child relationships: A decade review of research. *Journal of Marriage and the Family, 33,* 70–111.

WAMPOLD, B. E., CASAS, J. M., AND ATKINSON, D. R. (1981). Ethnic bias in counseling: An information processing approach. *Journal of Counseling Psychology, 28*(6), 498–503.

WARD, C. (1981). Prejudice against women: Who, when, and why? *Sex Roles, 7*(2), 163–171.

WARREN, R. C., JACKSON, A. M., NUGARIS, J., AND FARLEY, G. (1973). Differential attitudes of black and white patients toward treatment in a child guidance clinic. *American Journal of Orthopsychiatry, 43*(3), 384–393.

WASHINGTON, C. S. (1979). Men counseling men: Redefining the male machine. *Personnel and Guidance Journal, 57*(9), 462–463.

WASHINGTON, C. S. (1982). Challenging men in groups. *The Journal for Specialists in Group Work, 7,* 132–136.

WASHINGTON, K. R. (1977). Success counseling: A model workshop approach to self-concept building. *Adolescence, 12*(47), 405–410.

WEAVER, D. R. (1982). Empowering treatment skills for helping Black families. *Social Casework, 63*(2), 100–105.

WEIGEL, R. H., AND COOK, D. W. (1975). Participation in decision making: A determinant of interpersonnel attraction in cooperating interracial groups. *International Journal of Group Tension, 5,* 179–195.

WEINRAUB, M., AND WOLF, B. M. (1983). Effects of stress and social supports on mother-child interactions on single- and two-parent families. *Child Development, 54,* 1297–1311.

WEIRICH, T. W., AND SHEINFELD, S. N. (1982). The effects of recentralizing mental health services. *Community Mental Health Journal, 18*(3), 200–209.

WEISS, C. H. (1974). Research organizations interview the poor. *Social Problems, 22*(2), 246–259.

WEISS, R. L. (1978). The conceptualization of marriage from a behavioral perspective. In T. J. Paolino and B. A. McCrady (Eds.), *Marriage and marital therapy: Psychoanalytic, behavioral, and systems theory perspectives.* New York: Brunner/Mazel.

WEISS, R. S. (1973). Helping relationships: Relationships of clients with physicians, social workers, priests and others. *Social Problems, 20*(3), 319–328.

WEISS, S. L., AND DLUGOKINSKI, E. L. (1974). Parental expectations of psychotherapy. *Journal of Psychology, 86,* 71–80.

WEISSMAN, M. M., GEANAKOPLOS, E., AND PRUSOTT, B. (1973). Social class and attrition in depressed outpatients. *Social Casework, 54*(3), 162–170.

WEISSMAN, M. M., AND KLERMAN, G. L. (1977). Sex differences and the epidemiology of depression. *Archives of General Psychiatry, 34*(1), 98–111.

WEISSMAN, M., AND KLERMAN, G. L. (1981). Sex differences and the epidemiology of depression. In E. Howell and M. Bayes (Eds.), *Women and mental health.* New York: Basic Books, pp. 160–195.

WELKOWITZ, J., COHEN, J., AND ORTMEYER, D. (1967). Value system similarity: Investigation of patient-therapist dyads. *Journal of Consulting Psychology, 31*(1), 48–55.

WERBIN, J., AND HYNES, K. (1975). Transference and culture in a Latino therapy group. *International Journal of Group Psychotherapy, 25*(4), 396–401.

WERNER, P. D., AND BLOCK, J. (1975). Sex differences in the eyes of expert personality assessors: Unwarranted conclusions. *Journal of Personality Assessment, 39*(2), 110–113.

WESLEY, C. (1975). The women's movement and psychotherapy. *Social Work, 20,* 120–125.

WETZEL, J. W. (May 15–16, 1985). Global issues and perspectives on working with women: A call to social work. Paper presented at the 60th Anniversary of the George Warren Brown School of Social Work, Washington University, St. Louis, Mo.

WHEATON, B. (1983). Stress, personal coping resources and psychiatric symptoms. *Journal of Health and Social Behavior, 24,* 208–229.

WHITAKER, C. (1973). *The technique of family therapy.* Ackerman Memorial Address, Family Institute of Philadelphia Annual Conference.

V. TAKER, C., AND NAPIER, A. (1972). Conversation about co-therapy. In A. Ferber, M. Mendelsohn, and A. Napier (Eds.), *The book of family therapy.* Boston: Houghton Mifflin Company.

WHITELEY, R. (1973). Women in groups. *The Counseling Psychologist, 4,* 27–43.

WHITLEY, B. E., JR., (1979). Sex roles and psychotherapy: A current appraisal. *Psychological Bulletin, 86*(6), 1309–1321.

WHYTE, W. F. (1943). *Street corner society: The social structure of an Italian slum.* Chicago: The University of Chicago Press.

WIELY, M., AND ESKILSON, A. (1982). Coping in the corporation: Sex role constraints. *The Journal of Applied Social Psychology, 12,* 1–11.

WILKINSON, C. B. (1973). Problems in black-white encounter groups. *International Journal of Group Psychotherapy, 23*(2), 155–165.

WILKINSON, D. Y. (1984). Afro-American women and their families. *Marriage and Family Review, 7*(3/4), 125–142.

WILLIAMS, W. S., RALPH, J. R., AND DENHAM, W. (1978). Black mental health work force. In L. E. Gary (Ed.), *Mental health: A challenge to the Black community.* Philadelphia & Ardmore, Penn.: Dorrance & Co.

WILLIE, C. V. (1974). The Black family and social class. *American Journal of Orthopsychiatry, 44,* 50–60.

WILLIE, C. V., AND GREENBLATT, S. L. (1978). Four "classic" studies of power relationships in Black families: A review and look to the future. *Journal of Marriage and the Family, 40,* 691–694.

WILLS, T. A. (1978). Perceptions of clients by professional helpers. *Psychological Bulletin, 85*(5), 968–1000.

WILSON, W. J. (1978). *The declining significance of race.* Chicago: University of Chicago Press.

WINDER, A. E., AND HERSKO, M. (1955). The effect of social class on the length and type of psychotherapy in a veteran's administration mental hygiene clinic. *Journal of Clinical Psychology, 11*(1), 77–79, summarized.

WINSTON, A., PARDES, H., AND PAPERNNIK, D. S. (1972). Inpatient treatment of blacks and whites. *Archives of General Psychiatry, 26,* 405–409.

WINTER, S. K. (1971). Black man's bluff. *Psychology Today, 5,* 39–43, 78–81.

WOHL, J. (1981). Intercultural psychotherapy: Issues, questions, and reflections. In P. P. Pedersen, J. G. Draguns, W. J. Lonner, and J. E. Trimble (Eds.), *Counseling across culture.* Honolulu: the University of Hawaii Press.

WOLD, C., YOON, S., AND MAYO, S. (1977). Marital therapy with a Vietnamese couple: A cross-cultural melange. *Family therapy, 4*(3), 237–246.

WOLD, P., AND STEGER, J. (1976). Social class and group therapy in a working class situation. *Community Mental Health Journal, 12*(4), 335–341.

WOLKON, G. H., MORIWAKI, S., AND WILLIAMS, K. J. (1973). Race and social class as factors in the orientation toward psychotherapy. *Journal of Counseling Psychology, 20*(4), 312–316.

WOLMAN, C., AND FRANK, H. (1975). The solo woman in a professional peer group. *American Journal of Orthopsychiatry, 45,* 164–170.

WOMACK, W. M., AND WAGNER, N. N. (1967). Negro interviewers and white patients. *Archives of General Psychiatry, 16,* 685–692.

WONG, M. R. (1978). Males in transition and the self-help group. *The Counseling Psychologist, 7*(4), 46–50.

WOOD, W. D., AND SHERRETS, S. D. (1984). Requests for outpatient mental health services: A comparison of whites and blacks. *Comprehensive Psychiatry, 25*(3), 329–334.

WORCHEL, P. (1957). Catharsis and the relief of hostility. *Journal of Abnormal and Social Psychology, 55,* 238–243.

WORELL, J. (1978). Sex roles and psychological well-being: Perspectives on methodology. *Journal of Consulting and Clinical Psychology, 46*(4), 777–791.

WORTMAN, R. A. (1981). Depression, danger, dependency, denial: Work with poor, black, single parents. *American Journal of Orthopsychiatry, 51*(4), 662–671.

WRIGHT, C. T., MEADOW, A., ABRAMOWITZ, S. I., AND DAVIDSON, C. V. (1980). Psychiatric diagnosis as a function of assessor profession and sex. *Psychology of Women Quarterly, 5*(2), 240–254.

WRIGHT, F. (1976). The effects of style and sex of consultants and sex of members in self-study groups. *Small Group Behavior, 7*(4), 433–456.

WRIGHT, H., SCOTT, H. R., PIERRE-PAUL, R., AND GORE, T. A. (1984). Psychiatric diagnosis and the black patient. *The Psychiatric Forum, 12*(2), 65–71.

WRIGHT, T. L., AND SHARP, E. G. (1979). Content and grammatical sex bias on the interpersonal trust scale and differential trust toward men and women. *Journal of Consulting and Clinical Psychology, 47*(1), 72–85.

WYCKOFF, H. (1971). Radical psychiatry in women's groups. In J. Agel (Ed.), *The radical therapist.* New York: Ballantine.

WYNNE, L., RYCHKOFF, I., DAY, J., AND HIRSCH, S. (1958). Pseudomutuality in the family relationship of schizophrenics. *Psychiatry, 21*, 205–220.

YALOM, I. (1975). *The theory and practice of group psychotherapy.* New York: Basic Books, Inc.

YALOM, I. D., HOUTS, P. S., NEWELL, F., AND RAND, K. (1967). Preparation of patients for group therapy. *Archives of General Psychiatry, 17*, 416–427.

YAMAMOTO, J., AND GOIN, M. K. (1966). Social class factors relevant for psychiatric treatment. *Journal of Nervous and Mental Disease, 142*, 332–338.

YAMAMOTO, J., JAMES, Q. C., BLOOMBAUM, M., AND HATTEM, J. (1967). Racial factors in patient selection. *American Journal of Psychiatry, 124*, 630–636.

YAMAMOTO, J., JAMES, Q. C., AND PALLEY, N. (1968). Cultural problems in psychiatric therapy. *Archives of General Psychiatry, 19*, 45–49.

YBARRA, L. (1982). When wives work: The impact on the Chicano family. *Journal of Marriage and the Family, 44*(1), 169–178.

YERBY, J. (1975). Attitude, task, and sex composition as variables affecting female leadership in small problem solving groups. *Speech Monographs, 42*, 160–168.

YOUNGMAN, L. C. (1965). Social group work in the AFDC program. *Public Welfare, 23*(1), 25–31.

YUCHTMAN-YOAR, E., AND SHAPIRO, R. (1981). Sex as a status characteristic: An examination of sex differences in locus of control. *Sex Roles, 7*(2), 149–162.

ZAJONC, R. (1968). Attitudinal effects of more exposure. *Journal of Personality and Social Psychology,* pp. 1–27.

ZANDER, A. (1979). The psychology of group processes. *Annual Review of Psychology, 30*, 417–452.

ZELDOW, P. B. (1975). Clinical judgment: A search for sex differences. *Psychological Reports, 37*, 1135–1142.

ZELDOW, P. B. (1976). Effects of nonpathological sex-role stereotypes on student evaluations of psychiatric patients. *Journal of Consulting and Clinical Psychology, 44*(2), 304.

ZELDOW, P. B. (1978). Sex differences in psychiatric evaluation and treatment: An empirical review. *Archives of General Psychiatry, 35*(1), 89–93.

ZEREN, A. S., AND BRADLEY, L. A. (1982). Effects of diagnostician prestige and sex upon subject's acceptance of genuine personality feedback. *Journal of Personality Assessment, 46*(2), 169–174.

ZIETZ, D., AND ERLICH, J. L. (1976). Sexism in social agencies: Practitioners' perspectives. *Social Work, 21*, 434–439.

Author Index

Subject Index